The Psychotherapy of Carl Rogers

The Psychotherapy of Carl Rogers

CASES AND COMMENTARY

Edited by

Barry A. Farber
Debora C. Brink
Patricia M. Raskin

Foreword by Maria Villas-Boas Bowen

THE GUILFORD PRESS
New York   London

In memory of my father
–B.A.F.

In memory of Maria Villas-Boas Bowen,
a kind and wise friend
–D.C.B.

To Richard and Danny
–P.M.R.

© 1996 The Guilford Press
A Division of Guilford Publications, Inc.
72 Spring Street, New York, NY 10012

Printed in the United States of America

This book is printed on acid-free paper.

Last digit is print number: 9 8 7 6 5 4 3 2 1

Library of Congress Cataloging-in-Publication Data

The psychotherapy of Carl Rogers: cases and commentary / edited
    by Barry A. Farber, Debora C. Brink, Patricia M. Raskin;
    foreword by Maria Villas-Boas Bowen
        p.   cm.
    Includes bibliographical references and index.
    ISBN 1-57230-064-7
    1. Client-centered psychotherapy—Case studies. 2. Rogers,
Carl R.   (Carl Ransom), 1902–1987. Psychotherapy—Case
Studies.   I.   Farber, Barry A. (Barry Alan), 1947–   .
II. Brink, Debora. III.   Raskin, Patricia M., 1943–   .
RC481.P79   1996
616.89′14—dc20   96-38553
                                                      CIP

CONTRIBUTORS

Maria Villas-Boas Bowen, Ph.D. (deceased), Center for Studies of the Person, La Jolla, California

Jerold D. Bozarth, Ph.D., Department of Counseling, University of Georgia, Athens, Georgia

Debora C. Brink, Ph.D. (retired), School of Education, City College of the City University of New York, New York, New York (now living in New Orleans, Louisiana)

Barbara Temaner Brodley, Ph.D., Illinois School of Professional Psychology, Chicago Counseling and Psychotherapy Research Center, and Private practice, Chicago, Illinois

David J. Cain, Ph.D., A.B.P.P., Graduate Program in Psychology, Chapman University, San Diego, California

Robert E. Dingman, Ed.D., Private practice, Burlington, Vermont

Barry A. Farber, Ph.D., Department of Counseling and Clinical Psychology, Teachers College, Columbia University, New York, New York

Jesse D. Geller, Ph.D., Department of Psychology, Yale University, New Haven, Connecticut

Marvin R. Goldfried, Ph.D., Department of Psychology, State University of New York at Stony Brook, Stony Brook, New York

Edith Gould, M.S., C.S.W., Psychoanalytic Institute, Postgraduate Center for Mental Health, New York, New York

Leslie S. Greenberg, Ph.D., Department of Psychology, York University, North York, Ontario, Canada

v

Adele M. Hayes, Ph.D., Department of Psychology, University of Miami, Coral Gables, Florida

Samuel E. Menahem, Ph.D., Center for Psychotherapy and Spirituality, Fort Lee, New Jersey

Peggy Natiello, Ph.D., Private practice, Sedona, Arizona

Maureen O'Hara, Ph.D., Center for Studies of the Person, La Jolla, California

Nathaniel J. Raskin, Ph.D., Division of Psychology, Northwestern University Medical School, Chicago, Illinois

Patricia M. Raskin, Ph.D., Department of Counseling and Clinical Psychology, Teachers College, Columbia University, New York, New York

Debra Rosenzweig, M.S., Department of Counseling and Clinical Psychology, Teachers College, Columbia University, New York, New York

Julius Seeman, Ph.D., Department of Psychology, Peabody College of Vanderbilt University, Nashville, Tennessee

Fred Zimring, Ph.D., Department of Psychology, Case Western Reserve University, Cleveland, Ohio

FOREWORD

The work of Carl Rogers is prolific and diverse. From the time he published his first book in 1939 until his death in 1987, his ideas continually changed and expanded. Always faithful to his central theme—relationship—his interest in its range of meanings and applications broadened greatly over the years. From the one-to-one relationship in psychotherapy, he became interested first in applying his ideas in small groups, and later on in larger groups. He wrote about relationships in the context of education and intimate partnership, and he finally extended it to racial tension and international conflict resolution. During the last 10 years of his life he was invited to work in several countries in Europe and Latin America, as well as in Japan, South Africa, and the Soviet Union, thus extending his influence worldwide. When his life ended, he was in the midst of a total dedication to working for world peace.

Carl Rogers was a courageous man. At a time when what happened in psychotherapy sessions was only known through the account of the therapist, he broke the taboo of secrecy by allowing himself to be recorded and by publishing the verbatim transcripts of these recorded interviews. By doing so, he not only introduced one of the most valuable methods for teaching psychotherapy but also put himself under the microscope for scrutiny by his friends and foes.

It is this kind of examination that this book offers. Each commentator was invited to analyze Rogers' work in order to seek a fuller understanding of what made him effective and successful. Each reviewed Rogers' work through the lens of his or her own perceptions, biases, and theoretical framework. However, dissection presents risks. The whole may be sacrificed in order to facilitate a closer scrutiny of the parts. Parts may be taken out of context, giving a different meaning from that originally intended.

Aspects of cases that confirm the commentators' biases and illustrate their points of view may be chosen at the sacrifice of balance. Thus, the selective perceptions of the contributors must be kept in mind when reading these comments on Rogers' cases. Still, what readers gain from this collection is a fascinating variety of different opinions, judgments, perceptions, and points of view, all of which, ideally, will stimulate readers to form their own conclusions.

What must be kept in mind, too, is that as valuable as verbatim transcripts of interviews are as a means to study psychotherapy, key aspects of the therapist's work are lacking. In Carl Rogers' case, transcripts fail to convey the incredible quality of his presence, which he expressed through his eyes, posture, and tone of voice; this presence was certainly a central element of his therapy. Often, it was not so much what he said or did that made the difference, but how he said it and his way of being with the client.

The cases selected in this book show Rogers in different contexts. Some were part of a continuing process of psychotherapy, such as that of Jim Brown, who had been seen by Rogers twice a week for 11 months. The majority of them, however, were demonstration interviews, done specifically for the camera, or as a teaching device during workshops, some lasting a mere half-hour. We may question whether such a brief interview really reflects Rogers' style and whether it was of any help to the person being interviewed. Rogers himself answered this question a long time ago. When he first introduced his ideas about psychotherapy in 1942 in *Counseling and Psychotherapy,* he stated that even in a short period of time a very definite type of clarifying help could be offered: "We can enable the client to express his problems and feelings freely, and leave with a clearer recognition of the issues with which he is faced" (pp. 247–248). This is exactly what Rogers did in his demonstration interviews.

The cases in this book also span a long time period. A few of the cases selected for this book were interviews done in the 1940s and 1950s (e.g., the case of Jim Brown, the case of Mary Jane Tilden). It is notable, though, that during the 1960s through the middle of the 1970s Rogers was so absorbed in working with groups that very little is available regarding his work with individuals. It was mainly after Sylvia, interviewed at the request of the group during a 1976 person-centered workshop in Oregon, that Rogers systematically started to give demonstration interviews during workshops. He was always cautious about the choice of the client, and he made sure that another psychotherapist would be available in case the client needed any further assistance. After Rogers moved to California in 1963, there is no record of any long-term psychotherapy done by him. What we mostly have is a wide array of these demonstration interviews. It is unfortunate, then, that we have no idea how Rogers acted during a long-term therapy in the last 20 years of his life. In this regard, too, we might question how much his demonstration interviews reflected his way of doing "private" psychotherapy. My impression is that therapists' first contact with clients differs markedly from contact much later in therapy when they have established a deeper relationship. (On this issue, see also Patricia M. Raskin's Introductory Comments to Section II.)

The comments and critiques in this book may not offer conclusive answers about the work of Carl Rogers, but they may well raise new questions. If this book gives us food for thought and inspires us as therapists and as citizens of the planet to contribute to the welfare of others, we will be doing justice to Carl Rogers' heritage.

MARIA VILLAS-BOAS BOWEN

REFERENCE

Rogers, C. R. (1942). *Counseling and psychotherapy.* Boston: Houghton Mifflin.

ACKNOWLEDGMENTS

The editors and publisher would like to thank the following individuals and organizations:

For permission to reproduce transcribed versions of the audiotaped cases of Loretta (1958) and Jim Brown (1967): The American Academy of Psychotherapists.

For permission to reprint (as the case of Mark) the published article, Rogers, C. R. (1986). The dilemmas of a South African white. *Person-Centered Review, 1*(1), 15–35: David Cain, Editor, *Person-Centered Review.*

For permission to reproduce a transcribed version of the audiotaped case of Jill (Esalen Interview, 1983), transcribed versions of the videotaped cases of Mary and Louise (weekend meeting of the Expressive Therapy Training Program, 1986), and a transcribed version of the videotaped case of Sylvia ("Struggle for Self-Acceptance," produced and directed by John M. Whitely, American Personnel and Guidance Association, Washington, DC, 1980): Natalie Rogers, representing the estate of Carl Rogers.

For permission to summarize the videotaped case of "Carl Rogers Counsels an Individual on Anger and Hurt" (produced and directed by John M. Whitely, American Personnel and Guidance Association, Washington, DC, 1977): Natalie Rogers, representing the estate of Carl Rogers.

For permission to reprint the published chapter, Rogers, C. R. (1947). The Case of Mary Jane Tilden counseled by Carl R. Rogers, in William Snyder's *Casebook of non-directive counseling* (pp. 147–208): Houghton Mifflin Co.

The editors gratefully acknowledge the help of P. Michael Timpane, former President of Teachers College, Columbia University, who supported this project from the outset and provided the initial funds used for research assistance and transcriptions of the case material.

We would also like to acknowledge the efforts of Valerie Henderson, Nel Kandel, Bruce Meador, and John Whitely, all of whom were extremely helpful in making available the case material in this book. Our thanks also to Bill Coulson, who steered us to some helpful material about Carl Rogers, and to Dyer Bilgrave whose experiences helped inspire this book.

Thanks go to Kristy Nguyen and Byrne Pozzi, secretaries in the Department of Clinical Psychology at Teachers College, who were always available for countless tasks, and to Rocky Schwarz of the Teachers College Word Processing Center, whose staff did such terrific work with our documents. And special thanks go to Karyn Gerber Fischer and Debra Rosenzweig, talented doctoral students in counseling and clinical psychology, respectively, for their editorial and research assistance, organizational abilities, and general enthusiasm for this project. We are also indebted to those colleagues, students, and friends of ours who have passed on their considerable wisdom to us and who have taught us to keep our eyes open to new knowledge and alternative perspectives.

Finally, we would like to extend our grateful appreciation to Natalie Rogers for her ceaseless help, support, and encouragement over the years this book has been in progress.

CONTENTS

Section II. Rogers' Therapy Cases: Views from Within and Without

INTRODUCTION

Barry A. Farber

This book was written with two purposes: first, to present a series of counseling sessions conducted by one of this country's most prominent and influential psychologists, Carl Ransom Rogers (1902–1987), and second, to provide critical commentary by noted psychotherapists on these sessions.

Typically, books about psychotherapy are technique oriented and offer short vignettes to illustrate their points; rarely are multiple transcribed therapy sessions of a single therapist brought together in one volume. This book offers readers the opportunity to study sessions conducted by Rogers, eight of which are fully transcribed,[1] and to read discussions of these cases by therapists of varying theoretical persuasions. In the first half of the book we present five of Rogers' cases, each of which is commented upon by a client-centered therapist. In the second half, we present five additional cases, and we include commentaries on each by both a client-centered therapist and a therapist of a differing orientation. The contributors to this book—each of whom was given the transcript of a case session and, if available, a videotape of the session—were asked to comment on the strengths, weaknesses, theoretical assumptions, inconsistencies, and/or notable features of the session. We believe, based on conversations with Rogers, that he would have appreciated a close and respectful reading of his cases by practitioners of differing theoretical perspectives. Thus, the critical evaluations offered by the contributors to this book are intended to honor Rogers' memory while demystifying and demythologizing his extraordinary contributions to the field of psychology.

1

Carl Rogers' work has often been stereotyped and misunderstood by those whose knowledge of him begins and ends with either a single case (Gloria, the client whose successive clinical interviews with Rogers, Fritz Perls, and Albert Ellis in 1964 form the basis of a popular training film) or a single technique (reflection of clients' feelings). Rogers was, in fact, somewhat frustrated by the apparent mis-reading of his work by many of his contemporaries, and he seemed especially exasperated by descriptions of his work as simplistic or naive. "Because my writing is reasonably lucid and clear," he said (personal communication, May 1986), "does not mean that my ideas are less complex or profound than those whose writing is more difficult to understand." Not surprisingly, then, Rogers was receptive to an idea originally proposed by one of the editors of this book (Debora C. Brink): to compile a casebook as a means of demonstrating that client-centered therapy, as Rogers practiced it, embraced far more than reflection or rote mirroring of feelings. Indeed, Rogers made a list of cases to be included in such a book, which was found among his papers by his assistant, Valerie Henderson. Brink and I had the opportunity to further discuss this project with Rogers in 1986 when he was honored by his alma mater, Teachers College (Columbia University), and awarded the College's Medal of Honor. When Rogers died a year later, the casebook seemed a perfect response to a request from the president of Teachers College, P. Michael Timpane, for the college to find a suitable means of honoring one of its most esteemed and illustrious alumni. To further this goal, the college provided the initial funding to transcribe most of the cases included in this book.

The 10 cases in this book are remarkably diverse. They represent Rogers' work from 1946 (the case of Mary Jane Tilden) to 1986 (the cases of Mary and Louise). They reflect the wide range of clients with whom he worked—from schizophrenic patients (the cases of Loretta and Jim Brown) to a well-functioning, albeit conflicted clinical psychologist (the case of Mark). Two of these clients were seen in hospitals (Loretta and Jim Brown), one at a university counseling center (Mary Jane Tilden), one as part of a film series (Gloria), and the others as demonstration cases either at weekend workshops (Jill, Mary, Louise, Sylvia, Mark) or at a "closed" (no audience) filmed session (the case of "Anger and Hurt"). In some of these sessions, Rogers is consistently empathic (Loretta); in others, he more frequently asks questions, offers interpretations, and expresses his own feelings (Jill, Louise). The 40-year span captured in this material offers the opportunity to observe both the consistency with which Rogers was a keen and respectful listener and the increasing diversity in his response repertoire over the years. As Maria Villas-Boas Bowen points out in her discussion of Jill, Rogers became increasingly comfortable with interpretation, metaphor, humor, and even directiveness.

Although we believe that Rogers' contributions to the field are still underappreciated in academic circles (especially clinical psychology departments), as well as by the psychoanalytic sector of the psychotherapeutic community, there has been a revival of interest in his work in the past decade. Among other published works, there has been a fine, short biography (Thorne, 1992), an anthology of his writings (Kirschenbaum & Henderson, 1989b), an anthology of his dialogues with eminent psychologists, educators, and philosophers (Kirschenbaum & Henderson, 1989a), and several articles (e.g., Kahn, 1985, 1989) demonstrating conceptual links between Rogers' work and that of such psychoanalytic thinkers as Heinz Kohut. None of this material, however, provides direct access to that aspect of Rogers' work that he is best known for—his psychotherapeutic style. Whereas Rogers' contributions to the helping professions include significant work in such areas as group process, psychotherapy research, and conflict resolution, his most enduring legacy still centers on the ways in which his person-centered philosophy[2] created a new ethos for therapeutic work with clients.

What makes this book unique, then, is its focus on Rogers' therapy cases per se, including some previously unpublished ones. What further distinguishes this book from previous works on Rogers is its contributors: The authors within this book represent not just those who adhere to a person-centered or humanistic model (all of whom knew and/or worked with Rogers) but rather a wide spectrum of practitioners, including those who espouse psychoanalytic, cognitive–behavioral, Gestalt, experiential, and spiritual models of psychotherapy. Their comments on the cases presented in this book provide a sense of the differences, as well as commonalities, between person-centered and other psychotherapeutic approaches. And their criticisms of Rogers' work provide a tangible, pragmatic basis for viewing both the putative advantages and shortcomings in Rogers' model. Furthermore, the work of all the contributors to this book is extraordinarily diverse in tone and content, ranging from a feminist analysis (Maureen O'Hara) to a literary case commentary (Robert E. Dingman) to a critique based in part on a textual analysis study (Barbara Temaner Brodley). This range of ideas reflects the many creative ways in which Rogers' seemingly simple approach to individuals can be understood.

What emerges for us most strongly in reviewing these cases is Rogers' remarkable connection with his clients, even those with whom he was meeting for the first time. In distinct contrast to the classical analytic notion of a detached observer, Rogers was the apotheosis of the engaged listener. His thorough interest in understanding the nature of his clients' world—their feelings, thoughts, fears, conflicts—appears to have deeply moved these individuals, even those whose character we might now term as schizoid. His empathic responsiveness seems to encompass intellectual, emotional, and spiritual levels of understanding. His words, though often simple, seem to be chosen with great care and with great sensitivity to the immediate emotional tone of his client. Of course, neither the sound of his voice nor his body language can be conveyed in transcripts or summaries of these sessions, but, when seen on videotape, these characteristics, too, contribute to the feeling of how totally immersed Rogers was in trying to get a sense of the individual with whom he was sharing these minutes. At a time when great emphasis was laid upon a thorough intellectual understanding of a patient's dynamics, Rogers pioneered a clinical stance that seems to include equal doses of mind, heart, and soul.

For the most part, psychotherapy in the 1940s and 1950s was dominated by psychoanalysis and its conflict-laden, tragic view of life. At best, thought Freud, psychoanalysis could transform neurotic misery into common unhappiness. According to the then prevailing psychoanalytic tradition, personality is dominated by an irrational, apersonal id, and individuals are socialized only under heavy environmental pressures. Without the influence of an internalized superego, individuals are likely to give unbridled expression to their primary instincts, that is, sex and aggression. Ironically, though Freud rejected religion, he can be said to have secularized its born-in-sin assumption through his belief in the innate destructiveness of the id. In the post-World War II era, several social scientific works seemed to have confirmed many of Freud's ideas about the destructiveness of the id. For example, Lorenz (1963), in *On Aggression,* attempted to demonstrate that human hostility and aggression are inherent, carried in our genes, and expressed as instincts.

The primary mode of psychoanalytically oriented therapy was directive, and the therapist was clearly the expert in the room. Most of these therapists were emulating the prestigious medical profession in assuming a stance that necessarily fostered patients' beliefs about their therapists' omnipotence and omniscience. Wisdom and knowledge were viewed as the exclusive province of the therapist, often leaving patients feeling that they knew little or nothing about how best to live their own lives. In fact, patients in psychoanalysis were often discouraged from making any major decisions while in treatment—whether to get married or have children, for example.

How is it that a humanistic psychology emerged from the apparent hegemony of psychoanalysis? The progressive philosophical, religious, and educational ideas of John Dewey—his emphasis, for example, on personal experience, a religious attitude in life, and the innate ability of children to know what they need to learn—reflected a stance in many ways antithetical to psychoanalysis. In addition, observations in biology that demonstrated the remarkable capacity of living systems for self-regulation and self-repair was another challenge to the psychoanalytic vision. Goldstein's (1939) *The Organism* was a landmark contribution in this area, influencing the work of Rogers as well as that of other such notable psychologists such as Abraham Maslow, Andras Angyal, and Milton Erickson.[3] Rogers drew on these new currents in American thought, his own background in theology, his work with clients (particularly at the Child Guidance Center in Rochester in the 1940s), and the ideas of such innovative psychoanalysts as Karen Horney and Otto Rank (particularly Rank's notion of individuals being self-directing) to develop a psychotherapeutic paradigm remarkably distinct in its values and approach from psychoanalysis. Adopting the belief that clients (not "patients") are the ones who possess the resources for change, Rogers and his followers adopted a nondirective, more egalitarian, client-centered stance that aimed to promote growth in individuals. In practice, this meant that the therapist was to rely upon the client for the direction that the therapy would take, and that the emphasis in therapy would be more on the present than the past, more on feelings than thoughts, more on the client's resources than the therapist's, more on potential than pathology, and more on the ability of the therapeutic relationship to provide a positive human experience than an intellectually meaningful one. Rogers' trust in individuals' ability to understand and remediate their problems was at the core of this new therapy. Undoubtedly, his faith and belief that individuals would change in healthy directions fostered and reinforced that change. He was critical of those therapists whose theoretical model led them to make inferential leaps about clients' inner lives; he averred that therapists could not know more about their clients' functioning than the clients themselves.

Rogers' first book, *The Clinical Treatment of the Problem Child*, was published in 1939, but it was his second book, *Counseling and Psychotherapy*, published in 1942, that laid out the core concepts of client-centered therapy. It was in this book that Rogers first started using the term "client." Notably, too, this book contained the first fully transcribed psychotherapy case. In many ways the reaction to this remarkable book augured the treatment Rogers was to receive for much of his career: "There were those who found it immensely attractive, and many graduate students at Ohio State often referred to it as 'The Bible.' On the larger psychological community, however, it seemed to make little impact and it was not, in fact, reviewed by any major professional journal" (Thorne, 1992, p. 13).

Rogers was not the first to espouse a humanistically oriented psychotherapy. In the 1930s, Rank was describing a form of treatment ("will therapy") that emphasized creativity, individual uniqueness, self-directiveness, and personal growth. But Rogers was clearly the first to see the possibilities of a new form of therapy cast not in psychoanalytic terms but in an entirely different language. Moreover, if Rogers' work was not exactly sui generis—and no theory ever truly is—it nonetheless provided the focus for a view of life, including possibilities for growth and personal fulfillment, that was remarkably consonant with the values and aspirations of large segments of postwar America. The ethos inherent in client-centered therapy was in distinct contrast to Freud's view. To Rogers, individuals are basically rational, responsible, realistic, and inclined to grow. Freud postulated both a life ("eros") and death ("thanatos") instinct; Rogers, like Maslow, suggested instead that individuals possess an "actualizing tendency" that enables them to move creatively toward fulfilling their potential.

Near the end of his life, at the Evolution of Psychotherapy Conference held in Phoenix in December 1985, Rogers commented on the frequent criticism that his work took too positive a view of human nature:

> I am certainly not blind to all the evil and the terribly irresponsible violence that is going on. . . . There are times that I think I don't give enough emphasis on the shadowy side of our nature, the evil side. Then I start to deal with a client and discover how, when I get to the core, there is a wish for more socialization, more harmony, more positive values. Yes, there are all kinds of evil abounding in the world but I do not believe this is inherent in the human species any more than I believe that animals are evil. (cited in Zeig, 1987, p. 202)

According to Rogers, the natural process of change and growth is facilitated when therapists provide a climate of safety for their clients' self-explorations. Such an atmosphere comes about when the therapist is experienced as real or genuine rather than dissembling or acting out a role, as feeling positive regard for the client even when the latter's reported beliefs or actions are self-perceived as unacceptable, and as being empathic, that is, so sensitively attuned to the client's inner world as if walking in his or her shoes. These, claimed Rogers (1957), were the "necessary and sufficient conditions" (p. 95) for personality change. When the therapist is experienced by the client as real, caring, and understanding, significant and enduring change can occur.

Despite equivocal research findings (Watson, 1984), Rogers' delineation of these necessary and sufficient therapeutic conditions has had enormous influence within the field. This theory set the stage for a radical alternative view regarding the effective ingredients in psychotherapy: Unlike the classical psychoanalytic view that emphasized technical aspects of the work (e.g., well-timed interpretations), Rogers' formulation suggested that the relationship itself was mutative, an idea that has been borne out repeatedly in psychotherapy outcome studies over the past 20 years. That is, research has consistently found that patients' perceptions of the quality of the therapeutic relationship (sometimes operationalized as the therapeutic alliance) is positively and significantly correlated with positive clinical outcome (Bergin & Garfield, 1994).

During the 1960s, many of the proponents of psychoanalysis and behavior therapy were convinced that the "other" approach worked, if at all, because it clumsily provided what was truly therapeutic. That is, behavior therapists suggested that psychoanalysis worked only to the extent that it serendipitously desensitized patients to fearful experiences. Conversely, analysts contended that behavior therapy unintentionally provided interpretations, insights, and even perhaps "corrective emotional experiences"—all of which freed patients to choose new, more adaptive behaviors. In retrospect, both parties may have overlooked what may be most curative in all psychotherapeutic approaches: the provision of a good relationship. Rogers' delineation of the ingredients of such a facilitative relationship—genuineness, positive regard, empathy—may need qualifying and/or correcting. Research may well determine that the specific components of an effective therapeutic relationship are a function of myriad patient and therapist variables, including gender, age, culture, diagnosis, and previous treatment history. Nevertheless, Rogers' steadfast emphasis on the importance of the relationship has now been accepted by virtually all schools of psychotherapy.

For example, the psychoanalytic approach that has been ascendent for the past two decades—object relations—has shifted the focus of analytic inquiry from drives to relationships. The assumption underlying this approach is that both the origins of psychological disturbance and the means to healing lie in the nature of the patient's interpersonal relationships. (Whereas it might be argued that psychoanalysis has always emphasized the patient–therapist relationship in its focus on the transference, the role of the classical analyst in this relationship—"a blank screen"—is far removed from Rogers' use of the relationship not to understand the patient but to provide the facilitative conditions for the "patient" to heal him- or herself). Different schools of thought emphasize somewhat different aspects of the therapeutic relationship—for example, self psychology, as pioneered by Kohut, speaks of the need for the therapist to function as a validating "selfobject" to the patient; the interpersonal model, as articulated by Harry Stack Sullivan, focuses on the basic sense of relatedness between the two participants in the room. These variations should not obscure the substantial overlap among these approaches. Most seem to subscribe to the same basic notion—that "since the internalization of 'bad objects' has made the patient 'ill,' therapy succeeds to the extent that the therapist can become a 'good object' " (Strupp, 1978, p. 315).

Credit to Rogers as a pioneer in this critical change in therapeutic focus—from emphasis on technique to that of relationship—has been conspicuously lacking. As noted earlier, some of this is attributable to the relegation, indeed almost dismissal, of the entire corpus of Rogers' work by large segments of the academic and clinical psychology community. That is, while Rogers received considerable recognition by the overall membership of the American Psychological Association (APA)—he was the first person to receive both the APA's Distinguished Scientific Contribution Award and its Distinguished Professional Contribution Award—his enormous influence on the evolution of psychotherapeutic practice is largely overlooked in contemporary clinical psychology programs. There, at the university level, it seems as if attempts to trace the pattern of influence on current therapeutic practice are focused almost exclusively on modifications of either psychoanalytic or cognitive–behavioral principles. Rogers (1986a) himself noted that

> in universities I feel we are underrepresented, badly misunderstood, mistakenly seen as superficial. We are underrepresented partly because we constitute a threat to the academically minded. We espouse the importance of experiential as well as cognitive learning. Such learning involves the risk of being changed by the experience, and this can be frightening to one whose world is intellectually structured. (pp. 257–258)

Thus, with the exception of counselor education and counseling psychology programs, Rogers' work was not—and still is not—accorded the respect it deserves. Many of his ideas, of course, have been accommodated within the boundaries of a common psychotherapeutic culture. That is, among the plurality of therapists in this country who regard themselves as "eclectic" in orientation, Rogers' notions regarding empathy, egalitarianism, the primacy of the therapeutic relationship, and the value of research are accepted without controversy. But, as Thorne (1992) has aptly noted, "many of Rogers' theoretical concepts have been absorbed into everyday psychological parlance without any acknowledgement of their origin . . . and much that was revolutionary in the early years of client-centered therapy is now apparently taken for granted by practitioners of many different therapeutic schools" (p. 44).

In contrast to the technical armamentarium available to the psychoanalytically oriented therapist—for example, dream analysis, transference interpretations, uncovering and confronting resistance—the stance of the client-centered therapist may seem simplistic indeed. But the power of this approach ought not to be underestimated. Perhaps because so many individuals grow up feeling alienated from their "true selves," the experience of having another human being trying his or her best to listen—constantly checking the accuracy of his or her understanding in a caring, gentle style—can be a profound and moving experience. The therapist's openness, availability, expressiveness, and faith may all serve to validate a person's sense of worth. For some, this means of interaction can break through long-standing barriers of isolation to start a process of self-reorganization.

As the cases within this book make clear, Rogers was an extraordinary listener. He was fully present to his clients. His patient but active focus on the personal meanings of words seem consistently to bring sense and clarity to those vague or confused messages created by some clients as they groped haltingly for what was true for them. Perhaps this is why he could experience even the most disorganized client as "articulate." He was guided by his sense of his clients' needs from moment to moment. And he seemed free to do, within the limits of therapeutic principles and values, whatever seemed right and necessary at the moment—being accepting, providing a clarifying label, making an integrative statement, explicitly checking his perceptions ("Am I getting it right?"), or even occasionally interpreting client statements or being self-disclosing ("There was a time when—I felt that way about myself"). (See the next chapter for descriptions of the types of responses Rogers employed in the cases in this book.) If any response of his was off the mark, he let it go; he had no investment in persuading a client to see it his way. His assumption that the therapist can be wrong is consistent with the essence of the person-centered approach as a nonauthoritarian process.

Still, as indicated by the case material in this book, Rogers did have a penchant for empathic responses that was consistent with his theoretical perspective. Whereas on a manifest level, these responses often seemed to "reflect client feelings," Rogers (1986b) preferred to view them as "testing understanding" or "checking perceptions." Regardless of the label, in the great majority of instances, this clinical stance worked quite well. The client appears to feel understood and apparently moved to a deeper level of self-understanding or self-acceptance. But we are also aware—as are some of the contributors to this book—that exclusive reliance on empathic responses may limit a therapist's effectiveness. Even when this approach seemingly reflects the therapist's genuine caring and understanding, the client may not experience it that way. Some may even find it disturbing and perceive such responses as aloof, distancing, or mechanical. In this regard, Schonbar (1968) recounts her experience, while working as a nondirective therapist, of being perceived by a young woman client as "indifferent." Furthermore, the general reluctance of a person-centered therapist to be interpretive may have dysfunctional therapeutic consequences. Schonbar acknowledged feeling "handcuffed" when her young woman patient reported a dream:

> My limited armamentarium gave me no way to deal with it meaningfully, apart from a comment on the mood or feeling of the dream. I felt as if something valuable had been brought into the room and just shoved aside

into a corner—or, more properly that it lay between us untouched, thus depriving her of its potential values, and confirming her experience of my not caring. I was indeed rejecting a part of her. (pp. 55–56)

The extent to which "reflection" or "clarification" or "checking perceptions" is integral to the practice of client-centered therapy is a complex question with an interesting historical background. It is really empathy, expressed within the context of realness and caring, that is at the core of Rogers' work (Brink, 1987). Nondirective reflection of feelings is but one way of expressing empathy with clients. Brink's (1987) attempt to understand why the whole person-centered approach has been equated with the specific technique of reflection takes her back to the early days of the movement:

> In their early explorations of recorded therapy sessions, Rogers and his students tended to focus more on the content of therapist responses than on their empathic attitudes in listening, with consequent misunderstanding and distortion of their whole approach. Nondirective therapy came to be described as a technique of reflecting back the feelings of the client. Criticism was harsh (Rogers, 1980, pp. 138–139). However, this distortion of Rogers's early work, lambasted and caricatured though it was, has not only survived but has been firmly institutionalized. It is a very curious fact that all of Rogers's work over the past 30 years has not succeeded in correcting that distortion that reduced his broad underlying philosophy and triad of facilitative conditions to a narrow set of skills. . . . In regard to empathy as such, Rogers does not have a simple set of skills in mind, but a complex cluster of abilities (keen awareness and sensitivity), attitudes (nonjudgmental, open, respectful, flexible, confident, subtle, gentle, caring, willing to articulate the not-yet-spoken, and to be wrong) as well as skill in communicating. Empathy was conveyed, among other ways, by reflecting the clients' statements back, with special emphasis on articulating the feelings sensed. Since reflection was a conspicuous part of nondirective therapist behavior, the whole broad approach was equated with that specific technique. Mistaking the part for the whole is a common human fallacy. . . . Reflection, with or without attention to feelings, is a skill, an operation on the outside world. It is objective, easy to mimic or master, hence capable of being abstracted as a thing-in-itself apart from the empathic context in which it had its origin. (pp. 32–34)

Thus, although the preponderance of his therapeutic comments were of the "restatement" or "reflection" type, Rogers did, in fact, exhibit a variety of clinical responses. For example, with Jim Brown, Rogers expressed empathy not only by being reflecting but by waiting patiently with him through long silences. With this client, too, Rogers revealed that he too had at one time felt "no damn good to anybody." "I wanted," said

Rogers, "to let him know he was not alone." A little later he explicitly told Jim Brown that he cared about him, cared what happened. His sensitive, timely self-disclosures penetrated this client's walls of isolation, touching him at his core, setting off a storm of wracking sobs. With another client, Sylvia, he briefly held hands. And with Gloria, there is an extremely touching moment—one that would seem to violate analytic proscriptions regarding boundaries and self-disclosure—where Rogers, in response to Gloria's expressed wish for him to be her loving father, suggests that Gloria herself seems to look "like a pretty nice daughter." Several minutes later, in response to Gloria's statement that she can't expect him to feel very close to her because he doesn't know her that well, Rogers replies: "All I can know is what I am feeling, that is, I feel close to you in this moment." The point is that for Rogers, being truly person-centered meant not losing the flexibility demanded by the uniqueness of individuals. During one post-workshop discussion, a participant said to Rogers, "I noticed that you asked questions of the client. But just last night a lecturer told us we must never do that." Rogers responded, "Well, I'm in the fortunate position of not having to be a Rogerian" (Brink, personal communication, 1990).

It has often been assumed that Rogers, the private individual, merely was himself in therapy sessions, and that it was his personal "magic" that created the therapeutic climate. And, to a certain extent, this may have been true. Those who knew him outside of his professional life were often struck by the charismatic quality of his low-key intensity; his gaze, demeanor, and listening style all served to mark his presence as special. In fact, it's difficult to imagine how anyone without special personal qualities could launch a therapeutic movement that would successfully challenge the monolithic presence of psychoanalysis in the 1940s and 1950s. On the other hand, as his colleague Eugene Gendlin (1988) has commented, he also seemed "ordinary; he was not a sparkling conversationalist . . . he rarely exuded feelings, and hardly ever anger" (p. 127). It should also not be surprising that, having grown up in a household where being heard was not valued and where he was judged and criticized, Rogers could not help but echo on occasion the critical, judgmental conditions of his youth (see Thorne, 1990). Of course, Rogers himself would have been the first to acknowledge that he was not a saint and that he was not uniquely able to provide the facilitative conditions for client growth. The fact is that by describing the optimum conditions for therapeutic change and by establishing the means by which others could learn how to provide these conditions, Rogers attempted to dispel the notion that it was he himself who was responsible for client growth. Indeed, if it were true that it was Rogers' personality that was therapeutic rather than his method—or more accurately, his way of listening and responding—then client-centered therapy would not be replicable. And it clearly is replicable. It has been practiced successfully by many others (and with a good deal of variation), leading to improved lives for countless numbers of people. It is noteworthy, too, that even those individuals who have been clients (or even "patients") of non-person-centered therapists have likely benefited from Rogers' humanistic legacy. Genuineness, empathy, and positive regard have become much stronger parts of the overriding therapeutic culture.

As briefly alluded to earlier, Rogers was committed to psychotherapy research. In a departure from analytic tradition, he was willing to record therapy sessions and make them available for study. For this he was "accused of 'violating the sanctity of the analytic relationship' " (Gendlin, 1988, p. 127). But unlike Freud, who was essentially dismissive of attempts to study the therapeutic process, Rogers believed that such investigations would serve to improve therapeutic practice; indeed, "he insisted on testing his new therapy to show that it worked" (Gendlin, 1988, p. 127). In addition to the use of clinical material to study the psychotherapeutic process, Rogers pioneered the use of this material in training programs. Indeed, almost every counselor training program in the United States subscribes to some version of the training model created by Rogers: listening to tape recordings of experienced therapists; role playing between trainees; observing live demonstrations by supervisors; participating in personal therapy; and recording interviews conducted by trainees (Truax & Carkhuff, 1967). It is in this spirit—in the hope that the transcripts, case summaries, and commentaries in this volume will further the training and ability of our readers to improve the lives of those with whom they work and live—that we dedicate this book to the memory of Carl Rogers.

NOTES

1. We did not receive permission to print the full transcriptions of the case of Gloria and the case of "Anger and Hurt."

2. Originally, Rogers' therapeutic approach was termed "nondirective therapy." Later, it became "client-centered therapy," and still later, "person-centered therapy." As Rogers explained in 1979, the term "person-centered" was adopted to reflect that the boundaries of the client-centered movement had moved well beyond counseling and mental health. As Levant and Schlien (1984) have noted, "this relabeling recognized the increasing emphasis given to working with a wide range of people, few of whom would define themselves as 'clients' seeking therapy" (p. 14).

3. More recent works have also presented pictures of the universe and of human nature that are markedly at odds with the essentially pessimistic outlook associated with classical psychoanalysis. For example, in *The Unfinished Universe*, Louise Young (1986) points out that "whole-making" is an intrinsic tendency of

the physical universe: As soon as conditions are favorable, small units of matter, naturally attracted to others, come together to form larger wholes (e.g., quarks unite to form protons) that are stable, self-maintaining, and self-repairing when disrupted by outside impact. Similarly, Schmookler (1988) has argued from an anthropological perspective that the outstanding tendency of the process of evolution is the creation of "ever-larger wholes of ever-increasing harmony" (p. 305). The destructive violence of civilization is seen as a recent aberration, an "unprecedented disruption" (p. 308) of this larger process of whole-making.

REFERENCES

Bergin, A., & Garfield, S. (1994). *Handbook of psychotherapy and behavior change* (4th ed.). New York: Wiley.

Brink, D. C. (1987). The issues of equality and control in the client- or person-centered approach. *Journal of Humanistic Psychology, 27,* 27–41.

Gendlin, E. T. (1988). Carl Rogers (1902–1987). *American Psychologist, 43,* 127–128.

Goldstein, K. (1939). *The Organism.* Cincinnati: American Book Company.

Kahn, E. (1985). Heinz Kohut and Carl Rogers: A timely comparison. *American Psychologist, 40,* 893–904.

Kahn, E. (1989). Heinz Kohut and Carl Rogers: Toward a constructive collaboration. *Psychotherapy, 26,* 555–563.

Kirschenbaum, H., & Henderson, V. L. (Eds.). (1989a). *Carl Rogers: Dialogues.* Boston: Houghton Mifflin.

Kirschenbaum, H., & Henderson, V. L. (Eds.). (1989b). *The Carl Rogers reader.* Boston: Houghton Mifflin.

Levant, R. F., & Shlien, J. M. (Eds.). (1984). *Client-centered therapy and the person-centered approach: New directions in theory, research and practice.* New York: Praeger.

Lorenz, K. (1963). *On aggression.* New York: Harcourt, Brace, & World.

Rogers, C. R. (1939). *The clinical treatment of the problem child.* Boston: Houghton Mifflin.

Rogers, C. R. (1942). *Counseling and psychotherapy.* Boston: Houghton Mifflin.

Rogers, C. R. (1957). The necessary and sufficient conditions of therapeutic personality change. *Journal of Consulting Psychology, 21,* 95–103.

Rogers, C. R. (1979). The foundations of the person-centered approach. *Education, 100,* 98–107.

Rogers, C. R. (1980). *A way of being.* Boston: Houghton Mifflin.

Rogers, C. R. (1986a). Carl Rogers on the development of the person-centered approach. *Person-Centered Review, 1,* 257–259.

Rogers, C. R. (1986b). Reflection of feelings. *Person-Centered Review, 1,* 375–377.

Schmookler, A. B. (1988). *Out of weakness: Healing the wounds that drive us to war.* New York: Bantam.

Schonbar, R. A. (1968). Confessions of an ex-nondirectivist. In E. Hammer (Ed.), *Use of interpretation in treatment* (pp. 55–58). New York: Grune & Stratton.

Strupp, H. (1978). The therapist's theoretical orientation: An overrated variable. *Psychotherapy: Theory, Research and Practice, 15,* 314–317.

Thorne, B. (1990). Carl Rogers and the doctrine of original sin. *Person-Centered Review, 5,* 394–405.

Thorne, B. (1992). *Carl Rogers.* Newbury Park, CA: Sage.

Truax, C. B., & Carkhuff, R. R. (1967). *Toward effective counseling and psychotherapy: Training and practice.* Chicago: Aldine.

Watson, N. (1984). The empirical status of Rogers' hypotheses of the necessary and sufficient conditions for effective psychotherapy. In R. F. Levant & J. M. Shlien (Eds.), *Client-centered therapy and the person-centered approach: New directions in theory, research and practice* (pp. 17–40). New York: Praeger.

Young, L. (1986). *The unfinished universe.* New York: Simon & Schuster.

Zeig, J. K. (1987). *The evolution of psychotherapy.* New York: Brunner/Mazel.

CHAPTER 1

A SCHEME OF ROGERS' CLINICAL RESPONSES

Debora C. Brink
Barry A. Farber

It has often been assumed by the public and even by mental health professionals that Rogers' prototypical therapeutic response was "reflecting feelings." Responding to this misperception, Rogers wrote in 1986: "I'm *not* trying to 'reflect feelings.' I am trying to determine whether my understanding of the client's inner world is correct—whether I am seeing it as he or she is experiencing it at this moment. . . . I suggest that these therapist responses be labelled not 'Reflection of Feeling' but 'Testing Understandings' or 'Checking Perceptions' " (p. 376). This clarification is important inasmuch as it counters criticism that Rogers simply and simplistically echoed his clients' statements. Moreover, the clinical interviews in this book reveal that his response repertoire was extensive, going far beyond "testing" or "checking."

The following category scheme is based on the explicit methods or techniques used by Rogers to implement his guiding therapeutic values of congruence, empathy, and caring. Of course, the use of the word "technique" or "method" here is somewhat misleading, for both words connote behavior that is antithetical to the goal of authenticity and true understanding. Nevertheless, these typical interventions were the means by which Rogers worked; in addition, these "techniques" or "methods," especially that of restatement, are the ones taught to beginning counselors worldwide.

The list is not intended to be exhaustive and reflects only the techniques identified in the Rogers' interviews included in this book. It is interesting to note that his responses show considerably greater variability in some interviews than in others. Compare, for example, Rogers' work with Mary Jane Tilden and his work with Jill; or contrast his clinical style with Mary and Louise, who were interviewed on successive days during the same workshop.

PROVIDING ORIENTATION

Rogers started many sessions, notably first contacts, by orienting self and client: a brief quiet time to get himself ready, inviting his client to do the same, then a statement of his readiness to listen. Note this example from the case of Mark:

Carl Rogers (C.R.): Now, if you can get your chair settled—this has come rather suddenly. I need to take a minute or two to kind of get with myself somehow, okay? . . . Then let's just be quiet for a minute or two. *(Pause)* Do you feel ready?

Mark: I'm ready.

C.R.: Okay. I don't know what kind of issue or problem you might want to talk about. I'd be very glad to hear whatever you have to say.

AFFIRMING HIS ATTENTION

Every recording of Rogers at work indicates that he frequently let his client know that he was present and was listening in an accepting manner. Most often, he accomplished this with a simple "M-hm, m-hm." The videos show that he tended to lean toward the client, nodding affirmatively, looking at the client steadily and directly, with eye contact ever available.

CHECKING UNDERSTANDING

Rogers often checked explicitly whether he was correctly getting his client's meaning. Note this example from the case of "Anger and Hurt":

Client: Just like somebody took a big goddamned tree and just rammed it u—, ooh, so you know? *(Sighs)* Hard to describe, you know? You know?

C.R.: Took a great big stick and rammed it up your ass—is that what you're saying?

Client: *(Laughs)* I didn't say that.

C.R.: Is that what you meant?

Client: That's what I meant.

C.R.: OK. That's what I want to know, whether I was catching your meaning correctly.

Client: Yeah, for sure.

RESTATING (ALSO KNOWN AS "REFLECTING," "MIRRORING," OR "EMPATHIZING")

We have reserved the use of the word "restating" for those occasions when Rogers did not explicitly state that he was checking his perception, but his words nonetheless seemed to reflect or mirror the client's feelings, thoughts, or meanings. Restatement sounds simple, like an echo or reflection. But Rogers seems to have had a remarkable ability to match his responses to his clients' inner meaning–feeling state—however confused these clients' words may have been.

This technique is the one most often misunderstood and even satirized. Too often have we heard mental health professionals reducing person-centered therapy to the practice of restating clients' thoughts or words. And, just as some psychoanalysts' behavior seems all too consistent with caricatured ideas of the distant, "blank screen" individual, some client-centered therapists have probably relied too exclusively on restatements in their clinical practice.

Rogers' restatements took several forms: verbatim repetition, restatements that seemed to integrate and clarify client's responses, restatements that seemed to intensify certain client feelings, and restatements in a first-person voice.

Rogers seldom repeated verbatim what a client had said. When he did so, it seemed to have the purpose of adding emphasis to a clear, crucial client statement. From the case of Jill:

Jill: She's going to save me.

C.R.: She's going to save you.

More typically, his response was to the clients' *meaning* behind their words, expressed in his own economic and lucid manner. His restatements in such cases seemed to be an attempt to integrate and clarify clients' feelings and intents. This example is from the case of Louise:

Louise: And sometimes I feel like I don't know him [father] at all. And, um, the sadness of that was coming out as well as feeling the sadness for his, failing at things he wants to do, and also the sadness that I don't know him as well as I'd like to.

C.R.: M-hm, m-hm. So it's sadness for him in his situation but sadness on your part that you don't know him.

The following example is from the case of "Anger and Hurt":

Client: And I allow myself to, and I don't regret caring, and I don't regret loving or whatever, but you know, like, I'm like a kid, you know, I'm a kid in a way, I like to be loved, too, some reciprocity. And I'm going to start, I think, expecting that, you know, without being cold or anything like that. But I have to, you know, start getting something back in return.

C.R.: You want love to be mutual.

Client: For sure, for sure.

At times, too, Rogers' restatements seemed to intensify or exaggerate client statements. Again, this seems to be in the service of providing greater clarity and a sharper focus on the feelings expressed. From the case of Mark:

Mark: And I say, "I work for the [South African] government." . . . And then they sort of float away.

C.R.: So you feel you're sort of a social leper.

Mark: Yeah, yeah.

Finally, Rogers' restatements were occasionally phrased in a first person voice, as though he were the client. This may well have had the effect of enhancing the sense of empathic concern. Here are three such rephrasings from the case of Mary: "Part of the real block is, 'If I let my power loose into the world, I might be killed for that.' " " " 'If I let out the real inner me, how could that possibly be so wrong?' " " " 'That's the way the universe is. I'll never be able to come out as I am.' "

ACKNOWLEDGING CLIENTS'
UNSTATED FEELINGS

Rogers was attentive to both verbal and nonverbal behavior. His acknowledgment of subtle or nonverbal expressions of feelings most likely strengthened a clients's sense of being seen, heard, and attended to. The first example is from the case of Gloria, the second from Jill:

Gloria: Well I'm, right now I'm nervous. But I feel more comfortable the way you're talking in a low voice and I don't feel you'll be so harsh on me. But, uh—

C.R.: I hear the tremor in your voice.

Jill: Yeah, I get very angry, very angry with her.

C.R.: *(Pause)* You're also feeling a little tension at this point, I guess.

Jill: Yeah. Yeah. A lot of conflict.

PROVIDING REASSURANCE

When reassurance was needed, Rogers most often provided it by accepting the issue or problem and placing it in a broader perspective. This example is from the case of Sylvia:

C.R.: M-hm. You would in general feel, "I have to justify myself with proper reasons."

Sylvia: M-hm. *(20-second pause)* Well, do you do that? Do you—?

C.R.: I suspect we all do, some.

Or, another example, from the case of Gloria:

Gloria: I don't get that as often as I like. . . . I like that whole feeling, that's real precious to me.

C.R.: I suspect none of us get it as often as we'd like.

Sometimes, too, Rogers provided reassurance by disagreeing with a client's negative self-judgment. In commenting on his work with Sylvia, Rogers noted that he "simply couldn't permit her to scold herself for what she'd been doing":

Sylvia: Like I just went jabber-jabber-jabber-jabber.

C.R.: Sounds like you scold yourself for that, as though, "Oh, I just talk-talk-talk." (Sylvia: M-hm.) It didn't sound like just talk-talk-talk to me.

Sylvia: It didn't? *(Laughs)*

C.R.: No.

Sometimes reassurance was granted to a client through "permission giving." That is, Rogers granted a simple request or explicitly affirmed the client's "right" to have feelings that might be perceived as socially unacceptable. From the case of Louise:

Louise: I'd like to read you what I wrote. Would that be OK?

C.R.: OK. M-hm.

And from the case of "Anger and Hurt":

C.R.: I get what you're saying, and I also feel quite strongly that I want to say, "it's OK with me if you're angry here." *(Pause)*

Client: But I don't—you know, it's hard to know how to be angry, you know, hard to—

C.R.: Sure, sure, I'm not saying you have to be.

Client: Sure.

C.R.: I'm just saying it's OK with me. If you feel like being angry, you can be angry.

Client: You really believe that?

C.R.: Damn right!

At times, too, Rogers' reassurance seemed to provide the client the experience of receiving explicit "positive regard." The first example is from the case of Jill; the second from the case of Gloria:

C.R.: What's that smile?

Jill: It's your eyes are twinkling. *(Both laugh)*

C.R.: Yours twinkle too. *(Laughs)*

Gloria: I miss that my father couldn't talk to me like you are. I mean, I'd like to say, gee, I'd like you for my father.

C.R.: You look to me like a pretty nice daughter.

Finally, it should be noted that, occasionally, Rogers held hands with a client. Sylvia asked to hold his hands, and he agreed to it. When Jim Brown was in turmoil, Rogers reached out and held his hand, being physically in touch with him during his emotional crisis.

INTERPRETING

An interpretation is an extrapolation beyond the data. Despite the popular assumption that Rogers never made interpretations, in fact, he did. And although such comments seem to have been made rarely, they sound remarkably similar to those of any analytically oriented therapist. One important difference, however: whereas analysts' interpretations may be related to a theory of personality that emphasizes linkages of the past to the present, Rogers' interpretations seem designed not to "free up" psychic energy but rather to further his understanding of the client's world. This is from the case of Louise: .

C.R.: You really want very much for him [father] to go through the kind of process that you're going through. *(Long pause)*

Louise: *(Surprised tone) Yeah. Yeah.* I suppose I want him to be more aware of himself. *(Pause) (Teary voice)* Of what a fine person he is.

C.R.: Yeah. You wish very deeply *he* could paint a picture like that.

Louise: Yeah.

CONFRONTING

Although he was seemingly more comfortable providing reassurance to clients, Rogers would, at least occasionally, confront them when they appeared to be avoiding a painful issue. These are two examples from the case of "Anger and Hurt":

C.R.: That's what I sense is going on now, that you feel, "There's so many reasons why I really shouldn't express my anger. I'll talk about all those reasons."

Client: Yeah *(small laugh)*, for sure . . .

C.R.: I hear you explaining and explaining that "It's not in my nature to be angry, it's just that I am angry right now."

Client: For sure. *(Slight laugh)* For sure . . . I don't know how you'd be angry in a productive way. . . .

C.R.: You'd like to just tell off the bastard.

Client: Yeah, right, right, right. For sure. *(Laughs)* Oh my goodness! *(Laughs)*

C.R.: You can't even do that.

Client: *(Sighs)* Oh, it's incredible. I don't know. Whew! I'm getting warm.

DIRECT QUESTIONING

As was the case with interpretations, Rogers' use of direct questions would seem to belie his basic nondirective stance. At least occasionally, Rogers *is* directive. Although in these instances, his questioning is typically used to move clients toward greater acceptance of self. From the case of Jill:

C.R.: It sounds as though you don't have too many caring people in your life.

[Later] Can you care for yourself that much?

[Later still] Can she [the little child part] care for the other parts of you?

TURNING PLEAS FOR HELP
BACK TO THE CLIENT

In the face of pleas for guidance, answers, and help, Rogers—in a true nondirective manner—turned the question back to the client. From the case of Gloria:

Gloria: I really know you can't answer for me—but I want you to guide me or show me where to start or so it won't look so hopeless . . .

C.R.: I might ask, what is it you wish I would say to you?

Gloria: I wish you would say to me to be honest and take the risk that Pammy's going to accept me—

C.R.: See, yeah, you know very well what you'd like to do in the relationship.

MAINTAINING OR BREAKING SILENCE

Remarking on his work with Sylvia, Rogers stated that he valued silence as a hard-working time for his client. In fact, during a single one-hour session with Jim Brown, an inpatient seen twice per week, Rogers shared 25 silences ranging in duration from 18 seconds to 17 minutes, 41 seconds, totaling nearly 46 minutes of silence. On the other hand, during a single half-hour workshop session with Jill, he broke 15 of the 16 silences. Clearly, his stance regarding breaking or maintaining silences was partly based on the nature of the work (ongoing therapy vs. workshop demonstration); presumably, too, his decisions were affected by considerations regarding client need.

SELF-DISCLOSING

Self-disclosure on the part of therapists may feel quite affirming to patients. Rogers' self-disclosures can be roughly grouped into statements about his therapeutic work and other statements, more personally oriented. An example of the first type is from the case of Gloria:

C.R.: See, one thing that concerns me is, uh, it's no damn good your doing something that you haven't really chosen to do. That's why I'm trying to help you find out what your own inner choices are.

Occasionally, Rogers did share with a client some of who he was as a person. This vignette is from the case of Jim Brown:

C.R.: I don't know whether this will help or not, but I would just like to say that—I think I can understand pretty well—what it's like to feel that you're just no damn good to anybody, because there was a time when—I felt that way about myself. And I know it can be really rough.

(Commenting on his response later, Rogers noted: "This is a most unusual response for me to make. I simply felt that I wanted to share my experience with him—to let him know he was not alone.")

ACCEPTING CORRECTION

When any response by Rogers missed the mark, he accepted correction by the client and moved on. From the case of Mary:

C.R.: You feel sort of doomed that . . . this expansive real inner you has not and *never* will fit into the world as it is.

Mary: Well, . . . I've never given up hope that it *never* will.

C.R.: OK. Has not and does not fit into the world as it is.

Mary: Yeah. Yeah.

One might say, in reviewing the cases presented in this book, that Carl Rogers adhered consistently to the person-centered principles and values that he held to be universally true, and that he did so flexibly through using a variety of techniques. That is, his *attitude* toward his clients was a consistent, direct expression of his therapeutic values, with his specific *techniques* being suited to the individuality of his clients within their unique circumstances at the time seen. Hence as variable as the persons with whom he worked.

REFERENCE

Rogers, C. R. (1986). Reflection of feelings. *Person-Centered Review, 1,* 375–377.

Section I

ROGERS' THERAPY CASES
Views from Within

Debora C. Brink

Now more than 50 years old, the client-centered approach (CCA) has undergone significant shifts in thinking over time. In ways similar to other venerable schools of therapy like psychoanalysis and behaviorism, the client-centered approach has grown theoretically and technically while still retaining its distinctive philosophy and values. Such modifications in therapeutic styles are often healthy, serving to keep practitioners responsive to changing social conditions and research-based advances. Thus, the client-centered approach now covers a range of practices, from those following the classical Rogerian model to others representing innovative ways of implementing Rogers' humanistic beliefs, for example, the expressive arts therapy of Natalie Rogers (1993) and the experientially oriented focusing work practiced by Eugene Gendlin (1978). Furthermore, as Maria Villas-Boas Bowen notes so well in her chapter within this section, Rogers himself, while holding true to his fundamental principles, became increasingly flexible and varied in his responses to his clients as he grew older.

The growing diversity within the client-centered community has given rise to vigorous debate among its members as to what is and what is not truly client-centered. Our sense is that a therapeutic philosophy, with its attendant values, can be implemented in a variety of ways and that, for the most part, change in technique as such does not necessarily mean a violation of that philosophy. For example, a greater focus on cognitive rather than overt behavioral phenomena does not violate the basic assump-

25

tions underlying behavior therapy, and the increasing emphasis in recent years on internal representations of self and others in psychoanalytically oriented therapy has not changed the essential character of this form of therapy. Hence, therapists may be considered client centered if they act in accord with a profound belief in the ability of clients to grow and develop, if they view the client–therapist relationship as ideally egalitarian, if they attempt to create the stated Rogerian conditions of genuineness, caring, and empathy as the bases for deeply understanding and relating to their clients, and if they reflect a true readiness to accept correction by clients. All this was certainly true of Rogers.

In this section, five of Rogers' cases are presented, four in transcript and one (the case of Gloria) in summary. We have presented these cases in chronological order so that the reader may get a sense of the shifts in Rogers' approach over the years. All these cases are commented upon by client-centered practitioners, each of whom is able to view both the essential value, as well as the flaws, of Rogers' work.

With three of these cases (Loretta, Gloria, and Mary), Rogers was, for the most part, the "classical" Rogerian, adhering to his earliest stated therapeutic procedures. While we might expect this with the two individuals with whom he worked many years ago (Loretta in 1958; Gloria in 1964), his approach with Mary, whom he interviewed as recently as the summer of 1986, less than a year before his death, seems surprisingly orthodox in its approach. On the other hand, in his session with Jill, with whom he worked in 1983, he broke all but one of the silences, exaggerated her feelings, and interpreted some of her statements. And with Louise, with whom he worked the day after his session with Mary, he remarked at the outset that he did not "usually operate" in this particular way and proceeded to direct the session by way of questions about her paintings.

During the early years of the client-centered approach, Rogers and his colleagues put forward (and empirically tested) the "necessary and sufficient conditions" for therapeutic change. As Rogers viewed it, these constituted broad guidelines for the conduct of effective psychotherapy. By the latter part of his life, however, Rogers seems to have adapted his responses intuitively to the unique needs of each of his clients. Thus, he ranged on two consecutive days from his classical approach to a more directive orientation, each seemingly appropriate for his client at that moment. This flexibility seems to derive primarily from Rogers' genuine desire to get to know, as deeply as possible, the person before him right now, on that person's own terms; paradoxically, this stance freed Rogers from the absolute necessity of having to reflect, mirror, or restate clients' responses. Consequently, Rogers' responses to a particular client often could not be predicted from his philosophy; that is, his responses were not mechanical or perfunctory reflections but rather were his whole-person reactions to the presence of his clients.

LORETTA

Loretta was a hospitalized paranoid schizophrenic patient who, at the time of the interview, was very concerned about an impending transfer to another ward. She also expressed her concern about some puzzling symptoms and experiences beyond her control, her mistrust of the hospital staff, the effects on her of her treatment, and the disturbing behavior of another patient. She mentioned her disappointment at the lack of contact with her father and brother, and her desire to go home.

The transcript of the half-hour session creates an impression of an actively engaged, free-flowing process, with both parties inclined to interrupt each other. Rogers' approach, though very active, is gentle. He presents some of his statements questioningly (e.g., "Right now you feel kind of mixed up?") and others rather tentatively (e.g., "And if I, if I sense some of your feeling now, it is, uh, a little tenseness, that, that, uh, maybe . . . "). He frequently accepts correction from Loretta. Of note, too, is that of Rogers' responses to Loretta, a significant number are in the form of first-person statements, as if he were Loretta speaking for her in her own voice (e.g., "And really with most people you feel, 'I don't think I trust 'em.' "). Overall, Rogers presents a picture of someone who wants to understand the inner world of his client as fully and accurately as possible, wanting to minimize in this process the tendency to read into the material his own projections. Thus, he can say "M-hm," restate, direct, interpret, confront, and even express personal feelings as his intuitive sense of the person before him guides him in his desire to connect and understand.

In his discussion of Rogers' session with Loretta, Nathaniel J. Raskin points up the high degree of empathy he expressed toward her and the facilitative effects thus fostered. Raskin also notes, though, that Rogers bypassed Loretta's disappointments with her father and brother, and he connects this oversight with details of Rogers' personal life. In the last part of his discussion, Raskin presents data to suggest that, in comparison to therapists of other theoretical persuasions, client-centered practitioners are less likely to dominate the client–therapist interaction. He notes in closing that Rogers' work with Loretta is a "superb example of the client-centered approach applied successfully" to a psychotic patient.

GLORIA

The case of Gloria is arguably Rogers' most famous case and much has been written about it, both by Rogers (1984) and others (e.g., Weinrach, 1990). A recent divorcée, Gloria was concerned about the possible effects of her sex life on her children. Her half-hour session with Rogers enabled her to clarify her values and feelings. However, her pleas for advice as to how to resolve her conflict between her sexual desires and her concerns for her children were consistently reflected back to her. Even so, Rogers was not always "Rogerian" in this session. He frequently did not respond to Gloria's feelings; some of his responses were not restatements of hers; and he freely expressed some of his own opinions, values, and feelings.

Gloria came to the session with a tremor in her voice, her body shaking, in an evident state of nervousness, fearing "harshness" from Rogers. With the initial presentation of her problem, she said she wanted "an answer" from him, wanted him to tell her what to do. Perhaps this is not surprising considering that Rogers had introduced himself to her as *Doctor* Rogers, that is, as the expert, at the opening of the session. In various ways Gloria expressed her plea for expert help 10 times during the brief session.

Despite his self-designation as "doctor," Rogers came to the session with a humanistic, egalitarian philosophy, a belief in his clients' capacity for self-discovery and self-direction, and a commitment not to prescribing but to helping clients find their own way. How then to meet Gloria's need for authoritative answers (implicitly promised by his title) without depriving her of an opportunity for self-determination? The following are some of the ways in which Rogers worked with Gloria in this session:

• He was gently and fully present for Gloria, expressed through posture, gaze, voice, soft laughter, and repeated "m-hm"s—all of which, taken together, probably contributed to setting Gloria more at ease.

• He made sure that he understood her meaning accurately ("Is that right?" "Is that what you're saying?") and, when he did not, he accepted her correction (five times). For example, when Gloria remarked, "Gee, I don't feel like I'm saying that, no that isn't what I feel, really," Rogers responded with: "No. OK. OK." In this manner, Rogers' empathy seemed to facilitate her own self-understanding and articulation of her own values.

• He offered several interpretations (e.g., "You hate yourself more when you lie than [when] you disapprove of your behavior"); at least one of these seemed to touch Gloria deeply: "I sense that in those utopian moments you really feel kind of whole, you feel all in one piece."

• He firmly and gently set limits as to what he would and would not do: "No, I don't want to let you just stew in your feelings, but . . . I couldn't possibly answer for you, but I sure as anything will try to help you work toward your own answer." In this way, he offered her support without reinforcing her dependency.

• In response to Gloria's persistent pleas for help from him, he asked that she answer herself through him: "What is it you wish I would say to you?" And, when she did so, he affirmed her: "See, yeah, you know very well what you'd like to do."

• He was self-revealing, expressing some of his own values and feelings pertinent to Gloria's concerns: "One thing I feel very keenly is, it's an awfully risky thing to live." And: "It's no damn good your doing something you haven't really chosen to do." In doing so, he may well have afforded her some sense of "my feelings are natural" and tempered her self-accusation of "immaturity."

In his discussion of this case, Fred Zimring points out that Rogers often spoke from "his own frame of reference" and was selective in what he responded to, tending to overlook Gloria's negative feelings, and focusing on her actions rather than on her felt sense of the moment. Reference to her "felt sense" suggests a comparison with Gendlin's approach, in which the client's attention is focused on the nonverbal, bodily feelings at the base of the experience of the moment. Moreover, Zimring's critique of this case suggests to us that further theoretical work may well be necessary to understand the full implications of the conflict that sometimes occurs between the conditions of empathy and genuineness. Speaking from one's own frame of reference seems "genuine," on the one hand, but also seems—at least under certain conditions—to conflict with the empathic goal of attending to the client's frame of reference. Whereas Zimring criticizes Rogers' tendency to speak from his own frame of reference in this case, it seems to us that some of these interpretative comments were quite accurate and may well have been valuable to Gloria (e.g., Rogers' remark that Gloria's problem seems to be in her being honest with herself). Zimring's critique thus raises the important question as to the rightful place, if any, of occasional interpretations within client-centered therapy. (This issue is dealt with, in part, in Maria Villas-Boas Bowen's chapter.)

Zimring also comments insightfully on parallels between Gloria's relationship with her father and her relationship with her daughter, pointing out that Rogers did not explicitly attend to these similarities. Zimring speculates on the way such attention may have helped Gloria resolve her quandary with her daughter more satisfactorily. Zimring does conclude, however, that Gloria's continued posttherapeutic contact with Rogers implies that their interaction had real value for her that transcended the apparent technical shortcomings of the session.

JILL

Jill, an attendant at a Rogers workshop in 1983, was concerned about her difficulty in letting go of her college-age daughter. Her self-image was negative. Rogers not only restated her negativity but consistently exaggerated it, until she finally took a counterstand with a positive self-statement.

Maria Villas-Boas Bowen (who died in 1994) places her comments regarding the case of Jill within the context of an overview of Rogers' work over a 45-year period. She shows that, though true to his original values, he demonstrates in his work with Jill much greater diversity and flexibility in his ways of implementing those values than was true early in his career. She attributes this change in his work to his greater trust in his clients' strength and self-determination.

Bowen's interpretation rings true. But an additional factor may be involved as well—intuition. Performance at the highest level of skill develops through stages from novice to expert (Dreyfus & Dreyfus, 1986). With the facts and principles of a discipline long since mastered, the expert is no longer a detached, analytic observer and a rule-bound problem solver; he or she is deeply involved in the process, capable of holistic pattern recognition, of freeflowing, adaptive, intuitive responsiveness to the immediate situation. Intuition, however, is prone to error, in principle always requiring verification. Rogers seemed to have taken this for granted, being always ready to accept—and sometimes even soliciting—correction from his clients.

It is interesting to note that, after a demonstration interview, Rogers would occasionally tell his audience that his attention was so totally focused on his client that the rest of the world simply disappeared for him. He also had no memory, he said, immediately after the event, of the details of the process. Rogers' years of experience, his deep involvement in the interaction, his insistence on correction as a matter of course, his inability to recall the details of the session—all these suggest his having come to rely on intuitive processes in the mature stages of his work. Indeed, in one of his last published articles, Rogers (1986) noted that in recent years he had begun to give more importance to intuition in his clinical practice: "As a therapist, I find that when I am closest to my inner, intuitive self, when I am somehow in touch with the unknown in me, when perhaps I am in a slightly altered state of consciousness in the relationship, then whatever I do seems to be full of healing" (p. 130).

In his willingness to embrace intuitive processes, Rogers demonstrates that departure from certain rules or procedures is compatible with commitment to client-centered principles. This is not to be understood as a message that "anything goes." Each therapist departure from standard and well-validated procedures must stand the test of respect for the autonomy and integrity of the client.

MARY AND LOUISE

Mary and Louise were participants in a Natalie Rogers' Expressive Therapy Training Program in 1986. They were interviewed by Carl Rogers on consecutive days near the end of the workshop. The two of them were at different points when interviewed: Mary was troubled by her difficulty in finding a place for herself in the world, a world that she experienced as rejecting her. Louise, however, had just arrived at a point of emergence from darkness, of celebrating her "sunrise." Mary brought a very serious issue to explore, Louise a joyous achievement to share.

Rogers' responses to Mary were restatements and clarifications of hers, affirming her corrections when he had not quite gotten it. His acceptance and support enabled her to "swallow" what had stood in opposition to her, facilitating a resolution of her conflict. With Louise, Rogers let go of the way he "usually operates." Upon noticing her intent gaze at her pictures, he directed that they be brought over; Louise locked onto them visually, as if to drink them in, seemingly oblivious to Rogers. He entered into her absorption with humorous but unqualified acceptance, emphatically affirming that she *was* the sunrise of her painting. In a freewheeling style, he was directive (gently, with questions), interpretive (e.g., regarding her father), affirming, clarifying, and willing to let her *be with* her picture, the power of which she had not fully appreciated until her session with him.

Peggy Natiello points out with illuminating detail how closely Rogers' interventions matched Mary's concerns. His attunement encouraged her to probe more deeply, with his responses becoming more intimate as she did so, enabling her to arrive at a deeply satisfying resolution.

In a letter from Mary 6 years after this interview, she says:

> The two equally healing and transformational aspects of that whole [expressive therapy] experience were, first, the power of the creative arts processes in opening me up to myself and, second, the affirming and compassionately accepting nature of the person-centered approach which allowed me to venture forth, and which was capped by my interview with Carl. The healing begun [then] has continued to deepen and expand in me—My present experience of immeasurably expanded inner peace, freedom and actualization make the previous four decades of suffering seem a distant dream.

Rogers' work with Louise is more problematic for Natiello. She finds his directive manner suggestive of a possible hidden agenda of his own regarding her pictures. She suggests that this may have promoted a lack of connectedness between them and missed opportunities for Rogers to be of help to Louise.

However, maybe because of the unusual nature of the occasion—an opportunity for the celebration of growth rather than for seeking help—Louise found the session of crucial importance. In a telephone conversation in 1992, she said that she had worked with Natalie Rogers (in her

Expressive Therapy Training Program) since 1978, but this experience of hers with Rogers in 1986 was special for her. The session, with its "amazing climax," made her feel she could "do anything." About the session with Rogers she said, "I really was *with* the pictures, it was natural, felt marvelous." What she needed most at the time, she said, was celebration. Rogers helped her "to *see* the celebration. He made a leap in saying, 'you *are* the sunrise,' and it worked." But had Rogers not missed out on those valuable opportunities pointed out by Natiello, who knows how much richer her gain might have been!

REFERENCES

Dreyfus, H. L., & Dreyfus, S. E. (1986). *Mind over machine: The power of human intuition and expertise in the era of the computer.* New York: Free Press.

Gendlin, E. T. (1978). *Focusing.* New York: Everest House.

Rogers, C. R. (1984). Gloria—A historical note. In R. F. Levant & J. Shlien (Eds.), *Client-centered therapy and the person-centered approach: New directions in theory, research, and practice* (pp. 423–425). New York: Praeger.

Rogers, C. R. (1986). Rogers, Kohut, and Erickson: A personal perspective on some similarities and differences. *Person-Centered Review, 1,* 125–140.

Rogers, N. (1993). *The creative connection: Expressive arts as healing.* Palo Alto, CA: Science & Behavior Books.

Weinrach, S. G. (1990). Rogers and Gloria: The controversial film and the enduring relationship. *Psychotherapy, 27,* 282–290.

CHAPTER 2

THE CASE OF LORETTA (1958)

TRANSCRIPT[*]

Carl Rogers (C.R.): *(Screaming in the background)* I'm Carl Rogers. This must seem confusing and odd, and so on, but I, I felt really sorry that the interview had been kind of cut short 'cause I sort of felt maybe there were other things you wanted to say.

Loretta: I don't know. I'm being moved all right, transferred. And I was just wondering if I'm quite ready for a transfer. I've mentioned that—it's annoying, that woman talking, uh, she's been yelling like that *(referring to patient who keeps screaming in the background)*. I really rather like it on my ward. (C.R.: M-hm, m-hm.) And I have been helping . . . I had thought maybe I could go home from there. (C.R.: M-hm, m-hm.) I know being transferred means I'll probably be put to work in the laundry all day. *(Screaming in the background)* And I don't feel quite up to that.

C.R.: M-hm, m-hm. So that's one immediate thing of concern. "Am I ready to face whatever's involved in moving away from the spot where I've—?"

Loretta: You get kind of oriented to one place when you're here.

C.R.: M-hm, you get sort of used to it and—

Loretta: Oh, I meant to correct one thing. When I said "no" before, I didn't

---

[*]This interview with Loretta is Tape Number One in the Audiotape Library of the American Academy of Psychotherapists. This transcript was prepared by Marco Temaner and emended by Nathaniel J. Raskin.

mean I was tired of talking to that doctor. I just meant, "no," that I was ready to, that I wondered why I couldn't go home.

C.R.: Yeah, yeah. That you felt he didn't quite understand you on that *(screaming in the background)*, that really—

Loretta: Maybe he thought I was being blunt *(loud screaming in the background)* . . . and that I meant "no," I didn't want to talk to him anymore. *(Loud screaming)*

C.R.: Uh-huh. *(Screaming continues intermittently.)* And if I, if I sense some of your feeling now, it is, uh, a little tenseness that, that, uh, maybe he didn't really get that. Maybe he thought you were, sort of—

Loretta: I thought he thought I—

C.R.: Shutting him off, or something.

Loretta: Yes! That's what I had thought. (C.R.: Uh-huh.) And that isn't what I meant— (C.R.: Uh-huh.) Uh, I don't know. I'm wondering if that transfer is a good thing. I mean, they make you feel so important around here, and still you aren't, but— (C.R.: M-hm, m-hm.) Then when I go over to Two, I know that's an open ward, that's [a] dormitory, and I've been wearing not so many of my own clothes 'cause I don't like to launder them. Just wonder if I'm ready for that change.

C.R. M-hm, and that—

Loretta: 'Cause my father and that don't come to visit me or anything, so I don't get out at all on weekends or anything.

C.R.: M-hm. . . . And I'm not quite sure about this. Is it in the ward where you are now that you feel, yeah, they seem to make you so important, but then really you're not. *(Screaming in the background)* Is that—?

Loretta: That's really it. I'm important, but I'm really not. (C.R.: M-hm.) I probably wouldn't be on the other ward, either. Well I know that, you're not very important when you move to that ward.

C.R: I see. So that if you're not very important where you are right now, you feel then if you were transferred, even less so.

Loretta: Even less important.

C.R.: So that's something that concerns you.

Loretta: I think it means working all day in the laundry, too, and I'm not quite ready for that. I mentioned earlier that I had this tickling sensation in my knees when I was on Six C when I was getting Reserpine and a tranquilizer— (C.R.: M-hm, m-hm.) I think it was. And I asked the doctor at that time if he would move me, so I could go to work and work in the laundry. (C.R.: M-hm, m-hm.) And the transfer came today. I didn't ask to be transferred, though, this time.

C.R.: M-hm, m-hm. But it troubles you as to whether you're really ready to face some of the things that would be involved.

Loretta: I don't know, there isn't much to face, it's kind of confusing, I think.

C.R.: I see. It's more a question of facing the uncertainties, is that what you mean?

Loretta: I don't know what I mean *(little laugh)* . . . I just know that—

C.R.: Right now you feel kind of mixed up?

Loretta: Well, I know there's Anita on that ward that I didn't trust very far *(banging in the background)* because she's the one that put me on shock treatment.

C.R.: I see.

Loretta: Or I think she did, anyway. (C.R.: M-hm, m-hm.) And still she put her arm around my shoulder when I came back, but it . . . she was the one that told me I had to go on it and I had done nothing that I knew of to be put on that kind of treatment.

C.R.: So that there's something that's real confusing. It would be putting you next to a person who seemed to like you and put her arm around you and, by gosh, was responsible for shock treatment.

Loretta: That's right. . . . Of course she said it was doctor's orders, but I hadn't talked to a doctor that I knew of at the time. (C.R: M-hm, m-hm.) And I know that they gave them to . . . even though that was a work ward they had them go over to the treatment ward and then back to the work ward. (C.R: M-hm, m-hm.) *(Screaming in the background)* And then to work.

C.R.: M-hm, sure you heard, the explanation was doctor's orders and all that, but you can't help but feel, "Is she really trustworthy?" 'Cause here she seemed to—

Loretta: No, I don't trust people anyway, anymore. (C.R.: M-hm, m-hm.) That's why I don't want them to trust me. I either believe in them or I don't believe in them.

C.R.: M-hm, and all or none.

Loretta: And I don't quite think I believe in her very much.

C.R.: M-hm, m-hm. And really with most people you feel, "I don't think I trust 'em."

Loretta: That's the truth, I don't trust 'em. *(Screaming in the background)* Either believe 'em, or I don't believe 'em or I don't, I'm not quite certain whether I believe them yet or not. (C.R.: M-hm, m-hm.) But I don't believe in, trust anymore.

C.R.: M-hm, m-hm. That's one thing that you feel has really dropped out for you, that just to trust people. Not for you.

Loretta: No, I don't trust 'em. . . . You can get hurt much too easily by trusting people.

C.R.: M-hm, m-hm. If you really believe in someone, and let your trust go out to them, then—

Loretta: I don't have any trust, that's why I can't let any trust go out to 'em.

C.R.: M-hm, but evidently your feeling is that when that has happened in the past—

Loretta: You just get hurt by it.

C.R.: That's the way you can get hurt.

Loretta: That's the way I *have* been hurt.

C.R.: That's the way you *have* been hurt.

Loretta: I don't mind being moved. I mean if it's, uh *(pounding in the background)*, uh, another thing toward going home. (C.R.: M-hm.) *(Screaming in the background)* But I don't get out anyway, and I don't, I don't know that he, my brother, I wrote a letter, but I didn't get any answer from him. *(Screaming in the background)* (C.R.: M-hm, m-hm.) He never came.

C.R.: M-hm. It isn't that, at least what I understand you to be saying, is that it isn't the practical question of the move so much that, uh, but it's the question of—

Loretta: If I'm quite ready for that.

C.R.: Yeah, are you, are you ready for a next step, is that it?

Loretta: I don't think I'm going to like working in the laundry, that I know. 'Cause I didn't like it either [of] the other two times. *(Announcement on PA system in the background)* And I don't think I care too much [for] working on [the] food center over there, either, because I worked there before, and I didn't care for it. (C.R.: M-hm, m-hm.) Well, I didn't have anything . . . I . . . the first day I worked all right, the second day I worked about a half an hour, and I blacked out, and I tried it 3 more days, and I blacked out each day, so . . . I just quit trying to work there. There was too much electricity or something.

C.R.: M-hm, m-hm. You feel something was wrong over there? Too much electricity or something, "that really had a bad effect on me when I was working there."

Loretta: It did. I blacked out, completely. If I hadn't gone to sit down, I would have fainted.

C.R.: M-hm, m-hm. You feel really you were in, in kind of a desperate way, at those points?

Loretta: No, I didn't feel desperate. I just, I didn't understand it, I didn't know why I blacked out.

C.R.: I see.

Loretta: It did frighten me, though. I just couldn't work, so—

C.R.: It was just something very odd happening to you.

Loretta: 'Cause I don't have epilepsy seizures or anything like that, so I couldn't imagine what it was. I don't, I'm not, I don't usually have fainting spells.

C.R.: M-hm. It just made you feel real puzzled. "What is happening to me?"

Loretta: What it was, yeah, I tried, but I couldn't work, and they wanted me to work, so . . . sometimes I think you get put back on treatment if you refuse to work.

C.R.: Uh-huh. Well, maybe, maybe shock treatment is really something they may use for punishment if you don't do the things the way they want you to do?

Loretta: Well, it would appear that way from what everybody says, but I don't think I was even, I don't know why they even gave it to me in the first place. I was just beginning to come to, enough to realize that I was in an institution, I think. (C.R.: M-hm, m-hm.) And the next thing I knew, they said, "You're ready, you're on treatment." (C.R.: M-hm, m-hm.) And I said, "Why? I didn't do anything. I haven't had any fight or anything with anybody." (C.R.: M-hm, m-hm.) And they said, "Well, doctor's orders." And I said, "Well, I haven't even talked to a doctor."

Because I *hadn't* talked to one. (C.R.: M-hm, m-hm.) At least I didn't know it if I had. (C.R.: M-hm, m-hm, m-hm.) And so—

C.R.: So to you it seemed, "Here I was just beginning to come to life a little, really to know a little bit what was going on."

Loretta: I was just beginning to realize I was in the hospital— (C.R.: Uh-huh.) When they put me on it, and they put me to work the same day.

C.R.: And then you feel that for no reason you could discern, zingo, you were—

Loretta: And I began talking very badly and everything, and I still haven't forgotten some of the things I said.

C.R.: M-hm, m-hm, m-hm. It feels that, that sort of brought out the worst in you, is that what you mean?

Loretta: If I had a worst part. It was like it wasn't even me talking.

C.R.: Uh-huh. Almost seemed as though this—

Loretta: And then I went home weekends, and I got in trouble there, because I talked so much. Of course, I was getting Sodium Amytal, too, so it might have been the combination of the two, not just the one thing.

C.R.: But there, too, I guess I get the feeling that you're wishing you could understand that part of yourself; was it something that was not you talking, or was it just the effect of the drugs, or what was it that made you—?

Loretta: It was the combination, I think. (C.R.: Uh-huh.) If you notice, my . . . I move my feet.

C.R.: Yes, I did notice.

Loretta: As I said, my knees tickle. (C.R.: M-hm, m-hm.) And I, I don't know if it's the drugs I'm getting or what, but it's something I can't help. It isn't that I'm so terribly nervous that I can't sit still, that isn't it. I do that at group meetings or anything, and I can't control them. It's rather embarrassing *(laughs nervously)*.

C.R.: And you would like me to understand that it isn't just tenseness or something, it's, uh—

Loretta: No.

C.R.: It's simply the—

Loretta: Something I can't control.

C.R.: Uncontrollable tickling sensations. *(Screaming in the background)*

Loretta: In my knees and that far up, and my feet just move. If I'm sitting up there in the corner alone, that isn't so much, but my knees still tickle. (C.R: M-hm, m-hm.) But when I get in a group, and that, my, I don't know, they just move.

C.R.: It seems as though being in a group makes this worse.

Loretta: Well, I have it when I'm alone sometimes, too. (C.R: M-hm, m-hm.) I think it's the medication I'm getting.

C.R.: Well, probably it's just the drugs?

Loretta: I think it's the green medication I'm getting. I don't even know what it is, 'cause I haven't asked, but then— (C.R.: M-hm.) *(Pause)* I think these meetings are very enlightening *(little laugh)*.

C.R.: Do you?

Loretta: Well, if you can't think quite clear at the time, you can think about it later.

C.R.: M-hm, m-hm. And in that sense they, they're somewhat helpful in *(banging in the background)* making you think more clearly afterwards?

Loretta: I think I've been helped a lot by, more by talking than I have by the pills, and that.

C.R.: M-hm, m-hm. It really, it seems as though getting things out to some degree in talk—

Loretta: Seems to alleviate whatever the situation is. (C.R.: M-hm, m-hm.) If it's created a situation that seems to alleviate . . . I wish that woman would quit screaming.

C.R.: "Why doesn't she stop?"

Loretta: She can't stop though, that's the worst of it. . . . That gives you a terrible feeling, what's going to happen to you if you end up in a, like that.

C.R.: Yeah, yeah, part of the, part of the disturbance of that noise is the feeling, "My god, could this happen to me?"

Loretta: Yes. (C.R.: M-hm, m-hm.) Exactly. And you think you could just about go out of your head just from hearing that all the time. That's been going on for 3 days now, and why did they give her that much, she, if it's who I think it is, she was up on the ward for one of those QIM clinics, and I sat next to her, and she said something about liking to talk, and all of a sudden she was, she just began talking and didn't quit.

C.R.: So this seems kind of awful, that here is this person and—

Loretta: She was all . . . perfectly all right then, calm; she wasn't talking or anything—

C.R.: Next to you and so on, and now here it's just going on and on—

Loretta: You should think, I thought they could relieve those, not make them worse.

C.R.: It's kind of discouraging in a sense to feel that they, it seems to you, that they aren't helping her.

Loretta: Yes, considering it's an admission ward, and they shouldn't be that far out of their heads. It's more like the drugs they're giving after they're here are doing it to them.

C.R.: Almost makes you feel, "Are they making her worse with their drugs?" Is that—?

Loretta: That's right.

C.R.: And that's kind of a disturbing—

Loretta: I think it is.

C.R.: Thought, too—

Loretta: Because after all, I'm getting drugs, too, and I wouldn't want to end up like that.

C.R.: M-hm, m-hm. It can't help but raise the question in you, "Would the drugs they're giving me make me like that?"

Loretta: That's right. And then once you're that way, what can you do about it? Only, only I know what they're like and I can see it, so I have enough control to hang on to myself, enough to keep from just batting my head against the wall, like, uh. . . . Some of them had that feeling, and they just can't control it. They . . . I've seen so much of it and heard so much of it that I can hang on to myself a little bit.

C.R.: Those things are kind of—

Loretta: I think that's why, pardon me, I think that's why my knees tingle, though, because rather than batting my head against the wall, I have that type of reaction.

C.R.: M-hm, m-hm. So in a sense, you can hold yourself in enough so you're not going to bat your head against the wall, and yet it's as though it has to come out somewhere, and it, uh—

Loretta: Comes out in the tickling. It's terrible!.

C.R.: Comes out in the tickling of your knees.

Loretta: Because . . . well, I've seen on the outside, too, so I mean I know that . . . it's just futile to bat your head. Why anyway, I think my head's too valuable to bat against the wall *(laughs)*. It's my own head, and I like it.

C.R.: You feel by gosh, "I'm not going to smash my head against walls."

Loretta: That's right. After all, God gave me that head, that's the head I want. I'm not going to bang it against the wall, even if I like to, which I really wouldn't like to do, anyway. . . . Well, why, how does that help that girl to be in . . . locked up like that and screaming like that? What, I mean what . . . beneficial aid is she getting out of that? Anything?

C.R.: I guess that's the question you're asking yourself, "What earthly good—?"

Loretta: No, I'm asking *you*.

C.R.: You're asking me. Well, I'm not on the hospital staff, and I really guess I wouldn't try to answer because I don't know her, and I don't know anything about it. But what I can understand is, is the way that affects you and the feelings that it stirs up in you. 'Cause it sounds as though with you that, that is disturbing not only from the noise from her but the things that it *(screaming in the background)* stirs up in you.

Loretta: I don't know. I'm all mixed up. I want to *(loud screaming in the background)* go to Building One, but I know Building One's not the next to home. . . . But if I could go home from One, I'd be happy. . . . But I've been there before. I know it's going to be a great change from this building. I hate to leave this building, 'cause it's quite beautiful. . . . But still, it, maybe it's better than listening to that girl screaming all day, every day.

C.R.: It's a real tough choice to make.

Loretta: But I hate to think that I'm going to have to go to work in the laundry room. I'd rather . . . and there isn't as much to do around that ward as there is here, that much I know.

C.R.: M-hm, m-hm. You feel that, uh—

Loretta: You can relax and just sleep, because you do have beds, but I don't think they do. I think they expect you to work if you can. (C.R: M-hm, m-hm.) They don't go that far as to just let you rest like you're in a hospital for a rest. *(Screaming in the background)* Keep you working all the time.

C.R.: If it, if it represented a chance to rest, then you might like it, but if it's a chance just to work all the time, uh, then you're not sure that that's what you want.

Loretta: I don't think I'm ready for it. (C.R: Uh-huh.) Because my knees tickle, maybe that's. . . . I worked in the laundry before, and I know. I got along all right. I know I can get along now, but—

C.R.: "I could do it, but, uh, am I really ready for it?"

Loretta: Though why?

C.R.: "Why?" M-hm.

Loretta: I packed my own grip, so I'm all ready to go. I didn't say, "No, I won't go," because I'm always putting up a big fight about it. (C.R.: M-hm, m-hm.) If it's an improvement, well, I'm willing to go along with it.

C.R.: M-hm. A chance you're willing to take although within yourself, you feel a lot of question about it.

Loretta: I rather like seeing them admitted, although I can't say that I like to see 'em get worse. But when they improve it's quite a joy to, to be where they're all coming in and going out.

C.R.: It kind of helps you inside, when they, when they—

Loretta: To know that others get well and can go home.

C.R.: M-hm, m-hm. So that you're sort of discouraged and encouraged by what happens to others.

Loretta: I had thought, I had thought that I'd go home from here because I hadn't done anything very serious— (C.R.: M-hm.) I hadn't, uh, had any violent struggle with anybody, or anything like that.

C.R.: That's part of your feeling all the way through, "I haven't done anything wrong, I've held myself in, you know, I really have not been violent, I haven't broken many rules."

Loretta: I haven't broken any, I don't think.

C.R.: You haven't broken any—

Loretta: And half the time you have to find out what the rules are, because they don't tell ya.

C.R.: M-hm, m-hm. But your feeling is, "I've been good."

Loretta: But I haven't been *too* good, though. *(Screaming in the background)* You shouldn't go overboard about being good, too. (C.R.: M-hm.) I don't believe in that, either. (C.R.: M-hm.) I've been as good as I know how to be. (C.R.: M-hm) And I'm not letter-perfect. I would like to be, but I'm not.

C.R.: But in terms of what you can do, you feel you've done the best you can do.

Loretta: I'm doing as good as I know how.

C.R.: M-hm. Loretta, I know that some of these people have got to go, and I expect we've got to call it quits. I appreciate this chance to talk with you.

Loretta: And thank you very much. I know that you're very important people. That's what I've heard, anyhow.

COMMENTARY

THE CASE OF LORETTA
A Psychiatric Inpatient

Nathaniel J. Raskin

THE INTERVIEW AND ITS CONTEXT

"I'm Carl Rogers. This must seem confusing and odd, and so on, but I, I felt really sorry that the interview had been kind of . . . cut short 'cause I sort of felt maybe there were other things you wanted to say." Thus does Carl Rogers open his interview with Loretta, a state hospital inpatient, diagnosed as paranoid schizophrenic, in the summer of 1958. The American Academy of Psychotherapists was in the middle of its 4-day Second Annual Workshop at the University of Wisconsin in Madison. The 30 or so participating therapists were gathered in a small auditorium of the hospital to observe one another in actual practice. Loretta had been previously interviewed by Albert Ellis to demonstrate his rational–emotive approach and by psychiatrist Richard Felder to demonstrate the experiential method of his Atlanta group, which included Carl Whitaker, Tom Malone, and John Warkentin.

Ellis and Felder had had a difficult time with Loretta, and there was a clamor in this diverse group of experienced therapists for Rogers to try his hand with her. He was only too willing, as he had suffered through two interviews in which, from his point of view, this woman's expressed feelings and attitudes had not been responded to empathically. Ellis, the day before, had tried to help Loretta to see the irrationality of her behavior, and Felder, earlier on this day, had attempted to engage her in a person-to-person dialogue about, among other things, a dream he had had about her the night before. It was the interview with Felder to which Rogers referred when he said he thought Loretta might have felt cut short. After Rogers agreed to the interview, Loretta, who had returned to her ward, was asked how she felt about returning to talk to still another psychotherapist; her response was positive.

Aside from attending this workshop as the first president of the American Academy of Psychotherapists, Rogers had moved from the University of Chicago to the University of Wisconsin the year before for a joint professorship in Psychology and Psychiatry. This bears directly on the interview with Loretta, because Rogers saw his appointment at Wisconsin as providing an opportunity to test the hypothesis that client-centered therapy would work with a schizophrenic population. This would be explored comprehensively in a large-scale research project (Rogers, Gendlin, Kiesler, & Truax, 1967); the interview with Loretta was a single clinical test of Rogers' hypothesis.

THE SIGNIFICANCE OF THE INTERVIEW

The Case of Loretta is significant in at least two ways. First, it is one of the few verbatim recordings of a therapeutic interview, within any orientation, with a psychotic patient. Second, it provides a concrete example of the application of client-centered therapy to a psychiatric inpatient diagnosed as paranoid schizophrenic. The interview shows how a deeply disturbed individual may respond positively to the therapist-offered conditions of empathy, congruence, and unconditional positive regard.

One stereotype of client-centered therapy is that it is a superficial approach that works primarily with "normal people," for example, college students with minor problems. Rogers may have contributed to this belief in *Counseling and Psychotherapy* (1942) his first book-length exposition of his approach, in which he stated, as one of the tentative criteria for attempting psychotherapy of any kind, that the individual be "reasonably free from excessive instabilities" (p. 77). His position was radically different in his next book, *Client-Centered Therapy* (1951). Here he wrote:

> Present opinion on applicability must take into account our experience. A client-centered approach has been used with two-year-old children and adults of 65, with mild adjustment problems, such as student study habits, and the most severe disorders of diagnosed psychotics. . . . An atmosphere of acceptance and respect, of deep understanding, is a good climate for personal growth, and as such applies to our children, our colleagues, our students, as well as to our clients, whether these be "normal," neurotic, or psychotic. This

does *not* mean that it will *cure* every psychological condition, and indeed the concept of cure is quite foreign to the approach. (pp. 229–230)

The interview with Loretta lasted about 30 minutes. Some of the noteworthy occurrences in this brief encounter, each of which is amplified, include:

1. Loretta's explanation of her side of the process of ending the just-completed interview with Dr. Felder. It was clear that the opportunity to clarify this was important to her.
2. Her exploration of the problem of an impending transfer to another ward. This was her "presenting problem," a real one.
3. The transition from this specific issue to the question of whether she was able to trust people in general and whether she could trust the hospital staff in her treatment.
4. Her expressions of distress and confusion about the treatment of a patient heard screaming in the background continually throughout the interview.
5. Her descriptions of peculiar sensations of tickling in her knees and of a feeling of electricity in the air when she had worked in the hospital laundry.
6. Her emerging positive self-regard as the interview progressed.

Loretta explains her side of the process of ending the just-completed interview. After introducing the subject of her impending transfer to another ward, Loretta wishes to clear up a possible misunderstanding of her attitude about ending the interview just concluded with Dr. Richard Felder. She makes it clear that the opportunity to clarify this is important to her: "Oh, I meant to correct one thing. When I said 'no' before, I didn't mean I was tired of talking to that doctor. I just meant 'no,' that I was ready to, that I wondered why I couldn't go home." Rogers empathizes: "Yeah, yeah. That you felt he didn't quite understand you on that really."

At this point, screaming can be heard in the background, but Loretta responds to Rogers' comment: "Maybe he thought I was being blunt and that I meant, 'no,' I didn't want to talk to him anymore." To which Rogers responds: "Uh-huh. And if, if I sense some of your feeling now, it is, uh, a little tenseness that, that, uh, maybe he didn't really get that. Maybe he thought you were, sort of . . . shutting him off, or something." Loretta agrees: "Yes! That's what I had thought."

Rogers' empathic responses in this dialogue facilitate Loretta's explanation, and, apparently satisfied that she has clarified her position, she then returns to the issue of the ward transfer.

Loretta explores the problem of an impending transfer to another ward. Loretta now begins to explain her concern, her presenting problem: "I don't know. I'm being moved all right, transferred. And I was just wondering if I'm quite ready for a transfer. . . . It's annoying, that woman . . . yelling like that *(referring to patient who keeps screaming in the background)*. I really rather like it on my ward."

The ward transfer is clearly an issue of great importance to Loretta, She devotes about one quarter of the interview with Rogers to it. To summarize some of her attitudes about it:

> I don't know if I'm ready for the work that would be involved in the transfer. I'd hate to work in the laundry room; I'm not even keeping up with my own laundry now. And when I worked in the food center in that ward, I had real physical trouble. I blacked out.
> Even though the hospital makes a pretense that the patients are important, I'm not really important on my present ward and would be less so on the new one.
> At one time I wanted the transfer, but I didn't ask for it right now.
> I'm confused.
> If the transfer is a step closer to my discharge from the hospital, that would make me favor it more.
> I like the building I'm in, because it's beautiful, and there's more to do here, but it would be nice to get away from that screaming girl.
> I wouldn't mind going to the new ward if they let you rest there, but they keep you working all the time.
> I was able to work in the laundry when I was there before. I know I can do it now, but I'm not sure I'm ready for it.
> I won't refuse to go. I've even packed my own grip. If it's an improvement, I'm willing to go along with the move.

Rogers communicates his empathic understanding of these attitudes. Specifically, he recognizes Loretta's feelings of confusion and uncertainty about whether she is ready for this change in her life. He acknowledges that it is a tough choice to make and articulates Loretta's feeling that it might not be what she really wants. This seems to have the effect of helping Loretta, after considerable exploration, come to a resolution of a very difficult and troubling issue: She would be willing to give the transfer a try, even though she is not sure she is ready for it.

Loretta's exploration of the issue of the ward transfer leads her into the question of whether she is able to trust people in general. After Rogers empathizes with Loretta's feeling of confusion ("Right now you feel kind of mixed up?"), she moves to a new issue: "Well, I know there's Anita on that ward that I didn't trust very far . . . because she's the one that put me on shock treatment." Later in this segment, responding to Rogers' understanding and acceptance of her distrust of one person, Loretta shares with him the breadth of her distrust: "I don't trust people anyway anymore." A little later, she adds, "You can get hurt much too easily by trusting people." The attitudes she expresses in this segment can be summarized as follows:

> I don't trust the staff person who I think was responsible for my getting shock therapy. She acted friendly and said it was done on "doctor's orders," but as far as I know I hadn't talked to a doctor.
> In a very general way, I don't trust people anymore. I've been hurt when I did.
> I don't understand why they suddenly ordered shock therapy for me. I wonder if it was because I said I couldn't work and they didn't believe me.
> All of a sudden, I was given shock and assigned to work.

Rogers deals with Loretta's difficulties in trusting people by consistently trying to appreciate her feelings and perceptions. For example, when Loretta expresses her lack of trust about the staff member who orchestrated her shock treatment, Rogers replies, "So that there's something that's real confusing. It would be putting you next to a person who seemed to like you and put her arm around you and, by gosh, was responsible for shock treatment." He also empathizes with her feeling that the shock treatment is used to get her to perform her duties: "Well, maybe, maybe shock treatment is really something they may use for punishment if you don't do the things the way they want you to do?"

Implicitly, in the way he responds, Rogers invites Loretta to correct him when he has not gotten her feelings exactly right. This is exemplified when she begins to discuss her inability to trust people because it inevitably leads to getting hurt. When Rogers responds with what appears to be accurate empathy: "That's the way you can get hurt," Loretta goes further and states: "That's the way I *have* been hurt." Whereupon Rogers accepts her clarification: "That's the way you *have* been hurt."

Loretta expresses distress and confusion about the treatment of a patient frequently heard screaming in the background during the interview. A dramatic aspect of the audiotape recording of this interview is the sound of another female patient screaming in the background. After mentioning it in her first statement, Loretta does not bring up the subject again until more than halfway into her dialogue with Rogers, even though the sound is piercing and rather constant: "I wish that woman would quit screaming." Rogers' empathic response is in the form of a question: "Why doesn't she stop?" Loretta's answer takes her into a personal concern: "She can't stop though, that's the worst of it. . . . That gives you a terrible feeling, what's going to happen to you if you end up in a, like that."

Some of the attitudes expressed by Loretta in this section are:

> That woman's screaming really bothers me. You could go out of your head hearing that all the time.
> I'm worried that I could end up like that.
> I sat next to her, and she seemed perfectly all right. She was calm and not talking.
> You would think the hospital could help somebody like that, not make her worse.
> I think maybe it's the drugs they're giving her.
> I'm getting drugs, and I'm worried I could end up like that.

In his usual way, Rogers responds with explicit empathic understanding to these concerns. He verbalizes Loretta's fear that what happened to this screaming woman could also happen to her, as well as her suspicion that the hospital staff had caused her disturbance rather than relieved it. Note, for example, the following empathic response: "Almost makes you feel, 'Are they making her worse with their drugs?' " On the basis of Loretta's participation in the dialogue, one may reasonably conclude that she feels understood regarding her misgivings about the treatment of the screaming patient and her fear that she could end up the same way.

Loretta describes sensations of tickling in her knees and a feeling of electricity in the air. Loretta explains her experiences as follows: "I don't think I'm going to like working in the laundry, that I know. 'Cause I didn't like it either the other two times. . . . And I don't think I care too much working on food center over there, either, because I worked there before, and I didn't care for it. (C.R.: Mh-m, m-hm.) Well, I didn't have anything . . . I . . . the first day, I worked all right, the second day I worked about a half an hour, and I blacked out, and I tried it 3 more days, and I blacked out each day, so . . . I just quit trying to work there. There was too much electricity or something."

To this, Rogers replies: "M-hm, m-hm. You feel something was wrong over there? Too much electricity or something, 'that really had a bad effect on me when I was working there.' " And after Loretta describes how frightened she felt by her blackouts, Rogers responds, "It was just something very odd happening to you," and then, "M-hm. It just made you feel real puzzled. 'What is happening to me?' "

A little later, Loretta describes another symptom: "If you notice, my

. . . I move my feet." To which Rogers responds: "Yes, I did notice." And Loretta further explains: "As I said, my knees tickle. (C.R.: M-hm, m-hm.) And I, I don't know if it's the drugs I'm getting or what, but it's something I can't help. It isn't that I'm so terribly nervous that I can't sit still, that isn't it. I do that at group meetings or anything, and I can't control them. It's rather embarrassing *(laughs nervously).*"

Rogers listens respectfully to Loretta's experience that the sensations are specific to particular situations: "It seems as though being in a group makes this worse." He is also responsive to Loretta's belief that her symptoms are caused by her medication: "Well, probably it's just the drugs?" Later Loretta comes up with another explanation for the sensations in her knees. She has been discussing the patient who screams: "And then once you're that way, what can you do about it? Only, only I know what they're like and I can see it, so I have enough control to hang on to myself, enough to keep from just batting my head against the wall, like, uh. . . . Some of them had that feeling and they just can't control it. They . . . I've seen so much of it and heard so much of it that I can hang on to myself a little bit. . . . I think that's why my knees tingle, though, because rather than batting my head against the wall, I have that type of reaction."

Rogers then responds: "M-hm, m-hm. So in a sense, you can hold yourself in enough so you're not going to bat your head against the wall, and yet it's as though it has to come out somewhere, and it, uh . . . " Loretta finishes Rogers' sentence: "Comes out in the tickling." Rogers accepts her way of putting it: "Comes out in the tickling of your knees."

The striking feature of the interaction between Loretta and Rogers on the topic of her odd sensations is that he is just as respectful of this kind of experience on the part of a hospitalized schizophrenic as he would be of the everyday experience of a "normal" client. His unconditional positive regard for Loretta, together with his empathy and genuineness, appear to facilitate her movement toward a rational explanation of what initially appeared to be bizarre symptoms.

Loretta expresses greater positive regard for herself as the interview progresses. The interview with Loretta illustrates a dynamic observed by Rogers from the earliest days of client-centered therapy: If the therapist conveys an empathic understanding and acceptance of the client's negative feelings, the client is freed to experience positive aspects of self and others. For example, immediately after the dialogue about the tickling in her knees, Loretta says: "it's just futile to bat your head. Why anyway, I think my head's too valuable to bat against the wall *(laughs).* It's my own head, and I like it." Here is a dramatic expression of Loretta's belief that she is a worthwhile person. Similarly, in her next exchange with Rogers, she says: "That's right. After all, God gave me that head, that's the head I want. I'm not going to bang it against the wall, even if I like to, which I really wouldn't like to do, anyway. . . . Well, why, how does that help that girl to be in . . . locked up like that and screaming like that? What, I mean what . . . beneficial aid is she getting out of that? Anything?"

Rogers reply here is, "I guess that's the question you're asking yourself, 'What earthly good . . . ?' " Loretta interrupts Rogers at this point and says, "No, I'm asking *you*." Here, then, we see Loretta standing up to this noted psychologist, letting him know what she meant: She wants to know what *he* thinks of the treatment of the screaming patient. There are other examples in the interview of Loretta's insistence on being understood exactly. One such instance occurs when Loretta is describing her blackouts. One of Rogers' responses is "M-hm, m-hm. You feel really you were in, in kind of a desperate way, at those points?" Loretta corrects Rogers' statement: "No, I didn't feel desperate. I just, I didn't understand it. I didn't know why I blacked out."

These examples of Loretta's insistence on being understood exactly are the second indication of her emerging self-regard in this interview. A third, somewhat more indirect, expression is reflected in her assertion that therapy has been helpful to her: "I think these meetings are very enlightening *(little laugh)*. . . . I think I've been helped a lot by, more by talking than I have by the pills, and that . . . seems to alleviate whatever the situation is." Loretta's statement that talking to professionals is more helpful than medication suggests that her participation in the treatment process is valuable. The interview with Rogers provides an example of her active stance in such a situation.

It is noteworthy, too, that while talking to Rogers, Loretta expresses concern that others may perceive her as not being good or as acting antisocially, in some way. The first instance occurs soon after the interview begins, when Loretta notes that she wants to correct an impression she may have made: "Oh, I meant to correct one thing. When I said 'no' before, I didn't mean I was tired of talking to that doctor. I just meant, 'no,' that I was ready to, that I wondered why I couldn't go home." She explains that her intention was not to be blunt, that she didn't mean to be insulting, and that she did not want to be perceived that way.

Another instance of her wish to be perceived as someone who behaves in an acceptable manner occurs during her discussion of having received shock therapy. She says: "I had done nothing that I knew of to be put on that kind of treatment." Implicitly she is expressing a concern that she is being perceived as having done something "bad." This hypothesis is confirmed by what she says a few minutes later: "And the next thing I knew, they said, 'You're ready, you're on treatment.' . . . And I said, 'Why? I didn't do anything. I haven't had any fight or anything with anybody.' "

Later in the interview, Loretta brings out her perception that the decision about her release is related to whether she has acted out: "I had thought that I'd go home from here because I hadn't done anything very serious. . . . I hadn't, uh, had any violent struggle with anybody, or anything like that." In his response, Rogers recognizes that this is an issue that has run throughout the interview: "That's part of your feeling all the way through, 'I haven't done anything wrong, I've held myself in, you know, I really have not been violent, I haven't broken many rules.' " Loretta replies: "I haven't broken any, I don't think." And then she adds, "And half the time you have to find out what the rules are, because they don't tell ya." Rogers then reflects her underlying assertion: "M-hm, m-hm. But your feeling is, 'I've been good.' "

Loretta's response at this point is interesting and significant: "But I haven't been too good, though. . . . You shouldn't go overboard about being too good. . . . I don't believe in that, either. . . . I've been as good as I know how to be. . . . And I'm not letter-perfect. I would like to be, but I'm not." Rogers replies: "But in terms of what you can do, you feel you've done the best you can do." And Loretta affirms this comment, "I'm doing as good as I know how."

Here is an issue important to Loretta that she resolves in a way that expresses positive self-regard. She articulates an impressive acceptance of self: She is only as good as she really is, that she is not perfect, and that she does not believe in going "overboard about being good."

ROGERS' BEHAVIOR IN THE INTERVIEW

In the course of demonstrating how Loretta dealt with six areas of concern during this interview, many illustrations have been given of the way Rogers interacted with her. An examination of the entire interview reveals a remarkable consistency of empathic responsiveness on Rogers' part. Of all of his responses, there are perhaps only one or two in which Rogers did something other than try to convey to Loretta his understanding of what she was sharing with him.

Loretta was responsive to this empathic approach. She advanced from one area of discussion to another (e.g., from the presenting problem of a possible ward transfer to the issue of her lack of trust in the institution and in people in general), and she made progress within specific areas (e.g., resolving her conflict about moving by deciding that the transfer might be an improvement and that she would not fight it). In addition, Rogers' empathic approach seemed to facilitate increased self-understanding and acceptance as well as a greater ability to view problems more clearly. Finally, Loretta's responsiveness to Rogers' therapeutic style is evident in the comments she makes immediately following some of his responses; statements such as "That's really it," "Yes, that's what I thought" and "That's the truth," all indicate that she truly felt understood.

In addition to a high degree of empathy, Rogers provided two other therapist characteristics included in his classic formulation of "necessary and sufficient conditions of therapeutic personality change": unconditional positive regard and congruence. He accorded Loretta the same kind of respect he would any client; his motive for interviewing her was his sense that her feelings had been insufficiently understood and respected in the first two demonstrations. He displayed unconditional regard for her belief that there was electricity in the atmosphere of the laundry and for the tickling sensations she experienced in her knees. He respected her choice of topic, her manner of exploring each one, and her decisions to switch to other issues. I count 24 times in this short interview that Loretta took the initiative in introducing a new subject, going back to one she had been exploring earlier, coming up with an insight or new attitude, or exercising some other form of self-direction.

Another index of the client-centeredness of this interview is the number of lines in the printed transcript taken up by Loretta's statements (218) and the number taken up by Rogers' (131). Many psychotherapists pay lip service to respecting the strength of their clients. However, an examination of typescripts, when they are available, characteristically show Adlerians, Jungians, Gestalt therapists, cognitive therapists, family therapists, and others dominating the interaction between client and therapist. This is often true of psychoanalytically oriented therapists, as well. Client-centered therapists, because they eschew the role of expert, are consistently less verbose, in spite of the usual reliance on words to convey empathic understanding.

Some support for these assertions comes from an analysis of the interview material in *Case Studies in Psychotherapy* (Wedding & Corsini, 1989). This book includes cases treated by therapists from a variety of approaches. All cases that included verbatim interviews were tallied for the number of lines spoken by the therapist and the number spoken by the client or patient. As Table 2.1 indicates, the Adlerian, rational–emotive, and cognitive therapists outtalked their clients or patients by a significant margin. Qualitatively, they are also quite directive. This is true, for example, of Fritz Perls, the Gestalt therapist. Even though he does not dominate in the number of words spoken, his interview is replete with comments like, "Say this to them," "Now play the bedroom," "Now be the kitchen again," "Stay with what you experience now," "Be phony." Peggy Papp, the family therapist, is also quite directive; she speaks for a "Greek chorus" of observing therapists who are watching through a one-way mirror. (The 325 client lines in the table represent the output of all five members of the family being treated by Papp.)

By contrast, Rogers is consistently empathic with "Mrs. Oak," a client

Table 2.1. Number of Transcript Lines Spoken by Therapists and Clients

Orientation	Therapist(s)	Therapist lines	Client lines
Adlerian	Mosak and Maniacci	268	227
Client-centered	Carl Rogers	165	401
Rational–emotive	Albert Ellis	554	290
Cognitive	Aaron Beck	398	182
Gestalt	Fritz Perls	200	540
Family	Peggy Papp	253	325

Note. Based on verbatim interview material contained in Wedding and Corsini (1989).

he saw over a long period of time in the early 1950s and whose interview with Rogers was the one included in Wedding and Corsini (1989). Furthermore, Brodley (1991), in classifying Rogers' responses in 34 interviews between 1940 and 1986, found 1,659 empathic responses out of a total of 1,928 responses of all kinds, for an "empathy percentage" of 86. And, if Brodley's (1991) three 1940 interviews from the case of "Herbert Bryan" (the eight-interview case that took up approximately two-fifths of *Counseling and Psychotherapy* [Rogers, 1942]) are omitted, Rogers' empathic responses rise to a remarkable 90%.

Rogers came to view congruence or genuineness as "the most basic of the attitudinal conditions that foster therapeutic growth" (Rogers, 1980, p. 2158). I grant that the judgment of genuineness is very subjective. However, I was present at Rogers' interview with Loretta and I have carefully reread the typescript. From this I find Rogers to have been very much up front with Loretta and truly interested in her. He meant what he said, and he responded to her on the level of another human being rather than from the pedestal of an expert.

As consistently empathic as he was, I noted one lapse in Rogers' responsiveness to Loretta. Loretta referred to her family on a couple of occasions. Early in the interview, she says: "'Cause my father and that don't come to visit me or anything, so I don't get out at all on weekends or anything." Then, a few minutes later, Loretta remarks: "I don't mind being moved, I mean if it's, uh, . . . uh, another thing toward going home. (C.R.: M-hm.) . . . But I don't get out anyway, and I don't, I don't know that he, my brother, I wrote a letter, but I didn't get any answer from him. . . . (C.R.: M-hm.) He never came."

While Rogers responds, "M-hm" to Loretta's references to going home and to her brother's nonresponse, by returning to the issue of the move he does not add the explicit recognition he generally accords to Loretta's feelings and attitudes. If Loretta had pursued the topic, it is likely that Rogers would have come around, but at this point he failed to facilitate Loretta's going further with her disappointment about not seeing or hearing from her father and brother, and what appears to be a strong interest in being discharged from the hospital and going home.

Is this a significant failure in empathy? When one listens to the audiotape of this interview, as distinguished from reading the transcript, this and other errors do not appear so glaring. This is supported by the recorded discussion that followed Rogers' interview with Loretta. About 30 members of the American Academy of Psychotherapists, most of whom were not client-centered therapists, observed this interview and attended a question-and-answer session with Rogers immediately after Loretta left. While the reactions were polite, they were largely critical. Why had Rogers failed to support the staff of the hospital? Why had he not pointed out connections among some of the things Loretta had talked about? There were many other remarks of this sort, but nobody in this audience, which included a number of noted psychoanalysts, commented on Rogers' failure to respond to Loretta's references to her brother and father.

This said, it still may be worth speculating on the reasons that Rogers did not pursue this particular topic. Was there something in Rogers' life—in his background—that made him disinclined to follow up Loretta's references to her family? In Kirschenbaum's (1979) biography of Rogers, he notes the following:

> In my first interview with Rogers he told me, "I hate old people who reminisce." He has frequently made comments like, "We could count on the fingers of one hand the people of our own age we really enjoy. The rest are all too stuffy." When he worked on his "autobiography" in 1965 for a collection of autobiographical essays by well-known psychologists, he said it took him and Helen [his wife] months to recover from spending that much time looking in the past. Both the scientist and the artist in him were operating here; both sides needed new challenges and could not be content with past accomplishments. Beyond this, for Rogers, an interest in the future also went hand in hand with his association with young people. He had always valued his contact with graduate students, and this continued after he left the university setting. As he described it, "Probably the major factor in keeping me alive as a growing therapist is a continuing association with young people on a thoroughly equalitarian basis. I have always worked with young staff members; I have never found people my own age stimulating except for rare and fortunate exceptions. I find that younger people are full of new ideas, exploring the boundaries of our disciplines and raising questions about any sacred cows which I hold dear. This keeps me stimulated, moving, and I hope growing." (p. 396)

Rogers' family relationships seem to be consistent with these attitudes. He was closest to Helen, his wife of 55 years, his children, David and Natalie, and his six grandchildren. His interest in some of his own siblings appeared to decline with the years, probably because of a lack of shared values and interests.

It may be, then, that in responding to Loretta, Rogers' own issues influenced his "overlooking" Loretta's references to her brother and father; clearly, he was far more attentive to her current concerns such as her move and her difficulty in trusting the hospital staff. This lapse, however, detracts only slightly from an extraordinary interview—one that offers a superb example of the client-centered approach being applied successfully to a woman disturbed enough to be a patient in a psychiatric state hospital with a diagnosis of paranoid schizophrenia.

REFERENCES

Brodley, B. T. (1991, July 1–6). *Some observations of Carl Rogers' verbal behavior in therapy interviews.* Paper presented at the Second International Conference on Client-Centered and Experiential Psychotherapy, University of Stirling, Scotland.

Kirschenbaum, H. (1979). *On becoming Carl Rogers.* New York: Delacorte Press.

Rogers, C. R. (1942). *Counseling and psychotherapy.* Boston: Houghton Mifflin.

Rogers, C. R. (1951). *Client-centered therapy.* Boston: Houghton Mifflin.

Rogers, C. R. (1980). Client-centered psychotherapy. In A. M. Freedman, H. I. Kaplan, & B. J. Sadock (Eds.), *Comprehensive textbook of psychiatry/III* (pp. 2153–2168). Baltimore: Williams & Wilkins.

Rogers, C. R., Gendlin, E. T., Kiesler, D. J., & Truax, C. B. (Eds.). (1967). *The therapeutic relationship and its impact: A study of psychotherapy with schizophrenics.* Madison: University of Wisconsin Press.

Wedding, D., & Corsini, R. J. (Eds.). (1989). *Case studies in psychotherapy.* Itasca, IL: Peacock.

CHAPTER 3

THE CASE OF GLORIA

SUMMARY BY DEBRA ROSENZWEIG

This session is one in a series of filmed interviews with Gloria (Shostrom, 1965) that were conducted by three therapists of different orientations: Albert Ellis (rational–emotive therapy), Frederick Perls (Gestalt therapy), and Carl Rogers. The case of Gloria has probably been viewed by more mental health trainees than any other case history. Rogers' interview was the first conducted.

A summary of the case is included here because, as noted earlier, permission to publish the entire transcript was not granted. The full transcript of the case can, however, be found in Rogers and Wood (1974), and discussions of the case by both Rogers (1984) and Ellis (1986) are also available. The interested reader is also directed to Weinrach (1990) for a fascinating account of the history of this controversial film, including a transcription of 249 words of dialogue that were not included at the end of the film and some details of the enduring postsession relationship between Gloria and Rogers.

Rogers begins the session by saying, "Good morning," and explaining that he and Gloria have only a half-hour to talk but that he hopes they can make something of it. He says, "I'll be glad to know whatever concerns you." Gloria replies that she had been nervous but feels more comfortable now because of the tenor of Rogers' voice. She says that she expects that he will not be too harsh with her, and Rogers says he can hear the tremor in her voice. Gloria then tells of the "main thing" she wanted to discuss, "I'm just newly divorced and I had gone in therapy before, and I felt comfortable, and I left. And all of a sudden now the biggest change is adjusting to my single life." She then explains that she has been concerned about the impact of having men in the house on her 9-year-old daughter, Pammy, who has experienced emotional problems in the past. Gloria is very conscious of how things would affect Pammy and describes their frank and open communication, which extends even to the subject of sex. She and Pammy recently had a conversation wherein "she asked me if I'd ever made love to a man since I left her daddy. And I lied to her. And ever since then it keeps coming up to my mind 'cause I feel so guilty lying to her, 'cause I never lie and I want her to trust me." She then says, "I almost want an answer from you, I want you to tell me if it will affect her wrong if I told her the truth or what." Rogers responds that Gloria is concerned that this open relationship she has with her daughter is now threatened. Gloria then explains how *she* felt after first finding out that her mother and father made love. She says she thought it was dirty and terrible, and she disliked her own mother for a while after she found out. Thus Gloria feels torn between wanting to be truthful with her daughter and fearing the consequences.

Rogers responds, "I sure wish I could give you the answer as to what you should tell her . . . 'cause what you really want is an answer." Gloria says what she most wants to know is which would affect her daughter worse, being completely open and honest or lying. She says she feels that lying is bound to strain their relationship to which Rogers responds, "M-hm. You sort of feel she'll suspect that, or she will know, something is not quite right in the relationship." Gloria explains that she feels her daughter would not be able to trust her and adds, "Well, gee, what about when she gets a little older and she finds herself in touchy situations? She probably wouldn't want to admit it to me because she thinks I'm so good and sweet, and yet, I'm afraid she could think I'm really a, a devil." Later in the discussion, Gloria describes that she is ashamed of the "shady" side of herself, and Rogers replies, "M-hm. I see. It really cuts a little deeper. If she really knew you, would she, could she, accept you?" Gloria agrees with this and then describes how guilty she feels when she has a man over; how she arranges a "special set-up" so that her children could "never catch us in that sort of thing." She says she wishes she could feel comfortable with whatever she chose to do—whether it is deciding not to tell her daughter the truth or going ahead and being honest. Yet, she says, "I feel there are some areas that *I* don't even accept." Rogers restates, "If you can't accept them in yourself, how could you possibly be comfortable in telling them to her?", adding, "And yet, as you say, you do have these desires and you do have your feelings, but, but you don't feel good about them."

Gloria agrees and then says she has the feeling that he would just sit there and let her stew in her feelings, but she wants more from him. "I want you to help me get rid of my guilt feeling . . . about lying or going to bed with a single man . . . just so I can feel more comfortable," to which Rogers replies, "And I guess I'd like to say, 'No, I don't want to let you just stew in your feelings,' but, on the other hand, I also feel that this is the kind of very private thing that I couldn't possibly answer for you, but I sure as anything will try to help you work toward your own answer. I don't know whether that makes any sense to you, but I mean it."

Gloria says she appreciates what he has said and that he does sound like he meant what he said, but she just does not know how to answer these questions on her own. She talks about feeling disappointed in herself because she had previously thought that these issues about her guilt had already been worked through, but they still keep coming up. It is the same with her conflict about showing the more "ornery devilish" side of her personality. She does not want to deny it, but she cannot let others see that she is not always sweet. Rogers tells her that he understands her disappointment: She had thought that a lot of things were worked through, but now her guilt and her feeling that only part of her is acceptable to others were are all evident again. He continues, "That keeps coming out. I guess I did catch the real deep puzzlement that you feel as to what the hell shall I do, what can I do?"

Gloria confirms what Rogers has said and then describes that her impulse to do whatever feels comfortable seems natural until she remembers the way she, herself, had been affected as a child. "And the minute that comes up then I'm all haywire." She continues, then, talking about how she feels she is in a double bind: She wants to work at night and enjoys doing it; she also enjoys having the extra money, until she starts to feel guilty that she is not being good to her children or giving them enough of her time. She wants to do both: be a good mother and work nights. "I'm becoming more and more aware of what a perfectionist I am. . . . Either I want to become perfect in my standards or not have that need anymore." Rogers asks if she wants to seem like a good mother even if some of her actual feelings are different, but Gloria rejects this: "That isn't what I feel really," to which Rogers responds, "No. OK, OK."

Gloria then talks about her wish to approve of herself; however, she feels frustrated because her actions will not "let her." Rogers responds, "I'd like to understand that. You sound as though your actions are kind of outside of you. You want to approve of you, but what you do somehow won't let you approve of yourself." Gloria confirms his statement and explains that she would feel less guilty about her sex life if her partner were someone whom she loved. It is when she sleeps with someone just because she has a physical desire that she feels guilty. At such times, she says, "I hate facing the kids. I don't like looking at myself, and I rarely enjoy it. If the circumstances would be different, I don't think I'd feel so guilty because I'd feel right about it."

Gloria then remarks that it sounds as if what she wants is a perfect situation, but that she cannot help having such desires. She explains that she has tried to say to herself, " 'OK, I don't like myself when I do that, so

I won't do it anymore,' " but this leaves her feeling resentful toward her children. She begins to question why they prevent her from doing what she wants, and Rogers says, "And somehow, sometimes, you kind of feel like blaming them for the feelings you have, I mean, why should they cut you off from a normal sex life?" Then Gloria explains that there is something in her that makes her feel it is not healthy for her to have sex just because she feels a physical attraction.

Rogers states, "You feel really that at times you're acting in ways that are not in accord with your own inner standards, but then you were also saying a minute ago that you feel you can't help that either." Gloria says she wishes she could, but she cannot. She feels she does not have the control over herself that she used to have. She says, "I just let go and I—there's too many things I do wrong that I have to feel guilty for, and I sure don't like that."

She then asks Rogers, "Do you feel that to me the most important thing is to be open and honest? . . . If, for example, I could say to Pammy, 'I was, I felt bad lying to you, Pammy, and I want to tell you the truth now.' And if I tell her the truth and she's shocked at me and she's upset that that could bother her more? I want to get rid of my guilt, and that will help me, but I don't want to put that on her." Rogers responds, "I guess, I'm sure this will sound evasive to you, but it seems to me that perhaps the person you're not being fully honest with is you." He continues, "Because I was very much struck by the fact that you were saying, 'If I feel all right about what I have done—whether it's going to bed with a man or what—if I really feel all right about it, then I don't have any concern about what I would tell Pam or my relationship with her.' "

Gloria then says, "I want to work on accepting me then. I want to work on feeling all right about it. No, that makes sense, that will come naturally, and then I don't have to worry about Pammy." But then Gloria asks how it is that she accepts her impulse to do things that seem so wrong to her, to which Rogers says, "What you'd like to do is to feel more accepting toward yourself when you do things that you feel are wrong, is that right?" When Gloria agrees, he says that it sounds like a tough assignment.

Gloria says she feels that having sex with someone whom she does not truly love is wrong, regardless of what she learned in therapy, which was how natural her desires are. She says she has a hopeless feeling, and Rogers replies, "So you feel this is the conflict and it's just unsolvable, and therefore it's hopeless, and here you look to me and I don't seem to give you any help." Gloria affirms this and tells him that what she needs is for him to guide her or show her where to begin so that things will not seem so hopeless anymore.

Rogers asks Gloria what it is she wishes he would say to her, and she says she wants him to tell her to go ahead and risk being open with Pammy.

She explains, "If she really knows what a demon I am and still loves me and accepts me, it seems like it would help me to accept me more, like it's really not that bad." Then she wonders, if her own mother had been more open with her about sex, whether she might then have been more broad-minded. She says that she wants Pammy to see her as a full woman, with both a sweet and a more sexy, devilish side, but she also wants to be fully accepted by her.

Rogers says, "M-hm. You don't sound so uncertain," and then, "What I mean is, you've been sitting there telling me just what you would like to do in that relationship with Pam." Gloria responds that she does not want to take that risk unless an authority figure were to give her the OK. Rogers says he understands that it is "risky" to live. "You'd be taking a chance on your relationship with her. You'd be taking a chance on letting her know who you are, really." Gloria continues, "Yeah, but then if I don't take a chance, if I feel loved and accepted by her, I'm never gonna feel good about it anyway." Rogers then asks, "If her love and acceptance of you is based on a false picture of you, what the hell is the good of that? Is that what you're saying?"

Gloria agrees with him and then goes on to say that she feels so much responsibility as a mother. She does not want to be responsible for having caused her children any trauma. Rogers replies, "M-hm. I guess that's what I meant when I said life is risky. . . . It's a hell of a responsibility . . . a very frightening one." Gloria and Rogers then talk about how Gloria would feel proud of herself if she could say that she had always been honest with her children. Yet she feels jealous that their father is not as honest with them, and they consider him all sweetness and light. Rogers says that Gloria wishes her children would have just as nice a picture of her as they have of their father, and in order to do that, she would have to be a little phony.

Gloria describes herself as more "ornery" than the children's father and therefore likely to do more things of which they disapprove. Rogers responds, "Sounds as though you really find it quite hard to believe that they would really love you if they knew you." Gloria says she needs reassurance that she is doing the right thing before she can go ahead and take the risk, and Rogers responds by saying that she would sure like somebody to give her permission. Gloria agrees enthusiastically and then talks about how encouraged she gets when she reads books that say that what she wants to do is the right thing, that no matter what, honesty will win out. Rogers responds, "M-hm. It's so damn hard to really choose something on your own, isn't it?"

Gloria says she feels immature because she has such a hard time making decisions and sticking to them. She really needs somebody to help her and push her. Rogers responds that she reproaches herself for those needs, and Gloria agrees. She speaks about her wish to just accept herself, that she could respect herself if she could say, " 'No matter what you ask me, kids, at least I told you the truth. You may not have liked it but it was the truth.' " Rogers responds, "I guess, judging from your tone of voice, you sound as though you hate yourself more when you lie than you do in terms of things you disapprove of in your behavior." Gloria confirms this by saying that the lie she told Pammy had been over a month ago, but she continued to feel tormented by it. "Now," she says, "I feel like that is solved, and I didn't even solve the thing. But I feel relief."

Gloria then tells Rogers she senses that he is backing her up, giving her permission to follow her instincts. He responds, "I guess the way I sense it is you've been telling me that you know what you want to do, and yes, I do believe in backing up people in what they want to do. It's just a little different slant than the way it seems to you." Gloria is confused by this so he clarifies, "See, one thing that concerns me is it's no damn good you're doing something that you haven't really chosen to do. That's why I'm trying to help you find out what your own inner choices are."

Gloria says it is hard to tell which of her feelings is the strongest. If she actually behaves in certain ways, she does not know whether it means she feels strongly about it, because she often disapproves of herself afterward. Rogers responds, "It sounds like you're feeling a contradiction in yourself too, although what I heard you saying in part is the way you'd like it is when you feel really comfortable about what you're doing." Gloria says "yes" to this but says she still feels her question about how to decide what her true feelings are has not been answered. Rogers says, "M-hm. So that really is tough when, if you feel comfortable in the moment about it, but then after you don't feel at all comfortable, which course of action was really the one you should have followed?"

Gloria says that when she left her husband, she knew that she had made the right decision. She was not conflicted about her choice and knew that she was following her true feelings. Rogers suggests that what she is saying is that she knows perfectly well the feeling within herself that occurs when she is doing something that is really right for her. Gloria agrees and Rogers adds, "You can really listen to yourself sometimes and realize, 'No, no, this isn't the right feeling. This isn't the way I would feel if I was doing what I really wanted to do.' " Gloria says, "But yet many times I'll go along and do it anyway, and say, 'Oh well, I'm in the situation now, I'll just remember next time.' "

Gloria says that when she has a feeling that she knows is good for her, it is her own form of utopia. Rogers responds, "I sense that in those utopian moments, you really feel kind of whole, you feel all in one piece." Gloria says, "Yeah," and then adds that "It gives me a choked-up feeling when you say that because I don't get that as often as I'd like."

Rogers says he suspects none of us get that feeling as often as we would like. Gloria responds by saying she was also thinking about how nice it is to talk to him. She says she misses that her father did not talk to her like Rogers does. "I mean, I'd like to say, 'Gee, I'd like you for my father.' " Rogers responds, "You look to me like a pretty nice daughter. 'Cause you really do miss the fact that you couldn't be open with your own dad."

Gloria says she wants to blame her father for not being able to talk to him. She says he did not listen to her. She realizes that the reason she always had to be so perfect was because her father always wanted her to be better than she was. Rogers says, "You're just trying like hell to be the girl he wants you to be." And Gloria adds, "Yeah, at the same time rebelling."

She says she gloated at the idea of writing to her father that she worked nights as a waitress. She knew he would disapprove, but it felt like she could hurt him by telling him this; still, she also wants him to accept her and love her, regardless of her role in life. Rogers suggests, "I guess you really feel badly that you think there's very little chance he'll say that." Gloria says her father does not hear her. She describes how 2 years ago she tried to talk to him about her feelings, that she loved him although she had been afraid of him. His response was to say repeatedly things like, "Honey, you know I love you. You know I've always loved you." Rogers responds, "M-hm. Never really known and loved you, and this somehow is what brings the tears inside." Gloria says that when she talks about it, she feels "more flip," but when she sits still, she feels a great big hurt. Rogers replies, "It's much easier to be a little flip because then you don't feel that big lump of hurt inside."

Gloria then says the relationship between her and her father was another hopeless situation. She has tried working on it, but she feels it is just one more thing she has to accept. Her father just is not the type of man with whom she can communicate. She says he cares, but not so that they can cooperate or even communicate with each other. Rogers describes Gloria's feeling this way: " 'Well, I'm permanently cheated.' " Gloria says that this is the reason why she likes substitutes. She values talking to Rogers and other men she can respect. She describes that she keeps a feeling inside that she is very close to Rogers, that he is like a substitute father. Rogers says, "I don't feel that's pretending," and Gloria says, "But you're not really my father." He replies to this, "No. I meant about the real close business." Gloria says she does feel it is pretending. She cannot expect him to feel that close to her because he does not know her that well. Rogers finishes the interview by saying, "Well, all I can know is what I am feeling, that is, I feel close to you in this moment."

A separate audiotape recording of the session captured a few more exchanges not included in the film (discussed in Zimring's commentary). Gloria continues to speak of her need to have someone love her like a father. She notes that it is ironic that she dates men whom she does not respect. Rogers responds with a surprisingly confrontive interpretation: "You're slapping your father in the face, aren't you?" Gloria does not seem to understand: "Oh? By wanting mature men?" and Rogers explains, "No. By going out with those who are quite unlike the ones you'd really want." The last words recorded are Gloria's: "But I don't mean to. I don't understand why they keep coming around."

REFERENCES

Ellis, A. E. (1986). Comments on Gloria. *Psychotherapy, 23*, 647–648.

Rogers, C. R. (1984). Gloria—A historical note. In R. F. Levant & J. Shlien (Eds.), *Client-centered therapy and the person-centered approach: New directions in theory, research, and practice* (pp. 423–425). New York: Praeger.

Rogers, C. R., & Wood, J. K. (1974). Client-centered theory: Carl R. Rogers. In A. Burton (Ed.), *Operational theories of personality* (pp. 237—254). New York: Brunner/Mazel.

Shostrom, E. L. (Producer). (1965). *Three approaches to psychotherapy (Part 1)* [Film]. Orange, CA: Psychological Films.

Weinrach, S. G. (1990). Rogers and Gloria: The controversial film and the enduring relationship. *Psychotherapy, 27*, 282–290.

ROGERS AND GLORIA
The Effects of Meeting Some, But Not All, of the "Necessary and Sufficient" Conditions

Fred Zimring

We learn about a method not only by seeing what is done correctly by an expert but also by seeing what sort of behaviors the expert considers unproductive. Examination of complete transcripts of several of Rogers' rather lengthy cases has shown me that he, apparently effortlessly, consistently met his "necessary and sufficient" conditions. In the present discussion of his interview with Gloria I argue, however, that at several points he failed to meet his own goals (most often, that of empathic understanding). Because of Rogers' consistency in meeting his own goals, the interview with Gloria provides a rare opportunity to examine some of his errors and consider their effects. In addition, as the person-centered movement has grown from client-centered therapy, there has been an increased emphasis on genuineness and speaking from one's own frame of reference. Because Rogers does this at several points in the interview with Gloria—speaks from his own frame of reference about life and about his client—we have the opportunity to examine some of the implications of this trend.

Rogers was explicit about how he wanted to act in the interview with Gloria. Just before the session, he described three conditions for establishing a therapeutic atmosphere. One condition was that he be transparent and genuine, and express any feelings he might have about the relationship with the client. The second was that he feel a spontaneous prizing, feel positive regard for the client without judgment about the content of the client's discourse. The third was that he understand the inner

65

world of the client, know what it feels like to be the client. He should see the world through the client's eyes and empathically understand the client's internal frame of reference. In the therapist's being genuine and transparent as well as unconditionally prizing, the client can be sure that the therapist has no hidden opinions about the problem. In being empathic, the client-centered therapist focuses on how the client sees the world rather than on the client's problem.

In order to see whether Rogers' behavior in therapy fulfilled his stated conditions and expectations, we will make a detailed examination of how he did, and did not, respond to Gloria. In addition, we will look at the effect of his responses. We will see that when Rogers responded to the subjective, or felt, sense of Gloria's remarks, she explored aspects of her subjective world.

THE INTERVIEW

When Rogers starts the interview by introducing himself and says, warmly, that he does not know what use they will be able to make of the half-hour but that he hopes they can make some use of it, he is being genuine, is being open about his feelings regarding his interaction with Gloria. This is different from his tendency, especially in the first part of the interview, to speak about nonrelational topics. That is, on several occasions, Rogers subtly but importantly moves from sharing his thoughts and feelings about the relationship (true genuineness) to communicating, from his own frame of reference, thoughts and feelings about other issues not having to do with his relationship with Gloria.

The first thing Gloria says is that she feels nervous, to which Rogers makes no response, and then she comments on his tone of voice, saying that she feels comfortable because of it, that it seems he will not be critical or judgmental. Rogers, with warmth, comments on the tremor in her voice but does not respond specifically to her words. Notice, too, that Rogers, even this early in the interview seems to have decided to avoid responding either to Gloria's immediate negative feelings or to her comments about him, perhaps thinking that these temporary feelings were not what, in the main, she wanted to communicate and explore. Rogers may have been respecting what he sensed to be her intention about what she wanted to communicate at that moment in the interview.

Gloria then shifts the discussion to her "main" concern, which is the effect that having men come to her house might have on her children. She also comments that she wishes she could stop shaking. Although it is not possible to know for sure why she goes in this direction at this point, it frequently happens that clients will start to discuss an objective problem when they feel at a loss because the therapist does not respond to their immediate feelings. And though he laughs softly and warmly, Rogers makes no verbal response to her comment about shaking.

Rogers' approach to Gloria becomes clear during the next group of exchanges when she says that she feels "so guilty" that she lied to her daughter Pammy about not having slept with men since her divorce. When she asks Rogers whether telling her daughter the truth would be harmful, he responds to her concern about her daughter and their relationship, but not to her guilt or to her request that he "tell" her what she should do. Here he is doing two things. He is avoiding her negative feelings about herself and is resisting Gloria's tendency to want him to solve her problems.

Gloria then associates her dilemma over telling Pammy the truth with the negative feelings she had about *her* mother when she first found out that her parents made love, something she found "dirty and terrible." Perhaps sensing that Gloria is still pushing for him to give her advice, Rogers responds to her previous request that he tell her what he thinks ("I sure wish I could give you the answer to what you should tell her"). However, he still fails to respond to her negative feelings about sex and her mother and how this might affect her inability to decide whether to tell Pammy about her own sexual activities.

Gloria then explores the conflict that not being open with her daughter might cause Pammy to distrust her, but that being honest might adversely affect Pammy's acceptance of her. Gloria also admits that she is a little ashamed of what she calls her "shady side." Rogers responds to her desire for acceptance by her daughter ("If she really knew you, would she, could she accept you?"), but not to her shame, again avoiding the more subjective part of her experience, perhaps because it involves negative feelings.

A little later in the interview, when Gloria asks Rogers to help her get rid of her guilt feelings, he again responds that he cannot tell her what to do, but that he will try to help her work it out for herself. Gloria says she accepts this but that she still does not know what to do. She wants to feel good about herself but is disappointed in herself. Rogers responds to her disappointment ("Yes, I get the disappointment") but not to her helplessness. That is, he does not respond to the weakness she is feeling at the moment. Rogers again fails to respond when Gloria says that she feels comfortable about telling Pammy until she remembers how she was affected as a child, at which point she goes "haywire."

It seems clear that Rogers does not respond to what he may have seen as self-defeating statements, along with Gloria's entreaties to him to give her advice. Rogers' personal assumptions seem to interfere with his understanding of Gloria, when she says that she is a perfectionist and talks about her conflict between working at night and being a good mother.

That is, Rogers hears Gloria's conflict as her wanting to *seem* perfect; this interpretation seems to reflect a belief of Rogers' that people "get in trouble" when they reject their feelings and experience because of how they want to appear to others. For the first time in this interview Gloria disagrees, indicating that wanting to seem perfect is not something that she is feeling. What she is feeling is a desire to approve of herself, but her actions do not let her do so.

Rogers replies that it seems her actions are outside of herself. She ignores this remark, saying that she wants to approve of herself, especially regarding sex. If she was in love with the man with whom she was being intimate, she could approve of herself. Rogers communicates that he understands this by accurately restating it: "I guess I hear you saying, 'If what I was doing when I went to bed with a man was really really genuine and full of love and respect and so on, I wouldn't feel guilty in relation to Pam. I really want to be comfortable about, about the situation.' "

It might be useful to summarize the degree to which Rogers' therapeutic conditions have been applied up to this point in the interview. Starting with his explicit desire to make something of the time they will be together, he seems fully present as a person, is "transparent." However, his goals of unconditional regard for and understanding of Gloria's world do not seem to be fully achieved. There seems to be a pattern in his attempts at empathic responding. Starting with Gloria's initial nervousness and continuing through her statements of not being able to control her desires and feeling helpless, Rogers seems to avoid recognizing negative aspects of her present experience of herself. Although this may have been motivated by Rogers' desire to establish a relationship quickly and to avoid embarrassing Gloria, if a significant part of what the client is experiencing is not acknowledged, the therapist cannot fully express an understanding of the inner world of the client, nor fully reflect the client's internal frame of reference. This avoidance also has consequences for the therapist's unconditional prizing of the client as a person. If the therapist does not recognize the client's experience of weakness or helplessness, the client will not feel that these negative aspects of the self are as respected or accepted as the more positive aspects to which the therapist attends. In a more general sense, Rogers does not seem to have, as he usually would, the experience of the client at the moment as his central focus. Instead, especially in the first part of the interview, perhaps because of the pressure of her questions or of having to make rapid progress in what is a demonstration session, he seems to be concerned with her self-configuration, that is, with the relationship of self, behavior, and self-judgment.

When the therapist responds from his or her own frame of reference, the client tends to respond to the therapist's frame of reference and often asks for the therapist's opinion. Thus, at the point in the interview mentioned earlier, when Gloria repeats that she is unable to control herself and asks for Rogers' advice by asking him if it would hurt her daughter if she told her the truth about her sexual activity, he responds from his own frame of reference that the problem seems to be in her being honest with herself. Elaborating, he says that based on her prior comment if she felt all right about it, she would not have any trouble telling her daughter. Gloria accepts this and says that she has to work on accepting herself, but she questions how this can happen if she has the impulse to do things of which she does not approve; she is not sure whether her standards about sex are right or wrong.

Rogers consistently avoids her actual quandary but does acknowledge that she is in conflict. She agrees, and then says that she feels hopeless. Rogers responds to the fact that she feels the problem is insoluble and that he does not seem to be giving her any help. When Gloria says she needs him to show her where to begin so it will not seem so hopeless Rogers asks what she wishes he would say, and she replies that she would have him tell her to be honest. Gloria then speculates that if her mother had been more open about herself, maybe she (Gloria) would not have such a narrow attitude about sex. Rogers does not respond to Gloria's remarks about her mother. Instead, from his own frame of reference, he responds that she does not sound as uncertain as she had a few minutes before, that she has been spelling out just what she wants in her relationship with Pammy. When Gloria answers that she does not want to take the risk, Rogers expresses his own view of life, saying, "it's an awfully risky thing to live." She agrees, adding that not taking the chance and thereby being accepted on a true basis would not be much good. Rogers indicates that he understands this, and she says, however, that she does not want to cause any big traumas in the children. Whereupon he responds by explaining that what he meant in saying that life is risky is that being the person you want to be "is a hell of a responsibility . . . a very frightening one."

Here, Rogers is presenting his own views of self-acceptance and risk taking. There is little focus on Gloria's conflict between her impulses and her standards, nor of the standards that she respects. Also, there is little attention to her felt sense of her problem. The closest she gets to her felt sense is in talking about her hopelessness. Rogers does not respond and does not let her sit with her feeling of hopelessness; consequently, the felt sense of hopelessness is not developed.

As the interview proceeds, Gloria expresses a conflict between wanting to be accepted by her children for what she is and a desire to be seen by them as as "sweet" as they see their father. She says that because she is a little more "ornery" than her former husband her daughter might not have as nice a picture of her if Gloria were honest. Rogers says that she finds it hard to believe that the children would love her if they really knew her. She agrees emphatically, saying she needs reassurance before taking the risk. She feels better, she notes, when she reads a book that supports her standard of honesty. Rogers, not really taking up Gloria's need for reassurance, responds to her comments about books with a reflection that sounds like a personal attitude: "It's so damn hard to choose something on your own." This may have sounded like a rebuke to her for she says that it makes her feel immature and she wishes she could make a decision and stick to it. She says she is in a double bind, that she hates herself when she is bad but also when she lies. Rogers attends to her feelings, albeit from his frame of reference, and responds that from her tone of voice he judges that she hates herself more when she lies than when she does things of which she disapproves. She agrees but goes back to her indecision about action, about what to do about telling Pammy. She feels that she would like to tell Pammy about her previous lying and feels support from Rogers to do so.

Paradoxically, Gloria feels that the problem is resolved even though she thinks she has not solved it. She feels relieved, as if Rogers has been saying to her that she knows what she wants to do and that she should go ahead and do it. He says he believes in backing up people in what they want to do, for "it's no damn good" for people to do what they do not really want to do. She replies that she is in conflict about what she wants to do—that sometimes she knows what she wants to do, and feels right when she does it, and other times she is not at all clear.

When Rogers attends to her felt sense of this and communicates his understanding of her conflict and lack of clarity about her desires Gloria shifts her focus. As a result of his attending to these experiences of hers, she concentrates on her inner sense of the problem and says that when she is following her feelings she has a "utopian" feeling.

Being in touch with her feelings of the moment brings Gloria to several realizations: that it is nice that she can talk to Rogers, that she regrets that she could not communicate that way with her father, and that she would like Rogers for her father. It should be remembered that, for Rogers, true genuineness has to do with the relationship between therapist and client. Here he responds genuinely and tells her, "you look to me like a pretty nice daughter," and restates her feeling of regret that she is not able to be open with her father. Later he says that her father does not see and accept her as she is, that he has "never really known you and loved you." As Gloria explores the fact that she and her father do not communicate, she experiences a "big lump" of hurt inside and a feeling of being cheated. She realizes that when she talks about this, "it feels more flip." Rogers recognizes her flipness as a way of avoiding feeling hurt and cheated. "That is why I like substitutes," answers Gloria, indicating that she likes talking to Rogers and other men, like doctors, whom she can respect. But, she adds,

"I can't expect you to feel very close to me." Rogers responds genuinely, from his feelings about the realtionship, that he does not feel that his closeness is pretending and that he feels close to her "in this moment." A note of genuineness clearly pervades this last statement. And so the filmed interview ends.

FURTHER OBSERVATIONS

Many clients enter therapy concerned with the objective world and with the problems and standards of that world. If we focus on the client's objective world and problems, we succeed in reinforcing the importance of that world for them. Rogers' framework for therapy was to focus on and trust the person's subjective framework. By doing this the importance of the objective world for the person is lessened and, hopefully, the importance of the subjective world increased for them.

During much of the interview, Rogers and Gloria talked about actions and attitudes rather than feelings. To a surprising degree, Rogers talked about his attitudes about how life should be lived rather than talking about her felt sense of her difficulties. During the interview there were about 20 responses that were not empathic—responses that Rogers made from his own frame of reference rather than from his understanding of Gloria's frame of reference. About half of these were in response to questions, the other half were observations and assertions about Gloria and about life.

The effect of these observations was not to advance Gloria's understanding of her subjective world but rather to focus her attention on her perception of the objective world. Take for example 249 words of dialogue that occurred as Rogers and Gloria talked for a short while after the film stopped (not included in the summary in this book; see Weinrach, 1990). Gloria continued to talk about her need to have someone to love her like a father. She said it was ironic that she went out with men whom she did not respect. Rogers responded, "You're slapping your father in the face, aren't you?" and Gloria said, "Oh? By wanting mature men?" to which Rogers responded, "No. By going out with those who are quite unlike the ones you'd really want." This observation by Rogers was very much from his own frame of reference. Gloria responded, "But I don't mean to. I don't understand why they keep coming around."

There are several effects of the therapist responding from his or her own frame of reference. The most serious is that the therapist becomes more focused on his or her own framework and less on the client's. This may have been what happened here, resulting in Rogers' final (postsession) observation regarding Gloria's choice of men—a comment that seems very different from his usual therapy responses.

There is also an effect on the client when the therapist speaks from his or her own framework. One of the positive effects of responding to the client's internal frame of reference is that the client is likely to continue to speak about or from it. On the other hand, responses from the therapist's frame of reference may cause the client to stop attending to his or her internal world and focus instead on the external world. Note that after Rogers' observation that Gloria goes out with men "quite unlike" the ones she would really want, Gloria stated her intentions ("I don't mean to") rather than her feelings.

There was a noticeably different effect when Rogers was empathic and concentrated on Gloria's internal frame of reference. When he attended to her felt sense of things, as in most of the latter part of the interview, new feelings about her life at the moment occurred to her. These new feeling aspects were not necessarily about the problem she brought to therapy. Indeed, it is not at all apparent that there was an explicit resolution of the problem of what she would tell her daughter. Instead, it was the case, as is frequently true in both therapy and life, that increased attention to the felt sense of life at the moment gives rise to feelings and perceptions that had not seemed intellectually relevant to the central problem. Thus, when in the latter stage of the interview, Rogers attended to her felt sense of indecision and conflict, it was her feelings about the communication with Rogers and her father that suddenly came into focus and were most real to her.

It is noteworthy that Gloria spent much of the interview talking about communication with her daughter and the difficulties of knowing whether her daughter would accept her and then ended the interview by talking about her feelings about communication with her father and his not accepting her. This leads to an interesting speculation. If the interview had been longer, the similarity of acceptance and communication with her daughter and her father might have become apparent and have come together as one desire.

Somewhat similarly, consideration of the hurt she felt from being cheated by her father's lack of acceptance might have led Gloria to some new realizations about the situation with her daughter and why her daughter's acceptance was so important. It might have led to a course of action with respect to her daughter that would have been emotionally satisfying. One possibility is that after resolving some of her feelings about needing acceptance and love, she might have found that the problem of her daughter's acceptance was no longer as important. Or she might have framed a course of action in terms of her acceptance of her daughter rather than her daughter's acceptance of her.

This case is a good example of what happens when we do and do not respond to the client's subjective world, to his or her internal frame of reference. When Rogers was driven by his ideas about what it is good for a person to do, like taking risks, and so was not attending to Gloria's internal frame of reference, her attention remained focused on externals, on what she should do in the world, on what action she should take with her daughter. When Rogers was empathic, when his attention was focused on her internal frame of reference, her subjective landscape became richer.

Kantor and I (Kantor & Zimring, 1976) have investigated how increased subjective richness leads to the solution to a problem. When subjects focused on the felt sense of a problem, a solution did not occur. What emerged instead were new alternatives from which the solution could be fashioned. The feelings and meanings that occurred to Gloria near the end of the interview, as Rogers focused on her felt sense (i.e., was truly empathic), provided for her the raw material for reconsideration of her problem. She became able to move from considering her communication and acceptance by her daughter to focusing on communication and acceptance by her father.

Rogers' transparency and warmth during the interview had a lasting effect. Two years after his demonstration interview with her, Gloria enrolled in one of Rogers' workshops. She maintained contact with him until her untimely death some 15 years later.

This case provides evidence of the validity of Rogers' seminal insight about the "necessary" condition of empathy. When this condition is fulfilled, when the therapist attends to the client's internal frame of reference (including, of course, negative aspects of a client's experience), the client is more likely to attend further to his or her own internal frame of reference. Conversely, when such empathy is lacking—when a therapist's attempts at genuiness mistakenly lead to the therapist speaking about his or her own values or when a therapist fails to attend to the negative aspects of a client's experience—the client's attention is likely to shift outside of the self and attend to the therapist's framework rather than to his or her own.

REFERENCES

Kantor, S., & Zimring, F. (1976). The effects of focusing on a problem. *Psychotherapy: Theory, Research and Practice, 13,* 255–258.

Weinrach, S. G. (1990). Rogers and Gloria: The controversial film and the enduring relationship. *Psychotherapy, 27,* 282–290.

CHAPTER 4

THE CASE OF JILL (1983)

TRANSCRIPT

Carl Rogers (C.R.): OK, I think I'm ready. And are you ready?

Jill: Yes.

C.R.: I don't know what you might want to talk about, but I'm very ready to hear. We have half an hour, and I hope that in that half-hour we can get to know each other as deeply as possible, but we don't need to strive for anything. I guess that's my feeling. Do you want to tell me whatever is on your mind?

Jill: I'm having a lot of problems dealing with my daughter. She's 20 years old; she's in college; I'm having a lot of trouble letting her go. . . . And I have a lot of guilt feelings about her; I have a real need to hang on to her.

C.R.: A need to hang on so you can kind of make up for the things you feel guilty about. Is that part of it?

Jill: There's a lot of that. . . . Also, she's been a real friend to me, and filled my life. . . . And it's very hard . . . a lot of empty places now that she's not with me.

C.R.: The old vacuum, sort of, when she's not there.

Jill: Yes. Yes. I also would like to be the kind of mother that could be strong and say, you know, "Go and have a good life," and this is really hard for me, to do that.

C.R.: It's very hard to give up something that's been so precious in your life, but also something that I guess has caused you pain when you mentioned guilt.

Jill: Yeah. And I'm aware that I have some anger toward her that I don't always get what I want. I have needs that are not met. And, uh, I don't feel I have a right to those needs. You know . . . she's a daughter; she's not my mother. Though sometimes I feel as if I'd like her to mother me . . . it's very difficult for me to ask for that and have a right to it.

C.R.: So it may be unreasonable, but still, when she doesn't meet your needs, it makes you mad.

Jill: Yeah, I get very angry, very angry with her.

C.R.: *(Pause)* You're also feeling a little tension at this point, I guess.

Jill: Yeah. Yeah. A lot of conflict. . . . (C.R.: M-hm.) A lot of pain.

C.R.: A lot of pain. Can you say anything more what that's about?

Jill: *(Sighs)* I reach out for her, and she moves away from me. And she steps back and pulls back. . . . And then I feel like a really bad person, like some kind of monster, that she doesn't want me to touch her and hold her like I did when she was a little girl.

C.R.: It sounds like a very double feeling there. Part of it is, "Damn it, I want you close." The other part of it is, "Oh my God, what a monster I am to not let you go."

Jill: M-hm. Yeah. I should be stronger. I should be a grown woman and allow this to happen.

C.R.: But instead, sometimes you feel like her daughter.

Jill: M-hm. Yeah. Sometimes when I cuddle her, I feel I'm being cuddled.

C.R.: M-hm. *(Pause)* But you place a lot of expectations on yourself, "I should be different."

Jill: Yeah. I should be more mature. I should have my needs met so that I don't have to get anything from her.

C.R.: You should find other ways and other sources to meet your needs, but somehow that doesn't seem to be happening?

Jill: Well, I feel I get a lot of my needs met, but the need from her is very strong. It's the need from a woman really, I think. . . . It doesn't quite make up for the needs I get from men.

C.R.: There are some things that you just want from her.

Jill: M-hm. Yeah. Just from her. *(Sighs)*

C.R.: When she pulls back, that's a very painful experience.

Jill: Yeah, that really hurts. That really hurts. *(Big sigh)*

C.R.: *(Pause)* It looks like you're feeling some of that hurt right now.

Jill: Yeah, I can really feel her stepping back.

C.R.: M-hm, m-hm. *(Pause)* Pulling away from you?

Jill: Yeah. . . . Going away.

C.R.: You feel her sort of slipping away, and you . . . and it hurts . . . and—

Jill: Yeah. I'm just sort of sitting here alone. . . . I guess like, you know, I can feel her gone, and I'm just left here.

C.R.: M-hm. You're experiencing it right now—that she's leaving, and here you are all alone.

Jill: Yeah. Yeah. Yeah. I feel really lonely. *(Cries)*

C.R.: M-hm, m-hm. If I understand right, not lonely in every respect, but lonely for her.

Jill: Lonely for her. Yeah. Yeah. *(Cries)*

C.R.: I'm not a good therapist—I forget a box of Kleenex, but . . . I think I've got . . . *(Laughs)*

Jill: Thank you. *(Laughs)* I feel like I could cry a million tears about that. *(Laughs)*

C.R.: M-hm. It feels as if the tears could just flow and flow on that score.

Jill: Yeah. Never stop.

C.R.: That just to have her leave, have her pull away is just more than you can take.

Jill: Yeah. Yeah. It's really hard to go on without her. *(Cries)*

C.R.: It sounds as though that is almost the center of your life.

Jill: It's very close to that, you know. My husband, my children, my home. . . . My work is important too, but there's something about the heart that's connected to her. *(Sighs)*

C.R.: And there's a real ache in your heart with her leaving.

Jill: Yeah. Yeah. *(Cries) (Pause)* Oh . . . I just don't want her to go.

C.R.: "I want to keep her as my daughter, as my little girl, as the one I can cuddle."

Jill: Yeah, yeah. The one I can cuddle. She likes to cuddle too.

C.R.: M-hm, m-hm.

Jill: *(Cries)* And you know, I'm also scared for her. I'm scared for her out in the world. I'm scared for her to have to go through all the things that I did and how painful that is. I'd like to save her from that.

C.R.: You'd like to protect her from that life out there and all the pain that you went through.

Jill: Yeah, yeah. And all the new stuff that all the young people are going through. . . . It's very hard. She's struggling.

C.R.: It's a hard world.

Jill: Yeah, very hard.

C.R.: And you'd like to cushion it for her.

Jill: Yeah, make it perfect.

C.R.: Make it all right, just as you might when she fell down and banged her knee or something. You'd like to make it all right.

Jill: Make it better, try to make it better.

C.R.: *(Pause)* I guess it's very hard to face the fact that at this time you can't make it better for her.

Jill: I don't think I'm facing that very well. *(Laughs)*

C.R.: OK.

Jill: I think I'm still trying to do that.

C.R.: OK.

Jill: That's part of hanging on to her I think.

C.R.: But still in your own mind you can make it better for her, and, by God, you're going to.

Jill: Yeah. By God, I'm going to keep trying to make that better, to make it better no matter if she likes it or not. *(Audience laughter)*

C.R.: Save her even if she hates it.

Jill: Save myself, I—

C.R.: It's a question of who you're saving.

Jill: Yeah. So I won't feel so guilty. That I didn't do everything right.

C.R.: You feel, "I wasn't a perfect parent."

Jill: Made a lot of mistakes. *(Sighs)*

C.R.: And you can't forgive yourself, or you haven't forgiven yourself for making those mistakes.

Jill: No, no, I haven't. I'm really hard on myself.

C.R.: You give yourself a very rough time.

Jill: M-hm. Yeah, I really do. I really hurt myself, especially my body.

C.R.: It occurs to me you probably wouldn't think of treating your daughter as badly as you treat yourself.

Jill: That's probably true. I stop myself when I start treating her as badly as I treat myself.

C.R.: *(Pause)* Can you say what's going on in you?

Jill: *(With tears)* Well, when you look at me so kindly, I feel really heard, and it makes me feel really sad that I feel like someone really listens to me, really hears me.

C.R.: And that's sad because it's so rare?

Jill: Yeah. *(Cries)*

C.R.: You feel it isn't often that you've been really heard.

Jill: *(Cries) (Pause) (Sobs)*

C.R.: And that just brings the tears pouring out.

Jill: *(Sobs)* You know, my daughter really hears me, too.

C.R.: She really hears you, too?

Jill: She really hears me, too. *(Cries)*

C.R.: So that's. . . . M-hm. So that's what makes the relationship so precious; she hears you.

Jill: Yeah. She's one persons that does. That's very hard to let go of that.

C.R.: M-hm.

Jill: She really cares.

C.R.: Want a Kleenex?

Jill: I'm losing one of my caring people. That's what it feels like.

C.R.: It sounds as though you don't have too many caring people in your life.

Jill: No. Not too many.

C.R.: And to lose one of them—

Jill: Yeah, that's a big loss.

C.R.: I know.

Jill: A big loss.

C.R.: *(Pause)* Can you care for yourself that much?

Jill: *(Sighs)* That's really hard for me. I don't feel that I deserve it.

C.R.: So the caring for yourself just seems unreasonable. You don't deserve that.

Jill: No. . . . No, I don't. I want to, but I don't feel that I really do.

C.R.: You'd like to care for yourself, but it really seems to be something you have not been able to achieve.

Jill: No. I still have a lot of self-hate.

C.R.: You're a bad, bad person.

Jill: Yeah. A real monster. I did bad things. That's what it feels like.

C.R.: An awful person.

Jill: Yeah. An awful person. *(Sighs)*

C.R.: How could anybody care for a person like that?

Jill: Yeah. That's what it feels like. How could they? No wonder she pulls away, doesn't want me to touch her.

C.R.: It feels like she's pulling away from you because she sees you as a bad, bad person.

Jill: Yeah. Because I've done something really bad. That's what it feels like. And she knows, somehow she knows what I've done.

C.R.: She knows your secret and—

Jill: Yeah. She knows my secret. That's it. She knows my secret.

C.R.: So she's not going to have anything to do with this monster.

Jill: No. Once she starts moving back, she'll just keep moving away. She's going to be relieved to get away from the monster.

C.R.: After all, anybody would be glad to get away from such an awful person.

Jill: Yeah. Yeah. That's right. That's what it feels like. Something so bad that I can't make it right.

C.R.: Just no way that you can accept yourself.

Jill: *(Sighs)* I can accept parts of me, but not all of me. And I can take care of certain parts of me, but not all of me.

C.R.: There are some parts of you that are so awful you can't accept them, you can't care for them.

Jill: That's right. I can't take care of them. I have to punish those parts that are bad.

C.R.: They're just unforgivable.

Jill: Yeah. Unforgivable. Yeah. That's it. Unforgivable. What I've done is unforgivable. I don't even know what it is.

C.R.: M-hm. So it isn't something specific you're talking about, it's just a feeling that, "I know I've just done awful, unforgivable things."

Jill: M-hm. I must have—

C.R.: Must have—

Jill: I must have done awful, unforgivable things. Because no one wants to touch me. That's what it feels like.

C.R.: That's what it feels like, even though I gather that's not really true in all respects, but it's what it feels like.

Jill: That's what it feels like. . . . Yeah. . . . Yeah.

C.R.: That no one wants to touch you because you must have done some awful, awful things.

Jill: Yeah. Yeah. There has to be a reason that if no one wants to touch you and no one loves you and no one wants anything to do with you, you must have done something really bad. I must have done something bad. Then it makes sense. Then it makes sense.

C.R.: So that you feel your world only makes sense if somehow, sometime, someway, you did these monstrous things, these awful things.

Jill: Yeah. Yeah. That explains it.

C.R.: That explains everything.

Jill: M-hm, m-hm. Yeah.

C.R.: Does that mean that you feel no one cares, no one accepts?

Jill: No. I feel like now that there are people who do, who care and accept and hear and value me. But there's that little—

C.R.: So that the person who can't care and accept and value you is you.

Jill: M-hm. Yeah. It's mostly me.

C.R.: The person who sees those things as unforgivable is you.

Jill: Yeah. Yeah. Nobody else is that hard on me.

C.R.: M-hm. Nobody could be that cruel to you, or make such awful judgment.

Jill: *(Sighs)*

C.R.: Or hate you so.

Jill: Or hate me so. Yeah.

C.R.: Sounds like you're the judge, the jury, and the executioner.

Jill: Yeah. My own worst enemy.

C.R.: You pass a pretty tough sentence on yourself.

Jill: Yeah. Yeah, I do. Not a very good friend to me.

C.R.: No. You're not a very good friend to yourself. M-hm. (Jill: M-hm.) And you wouldn't think of doing to a friend what you do to yourself.

Jill: That's right. I would feel terrible if I treated anyone the way I treat me.

C.R.: M-hm, m-hm, m-hm. *(Pause)* Because to you, your self is just unlovable.

Jill: Well, there's a part of me that's lovable.

C.R.: OK. OK.

Jill: Yeah.

C.R.: OK. So in some respects you do love yourself.

Jill: Yeah. I love and appreciate the little child part of me. (C.R.: M-hm.) That's really struggled and come through. (C.R.: M-hm.) And survived. (C.R.: M-hm.) An awful lot.

C.R.: M-hm. That's a damned nice little girl.

Jill: Yeah. She's really special. (C.R.: M-hm.) She's like my daughter.

C.R.: Ah ha.

Jill: *(Sighs)*

C.R.: And she's a daughter you can hold on to.

Jill: Yeah. Yeah. I can still cuddle her. And tell her she's beautiful. And love her.

C.R.: And she's a survivor, and she's strong, and she's been through a lot, but she's OK.

Jill: Yeah. Yeah, she is. She's real special.

C.R.: *(Pause)* It must be nice to have such a special person in your life.

Jill: Yeah. It is. That is nice. Yeah. She's very nice.

C.R.: Can she care for the other parts of you?

Jill: She [is] starting to.

C.R.: She's starting to?

Jill: Yeah.

C.R.: M-hm.

Jill: Just beginning.

C.R.: M-hm. She's not as hard on you as the adult you.

Jill: No. That's right. (C.R.: M-hm.) She's much more understanding. (C.R.: M-hm.) And compassionate. (C.R.: M-hm.) *(Sighs)*

C.R.: *(Pause)* Sounds like she loves you.

Jill: Yeah. She gives me all that unconditional love that I didn't feel like I got.

C.R.: M-hm, m-hm, m-hm. *(Pause)* And she loves all of you.

Jill: Yeah. Yeah. She loves all of me.

C.R.: To her, none of it is unforgivable.

Jill: No. It's all OK.

C.R.: All OK?

Jill: Yeah. *(Sighs)*

C.R.: *(Pause)* I like her.

Jill: I like her too. *(Sighs)* She's going to save me.

C.R.: Hmm?

Jill: She's going to save me.

C.R.: She's going to save you.

Jill: *(Laughs)* From hurting myself anymore.

C.R.: M-hm. *(Pause)* She may really be able to keep you from being so hard on yourself. Really save you.

Jill: Yeah. I think she will; I think she will; I just have to give her a little help too.

C.R.: M-hm, m-hm. Like we'll work together . . . to save me.

C.R.: She's a good companion to have, isn't she?

Jill: Yeah, she is. *(Sighs)* It's good to have a friend.

C.R.: Yeah. M-hm. To have that kind of a friend inside really touches you.

Jill: Yeah. It really does. It'll never go away. (C.R.: M-hm.) It'll always be there for me.

C.R.: M-hm. She's not going to pull away and—

Jill: Go out into the world and do her thing. *(Laughs)* She's gonna stay home with Mama.

C.R.: M-hm, m-hm. And be a mother to Mama too, huh?

Jill: Yeah. Yeah. *(Pause)* *(Sighs)*

C.R.: What's that smile?

Jill: It's your eyes are twinkling. *(Both laugh)*

C.R.: Yours twinkle too. *(Laughs)*

THE MYTH OF NONDIRECTIVENESS

The Case of Jill

Maria Villas-Boas Bowen

When Carl Rogers first introduced the term "nondirective counseling" in 1942 in his book *Counseling and Psychotherapy*, it was in reaction to the directive diagnostic–prescriptive approach that was prevalent in the 1930s. He had just recently discovered at the Rochester Guidance Center that he was more effective in helping when he listened to what the client had to say than when he interviewed, diagnosed, and gave advice (Rogers 1980).

Rogers used a study done by Porter (1941) to demarcate the differences in techniques and values between the directive and nondirective viewpoints. In Porter's study directive counseling was characterized by frequent, highly specific questions to which specific answers were expected and by information and explanation given by the counselor. Directive counselors proposed the action the clients should take to bring change, and they used evidence and personal influence to insure that such action would be taken. In contrast, in nondirective counseling the clients did most of the talking, and the counselors used techniques that helped the clients to recognize, understand, and talk about their feelings, attitudes, and reaction patterns. To achieve this aim, the most common techniques of the nondirective therapists were to restate or to clarify the content of the client's responses and to give the client an opportunity to express feelings. Based on Porter's (1944) study, as far as differences of values were concerned, Rogers (1942) concluded that directive counseling placed high value upon social conformity and the idea that the more able could effectively guide the less able. The nondirective approach, on the other hand, placed a high value on the right of every individual to be psychologically independent and to maintain his psychological integrity. In the person-centered approach now, there are two legacies from this initial work of Rogers: first, the emphasis on the techniques of restatement of meaning and clarification of feeling as *the* way to convey empathy; and, second, the concern about not being directive.

Over 40 years passed between the time Rogers wrote *Counseling and Psychotherapy* and his interview with Jill, a volunteer at a demonstration workshop held in La Jolla, California, in 1983. This half-hour session demonstrates how much Rogers' work changed over this period. His work was still characterized by deep empathy, by unwavering respect for the client and her autonomy, and by an uncanny ability to access what goes on at the client's subliminal level of awareness. Yet, two changes are evident when his work with Jill is compared with the case material in *Counseling and Psychotherapy*. First, he uses a much broader array of techniques than simple restatement of what the client says and clarification of feelings. He uses interpretation; he uses the client's body cues to bring her to the here and now; he uses metaphors, humors her, and exaggerates and repeats her self-deprecating comments to accentuate their absurdity and promote greater accuracy in her self evaluations. Second, he allows himself to be directive. He forms hypotheses about the source of problems and very openly checks his hypothesis. Moreover, he introduces topics, he breaks silences.

There is a general belief that Rogers opposed the use of interpretation in psychotherapy. It is true that in *Counseling and Psychotherapy* (1942), as a reaction to psychoanalysis, he made a strong case against intellectual interpretation. He believed that the imposition of interpretations of the childhood causes and meanings of symptoms was not very helpful to the client. On the other hand, in this same book, he qualified his position by stating that interpretations "may have no effect, or an adverse effect, on therapy unless the client can accept [them]" (p. 27). Thus, we may deduce from this quote that, if the therapist is empathic and well synchronized with the client—and the interpretation makes sense to, and is accepted by, the client—it may be effective.

In the interview with Jill, Rogers' very first response is an interpretation. Note how the interview begins:

Jill: I'm having a lot of problems dealing with my daughter. She's 20 years old; she's in college; I'm having a lot of trouble letting her go. . . . And I have a lot of guilt feelings about her; I have a real need to hang on to her.

C.R.: A need to hang on so you can kind of make up for the things you
feel guilty about. Is that part of it?

Rogers interprets a relationship of cause and effect between her guilt
feelings and her difficulty in letting her daughter go; it is not she who makes
this connection. Nevertheless, it is interesting to notice the tentative way
in which he presents the interpretation, and the way in which he checks
whether it is acceptable to Jill. And she partly accepts the interpretation:
"There's a lot of that." Had she not accepted it, I am sure Rogers would
have let it go. He would not have insisted on his point. Unlike less humble
colleagues, or inexperienced therapists, who would judge the client's lack
of acceptance of the interpretation as stemming from denial or resistance
(never from the therapist's own inaccurate interpretations), Rogers was
more concerned with being helpful to the client than with who was right
or wrong.

The following is an example of a situation wherein Rogers' clarification is not accepted by Jill. He immediately abandons it to only come out
with a new interpretation which is then accepted by her. He even interrupts
her in order to interject his interpretation:

C.R.: Does that mean that you feel no one cares, no one accepts?

Jill: No. I feel like now that there are people who do, who care and accept
and hear and value me. But there's that little—

C.R.: So that the person who can't care and accept and value you is you.

Jill: M-hm, m-hm. Yeah. It's mostly me.

Instead of maintaining a dogmatic and unyielding opposition, he
seems to allow interpretation when two conditions are met. First, the
interpretation must flow from and with the ideas and the feeling that the
client was expressing at the moment, rather than consisting of intellectual
explanations of the causes and meanings of the client's behavior. Second,
the therapist must not be attached to the interpretations but be willing to
let them go if not accepted by the client.

When Rogers introduces Jill to the idea—"So that the person who can't
care and accept and value you is you"—he is making a hypothesis about a
source of the client's problem. At the same time that this hypothesis is
intuited directly from what the client has been saying, his own theory of
personality—in which he sees lack of self-acceptance as an important source
of problems—guides him in his interpretation. By directing the client's
attention to the hypothesis that her dependence on her daughter stemmed
from the fact that she herself was unable to take good care of herself and

lacked self-acceptance, he was inviting her to shift the focus of exploration from her daughter to herself.

Contrary to the belief that a person-centered therapist never introduces anything that the clients themselves have not brought up before, in this interview it is Rogers who brings up Jill's inability to care for herself:

C.R.: It sounds as though you don't have too many caring people in your life.

Jill: No. Not too many.

C.R.: And to lose one of them—

Jill: Yeah, that's a big loss.

C.R.: I know.

Jill: A big loss.

C.R.: *(Pause)* Can you care for yourself that much?

Jill: *(Sighs)* That's really hard for me. I don't feel that I deserve it.

Repeatedly during the interview Rogers encourages the client, sometimes quite insistently, to focus on her inability to care for herself and on her own low level of self-acceptance. He does this in an interesting way. He either repeats over and over again the negative aspects that Jill has been presenting about herself, or he exaggerates them still more, either by accentuating them through voice intonation or by using a stronger word than she had used. There comes a point when Jill's self-deprecating comments become so extreme that she recognizes their absurdity and begins to bring balance by introducing positive aspects of herself. Here is a good example:

C.R.: The person who sees those things as unforgivable is you.

Jill: Yeah. Yeah. Nobody else is that hard on me.

C.R.: M-hm, m-hm. Nobody could be that cruel to you, or make such awful judgment.

Jill: *(Sighs)*

C.R.: Or hate you so.

Jill: Or hate me so. Yeah.

C.R.: Sounds like you're the judge, the jury, and the executioner.

Jill: Yeah. My own worst enemy.

C.R.: You pass a pretty tough sentence on yourself.

Jill: Yeah. Yeah, I do. Not a very good friend to me.

C.R.: No. You're not a very good friend to yourself. M-hm, m-hm. (Jill: M-hm, m-hm.) And you wouldn't think of doing to a friend what you do to yourself.

Jill: That's right. I would feel terrible if I treated anyone the way I treat me.

C.R.: M-hm, m-hm. M-hm, m-hm. M-hm, m-hm. *(Pause)* Because to you, your self is just unlovable.

Jill: Well, there's a part of me that's lovable.

C.R.: OK. OK.

Jill: Yeah.

C.R.: OK. So in some respects you do love yourself.

From this point on they explore together Jill's lovable qualities.

A word of caution is important here. Since Rogers uses the paradoxical exaggeration of the negative several times during the interview with Jill, there is a temptation to consider it a technique. A technique is a preset strategy of behavior that is used in certain specified circumstances in order to produce a desired result. One thing is true of Rogers' approach to his work in therapy: He was not given to the use of techniques as such. His responses emerged spontaneously out of his participation in the client's world at the moment. I believe the secret of his success was that he so completely focused on the moment and on his presence with the client that the question "What should I do now?" probably never occurred to him. It is perhaps unfortunate that when he wrote *Counseling and Psychotherapy,* in an attempt to conceptualize what he was doing, he described his spontaneous responses as a technique, calling them "clarification of feelings." Since then his spontaneous patterns have been heralded indiscriminately as the only way to respond to clients. Even his ever-present "M-hm, m-hm" was transformed into a technique. My guess is that client-centered therapists say "M-hm, m-hm" more than any other subset of human beings.

His interview with Jill, 4 years before he died, demonstrates the changes in Rogers' work over the decades. He became less concerned with the nondirective label, became more flexible, and his responses to clients more varied. For example, in all but one instance, it was Rogers who broke the 16 silences that occurred during the session, often by referring to body cues as a way to bring the client to the here and now. Here are some examples:

Jill: Yeah, I get very angry, very angry with her.

C.R.: *(Pause)* You're also feeling a little tension at this point, I guess.

Jill: Yeah. Yeah. A lot of conflict.

In another part of the interview:

Jill: Yeah, that really hurts. That really hurts. *(Big sigh)*

C.R.: *(Pause)* It looks like you're feeling some of that hurt right now.

Jill: Yeah, I can really feel her stepping back.

Later on:

C.R.: It occurs to me you probably wouldn't think of treating your daughter as badly as you treat yourself.

Jill: That's probably true. I stop myself when I start treating her as badly as I treat myself.

C.R.: *(Pause)* Can you say what's going on in you?

Jill: *(With tears)* Well, when you look at me so kindly, I feel really heard, and it makes me feel really sad that I feel like someone really listens to me, really hears me.

At the very end of the session Rogers again breaks the silence by bringing the attention to body cues:

Jill: *(Pause) (Sighs)*

C.R.: What's that smile?

Jill: It's your eyes are twinkling. *(Both laugh)*

C.R.: Yours twinkle too. *(Laughs)*

The above interactions are also good examples of Rogers' asking direct questions of the client, taking into consideration nonverbal cues and giving direction to the interview by bringing the client back to her present experience. It is also evident that his personal warmth, empathy, and near-perfect attunement with the client were not sacrificed in the process. He was directive and yet remained profoundly respectful of the client's autonomy.

I believe that nondirectiveness is an illusion, except where therapists are overly passive, have such a slow reaction time that to identify what is going on within themselves and with the client is difficult, or are technique-bound. When there is a relationship between client and therapist, as there should be in psychotherapy, it is impossible for therapists to prevent their own personalities from playing a significant part. Therapists are constantly making choices, conscious or unconscious, as to which aspect of what the client is saying they are going to respond. Consider this example in the interview with Jill, when she talks about her need for her daughter:

Jill: Well, I feel I get a lot of my needs met, but the need from her is very strong. It's the need from a woman really, I think. . . . It doesn't quite make up for the needs I get from men.

C.R.: There are some things that you just want from her.

Jill: M-hm, m-hm. Yeah. Just from her. *(Sighs)*

I could easily imagine a therapist attuned to feminist issues asking a question that, although still empathic, might lead the client to an exploration of her own femininity as a way of understanding her need for her daughter. For example:

Therapist: There are some things that you need from women.

The point here is not to say that one direction would be better than the other. It is simply to point out that different therapists may respond differently, although still with the same degree of empathy, to the content the client presents. Rogers himself addressed this issue in 1983, in response to some reactions I had about his interview with Jill, which he had recently completed.

I first heard the Jill audiotape when he played it during a seminar he was conducting at his home. One of the students asked how he chose what to respond to. His answer was: "I try to respond to what is most important to the client." Later, I wrote him a letter taking exception to this remark. I explained to him that although I had listened to the same tape, I frequently imagined myself responding to aspects of what the client said quite differently from the way he had. I surmised that it may have been because he and I had different judgments of what was important to the client. He wrote back:

> When I try to respond to the feeling that is most important to the client, my choice of what is most important is certainly influenced by my own personality, past history, and so forth. I agree that that is most assuredly true and I don't think I have ever said [otherwise]. . . . If it is openly recognized that such responses are partly shaped by the therapist's *perception* and that this

perception is shaped both by the client's expression and by the therapist's personality, we may be able to avoid imitative "modeling." (personal communication, January 16, 1983)

The assumption that the personality of the therapist does not influence the course of therapy is unrealistic. The process is centered on the interaction *between* client and therapist rather than on the client or the therapist. In Buber's sense, it is an "I–thou relationship" where the hyphen reflects the profound interrelationship between the participants.

One of the choices that Rogers consistently made was to ally himself with the healthy side of the person. On the one hand, this alliance facilitated the development of self-acceptance and provided for a more peaceful environment. On the other hand, it may have prevented clients from going deeper into themselves to explore their "dark side," thereby avoiding the development of a more well-integrated and balanced self-concept.

In his interview with Jill, it is easy to notice Rogers' tendency to avoid exploring the negative side. For example:

C.R.: It's a question of who you're saving.

Jill: Yeah. So I won't feel so guilty. That I didn't do everything right.

C.R.: You feel, "I wasn't a perfect parent."

Jill: Made a lot of mistakes. *(Sighs)*

C.R.: And you can't forgive yourself, or you haven't forgiven yourself for making those mistakes.

Jill: No, no, I haven't. I'm really hard on myself.

C.R.: You give yourself a very rough time.

Rogers was already introducing the idea of forgiveness before giving Jill the chance to reexamine her mistakes and learn more from them. Maybe forgiveness would come more easily if she had had the opportunity to talk about and explore more fully the mistakes she had made. Rogers' comment "You give yourself a very rough time," seems in itself a forgiving comment. The fact that he forgives the client before she does it for herself is reassuring and affirming. However—and this question is often posed to client-centered therapists—what if the client had been a child abuser, for example, and had good reasons to feel bad about herself? Would Rogers' response not have been premature, possibly preventing the client from facing a part of herself that she needed to change? Rogers himself would likely have claimed that he was not *forgiving* morally reprehensible behavior but rather making it safe to talk about it.

Still, with his unwavering trust in the "goodness" of human nature, Rogers seemed to imply that her mistakes were easily pardonable. As a matter of fact, often during the interview he became quite insistent on minimizing Jill's perception of her "dark side" instead of helping her explore the reality of her perceptions. In the section that follows, he again allies himself with her healthier side by paradoxically exaggerating her self-deprecating comments:

C.R.: You'd like to care for yourself, but it really seems to be something you have not been able to achieve.

Jill: No. I still have a lot of self-hate.

C.R.: You're a bad, bad person.

Jill: Yeah. A real monster. I did bad things. That's what it feels like.

My guess is that if Rogers had reflected her feelings here by saying something like, "You feel like you did bad things," Jill might have talked about what she thought was so bad, and she might have had a better chance to reexamine her "badness". Instead he exaggerates it, making it still worse than Jill described. From her self-description as "bad," she escalates to "awful":

C.R.: An awful person.

Jill: Yeah. An awful person. *(Sighs)*

C.R.: How could anybody care for a person like that?

Jill: Yeah. That's what it feels like. How could they? No wonder she pulls away, doesn't want me to touch her.

C.R.: It feels she's pulling from you because she sees you as a bad, bad person.

Jill: Yeah. Because I've done something really bad. That's what it feels like. And she knows, somehow she knows what I've done.

C.R.: She knows your secret and—

Jill: Yeah. She knows my secret. That's it. She knows my secret.

Again, instead of facilitating Jill's exploration of her supposedly "dark" secret, Rogers opts to continue his exaggeration of the client's negative self-concept comments:

C.R.: So she's not going to have anything to do with this monster.

Jill: No. Once she starts moving back, she'll just keep moving away. She's going to be relieved to get away from the monster.

C.R.: After all, anybody would be glad to get away from such an awful person.

Jill: Yeah. Yeah. That's right. That's what it feels like. Something so bad that I can't make it right.

C.R.: Just no way that you can accept yourself.

Jill: *(Sighs)* I can accept parts of me, but not all of me. And I can take care of certain parts of me, but not all of me.

Jill finally breaks away from her self-deprecating judgments, and establishes a more balanced view of herself which is more self-accepting.

The personality of the therapist does indeed influence the therapist's choice of what to respond to. It is not surprising that Rogers consistently chooses to avoid the exploration of the negative, even though it seems that he was going along with it by exaggerating what Jill was saying. Those who knew Rogers personally know he was very warm, was quite appeasing, and a difficult person to get angry at. It is not by accident that, if they exist, there are very few instances of clients expressing negative feelings toward him. He himself seemed to have some awareness of this issue, maybe even some confusion about it, and that is how he responded when I expressed to him the same thoughts I am expressing in this chapter:

> Since you are certainly not the only one who feels that I don't really face up to the dark side of my nature or the dark side of others, there must be some truth in it. I don't experience myself that way since if I did, of course, I would change my behavior. Such criticisms have, however, made me more sensitive, I think, to the dark side, perhaps more often the dark side of others than my own. (personal communication, January 16, 1983)

In all fairness, it is important to keep in mind that the interview with Jill lasted only half an hour, and was a demonstration, and was probably Rogers' first and, most likely, last one-to-one contact with Jill. It would have been inappropriate for him to encourage her to go deeper into the recesses of her inner life if he was not going to be there to follow up with her. He was always cautious about this in his demonstration interviews.

In summary, the case of Jill demonstrates many of the changes in Rogers' work since he first expressed his ideas about psychotherapy in *Counseling and Psychotherapy,* until four years before his death in 1987. He wrote in 1942 that the counselor should never go beyond what the client had already expressed: "This is highly important, since real damage can be done by going too far and too fast, and verbalizing attitudes of which the client is not yet conscious. The aim is to accept completely and to recognize those feelings which the client has been able to express" (p. 39).

Forty-five years later we hear him verbalizing attitudes that the client had not yet introduced, offering and testing interpretations, and often being quite directive with the client. I think the biggest change of all is that he trusted his clients more. He considered them to be less fragile and less easily damageable by comments made by the therapist. He was more trusting of the clients' self-determination and self-regulation and saw his clients as less at the mercy of the therapist's influence. This gave him, I believe, more flexibility, freedom, and congruence with the kind of person he had become. But one thing he never changed was his belief in the core values underlying his work in psychotherapy. In 1942, he wrote that "the non-directive viewpoint places a high value on the right of every individual to be psychologically independent and to maintain his psychological integrity" (p. 127). Paradoxically, by adhering less strictly to a nondirective approach, he ultimately demonstrated an even greater trust in his clients' independence and psychological integrity.

REFERENCES

Porter, E. H. (1941). *The development and evaluation of a measure of counseling interview procedures.* Unpublished thesis, Ohio State University, Columbus, Ohio.

Rogers, C. R. (1942). *Counseling and psychotherapy.* Boston: Houghton Mifflin.

Rogers, C. R. (1980). *A way of being.* Boston: Houghton Mifflin.

CHAPTER 5

THE CASES OF MARY (1986) AND LOUISE (1986)

MARY: TRANSCRIPT

Carl Rogers (C.R.): Now that everybody's settled and the mikes are on and so on, I'd like to be quiet for a minute or two and kind of get myself ready for our interview. So I'd like to just be quiet for a minute or two; maybe you'd like that too.

Mary: Fine. *(Pause)*

C.R.:, OK. I've gotten to know some of the people in the workshop a little bit, but I really haven't had any contact with you at all so—at least not that I'm aware of—so I don't know you, and I'm looking forward to knowing you and whatever you'd like to talk about I'm very ready to listen to.

Mary: *(Sighs)* *(15-second pause)* Well, I guess, m-hm, the thing for me to talk about now is where I am, where I've come to in this workshop. I keep wanting to look at my, my latest drawings up there. (C.R.: M-hm, m-hm.) Um, uh, when I came into the first level I had a sense that, um, that I was sleeping, um. (C.R.: M-hm, m-hm.) In my life. Like I've come to a point in my life where—that I thought I had wanted to get to, um, in clearing out a lot of negativity that I had around me and a lot of patterns and, uh, I feel like I've done a lot of that. But it's, but it's not like I thought it would be. Now I'm in a place that I, I feel like I'm ready to create my life, but I don't know how to do it. I don't have the models to do it. (C.R.: M-hm, m-hm, m-hm.) And, um, in my drawings I, I, I've worked through that to the point where I feel like, um, I'm ready to, I'm ready to blossom and to do that somehow. (C.R.: M-hm, m-hm.) Um—

C.R.: Sounds like you cleared away a lot of the rubbish. Now what are you going to build there?

Mary: Yeah, right. I, I think, I think I still have certain blocks about, um, on, on my own power.

C.R.: Yeah, m-hm.

Mary: And, um, whatever that connection is that I want with my, my deeper self or my truer self. (C.R.: M-hm, m-hm.) I, I feel like, uh, my life in the world has been, um, it's been strange—it's hard for me to talk about it because I always feel like, like it's different from what other people have experienced or like, uh, um, like I'm trying to get to a different place, too.

C.R.: They might not understand 'cause, 'cause whatever you're after is something that perhaps other people aren't trying for, that they wouldn't really recognize what it is you're, you're trying to do for yourself.

Mary: Yeah, right. I don't see models around me for it.

C.R.: Uh-huh, uh-huh, uh. So whatever you're trying to create, there really is no model for that. It's something, something different.

Mary: That's, that's what I feel like. I mean, it may be, it may be there but I'm not recognizing it—

C.R.: Yes.

Mary: Or I mean, I wonder if I still have a block that's keeping me from recognizing it. (C.R.: M-hm.) Or if I just don't know how to create the model. (C.R.: M-hm, m-hm, m-hm.) For it. (C.R.: M-hm.) So—

C.R.: But you feel as though something is sort of holding you back from getting started? Is that—?

Mary: Yeah, I, I've had a lot, I've dealt a lot with, um, being in this world and, um, and, and resisting it because it's such a bizarre world. (C.R.: M-hm, m-hm, m-hm.) Um, the society is so bizarre and, um, you see, now it's hard for me to talk about it because I start getting into all the levels of uncertainty about what, what, what is the, my truth and then what is around me. (C.R.: M-hm.) It's like those all got mixed together.

C.R.: M-hm. And you're not quite sure whether you want to be in this crazy world.

Mary: Well, I've come to the point where I accept that I do. I, I feel like, I'm at the point where I, I want to, um, to express myself, to be myself, and to be of service. (C.R.: M-hm.) And, and, and to do that, I have to find my, what is my truth, my whatever that is, is, what my service will be about.

C.R.: So, "what, what is the way that I want to be of service in this world, strange and bizarre as it is?"

Mary: Well, I feel like that involves being in touch with myself, my—

C.R.: M-hm, m-hm.

Mary: *(Sighs)* Um, I don't know if I even want to say my higher self, I don't know if it's an—

C.R.: You want to be close to your inner truth, whatever it is.

Mary: Yeah, yeah. And, um *(sighs)*, I don't know, it's always been just, uh, I think that's what my life's about, finding out how to do that. It's just very difficult for me. (C.R.: M-hm, m-hm, m-hm.) Uh, there's been a lot of fear around that, and I, I'm dealing with that, but there's still a lot of sense of, um, of being vulnerable and um— (C.R.: M-hm.) Being, being easily, um, squashed.

C.R.: M-hm, m-hm. So to creep out into the world, that's a very dangerous procedure because you're vulnerable, you might be squashed, it's frightening.

Mary: *(Sighs)* And then too, I think too, it's, it's also the sense of not being valued like what I value so much about myself, to put that out and, um, have it be invisible to others because they don't see the value in it or they don't connect with it, um.

C.R.: M-hm, m-hm. I, I get a sense that you feel, uh, kind of alone in that, not at all sure that anyone else would value what, what you might see as the way you want to be.

Mary: *(Pause)* Yeah, there is a lot of that, there is a lot. I, I have been a very solitary person. (C.R.: M-hm, m-hm.) And very independent because I have not wanted to be dependent on that kind of approval from the world. (C.R.: M-hm, m-hm, m-hm.) But, yet, on the other hand, I think I am.

C.R.: But I guess there is a real question. "Does this world have any place for me, for somebody that's solitary, that's different?"

Mary: *(Pause)* Right. Right. I, I have, I've felt that the only way that I can really have anything to give or be of service is *(sighs)*, I have to change myself somewhat to f—, to fit what others can perceive and make use of, you know, to fit into others, somewhat into the framework and the values and that kind of thing in the world.

C.R.: I don't know whether I'm hearing that correctly but it sounds as though you feel " I've got to somehow fit their concepts of what I should be or I've got to fit in somehow."

Mary: Right, or other people's perceptions or expectations of what they need. I, yeah, the sense that I, I have to change it somehow. That there's not the room to really explore and find out where I am and so what is the value of that to, to then—

C.R.: So that you're quite sure there's no room really for the real you, you've got to modify that a little bit to fit what people expect.

Mary: Yeah, yeah. (C.R.: M-hm.) I don't know. When, when I hear it said, it ·sounds a little bit like ego, but maybe it, maybe it is that, but, um, I don't know. No, I feel like it comes from a deep, a deeper fear.

C.R.: M-hm, m-hm. So it sounds like to me a very real feeling that you're not quite sure there is any place for the real you, you've got to shape it a little bit and fix it a little to fit what other people are looking for, or could understand.

Mary: Right. And I think maybe in that real me, maybe this is—uh, yeah, I think this is also it, that there, that the real me is not necessarily perfected and, and while there is a lot of power and a lot of, um, energy and, um, goodness and, um, truth and beauty and all that, there's also a side that, that is not perfected.

C.R.: M-hm, m-hm, m-hm. So you don't—

Mary: And, and that I'm afraid *(sighs)*, and that I'm afraid of putting that out uh, uh, I'm afraid of having that condemned and, um, and I, I also think I'm afraid of the, the power of that too. (C.R.: Uh-huh, m-hm.) And, uh, and I know on a spiritual level that I've looked at this, I'm, I'm afraid of *(sighs)*, I'm afraid of any more karma with that, is, is what it is, that of, of the backlash that's going to come back on it, um, like I've done that, I'm aware of having misused what I am, my power, and, uh, and I'm aware that there's a part of it that I don't know how to use properly and—

C.R.: M-hm, m-hm. So there's no—

Mary: And that has consequences. (C.R.: M-hm, m-hm.) And uh—

C.R.: So there's no question about the strength of the inner power that you have. That, that you're sure of, but to let it out in its imperfect state, wow, that's dangerous.

Mary: Right. I, I don't even know if I have the right to do that actually.

C.R.: M-hm. Because it's so powerful?

Mary: Because I don't, um, because I'm not sure of being able to use it properly—

C.R.: I see.

Mary: Without hurting others or doing something that that will not be right.

C.R.: Not, not only imperfect in itself, it might have imperfect consequences. It might harm or not really be always helpful.

Mary: Right. And I'm afraid of harming myself as well as others. (C.R.: M-hm, m-hm, m-hm.) I, I guess I'm afraid of my own power.

C.R.: I get a sense of that, that you're a reservoir of enough power that that means that—God, what does it mean? It could be dangerous, it could be hurtful, it could be marvelous, but, but it's not perfect.

Mary: Yeah. I'm aware that it has been dangerous. (C.R.: Uh-huh.) That I have used it that way. (C.R.: Uh-huh, m-hm, m-hm, m-hm.) I feel that, um, my, some of my fears with that and the prohibitions and the controls and I, uh, the way in which I'm trying to grapple with it, uh, has religious connections. (C.R.: M-hm.) Um, I think maybe that the fear comes more from the religious connections than from the spiritual connections. Uh, and I, and by that I mean my sense of having, um *(sighs)*, I, I don't know—I feel like I'm getting into a heavy area and *(20-second pause) (Sighs)* Well, I get images of, of like being a witch and being um— (C.R.: M-hm, m-hm, m-hm.) Being condemned for that. (C.R.: Uh-huh.) For, for being what my power is and yet having it, um, uh, with, with its own integrity, you know, I mean, it is what it is, and if it's imperfect that is what it is.

C.R.: So it might come out pure and, and really what it is, but "my gosh, that might be, that might be a witch."

Mary: Right.

C.R.: A witch would be condemned by everybody.

Mary: Yeah.

C.R.: Or a lot of people.

Mary: And not in, not in just a, a moral way but in a, a life-and-death way.

C.R.: M-hm, m-hm, m-hm. You might in some very real sense be condemned to death for being the power that you are.

Mary: M-hm, m-hm. Yeah. Right, and so I think all those fears, now, now as I talk about the–, are really more, uh, physical and emotional than they are a sense of like–

C.R.: That they're what?

Mary: They're real physical, they're on a survival level. (C.R.: M-hm.) Um.

C.R.: "I don't want to be killed."

Mary: Yeah. So I think they're, you know, they're kind of ingrained in my subconscious, and it holds me back, or, or whatever it is, wherever those patterns are that, um, I can't consciously deal with.

C.R.: Part of; part of the real block is, "If I let my power loose into the world, I might be killed for that."

Mary: *(Pause) (Sighs)* Or something horrible. In a way, it's a little more nameless than that.

C.R.: Yeah, OK. Something terrible.

Mary: And, and so it's a little more unknown, and that's even a little worse.

C.R.: Uh-huh, uh-huh. "It might lead to some terrible fate for me."

Mary: Right. *(Pause)* And then there's, there's also the sense in it of, of being so wrong, I mean, of being puzzled at that. How could something that is so *me* be so *wrong*? (C.R.: M-hm, m-hm, m-hm.) And so unacceptable and have consequences that are so surprisingly, um– *(sigh)*.

C.R.: "How could it be that the real true inner me could have such awful, fateful consequences," perhaps? "Could that really be?" That seems a real puzzle.

Mary: Right. Or, or could just be so wrong.

C.R.: Yeah.

Mary: Could, could be in a way so, yeah, wrong.

C.R.: Yeah. M-hm, m-hm. "If I let out the real inner me, how could that possibly be so wrong?"

Mary: *(Pause)* Yeah. Yeah. So, so I have a, a real sense of, of really wanting to embrace my, my own truth and my, my own connections and my, my *whole* self, which is, uh, you know, a big huge expansive self and has a lot of connections of all kinds. (C.R.: M-hm, m-hm, m-hm, m-hm.) Um, both earthy and spiritual. (C.R.: M-hm.) Or both with nature and with the spirit. (C.R.: M-hm.) Uh, and I have a real strong impulse toward that and that, but I have this very strong or, um, I mean this big, there's this big No!

C.R.: You really love yourself, rooted in the earth and reaching to the sky.

Mary: Yeah.

C.R.: And very large and very whole.

Mary: Yeah. I've, I've always had that sense of I'm OK, but in the *world*, in the *world*, I'm not OK, and I'm very insecure— (C.R.: M-hm, m-hm, m-hm.) About myself in relation to other people and to the, the world, the world, and also, um, what has been difficult for me is that sense of being, um, being, um, consonant with myself in myself and to me that's, that's being one with, with God or with the world, the universe, whatever that is.

C.R.: And, and this would be being confident with yourself?

Mary: Consonant, uh, at, at one with or in harmony with.

C.R.: At one with, uh-huh, m-hm.

Mary: And, um, at the same time, on another spiritual level, more that of the religious level, being, um, being just completely wrong. (C.R.: M-hm.) So that's a big split in me. (C.R.: M-hm.) It's a—

C.R.: So on the, on the spiritual level it seems OK, really you're, you're pleased with yourself.

Mary: On one spiritual level, and on my own inner spiritual level, and yet with—

C.R.: But on the religious level.

Mary: The kind of religious level, religious spiritual level that I have been imbued with—

C.R.: Yeah, uh-huh, uh-huh, the religious spiritual level that comes from the outside.

Mary: Yes and—

C.R.: That's wow.

Mary: And I have a sense, a sense of the whole history of that on me, like I have a whole history that goes back to the beginning of, of, um, religion and the world or wherever.

C.R.: Beginning of time.

Mary: And always having that, that kind of split, that sense of here I'm OK, and here I'm not.

C.R.: So that in some sense—

Mary: So I mean it's not just like, like in this lifetime I, I was in the, you know, I was born in the Catholic church, and I have, and I have a sense of, of centuries of that on me.

C.R.: M-hm, m-hm. From the beginning of time you feel there's been this split in you between the, the—

Mary: Yeah.

C.R.: Real spiritual essence of you—

Mary: Yeah.

C.R.: Which is really OK, and the religious spiritual ethos of the, of the time, which is bad, wrong.

Mary: Right, of, of all of my society, and so how can I be a part of my society— (C.R.: M-hm.) If, I mean in that way, I just absolutely don't fit in and will never fit in, unless I deny myself?

C.R.: You feel that—

Mary: And, and yet, and yet, so what that does, is it, it cuts off my sense of wanting to be one with the world around me and with, with, um, the whole movement of, of my society, my culture, the human race, and all of that, kinds of things I feel the need to be in, um, to be in harmony with and to be a part of and to be working towards, um, wherever we're going.

C.R.: You feel sort of doomed that, that, uh, this expansive real inner you has not and *never* will fit into the world as it is.

Mary: Well, I, I, I've never given up hope that it *never* will.

C.R.: OK. Has not and does not fit into the world as it is.

Mary: Yeah. Yeah.

C.R.: M-hm, m-hm.

Mary: *(Sighs)*

C.R.: But you haven't given up hope.

Mary: No.

C.R.: It might fit.

Mary: I keep working at it. But I have not resolved it, with *all* the work I've done. I have not come to that feeling. *(Pause)* Only on certain levels can I do that, I'm, I'm more outer—I mean, I *began* to be able to create outer levels of myself that can do that, but I, I don't want it to be that way, I want it to be whole.

C.R.: M-hm, m-hm. The idea of sort of, the image that comes to my mind, sort of shaving off parts of yourself in order to fit really doesn't appeal, you want to be your whole self.

Mary: Yeah, because I feel that's my gift.

C.R.: M-hm, m-hm. That's your gift, that's your uniqueness, you'd like to *be* that.

Mary: And in a way, I feel like it's my, um, my, my *directive* from the universe or from an, um— (C.R.: M-hm, m-hm, m-hm.) And it's part of the race, the human race.

C.R.: So the universe really wants you to be that whole person.

Mary: Well, that I don't, um, well again that—

C.R.: That's putting it too strongly.

Mary: That split applies there too. (C.R.: M-hm, m-hm.) Um. I don't know, it doesn't make sense, it's not logical, but— *(Sighs)*

C.R.: Nevertheless, you do feel that it's *part* of the directive, part of the way the universe is constructed, that you might be your whole self and yet—

Mary: *(15-second pause)* Somewhat I, I have made this, um, into a conflict in myself, I, I've kind of, um, seen this sort of conflict between the male and female although I, I, in some ways that's not completely true, but the sense of being in touch my, uh, my deepest nature and of being willing to go along with that and be that in the sense of having to be out and fit myself into the universe outside of me. I'm coming to resolve that though, that, that's something I've kind of put on it and—

C.R.: M-hm. And you've seen it in terms of male and female—

Mary: I, I, I have in the past a lot, yeah. Um, yeah, it hasn't been, it has been a lot of that, yeah, it has been a sense of as a *female* I cannot experience those, uh, those connections.

C.R.: What is it? As a female you really don't have the right to be that whole self in the universe?

Mary: Right, because, um, religion is after all very male ori—, ori—, um—

C.R.: Oriented.

Mary: Oriented, and dominated, male dominated. (C.R.: M-hm.) And, um, and so, so on a spiritual level, it's a struggle for me too because, um, I, I'm trying to get back in touch with that, but yet I, a lot of me for a long time has been angry at God, the God that I have had to deal with in the world, which is a male God.

C.R.: The God that has said, "You're only a woman, you don't really have the right to be fully out there."

Mary: Yeah. And so, so I feel blocked between that, that sense that I have of whatever is really the, the spirit, the source *(sighs)*.

C.R.: *(Pause)* Some sort of a sigh—something.

Mary: Yeah, it's *(sighs)* well, I feel like I've clarified some of what it is, but I still feel like it's, it's, um, the immovable, immovable force, I mean, the two things that that are butting against each other.

C.R.: Sort of—

Mary: I don't see resolution in it.

C.R.: Sort of a sigh of resignation that, yeah, OK, uh, that's what it is, but it's still there, still there *(pause)*, still impossible to move out.

Mary: I feel like I incorporate it so, um, on all of my levels, like down to my cells it's in me. (C.R.: M-hm.) That way of, um, being conflicted in—

C.R.: Seems like you can't possibly free yourself from something that is so deep it's right down to the level of every cell in your body. That you're not permitted to be out there.

Mary: Yeah, it seems to me to be the way the universe is constructed, and I don't know— (C.R.: M-hm, m-hm.) I don't see resolution.

C.R.: M-hm, m-hm. Little bit of resignation or even hopelessness.

Mary: Yes.

C.R.: M-hm. "That's the way the universe is. I'll never be able to come out as I am."

Mary: Yes. That's it. *(Pause)* And there's also the spark in me that won't die, that won't, that won't give up.

C.R.: You're resigned, you're a little bit hopeless, but still there is something that says, "No, I'm not, I haven't given up."

Mary: Well, a part of me knows that there *(sighs)*, that there is wholeness.

Part of me knows. I don't know how to create it— *(Pause)* Or let it be created. (C.R.: M-hm.) *(Sighs)*

C.R.: M-hm. You don't quite know how to give yourself permission or to, how to create the opportunity or how to really let yourself loose.

Mary: I'm just getting a sense that maybe, um, what I have to do is—open up and, uh, and accept that whole world, that I want to— (C.R.: M-hm, m-hm, m-hm.) That *I* want to reject and that wants to reject *me*. (C.R.: M-hm.) Somehow to swallow that. (C.R.: M-hm, m-hm.) And, uh—

C.R.: Sounds like you're saying maybe you sort of have to bypass that feeling that, that you're rejecting the world and the world is rejecting you, that somehow you have to open up to something larger than that.

Mary: Yeah. Maybe that's the only way to do it.

C.R.: Hmm?

Mary: Uh, that maybe that's the, that that, I don't know, I'm getting an image of that. (C.R.: M-hm, m-hm, m-hm.) That that's, that *this* doesn't work. (C.R.: M-hm, m-hm.) Well, I've certainly tried this, but it—

C.R.: It doesn't work, and that maintaining it, somehow "I'm maintaining that."

Mary: M-hm. By *(sighs)*, by resisting, by resisting it being that way. I have an image of a snake— (C.R.: M-hm.) Um, for some, of a snake swallowing some big kind of, of a snake swallowing a big animal of some kind— (C.R.: M-hm, m-hm, m-hm.) And digesting it—

C.R.: I was going to say.

Mary: All of it.

C.R.: Digesting the whole damn bit, uh-huh. Bones and all.

Mary: Swallowing it whole.

C.R.: M-hm, m-hm. Taking it in, m-hm, right. M-hm.

Mary: And being nourished by it, it becomes a part of it.

C.R.: Be—?

Mary: Becomes part of the snake.

C.R.: M-hm, m-hm, m-hm.

Mary: *(Sighs)*

C.R.: Sounds like a pretty healthy snake!

Mary: M-hm. In a way it's the world, it's an image of the world– (C.R.: M-hm.) The planet.

C.R.: M-hm. They tell me your time is about up.

Mary: *(Laughs) (20-second pause)* Yeah, I feel myself straddling now, right now, straddling in the sense of just letting go of this, these two– (C.R.: M-hm, m-hm, m-hm.) Things and, um, and moving to this.

C.R.: M-hm. It's really a different thing than finding a solution to this conflict. It's a, it's a–

Mary: There is no solution as long as I hold the conflict.

C.R.: Uh, like, swallowing that thing and moving on.

Mary: Yeah. So I have to do it another way. (C.R.: M-hm, m-hm, m-hm, m-hm.) I feel right in the center now. (C.R.: M-hm.) The conflict is over here, and this one's over here.

C.R.: Yeah, it's a different, it's a new option or a different alternative or something.

Mary: *(Sighs)* M-hm. Yeah. A new model.

C.R.: M-hm. New model.

Mary: Yeah.

C.R.: OK. M-hm. OK to bring it to a close?

Mary: Yes. (C.R.: M-hm.) Thank you.

C.R.: M-hm. Thank you.

Mary: Thank you.

C.R.: Let's, uh, let's stay here a moment, and let's see, uh, after a minute or two if you, uh, feel like it or are able to, you could tell the group something of how this interaction felt to you, and I'll tell them how it felt to me. Then we could let them in on it perhaps.

Mary: OK. Do you want me to? I mean.

C.R.: If you're willing to, if you're able to.

Third party: Do you need a break at all?

Mary: No, no, no.

C.R.: Um.

Mary: Well, it felt very easy for me to to go into this, um, and it's something that that I have felt is . . . uh, um, been wanting to talk about. And it's difficult for me to talk about with other people because of the nature of it being, um, I mean, I don't know, it's something that I've not wanted to put out. I, I felt like few people would understand it or connect with it or, I don't know, there's elements of it being kind of a, odd, odd, fantastic.

C.R.: Little strange. M-hm.

Mary: Yeah. But you were right there, and, and I was willing to also let go of that and go with it. I had no idea I was going to get to there, to that. Uh, it, it, it just it went, I mean I don't know what to say about it. It was just kind of perfect. Went right to a conclusion and just—

C.R.: Uh, I felt, uh, very much with you, partly I'm sure because of, uh, my own personal feelings of being a loner and not quite . . . so I related on that basis, not on some of the other things you were saying, but, uh, I didn't find it difficult to *be* with you. And I, I really felt I could *feel* what it was like to, uh, uh, to perhaps, you know, if you came out really, maybe you would be a witch, uh, uh, and then just then to see that gradually get clear, until finally that part was set aside and a different way of perceiving the world really crept in. That was exciting.

Mary: You were very empathetic.

C.R.: Yes, I was. I felt, I felt that.

Mary: That was what enabled me to do that, uh, because this, this thing in me stops at the least bit of direction.

C.R.: M-hm, that's right. I, I felt that, uh, it's one of the, one of the angles that has, has a lot of meaning to me, that, uh, empathy needs to be very delicate. I mean that, uh, you are exposing a very vulnerable part of yourself and the least little thing that looks like misunderstanding or rejection or judgment or something can just shut it all off.

Mary: There's not one bit of that. Not one molecule.

C.R.: No, I didn't feel there was. That's true. M-hm, m-hm. Once you try—I went a shade beyond what you were feeling, but you corrected that, and it, uh, no, I felt a, I felt a real, real bond, uhh-uh. It was, uh—

Mary: Well, it helped me the way you were searching to—

C.R.: M-hm, m-hm. I was wanting to understand that. Yeah, to understand. I don't know if it was so much understanding, more, uh, something more, more than that it seems like.

Mary: OK. I know it.

C.R.: Yeah, I really wanted to experience what you were experiencing, and uh, your conversation is quite vivid, and that helped me to really get the *feel* of it, uh-huh, uh-huh.

Mary: And your willingness to do that, um, opens it up for me. It, it just clears—the space is clear.

C.R.: And just as you had no notion that you might arrive where you arrived at, neither did I. Uh, whatever else is evident in this interaction is that *the client knows best*. You don't know that you know best, you don't consciously know where you're going, but if I can trust that and just be with you wherever each strange step of the way, why it leads somewhere and, uh, just to be a little absurd: If I had had some goal for this interview, I would have wrecked it, it would have completely wrecked it. But just to try to be completely with you wherever you went, and you went in different ways, and, and then really saw a new door opening and that was, uh, that was *your* doing, you know.

Mary: I'm, I'm really sensitive to being directed in any way. (C.R.: M-hm.) Or pushed in any way. (C.R.: M-hm, m-hm.) So this is the only way it could have worked for me. I know that, and, and I had a little bit of unspoken fear, very little though, because I had a sense that, that with you it would be OK. But, um, I know with others, um, that it would come to a place where somehow there would be a little bit of a block or a, uh, pushing away on the other person's part that would just stop me cold.

C.R.: M-hm, m-hm, m-hm. And it wouldn't have taken long.

Mary: And out of that I would come to a more superficial level on something, you know, I'd have to grope for something else that might be more acceptable to that.

C.R.: Something nice. Shall we let them in on it for a bit?

Mary: Yes.

LOUISE: TRANSCRIPT

Carl Rogers (C.R.): I appreciate your being willing to be the client, and I don't know what you might want to talk about.

Louise: Um, I don't either. Just a moment, um. I guess I'd like to say how I feel right now. (C.R.: M-hm.) Um, which is, uh, which is a little, I'm thinking about, I'll talk about anxiety. Yesterday I remember saying my palms are sweating. (C.R.: M-hm.) And, um, when N. asked me, and we were doing, just after we did the dance, I suddenly became aware I wasn't wearing very much and, and I thought, "Well, that's how I feel, I feel vulnerable." (C.R.: M-hm.) And, and a bit naked, yeah. (C.R.: M-hm, m-hm.) Um—

C.R.: Both both anxious and exposed.

Louise: Yeah.

C.R.: M-hm. *(Laughs a little)*

Louise: In some ways that's a good feeling and that, and it comes off what we just did in our small group, um, similar to the process that we did this morning with three drawings. And at the end of it I, um, I felt, well, when I was looking back particularly at two of the drawings, I felt aware of my, I was quite overwhelmed at what I, at what had come out of those drawings. (C.R.: M-hm.) Um, the, the beauty of them, and that's something I can see with my eyes closed. (C.R.: M-hm.) So it was good to, I suppose it was good to be aware and in touch with and rejoicing at my inner beauty. (C.R.: M-hm, m-hm.) Um, so it's a continuation of the, this morning's process. *(Cranes her neck toward corner of room where her paintings are stashed.)*

C.R.: It's not part of the way I usually operate. If you'd like to—would you like to have the drawings here to talk about them or not?

Louise: Um, yeah, I'd like to show you them.

C.R.: OK, I don't know. . . . Let somebody else get them.

Louise: There, well, that pile, the orange pile, yeah. OK, that's one. Yeah, the three, the three, yellow one, no—yeah. *(Pause)* Those are the two that I was impressed with. *(Drawings brought over and laid out in order on floor next to the chairs.)* Um, that was the one, that was, this is the first one. (C.R.: M-hm, m-hm.) *(Pause)* I can't remember which, I think this one. *(Pause)* And I noticed that it, it's not *new* to me, those shapes, those colors, so it's like something that's been going on for a long time that I've only just fully noticed. (C.R.: M-hm.) Yeah.

C.R.: And you want to say something about each one? *(Pause)* You say this is the first one, huh?

Louise: Yeah. Well, what C. was suggesting to us was that we took two, we took two, uh, something that was bothering us or something that was in us and draw the two extra—the two sides of that. (C.R.: M-hm.) And something that's, um, something that has just occurred to me, everyone will laugh but anyway, the, the, um, somebody who's been picking up leaves and been around in the garden this week that I've been saying hello to suddenly asked me for a date just before I came to the small group. (C.R.: M-hm, m-hm, m-hm.) And, uh, I like talking to him but when he asked me out I was terrified, and, uh, that's—I realized I don't have to go out with him—there's no time—so I said that to him and, uh, and came up here. But it made me think of, um, those polarities in my life, that I long for a partner and yet I fear that as well. (C.R.: M-hm.) Yeah.

C.R.: It may have been a very small incident but still it symbolized some things for you.

Louise: Right.

C.R.: Both the longing and the fear.

Louise: That's right, yeah.

C.R.: M-hm. *(Pause)* So this is the first drawing—

Louise: What I took was exactly that, the longing and the, and that fear and that was, that was the longing— (C.R.: M-hm.) And what I was going to draw next was the fear, and I thought, what was going to come out was another black picture of some sort, and instead, well, I guess my joy and beauty came out. (C.R.: M-hm, m-hm.) Which, uh, just seemed in a way like an extension of that one. (C.R.: M-hm, m-hm.) Rather than— (C.R.: M-hm.) Rather than opposite.

C.R.: They somehow seem to belong together, and yet they came out quite differently.

Louise: Yeah, yeah.

C.R.: And one, if I understand it, one is sort of polarized, the other is, is real joyous.

Louise: That's right, yeah. They seem like a progression instead of opposites in a way. (C.R.: M-hm, m-hm.) *(25-second pause)* Something, um, that occurred to me about what I wrote this morning, when I was, uh, feeling the failure of my father. And, uh, I don't know, this is just real searching and just something that came out but— (C.R.: M-hm, m-hm.) I wondered if, uh, how my relationship with him affects my relationship in general with men. (C.R.: M-hm, m-hm, m-hm, m-hm.) The fact that I'm much closer to my mother— (C.R.: M-hm.) And sometimes I feel like I don't know him at all. And, um, the sadness of that was coming out as well as feeling his, all the sadness for him failing at things that he wants to do, and also the sadness that I don't know him as well as I'd like to.

C.R.: M-hm, m-hm. So it's sadness for him in his situation but sadness on your part that you don't know him.

Louise: Yeah, yeah.

C.R.: And I don't know, you mentioned failure. I don't know, are you speaking about his or about yours in his eyes?

Louise: Um, I think I felt his, uh, yeah, I guess he would say, he would acknowledge his failure. I guess I felt it very much since he had a very good position in R_____. I was all concerned with out, with the outward world, but that's what I was concerned with then. (C.R.: M-hm, m-hm.) And then we came back to E_____ and he was 40 and he had to take a very much, a job that much inferior to his ability. And that's how it's been really, and he's now 65. (C.R.: M-hm, m-hm, m-hm.) Um, and well, I just think of my own failure that, that went along with his really, that I, I didn't do as well as people expected of me at school and as I expected of myself, I guess. (C.R.: M-hm.) Because my parents certainly didn't lay anything heavy on me. (C.R.: Hmm?) My parents didn't lay anything heavy on me about what I should get. (C.R.: M-hm, m-hm.) And then that continued until I was, for the next 10 years, more or less. I failed the degree I was doing at college. Um, then I fumbled around trying to think what I would do, and then finally I went back to college, and I did this degree, and I have this bad experience with this tutor. (C.R.: M-hm, m-hm.) Um, who more or less told me that I was a failing teacher. You know, I think deep down inwardly I didn't believe that, but it's taken a while to work that off. (C.R.: M-hm.) Yeah.

C.R.: So in the eyes of your father, in the eyes of your tutor, sometimes in the eyes of yourself, you've often been a failure, even though in regard to the tutor, you feel "I'm right and he's wrong. I'm not a failure."

Louise: Yeah. In my head. (C.R.: Hmm?) In my head I can say that easily. (C.R.: Uh-huh, m-hm.) But in my heart— (C.R.: M-hm, m-hm.) It's still being accepted.

C.R.: Your heart says he might be right, he might be right.

Louise: Yeah, that's right.

C.R.: "Maybe I'm a failure."

Louise: Yeah. Well, I guess doing this has begun to change that. I mean, just last night becoming much more in touch with that. (C.R.: M-hm.) And, and even just doing *this* this afternoon, acknowledging my own strength and all that positive side.

C.R.: And I notice you didn't mention the third picture.

Louise: Hmm? This one?

C.R.: I assume.

Louise: Well, I felt like it was a continuation of, of the yellow one. Yeah. And, um, when N. suggested that we move to it, or express that in movement, I saw myself, um, standing on a cliff, uh, kind of, huh, it's interesting, welcoming the sunrise.

C.R.: M-hm, so that's that. *(Looks at one of the pictures.)*

Louise: That's that, yeah.

C.R.: M-hm. It looks like the strongest of the three. *(Looks at the pictures.)*

Louise: Yeah.

C.R.: So in your feelings, that's you welcoming the sunrise, and standing on a cliff.

Louise: Yeah. *(Pause)* I was thinking about the metaphor, and I understood that before, I was thinking about the metaphor of the sunrise like that being me— (C.R.: M-hm.) Um, acknowledging myself.

C.R.: That you *are* the sunrise.

Louise: Right. Yeah.

C.R.: Emerging from darkness.

Louise: Yeah. (C.R.: M-hm.) A good feeling.

C.R.: I say, it looks like, it looks like that was sinking in.

Louise: Yeah. (C.R.: M-hm.) Yeah. A very good feeling. I'd like to read you what I wrote. Would that be OK?

C.R.: OK, m-hm.

Louise: Um, I'm surprised, I'm awed, this is me. Feelings and shapes of beauty that came out of me. In spite of that large dark black brooding woman sitting there condemning, in spite of that, in spite of her being there, in spite, in spite of it all, here I am writing poetry. Wonderful. Bloody marvelous. *(Pause)* I felt really good.

C.R.: Bloody marvelous is right. Was your tutor a woman?

Louise: Yes.

C.R.: Oh, funny, I had visualized he was a man.

Louise: A man, yeah.

C.R.: I see, m-hm, m-hm, m-hm.

Louise: So I happened.

C.R.: So that's another version of the sunrise.

Louise: Yeah, yeah. *(Pause)*

C.R.: M-hm. And quite bloody marvelous, hmm? *(General laughter)*

Louise: *(Laughs) (Pause)* Huh. I was just thinking of the dark woman there. Last night when I was, um, working with S., she, she, um, suggested that we work in a Gestalt way. I worked with the woman, talking to her, and through that I realized that, um, that was when I got in touch with this condemning part of myself that she, that I like, internalized her. (C.R.: M-hm, m-hm.) And, um, well, I just feel like she has much less power now. I mean— (C.R.: M-hm, m-hm.) I feel that that critical side of myself is still there, but it's much more healthy, healthy side.

C.R.: Sounds a little bit as though that dark woman inside of you has been moved outside somewhat. Maybe that's not right.

Louise: Mmm. Well, it's funny, I w—, I was almost thinking that she wasn't there.

C.R.: OK.

Louise: And then I was thinking of what D. said, that it's good to have a critical person there. And I thought, "Yes, there's probably something there." Like that I think she's almost part of *this*. (C.R.: M-hm.) Yeah.

C.R.: Maybe some other strength is in there?

Louise: Yeah. (C.R.: M-hm.) That part of being self-critical in a healthy— (C.R.: M-hm.) Not overpowering way, m-hm.

C.R.: Maybe you can retain some of the healthy parts of her but not the condemning part.

Louise: Yeah, yeah. *(20-second pause)* M-hm, m-hm. I'm really drawn to it. *(General laughter)*

C.R.: Yes, I can see that. M-hm, m-hm. It looks as though you look at it and look at it and, "That really is *me.*"

Louise: Yeah, yeah. Hmm. I was thinking, um, it seems strange in a way to have taken so long to come to that realization. *(Long pause)* And I think before the black woman would have said, "Louise, honestly, it's taken so long to come to this point."

C.R.: Uh-huh, uh-huh, "Why have you been so slow, for heaven's sake?"

Louise: "All this money spent on workshops."

C.R.: I know. Terrible.

Louise: Hmm. It's a real magnet! Huh. *(General laughter, pause)* There was some sense when, um, after N. had asked me about doing this [interview], that I arrived at a very good place and didn't have anything more to say, you know, like I immediately wanted to do this, and yet I thought, that my process in some ways was complete.

C.R.: You thought, "I'm in a good place so what in the world is there for me to say?"

Louise: Yeah, yeah.

C.R.: And I get the feeling this is sort of a celebration.

Louise: Yeah. Yeah. It certainly is.

C.R.: You *are* drawn to that! *(General laughter)*

Louise: That's right. It's like I feel guilty now, I should be giving my attention to you!

C.R.: I know the feeling. Can't take your eyes off your masterpiece! *(General laughter)*

Louise: *(Laughs)* Was that how it was for you with your painting?

C.R.: I'm sorry?

Louise: When you did your, um, painting that you really liked?

C.R.: Yes, yes. I, I like to look at that. M-hm, m-hm. *(Pause)* M-hm. It looks like you're really appreciating it and appreciating you.

Louise: Yeah, yeah. Yeah. I still find it strange that I haven't got that sense of awe before but—suddenly that came out of *me.*

C.R.: M-hm, m-hm. A sense of wonder and a sense of "really?"

Louise: Yeah.

C.R.: "I gave birth to that."

Louise: Yeah. That's true. I was just thinking of birth. M-hm. It makes me feel that I really could *do* something. (C.R.: M-hm, m-hm.) Yeah.

C.R.: A person like that could *do* something.

Louise: Yeah, could *do* something, yeah. (C.R.: M-hm.) Last night, one of the things that surprised me was the Gestalt thing with C., with, um, I was talking to this, uh, tutor, professor of mine. (C.R.: M-hm.) And, um, and one of the things I, I wanted her to acknowledge was that I had potential and, um, creativity and that I could be a real leader in my field. And it was, I was kind of shy about saying that to her but, but I also wanted to say it and, uh, and that I was just thinking of that then. (C.R.: M-hm, m-hm.) Yeah.

C.R.: I wasn't sure of what you said. You wanted to acknowledge that in yourself or you wanted her to acknowledge that in what, in what you did last night?

Louise: Well, I guess it amounts to the same thing, yeah.

C.R.: OK, OK. Yeah.

Louise: Yeah.

C.R.: You wanted the dark woman in you to acknowledge that.

Louise: Acknowledge that, yeah. *(Pause)*

C.R.: I guess you can see she acknowledged it.

Louise: Yeah. I hadn't thought of that. *(Pause)* Yeah. I was thinking, um, if this means that I accept my own failure more and as like a thing of the past, and now I can really do something. (C.R.: M-hm, m-hm.) I was thinking I could perhaps help my father to do the same. (C.R.: M-hm, m-hm, m-hm.) Um, I know that, uh, I know one of the reasons I'm not close to him is that to some extent I back away from his, his pain which he hides very mu—, very well. Uh, one of the most difficult things about him is that he, he talks and talks about th—, well, about, what sounds to me about no—, nothing, about politics and about, um, well, mostly politics. *(Sighs)* Um, but that's, when I can really hear that, I hear it being a defense for everything that's going on behind it, but, um, often I'm not able to bear it, I want to run away.

C.R.: M-hm, m-hm, m-hm. You really can't stand this talk because of what are the feelings you sense behind it?

Louise: Behind them, yeah.

C.R.: And yet now you're wondering, "Maybe I could get close to him, maybe I could even be of help to him?"

Louise: Yeah, yeah. Like I go back there and just reassure myself that that *(indicates person in the sunrise picture)* person could do that. *(Laughs)*

C.R.: M-hm, m-hm, m-hm. If you can take that back with you inside. Why, m-hm. I guess in the way you put that, you're not quite sure, but that's what you'd like.

Louise: That's right.

C.R.: *(20-second pause)* I can't help but say that picture's going to be engraved on your brain, isn't it?

Louise: *(Laughs)* I was just thinking he's coming up for retirement soon. (C.R.: Hmm?) My father's just coming up for retirement, so there's going to be a lot more time for him.

C.R.: Oh. M-hm.

Louise: Well, let's see, yeah. *(Pause)* It changes me thinking about him. I can feel like I'm, I'm not like glowing with the sun; I feel sad.

C.R.: M-hm, m-hm, m-hm. Thinking about him takes the sunshine away, sort of. You feel, feel for him. Sounds like he's *very* much in your thoughts and feelings.

Louise: *(Teary voice)* I suppose it makes me feel like I've had all this opportunity and and he got stuck so early and he stayed in that stuckness.

C.R.: M-hm, m-hm, m-hm.

Louise: *(Cries)* He's been to one workshop, and, uh, he's much more open to kind of growth ideas now. (C.R.: M-hm.) He broke a tele–, he broke a telephone after. It was a retreat workshop, I think you were there in fact—he broke a telephone when he came back because he couldn't kind of bridge—he was mad at the world after this wonderful experience that he had. I think that made him stop exploring further.

C.R.: So his freedom of expression stopped with the telephone? *(General laughter)*

Louise: Right.

C.R.: But you feel he did have a taste of it.

Louise: Yeah. Now I feel with me now he really tries to—what he'll do if my mother is in is if I phone, he'll talk briefly to me and then he'll say, "Right, your mother's here," as if he has nothing to offer me. But if she's away and I phone and, uh, I'm in trouble, I'm wanting support of some sort, he'll, he'll really *try*. *(Pause)* Um, it reminds me of one time he got up to dance and, uh, he stopped because he felt like Pinocchio and I feel that somehow he's—wanting support is like that, he really *(sighs)*, well, just needs to loosen up a bit and *(voice trails away)* have more faith in himself.

C.R.: You really want very much for him to go through the kind of process that you're going through. *(Long pause)*

Louise: *(Surprised tone) Yeah. Yeah.* I suppose I want him to be more aware of himself. *(Pause) (Teary voice)* Of what a fine person he is. (C.R.: Hmm?) Of what a fine person he is.

C.R.: Yeah. You wish very deeply *he* could paint a picture like that.

Louise: Yeah. (C.R.: M-hm, m-hm, m-hm.) He's so very self-critical. And he puts it out there sometime, and it's Thatcher he's attacking or Reagan or some political figure like Khadafy. But, uh, it has to do with the attacks that he makes on himself, I feel.

C.R.: M-hm. You feel he has a dark critic inside of him.

Louise: Yeah, very dark.

C.R.: It seems very short to me, but they say that our time is about up.

Louise: Right. It's amazing. Seemed like 10 minutes.

C.R.: *(Laughs)*

Louise: M-hm. Well, I certainly haven't—hadn't fully acknowledged the power of that picture.

C.R.: You really drank in that picture, didn't you?

Louise: Yeah. (C.R.: M-hm.) I felt almost like, like it wasn't a part of what I should be doing here; since I was with you I should be talking to you, and it was just it, just kept drawing me.

C.R.: M-hm, it just had a magnetic power.

Louise: Yeah.

C.R.: M-hm, m-hm. Can we leave it with you looking at your painting?

Louise: Sure. *(Laughs)*

C.R.: OK.

Louise: Thank you, Carl.

C.R.: That's very good. Uh, again if you feel like it, you can say a little bit about what the experience seemed like to you, and I'll do the same.

Louise: Right. Well, I felt at the beginning like in some sense I didn't have anything to talk about. (C.R.: M-hm.) Um, and then when I made that known to you, I felt certain you accepted it, it was OK just to be here. Um, that made, that made me feel easier. Um, it was a strange mixture for me of, uh, feeling like maybe I wasn't doing quite the right thing and yet doing it in spite of, in spite of myself, or in spite of that same judge thing.

C.R.: M-hm, no dark woman is going to tell you whether it was right or not.

Louise: That's right. I just said, "to blazes," and I just did it. But all the same, it was reassuring what I felt when it was OK to you to be continually drawn to that. Yeah. And, uh, I suppose it was sort of mysterious to me how, although I can see how it happened, but "amazing" would be the word I'd use, when I made the connections, I mean, everything seemed, I could be talking about so much in my relationship with men, my own failure, my father's failure, my sense of joy, um, and somehow how they came together, um, especially with my father and feeling how that connected with him, um. So it's been very helpful to see that. (C.R.: M-hm.) And, and to be aware of his darkness, yeah. (C.R.: M-hm, m-hm.) I guess also I didn't feel, I didn't feel completely relaxed all the way through, but somehow it was OK, um, I mean that's, gosh, I'm a, I'm a, I'm just seeing how little power that that critic has because I think, you know, that's the same thing: "Louise, you weren't relaxed!" and somehow it was OK, I didn't, um—

C.R.: You weren't talking about problems, you weren't sufficiently relaxed, all kinds of things wrong.

Louise: Yeah, right.

C.R.: Only they weren't.

Louise: And yet I don't feel they had too much weight. (C.R.: M-hm.) Yeah.

C.R.: M-hm, not properly dressed! *(Laughs)*

Louise: Oh God, no wonder I have aching shoulders! (C.R.: M-hm, m-hm) Ah!

C.R.: M-hm. It was an unusual experience for me, uh, because usually people do come because they have some problem, and, uh, it was really very refreshing to have, I don't know, to sort of be present at the emergence of the new woman. That's, m-hm, m-hm. And, uh, it's a little bit weird that here we were making use of all of the procedures of Expressive Therapy! *(Laughs)*

Louise: So maybe it's OK after all!

C.R.: So maybe it's OK after all. That's right. Really.

Louise: Yeah. I liked it when you said that it's not the way you usually work, but we could do it.

C.R.: That's right. I felt, uh, what you were, what was happening would be OK with the group. So I felt relaxed too, I I did feel relaxed and sort of, uh, sort of an amused note in my feeling. I don't know quite, I don't want to be taken wrong, but yeah, I could, I could be a little light about it, like admiring your masterpiece and things like that.

Louise: Yeah, yeah.

C.R.: M-hm, and that I could relate as much to that and as easily to that as if you were in pain and that uh, that pleased me about myself. M-hm. Shall we see what they think about it?

Louise: Sure.

C.R.: *(To audience)* You have some questions or comments?

AN ARGUMENT FOR CLIENT SELF-DETERMINATION

Peggy Natiello

The therapist's commitment to the self-determination of the client is the outstanding feature of client-centered therapy. Rogers (1977) described this commitment as

> a conscious renunciation and avoidance by the therapist of all control over, or decision-making for, the client. It is the facilitation of self-ownership by the client and the strategies by which this can be achieved; the placing of the locus of decision-making and the responsibility for the effects of these decisions. It is politically centered in the client. (p. 14)

This concept seems absolutely crucial to me in the practice of client-centered therapy (Natiello, 1987). At first glance, it seems like a simple enough concept. But, upon reflection, it is not. The belief in the self-determination and personal power of the client is a radical departure from other styles of therapy that depend on the expertise and authority of the therapist. Rogers, in my experience, rarely departed from his belief in client self-determination and was genuinely committed to its practice.

The deep respect that the client-centered therapist has for the client's personal empowerment and self-determination is demonstrated by the therapist's willingness to follow the client's lead—stay with him or her during every step of the shared psychological journey. This style of therapy is not a technique (Brink, 1987). Indeed, Grant (1990) considers it a moral virtue. It evolves from a deeply held value and philosophy that persons are the world's best experts on themselves; that they are far wiser about their own needs than others can be; that they can be trusted to be self-directed; and that their beliefs and feelings are worthy of acceptance and respect. As Rogers (1977, p. 14) said, "the placing of the locus of decision-making and the responsibility for the effects of these decisions" are politically centered in the client. Thus the term client-centered.

Commitment to the self-determination of the client does *not* mean that the therapist behaves like a parrot, reflecting or repeating everything the client says, nor does it mean that the therapist is uninvolved as a person in the therapeutic relationship. In the client-centered approach, therapists will sometimes respond to a self-initiated question or request of a client, make a joke, reach out and touch, ask a question, say how they feel or what they are thinking, intuit something that the client has *not* said, say nothing at all, or choose a myriad of other behaviors that reflect genuineness. What they attempt *not* to do is take control away from the client; interpret, guide, or manipulate the client; give unsolicited advice to the client; attempt to change the direction of the session or the experience of the client; or make something happen that will satisfy an agenda of their own.

To the degree that Rogers' work is used as a model for how a client-centered therapist behaves, there is an obvious problem, and it has been the source of many misunderstandings. Rogers' well-known cases, because they come from later in his career when he did not have a psychotherapy practice, consist of one- or two-time interactions. They model the empathic, reflective response appropriate to and consistent with one- and two-time interactions, and do not adequately represent the more mature, long-term therapeutic relationships in which most therapists are involved.

Still, even within the limited context of a one-time interview, there was a variety and richness in Rogers' behaviors that went far beyond the reflective parroting often attributed to client-centered therapists.

The two videotaped interviews reviewed in this chapter are one-time sessions. Because each is conducted by Carl Rogers, they present a rare opportunity to contrast the difference in impact between a therapeutic process that is client-centered and one that is, at least partially, therapist-centered. In addition to looking at that impact, and in order to dispel some of the misconceptions about the unimaginative responses of the client-centered therapist, I will pay special attention to the artistry, variety, and increasing scope of Rogers' responses in the limited context of the one-time interview.

THE INTERVIEWS

The interviews took place in August 1986, just 6 months before Rogers' death. They occurred during a weekend meeting of an Expressive Therapy

Training Program. Both interviewees were therapists in training. Although it was not consistent with Rogers' style of therapy, certain forms of creative expression such as drawings, writings, body movement, and so on were used in *this* program to facilitate insight and intensify personal awareness. I surmise that the drawings referred to in both these sessions were created by the clients as part of their personal training work prior to their session with Rogers.

In the first interview—with Mary—Rogers, without exception, demonstrates his belief in the wisdom of the client. He waits for her to take the lead, and never guides her in a different direction from the one she chooses. The interview is extremely sensitive, and the client is in charge of the process every step of the way. (In the group discussion that followed the interview, one of the observers said to Rogers, "You were her soulmate.") The outcome included a shift in and integration of the client's experience, acknowledged in the processing discussion with Rogers at the end of the session. (In that discussion Mary said, "I had no idea I was going to get there, to that. . . . It was just kind of perfect, went right to a conclusion.") Thus, this is an outstanding example of a client-centered therapy session that is absolutely consistent with the theory.

In the second interview—with Louise—Rogers departs from his resolute commitment to the self-direction of the client and takes the lead almost immediately, suggesting that Louise might want to work with the pictures she had drawn on the morning of the interview. Several times later, he redirects her back to her pictures, rather than waiting for her to take the lead. Although his responses in this interview were generally empathic, as in the session with Mary, in my opinion, he failed to establish the depth of connection with Louise that he did with Mary, and the interview falls far short of its possibilities for healing and growth.

Let us look at the interview with Mary in more detail, paying special attention to the nature of Rogers' responses as well as his willingness for her to take the lead.

Interview with Mary

The session begins with Rogers inviting Mary to talk. He says he is ready to listen to anything she wants to discuss and makes it clear that the direction they will take and the way they will proceed are in her control. He has no agenda whatsoever.

Mary sighs and says:

Mary: Well, I guess, m-hm, the thing for me to talk about now is where I am, where I've come to in this workshop. I keep wanting to look at my, my latest drawings up there. (C.R.: M-hm, m-hm.)

It is important, for comparison with the case of Louise, to note here that Rogers does not negate or support Mary's reference to her pictures. He leaves the decision about how to proceed entirely up to her. And it turns out that she uses the pictures only as a point of orientation, referring to them again only very briefly.

Mary's story then begins to unfold. Through her participation in the expressive therapy program, she says, she has rid herself of a lot of negativity and is now "ready to create my life," to be of service, to be more fully herself. In examining her failure to have done this so far, she uncovers a distrust of her own power—a fear that, if she claims her own power, she might suffer rejection or worse. She has a belief that there is really no place for her "*whole* self" in society.

In the beginning stage of the session with Mary, Rogers' responses express simple attentiveness—"m-hm," "yeah"—or are restatements of what Mary has said, for the purpose of checking or deepening his understanding. As the session unfolds and Rogers gets a feel for her, his restatements become often metaphoric rather than literal, such as, "Sounds like you cleared away a lot of the rubbish. Now what are you going to build there?" and "You really love yourself, rooted in the earth and reaching to the sky."

If his understanding of her experience is even slightly distorted, Mary corrects it.

C.R.: And you're not quite sure whether you want to be in this crazy world.

Mary: Well, I've come to the point where I accept that I do. I, I feel like I'm at the point where I, I want to, um, to express myself, to be myself, and to be of service.

Mary's ease in correcting Rogers' perceptions indicates that she fully trusts that his responses are intended for accuracy of understanding and feeling, at a deep experiential level, what it is like to *be* her rather than merely mirroring back her experience. She seems very sure that Rogers sees *her* version of her reality as the important one and considers *her* to be the director of this session.

Sometimes Rogers seems to understand Mary at a deeper level than she is able to articulate. In those instances, his empathy helps to raise the unacknowledged parts of her experience into awareness.

Mary: *(Sighs)* And then too, I think too, it's, it's also the sense of not being valued like what I value so much about myself, to put that out and, um, have it be invisible to others because they don't see the value in it or they don't connect with it, um.

C.R.: M-hm, m-hm. I, I get a sense that you feel, uh, kind of alone in that, not at all sure that anyone else would value what, what you might see as the way you want to be.

Mary: *(Pause)* Yeah, there is a lot of that, there is a lot. I, I have been a very solitary person. (C.R.: M-hm, m-hm.) And very independent because I have not wanted to be dependent on that kind of approval from the world. (C.R.: M-hm, m-hm, m-hm.) But, yet, on the other hand, I think I am.

Several interesting phenomena occur as the session progresses. Rogers' understanding of Mary's experience, and thereby his responses, become more complex. Instead of simple empathic attention, he begins to weave some of the history from the early part of the interview into his attempt to understand. For instance, when Mary talks about being afraid of misusing her power, and of the consequences of that, Rogers ties this to an idea earlier in the session when she had asserted her belief in her power.

C.R.: So there's no question about the strength of the inner power that you have. That, that you're sure of, but to let it out in its imperfect state, wow, that's dangerous.

There is another change in Rogers' responses as the interview proceeds. As Mary becomes more self-disclosing and moves more deeply into her experience, Rogers seems to become more connected to her. This is evident in the growing warmth in his voice (even in the "M-hm"s) and, nonverbally, in his increasingly intent gaze and posture. Sometimes he actually sits on the edge of his chair. But perhaps the most dramatic evidence is in his growing use of "I" rather than "you." He begins to speak as though he *is* the client. "I don't want to be killed," "If I let my power loose into the world, I might be killed for that," or "If I let out the real inner me, how could that possibly be so wrong?" Several times he finds the word she was looking for or finishes her sentences.

Mary: Well, I've certainly tried this, but it—

C.R.: It doesn't work, and that maintaining it, somehow "I'm maintaining that."

Mary continues to elaborate her feelings of never being able to use herself fully in the world. When she seems to dip more deeply into her discouragement, Rogers never tries to talk her out of her feelings or change the way she sees things. His acceptance of her experience is unwavering.

Toward the end of the half-hour allotted for the interview, she acknowledges that she has clarified the issue for herself but does not see any
resolution. She sighs heavily and falls into silence.

C.R.: Sort of a sigh of resignation that, yeah, OK, uh, that's what it is, but
it's still there, still there. *(Pause)* Still impossible to move out.

Mary: I feel like I incorporate it so, um, on all of my levels, like down to
my cells it's in me. (C.R.: M-hm.) That way of, um, being conflicted
in—

C.R.: Seems like you can't possibly free yourself from something that is so
deep it's right down to the level of every cell in your body. That you're
not permitted to be out there.

Mary: Yeah, it seems to me to be the way the universe is constructed, and
I don't know— (C.R.: M-hm, m-hm.) I don't see resolution.

C.R.: M-hm, m-hm. Little bit of resignation or even hopelessness.

Mary: Yes.

C.R.: M-hm. "That's the way the universe is. I'll never be able to come out
as I am."

Mary: Yes, that's it. *(Pause)* And there's also the spark in me that won't die;
that won't, that won't give up.

C.R.: You're resigned, you're a little bit hopeless, but still there is something that says, "No, I'm not, I haven't given up."

It is at this point that the session shifts. Mary acknowledges that she
knows that there *is* a place for wholeness in the world and that she is even
beginning to suspect that she can create it in her own life.

Mary: I'm just getting a sense that maybe, um, what I have to do is—open
up and, uh, and accept that whole world, that I want to— (C.R.: M-hm,
m-hm, m-hm.) That *I* want to reject and that wants to reject me.

Mary then proceeds to describe metaphorically how that can come
about. Her metaphor contains a snake coming up against a big animal,
swallowing it whole, digesting it, and being nourished by it. As she develops
the metaphor and its significance, her entire physical presence changes.
Her intensity—characterized by a tight face, a hand sometimes pulling at
or covering her mouth, deep sighs and grimaces, and arms tightly hugging
her own body—seems to subside and is replaced by chuckles, smiles, a
softening of all her facial features, and a relaxation of her body in the chair.

Later, in her reflections on the session, she says, with an eloquent smile, "I don't know what to say about it. It was just kind of perfect. Went right to a conclusion."

An examination of the interview with Mary sheds some light on the range of responses available to the client-centered therapist. Even in the half-hour relationship presented here, there is a subtle change and expansion of Rogers' style of response. Most of his responses are geared toward empathic understanding, but there is a good deal of variety in the form they take. He asks direct questions to further his understanding; repeats what he thinks he is hearing, sometimes literally, sometimes metaphorically; links ideas from earlier in the session to later disclosures; completes the client's sentences; helps her find the right words; speaks in the first person as though he were her; and even jokes a little.

Whatever form Rogers' responses take, there is one thing that is consistent. None of them steer the client in a direction of his choosing or indicate that he has any agenda for the session. He makes each response on the basis of an implicit trust in the client's choice about the next step of the interaction and an absolute respect for her experience. In fact, during the group discussion following the interview, he said that it would be "horrible to seem to try to direct this. It just seems sacrilegious." One person, responding to this, confronted Rogers and said that this Expressive Therapy training group was trying to learn different ways to respond to clients and that his use of the words "horrible" and "sacrilegious" seemed judgmental. The observer said that if she had conducted the interview with Mary, she would have wanted to have the client's drawings in front of them so they could be used in the process if appropriate. Rogers hastened to explain that he felt it would be "horrible" for *him* to direct the client because it is not his style or in accordance with his belief. But he added that it was important for all students to find their own way of doing therapy and then to stick with it.

In what may have been a reaction to the above discussion, Rogers departed from *his* own way of doing therapy in the interview with Louise, perhaps in order to accommodate the kind of therapeutic processes used in the training program he was visiting. In the next session, I will demonstrate that Rogers took the lead and set the direction of the interview toward the subject of the client's drawings; that his suggestions interfered with the client's empowerment, as well as with his own connectedness to her; and that the client did not enjoy the feeling of completeness and release that Mary felt at the end of her interview.

Interview with Louise

In this interview, Rogers departs, to some degree, from his general way of working with clients in that he directs Louise to think about the pictures she had drawn earlier in the day as a part of the expressive therapy training context in which the interviews took place. In contrast to the simple acceptance of Mary's mention of her pictures, he seems to have an agenda to use Louise's pictures. There is more evidence of this agenda at the end of the session when he asks if the camera is still on. Told that it is, he suggests that Louise hold up her other pictures so that they can be seen on the videotape.

At moments during the interview, Louise seems connected to her personal experience, and Rogers responds with empathy and understanding. Much of the time, however, she seemed distracted by her pictures, and perhaps because of this does not provide much personal material for Rogers to empathize with. During the times she seems distracted, Rogers uses a light tone to reflect her absorption in and affirmation of the drawings. "You *are* drawn to that!" "Can't take your eyes off your masterpiece!" "That picture's going to be engraved on your brain, isn't it?" At other times, when Louise talks about her inner critic, "the dark woman" inside her, he joins her in mocking the critic with warm humor.

Louise: And I think before the black woman would have said, "Louise, honestly, it's taken so long to come to this point."

C.R.: Uh-huh, uh-huh, "Why have you been so slow, for heaven's sake?"

Louise: "All this money on workshops."

C.R.: I know. Terrible.

Despite the variety of types of responses in this interview, I believe that the deep connection which developed in his work with Mary, which was characteristic of Rogers' work and which he saw as healing, was adversely affected here by his agenda regarding the pictures. Several times during the session he abandoned his commitment to the self-determination of the client that he articulated during the group discussion following the interview with Mary.

> Whatever else is evident in this interaction is that the client knows best. . . . You don't consciously know where you're going, but if I can just trust that and just be with you on each strange step of the way, why it will lead somewhere. Just to be a little absurd. If I had had some goal for this interview, it would have completely wrecked it.

Rogers' departure from his personal style of therapy is evident very early in the interview when Louise, just like Mary, refers to her drawings. Rogers says,

C.R.: It is not part of the way I usually operate. If you'd like to—would you like to have the drawings here to talk about them or not?

Louise says she would like that. Given Rogers' status and the awkwardness of doing a public interview, it is no surprise that Louise attached herself to his suggestion. She follows, however, by saying very little about the pictures and does not seem interested in pursuing the subject. But Rogers *does* seem to want to pursue it.

C.R.: And you want to say something about each one? *(Pause)* You say this is the first one, huh?

Louise speaks briefly about the pictures, although somewhat falteringly. Actually, after one sentence, she changes the subject from the pictures to an interaction she had with a man during the preceding week. She pursues this while Rogers gives her empathic responses, but then there is an awkward pause. Seeming not to have anything to say, Rogers returns to the pictures: "So this is the first drawing—"

From this point on, Louise spends a great deal of time craning her neck around to look at the pictures to the right of her chair. She rarely looks directly at Rogers. Except for the times when she talks about her relationship with her father, there is very little eye contact between them. This causes them to be disconnected and deprives them of intimacy.

They talk some more about the pictures, and then there is a silence of about 25 seconds. Louise looks up at Rogers and talks about her father without any reference to the pictures. It seems quite clear, here and in several other places, that she is eager to explore that relationship.

Louise: Something, um, that occurred to me about what I wrote this morning, when I was, uh, feeling the failure of my father. And, uh, I don't know, this is just real searching and just something that came out but— (C.R.: M-hm, m-hm.) I wondered if, uh, how my relationship with him affects my relationship in general with men.

This is the second time she has drifted away from talking about the pictures and attempted to explore her feelings about her father and about her relationships with men. These incidents, and several others like them, provide some indication that, if Rogers had not directed her toward the pictures, she would have used them merely as a launching pad to move forward into other concerns. She continues to talk about her relationship with her father and her sadness about the failure of his professional life.

Louise: And sometimes I feel like I don't know him at all. And, um, the sadness of that was coming out as well as feeling his, all the sadness for him failing at things that he wants to do, and also the sadness that I don't know him as well as I'd like to.

Trying to pursue this last idea, Rogers asks Louise if she is speaking about sadness for her father's failure or for her own. This question comes as a complete surprise to me, and it hints at Rogers' lack of connection to Louise. It is so clear that she is speaking about her father's failure. Indeed, up to this point, Louise had not even hinted at her own failure. There are two other striking places in the interview where Rogers reveals a lack of connection to Louise and what she is saying. Once he says, "I'm sorry?" to get her to repeat what she had asked him, and once he says, "I wasn't sure of what you said." I believe these gaps occurred because the focus kept shifting back and forth between the pictures and the discussion with Rogers, and, as a result, there was no compelling theme or deep personal connection between therapist and client.

Louise responds to Rogers' question about whether she is speaking of her father's failure or her own by saying a little about her father's failure. But after a few sentences, she shifts direction and begins for the first time to examine her feelings about her own failures. Although this examination doubtless is useful to Louise, it seems evident here that, unlike Mary, she is not directing her own interview. She is easily led by the things that Rogers says or, in this case, asks. It is almost as though, after taking the lead in the beginning, Rogers has set up a power imbalance in his favor.

After continuing to explore her own feelings of failure, Louise says she thinks she is turning things around by joining the Expressive Therapy Training Program and even by agreeing to do *this* this afternoon, acknowledging my own strength and all that positive side." Rogers again responds to her in a way that is completely out of character, "And I notice you didn't mention the third picture," going in a different direction from the one she had chosen.

Louise says a few sentences about the picture—so few that Rogers responds, "M-hm, so that's that?" The next segment of the interview is awkward and stilted. Louise's gaze is riveted to the pictures on the floor. There is little contact between her and Rogers except for his recurring comments about her fascination with her "masterpiece" and her laughing agreement.

Toward the end of the half-hour allotted for the interview, Louise returns to her pain about her father and her relationship with him. Even at the beginning of this segment, the pauses are awkward, and she again looks down at her pictures. Rogers says with some humor, "I can't help but say that picture's going to be engraved on your brain, isn't it?" Her response indicates that she is not really studying the pictures at all, but still thinking about her father.

Louise: *(Laughs)* I was just thinking he's coming up for retirement soon.
(C.R.: Hmm?) My father's just coming up for retirement, so there's
going to be a lot more time for him.

From this point on, Louise talks about her father. She faces Rogers,
seeming deeply connected with her experience, and her tears well up as
Rogers empathically says, "You feel, feel for him. Sounds like he's *very* much
in your thoughts and feelings." For these few moments at the end of the
session, there is the kind of connection between Louise and Rogers that
she wished for with her father.

It seems clear that this segment of the interview, as well as Louise's
celebration of self and her confrontation of her inner critic, have value
for Louise. However, my appraisal that much of the session lacks the
depth and connectedness that characterized the session with Mary
seems to be substantiated by the group discussion following the interview.

There was none of the enthusiastic participation that followed the
Mary interview. Only two observers shared any thoughts or reflections
about the interview. The rest of the group was silent.

Although Louise herself was positive about some aspects of the
interview, she also said that she did not "feel completely relaxed all the way
through." She referred to her aching shoulders, "Oh, God, no wonder I
have aching shoulders!" These remarks do not seem to reflect the experience of a client who has gone through the kind of release and integration
that Mary spoke about after her session with Rogers.

Rogers reflected on the interview as if it were all a celebration of the
"emergence of the new woman" represented in Louise's drawings.

C.R.: It was an unusual experience for me, um, because usually people do
come because they have some problem, and, uh, it was really very
refreshing to have, I don't know, to sort of be present at the emergence
of the new woman.

A study of the video of this interview, however, provides little evidence
that the subject of the interview was not a problem, but only "the emergence of the new woman." Rogers seemed unaware of the pain and
confusion around Louise's relationship with her father, much as he did
during some of the session. He declared that his experience of himself
during the interview was that he had a "sort of an amused note in my
feelings. . . . I could be a little light about it."

There are two specific indications during the discussion following the
interview that Rogers, himself, was focused on the drawings (procedures
of Expressive Therapy) and had an agenda to use them:

C.R.: And, uh, it's a little bit weird that here we were making use of all of the procedures of Expressive Therapy! *(Laughs)*

Louise: So maybe it's OK after all!

C.R.: So maybe it's OK after all. That's right. Really.

And again, it is quite clear that he is pursuing his agenda to use the drawings when, at the end of the discussion, Rogers asks if the camera is still on and suggests that Louise hold up all her drawings so that they can be captured on the videotape. He has abandoned his commitment to a client-centered process in favor of a therapist-centered one.

CONCLUSION

Trust in and commitment to the self-determination of the client is crucial to the practice of client-centered therapy. Barbara Temaner Brodley (1988) explains how such trust is demonstrated in client-centered practice: "In practice, the therapist, guided by the non-directive attitude, has *no* directive intentions. His/her intentions are distinctly and only to provide the attitudinal conditions" (p. 7).

Rogers (1977) also described clearly that the concept of trust in the self-determination of the client radically alters the therapeutic relationship:

> It is hardly necessary to say that the person-centered view drastically alters the therapist-patient relationship, as previously conceived. The therapist becomes the "midwife" of change, not its originator. She places the final authority in the hands of the client, whether in small things such as the correctness of a therapist response, or large decisions like the course of one's life direction. The locus of evaluation, of decision, rests clearly in the client's hands. (p. 15)

In the interview with Louise, Rogers *did* have a directive intention—namely, to use the drawings that Louise had created as part of the Expressive Therapy Training Program. His subtle but consistent direction of Louise's focus back to her drawings prevented the relationship from having the characteristics he described in the quote above. In several places he was clearly the "originator" of change in the session rather than its midwife. As a result, Louise did not act as if she had the final authority during her session, but seemed heavily influenced by his direction until near the end when she determinedly stayed with the subject of her father. In the discussion following the interview she spoke of not having been relaxed. She said, at one point, that her relationships with men, her father's failure, her own failure, and her sense of joy all somehow came together "especially with [her] father and feeling how they connected with him," and this seemed to be an important idea. The transcript indicates, however, that she had to struggle quite a bit to stay with these reflections about her father rather than work with the drawings in the way that Rogers seemed to insist on. (Incidentally, I do not believe that even a trained Expressive Therapist would have taken the lead so persistently from Louise, but rather would have allowed her to find her own way in the session.)

In contrast, Mary was the "originator" of change in her session from the outset. Rogers followed her every step of the way, never interrupting or changing the direction. Mary spoke of the session being "just kind of perfect." She said, "I had no idea that I was going to get there, to that," and acknowledged, to Rogers, "But you were right there, and I was willing to also let go of that and go with it." She also said, "if somehow there would be a little bit of a block or a, uh, pushing away on the other person's part that would just stop me cold."

Especially since Rogers' death in 1987, I have felt that the commitment to, and trust in, the self-determination of the client is at risk in the ranks of client-centered therapists. It is the most radical aspect of the approach and the most difficult to practice in a world where the lures of expertise and authority are so pervasive. In the interviews with Mary and Louise, done in the same context, in the same time frame, and with the same observers, Rogers has given us powerful examples of (1) how an approach to therapy grounded in trust in the self-determination and directedness of the client and (2) how an approach that puts the therapist in the role of leader or director have such different processes and such different impacts. The interviews warrant careful study and reflection, particularly in the training of client-centered practitioners.

REFERENCES

Brink, D. (1987). The issues of equality and control in the client-centered or person-centered approach. *Journal of Humanistic Psychology, 27*(1), 27–37.

Brodley, B. (1988). *Client-centered and experiential–Two different therapies.* Paper prepared for the International Conference on Client-Centered and Experiential Psychotherapy, Louvain, Belgium.

Grant, B. (1990). Principled and instrumental non-directiveness in person-centered and client-centered therapy. *Person-Centered Review, 5*(1), 77–88.

Natiello, P. (1987). The person-centered approach: From theory to practice. *Person-Centered Review, 2*(1), 203–216.

Rogers, C. R. (1977). *Carl Rogers on personal power.* New York: Delacorte.

Section II

ROGERS' THERAPY CASES
Views from Within and Without

Patricia M. Raskin

Although this book is intended for those interested in learning more about Carl Rogers' work, we expect that some who read it will be of the school of thought that is not convinced that Rogers attended sufficiently to the nuances of human behavior, or that his theory was smart enough, analytic enough, deep enough, or technically effective. Rogers, like all major theorists, has had his detractors, as well as ardent supporters, and we suspect that at least some readers of this book also have their doubts regarding the "rightful" place of his contributions within psychology. Thus, it is not surprising that, within this book, authors writing from other theoretical perspectives would be critical of Rogers' work. As noted below, these contributors have outlined, at times rather pointedly, the deficiencies or excesses in Rogers' clinical work. More surprising is that, even among the authors in this book espousing a client-centered perspective, Rogers' work is often seen to be flawed. However, we regard this as positive. That these authors, many of them quite prominent figures within the person-centered community, are offering constructive criticisms of the "founding father" suggests a vitality and confidence in client-centered therapy that has often been lacking in other theoretical approaches.

Apart from theoretical criticisms that might be leveled at Rogers' approach, from a methodological standpoint one might question the extent to which his work with many of his most well-known clients (e.g.,

Gloria) was "real" therapy. That is, many of his cases were demonstrations, either filmed for learning purposes (e.g., Gloria) or single sessions conducted before attendees at workshops, with the "client" a paid registrant at the workshop. One problem with these cases is that, because they differ in crucial ways from the usual therapeutic situation, one cannot conclude that therapeutic success under these somewhat artificial conditions would necessarily occur under more typical therapy conditions. That is, Rogers' clients in many of these cases were already "under his spell," believers in his system. As such, they were primed to be self-revealing and to respond to his empathy, positive regard, and congruence. Further, many of these clients had had contact with Rogers shortly before the session, and one could argue that rapport, an essential condition for therapeutic change, had already been established.

Mental health practitioners are well aware of how important initial therapy sessions are. The immediate impression therapists make on clients affects the creation of an effective therapeutic alliance, which, in turn, influences a client's decision to reveal his or her concerns and return for further work. If Rogers knew his demonstration clients beforehand, and more importantly, if they knew who he was, were familiar with his work, and had paid to attend workshops with him, much of the task of the creation of optimal conditions may have been accomplished before the sessions began. This criticism, of course, also extends to other therapeutic approaches that invite the public to participate in open therapy demonstrations (e.g., rational–emotive therapy, psychodrama). What must be taken into consideration as well is that, by the later years of his life, when his fame was considerable, it would have been difficult for Rogers to have seen someone who was not in some way familiar with his ideas and work.

Rogers' contributions, at least in global terms, are acknowledged well beyond the client-centered community of psychotherapists. His open demonstrations of the process of psychotherapy, his interest in research, his respect for clients, his gentleness, and the accessibility of his writing to the general public are often noted by therapists who embrace different approaches. As noted in the Introduction to this book, however, one senses that underneath this general, somewhat diffuse praise, there is a reluctance—at least in the more traditional psychotherapeutic community—to ascribe real value to his approach. "Lightweight," "benign," "without real substance"—these are the comments one regularly hears about his approach.

In this regard, our purpose in Section II of this book is to present contrasting views of Rogers' work. Comments by a client-centered therapist on a particular case are followed by comments by a therapist or therapists of a differing theoretical perspective. The majority of Rogers' published cases come from the later part of his career, during which he did not conduct therapy with long-term clients because his time was taken up with research and in his role as founder and leading theoretician of the client-centered movement. It would have been desirable to include in this section sessions with clients relatively unaffected by his fame; however, if there were such cases, they were not recorded. Therefore, in Section II of this book, only the case of Jim Brown, and perhaps of Mary Jane Tilden, who saw Rogers when he was much less widely known, meet this criterion. Our assumption was that in considering the particulars of a specific session, the reviewers would be forced to go beyond their prejudices and assumptions about what Rogers wrote and would evaluate his material in new ways. Specifically, we requested that they provide "critical commentary," discussing the strengths, weaknesses, theoretical assumptions, notable features, and/or inconsistencies within the material. Virtually all found some intervention or interaction deficient in some manner. For the most part, however, the authors who describe themselves as client-centered took the opportunity to clarify and explicate client-centered principles, whereas those from outside the movement explored alternative facets of both process and content. As in Section I, the cases here are presented in chronological order.

The case of Mary Jane Tilden (published in 1947) focuses on a seriously withdrawn woman of 20, who complained of feeling different from others and whose ever-present self-condemnations were increasing; she was brought into therapy by her mother. What is particularly valuable about this case is the opportunity to view Rogers' early work over a series of 11 counseling sessions. Several of these sessions are transcribed in full (others are summarized), and many of the responses of both client and therapist are commented on in footnotes by Rogers himself. These footnotes reveal that Rogers, 5 years before the publication of *Client-Centered Therapy*, saw his work in terms of a "nondirective technique," with near-exclusive reliance on "reflecting feelings." His approach still new, these footnotes served to inform counselors of the rationale behind his interventions.

This case is an excellent example of the "classical Rogerian" approach. In these transcriptions, one can perceive Rogers at his essence. Mary Jane Tilden was so despairing and so ambivalent that the temptation to say more, do more, interpret more, would be enormous for a therapist who did not truly believe in the growth-enhancing potential in genuine existential acceptance. Indeed, Rogers himself, in describing his work, referred to the importance of the depth of these beliefs, rather than technique. Yet even then Rogers' practice was richer than his stated theories. Note, for example, how statements such as "You stood on her two feet" go far beyond reflecting feelings.

In his discussion of this case, Robert E. Dingman describes, from a client-centered perspective, this client's initial desire to be "fixed" and her slow movement inward. Dingman notes that in the face of Mary Jane's desperate need to "embody the attitudes and behaviors she thought appropriate for someone her age," Rogers refrained from advising or guiding. Instead, he chose "to remain empathically present, to understand her frustration and confusion without prescription for change. He simply would not undermine Mary Jane's movement toward encountering fully" her own needs, her own sense of self. According to Dingman, Rogers' noninterference—his refusal to be an expert—is particularly clear, and helpful, in this case.

Jesse D. Geller and Edith Gould observe the same sessions from a contemporary psychoanalytic perspective. Their reading of this case emphasizes two themes: "the centrality of Mary Jane's struggle to establish a positive feminine sense of self" and the difficulty of her efforts to discover her "true self" as a result of the "interaction between her relationship with her mother and the sociocultural conditions that were in existence when she entered psychotherapy." While acknowledging that Rogers' egalitarian style of exercising authority "succeeded in strengthening her [Mary Jane's] capacities for autonomy and mutuality," they also believe that "a therapy relationship between a 20-year-old unemployed female high school graduate and a middle-aged male doctor, in 1946, could not have been truly egalitarian." And while acknowledging that this client had, by the end of therapy, became increasingly self-accepting, they also contend that "Rogers and Mary Jane never did achieve full agreement about the goals of treatment, their relative responsibilities, or the kind of attachment or relationship required to do the work of therapy." Geller and Gould also suggest that "Rogers was at his weakest therapeutically with respect to his handling of issues related to gender and sexuality." They point out that Rogers responded to Mary Jane's strengths rather than to her pathology, and they also point out that he was neither empathic nor perceptive about her more negative feelings, limiting the depth of her explorations in these domains.

In the second transcript—actually consisting of two sessions within a given week in 1962—Jim Brown, a 28-year-old, hospitalized, often silent, schizophrenic patient, expressed the feeling that he was "no good" and beyond help. Rogers was very giving (e.g., he gave Jim cigarettes and magazines) and was consistently empathic. But it was his self-revelations that seemed to make a difference, precipitating what Rogers characterized as a "moment of irreversible change." This case represents one of the very few available transcripts of psychotherapeutic work (by Rogers or anyone else) with hospitalized psychotic patients. Jerold Bozarth represents the person-centered approach in his comments on this case, focusing on the relationships among Rogers' theory, his practice, and the therapeutic movement of the client. In his commentary, Bozarth points to Rogers' "consistency" within this session: "He was consistently striving to experience the client's frame of reference and to communicate this as well as his unconditional positive regard to the client. Rogers doggedly strove to understand this man within the confines of long silences and negativistic responses." Bozarth also emphasizes that a personal comment of Rogers— "I guess I'd just like to say—I care about you. And I care what happens"—may well have been the crucial turning point in this therapy. Interestingly, in contrast to Geller and Gould's perception that Rogers failed to pursue negative feelings, Bozarth contends that Rogers consistently followed Jim Brown's "lousy feelings."

Leslie Greenberg comments on this case from a Gestalt/experiential approach. He notes that it was Rogers' "caring presence" that appears to have been "central in breaking through Jim's defensive shell." But he also takes issue with client-centered theory—specifically, with the assumption that the principles of empathy, prizing, and congruence account in full for therapeutic change: "I am not suggesting here that I disagree with the importance of the three conditions . . . but rather that the elements of his [Rogers'] formal theory do not fully explain the curative elements of the process." According to Greenberg, Rogers' actual work was considerably more complex than his writings about his work, and that the utterances he responded to, the timing of those responses, and their content, all subtly communicated a deeply sophisticated (albeit unarticulated) well-timed directiveness. He writes: "Rogers, I suggest, is intentional and directed in his own process, . . . providing a gentle consistent pressure on Jim to focus on his internal experience and to focus on particular feelings at particular times." According to Greenberg, Rogers was doing far more than simply accepting his client or reflecting his client's feelings; rather "he empathically explores, and conjectures about, what the client might be experiencing at the edges of his awareness."

The third case in this section is a demonstration session that Rogers conducted in 1976 at Texas Woman's University with Sylvia, a woman who discussed her pride in her recent growth and learning as well as her conflicts regarding her feelings toward black men. This session, the second with Sylvia as part of this workshop (she had worked with Rogers three times in the previous year) was released as a videotape in 1980, entitled "Struggle for Self-Acceptance." The contrast between this transcript and the prior two is quite remarkable, both in content and process. Although Rogers' comments do not differ significantly in tone, style, or substance, he appears to be less formal and feel more connected to Sylvia than he did to Mary Jane Tilden or Jim Brown. Furthermore, Sylvia has clearly internalized the "rules," that is, that it is her job to permit herself awareness and to experience, and that it is not the therapist's job to provide answers.

What makes the transcript of this case so valuable is the inclusion of the postinterview comments of both participants on many of their in-session statements. As readers, we get an opportunity to understand the immediate experiences of both client and therapist. David Cain, the former editor of the *Person-Centered Review,* is particularly impressed by the intensity of the interaction in this session: "Rogers and Sylvia seemed to be in an almost impenetrable bubble in which the rest of the world . . . faded away into the background." Like Bozarth, he lauds the extent to which Rogers was "deeply and accurately empathic, receptive, supportive, and fully present and engaged" with his client. Like Greenberg, Cain notes Rogers' penchant for what Cain refers to as "inferential empathy"—responses that go beyond the client's manifest statements and seemingly reflect an underlying feeling. Like Greenberg, too, he feels that Rogers' triad of conditions provides insufficient explanation for therapeutic success. According to Cain, Rogers' hypothesis underemphasizes the client's contribution to the success or failure of therapy. This session with Sylvia was as successful as it was, points out Cain, because of Sylvia's receptivity and reflection. Cain also underscores Rogers' belief that "acceptance is more important that understanding" but notes that this bias of Rogers' may have worked to the detriment of Sylvia in this session: "Even a master therapist like Rogers will at times fall prey to his personal beliefs when they conflict with the client's needs or beliefs." Overall, however, Cain feels this session was remarkably powerful, in great part because of its "collaborative nature, the mutuality of client and therapist working in a partnership in which each brought to bear his or her personal resources for learning and growth."

Maureen O'Hara presents an alternative view, a feminist analysis, in which she explicitly comments on Rogers' traditional white male perspective and the extent to which Sylvia has internalized critical aspects of this perspective. Thus, while expressing deep affection and respect for both the man and his work, O'Hara also points out aspects of his approach that serve to "preserve, maintain, and protect the interests of the Eurocentric, patriarchal, Judeo-Christian world." For example, she wonders how much more empowering it would have been if Rogers had viewed Sylvia's newfound sexuality not in terms of "risking" but rather in terms of "self-assertiveness, self-confidence, authenticity, or politically revolutionary behavior." She questions, too, why neither Sylvia nor Rogers addressed the issue of Sylvia's troubling attraction to black men in terms of racism and sexism. Although O'Hara acknowledges Rogers' overall helpfulness—particularly the way his "exquisite interpretation of her words . . . helps Sylvia deeply listen to her self"—she also notes the limitations of a "strictly reflective, empathic therapy" and wishes that Rogers were able to view Sylvia's dilemmas as more societal than intrapersonal in origin.

In the fourth case, the second of two demonstration interviews known as the case of "Anger and Hurt," filmed in 1977, a man who reported having leukemia (in remission) talked in the first interview about his anger, but showed little affect. The transcribed session in this book is the second of the two interviews Rogers conducted with this client. Because the client was black, the case provides an intriguing opportunity to view Rogers' work with a minority client and to observe how he dealt with, indeed encouraged, his client's anger about being mistreated in this society. Barbara Temaner Brodley comments on this "rich and intense" session from a person-centered perspective. She is impressed with Rogers' "highly focused empathic responsiveness" and his ability to be "sensitive and adaptive to the issues and vulnerabilities that appear in the client," but she also comments on his somewhat surprising departures from his usual nondirective stance. She suggests that Rogers "had specific goals for the client at times during the session" (i.e., to have him express his angry and sad feelings) and that this directive stance confused the client, and it may have led him to feel somewhat manipulated. Moreover, she documents her assertions that Rogers acted differently here by comparing his responses with this client to his responses to nine other clients with whom he had worked through the years.

Samuel E. Menahem approaches this case from the point of view of transpersonal therapy, pointing out that Rogers' views were one of the foundations of transpersonal therapy and that his connection to spirituality was lifelong. Like Brodley, Menahem feels that Rogers was uncharacteristically directive in this session. Rogers' encouragement of this client to express his anger was a result of Rogers' "genuine caring and concern for this man" as well as the trust that Rogers himself had in his own ability to make "intuitive interventions." But, in contrast to Brodley, Menahem suggests that this stance of Rogers' was helpful, leading the client to rapid insight. To Menahem, "Spirituality starts with emotional healing," a process that Rogers initiated in this client.

A cross-cultural analysis, similar to O'Hara's feminist analysis in the case of Sylvia, could also be applied to the case of "Anger and Hurt." As O'Hara noted, Rogers was a product of his time—a white, middle-class male who assumed his place of privilege in a white, male-valuing society. Because he was white and male, his capacity for empathizing with women, by definition, was limited. So, too, was his capacity for empathizing with black people. Indeed, if one views the case from a cross-cultural counseling perspective, one cannot help but note these limitations. As Draguns (1989) suggested, culture is always a silent participant in therapy.

One salient aspect of Rogers' approach and personal style was his ability to enter into the client's frame of reference as completely as possible—but, in this case, his capacity to do this was limited. Espin (1987) has pointed out that when therapists are aware of the influence of race or ethnicity on their personality and interpersonal style, they may be more sensitive to those influences in their clients. The client was a black male who had apparently been married to a white woman. (He makes reference in the videotape to being married to someone "of a different race"). The marriage failed, and one has no idea about, nor does one necessarily need to know, why. What we do learn is that the client valued his father-in-law (a white male) and, at the same, was beginning to identify more closely with more disenfranchised men. Was the client's anger and hurt in part related to his growing awareness of his blackness and its meaning in a white society? Could Rogers have opened the door for the client to explore this aspect of his pain? There were, in fact, several opportunities for Rogers to do so. For example, in the first few moments of this interview, the client says: "It almost seems like that, uh, whatever is happening in my environment or whatever happened in my environment is pulling me into again, uh, that kind of a trap, that kind of a system." Rogers replies, "I think I get that but your mind is taking the place of the system in saying now, uh, 'play it right, do the proper thing.' " Here Rogers chose not to reflect, nor to inquire about, the client's thoughts and feelings about the "system." In order to have done so in an empathic and congruent manner, he would have needed a more culturally expanded self-awareness.

Because the session occurred in 1977, when black consciousness and issues of race were both influential and controversial, the client's reluctance to express the extent of his anger within the session may have reflected a sense on his part of the importance of the relationship between race and power in our society, a feeling he probably would not have articulated without encouragement from Rogers. Although Rogers did try to encourage the client to express his anger, he (Rogers) may not have been aware of the extent to which black culture, particularly at that time, proscribed the display of strong emotion in the presence of white people.

The final case presented in this section is that of Mark, a clinical psychologist who feels alienated from others and deeply conflicted about his role working for the racist South African government. What makes this case especially valuable is the availability of a postinterview discussion between Rogers and Mark, two follow-up letters from Mark (one written 3 years after the interview itself), and the personal reactions of Rogers to these letters. Julius Seeman, an early proponent of person-centered career counseling, who has written extensively throughout the years on Rogers and his work, comments on this session. He suggests that Rogers' work with Mark—his ability to utilize his "own total awareness to enter into the client's world in a phenomenological mode"—is characteristic of his approach to psychotherapy. This approach, says Seeman, "engendered rapid exploration on Mark's part," enabling him to "explore his inward doubts." Seeman also points out, though, that both Mark and Rogers were disappointed at the conclusion of the interview. Seeman attributes this both to the general effects of an "audience presence" and to a questionable, though defensible, decision of Rogers', that is, not to respond empathically to Mark's plea for more support. Still, for Mark, the session had great significance. Drawing on an analysis of several brief psychotherapies, Seeman finds several notable parallels between this session and those of other successful brief therapies. Overall, contends Seeman, "this brief and complex encounter between Mark and Rogers may fairly be seen as having been an enduring, life-enhancing experience for Mark."

Adele M. Hayes and Marvin R. Goldfried make their observations about this case from a cognitive-behavioral perspective, applying their Coding System of Therapeutic Focus (Goldfried & Hayes, 1989) to analyze Rogers' feedback to Mark. They present empirical evidence of Rogers' consistency with his stated theoretical approach, and they acknowledge that Rogers' work allowed Mark "to look at some of the previously denied and unacceptable parts of himself, decrease his sense of isolation, and begin the process of integrating and strengthening his fragmented sense of self." They recognize, too, that this demonstration session had a "profound impact on Mark." On the other hand, they question Rogers' decision to "explore Mark's sense of self, rather than to clarify his values and beliefs," and they suggest potential alternative approaches, including cognitive-behavioral and Gestalt, that might have focused more directly on "perceptual rigidities" and the modification of "problematic reactions to experiences." They also recognize, however, that this client presented difficult material that would not lead to easy resolution.

As you will see, there is little disagreement on the effectiveness (or lack thereof) of Rogers' interventions between representatives of the client-centered perspective and others. Rather, alternative approaches are suggested or alternative rationales are offered to explain the effectiveness of those interventions. The authors of these chapters—both those within and without client-centered therapy—pose intriguing questions about the essential nature of therapeutic effectiveness.

REFERENCES

Draguns, J. G. (1989). Dilemmas and choices in cross-cultural counseling: The universal versus the culturally distinctive. In P. B. Pedersen, J. G. Draguns, W. J. Lonner, & J. E. Trimble (Eds.), *Counseling across cultures* (3rd ed., pp. 3–21). Honolulu: University of Hawaii Press.

Espin, O. M. (1987). Psychotherapy with Hispanic women: Some considerations. In P. B. Pedersen (Ed.), *Handbook of cross-cultural counseling and psychotherapy* (pp. 165–171). New York: Praeger.

Goldfried, M. R., & Hayes, A. M. (1989). Can contributions from other orientations complement behavior therapy? *The Behavior Therapist, 12,* 57–60.

CHAPTER 6

THE CASE OF
MARY JANE TILDEN (1946)

TRANSCRIPT[*]

The first contact with the case of Mary Jane Tilden was a telephone call from her mother, who desired help for her daughter. She raised a number of questions about counseling services, which had been described to her by a friend. She described her daughter as "needing to be set straight on some matters," as "staying in too much," and as "acting strange." She was sure Mary Jane could not come in alone, and finally made an appointment to come in with her, with the plan of talking to a counselor herself, although she was ambivalent about this.

The mother and Mary Jane arrived for their appointment a few minutes late. Mary Jane was attractive in appearance, a twenty-year-old young woman, who came willingly with the counselor for the first interview, cited below. The mother talked with a second counselor, and during the first interview enlarged on the difficulties which the family was having with Mary Jane. Some statements from her conversation will give the picture. "She sleeps all the time. If I wake her she just broods and introspects and is harder to get on with." "Should I let her sleep until twelve o'clock? I don't know. She can't just do that, then not get dressed. She just sits by the radio or goes back to bed. Then sometimes I force her to get dressed and take a walk. Then she meets someone and they ask why she isn't working, she gets so ashamed—she's afraid of people's opinions of her." "Oftentimes she

[*]The summaries of this case material were done by Carl Rogers. The footnotes were written by William Snyder, editor of the *Casebook of Non-directive Counseling* (1947), the book in which this case was originally published.

143

says she's fearing insanity." The mother confessed that she also worries about this because a relative who exhibited similar behavior became psychotic. She explained that Mary Jane gave up her job some time ago, and has also given up her social life.

The mother came for two interviews, but then felt she did not wish to return for more. She brought Mary Jane for the third interview, but simply waited during the interview. From the fourth interview on, Mary Jane came by herself.

FIRST INTERVIEW

October 7

C.R.: I really know very little as to why you came in. Would you like to tell me something about it?[1]

Mary Jane: It is a long story. I can't find myself. Everything I do seems to be wrong. I can't get on with people. If there is any criticism or anyone says anything about me I just can't take it. When I had a job, if anyone said anything critical, it just crumpled me.

C.R.: You feel things are all going wrong and that you're just crushed by criticism.

Mary Jane: Well, it doesn't even need to be meant as criticism. It goes way back. In grammar school I never felt I belonged. Oh, sometimes I would try to feel superior, but then I'd be way down. I used to be the teacher's pet, but that didn't help with the other girls.

C.R.: You feel the roots go back a long way but that you have never really belonged, even in grammar school.

Mary Jane: Lately it's been worse. I even feel I ought to be in a sanitarium. There must be something awfully wrong with me.

C.R.: Things have been so bad you feel perhaps you're really abnormal.

Mary Jane: Yes. Of course, in school I used to get high grades, but I think I sort of memorized things.

C.R.: Excuse me. You speak pretty rapidly and I can't get it all down in my notes. Would it bother you if I set up a microphone and recorded the interview on this machine?[2]

---

[1] This is a good opening lead which allows full freedom for the client to develop the material in his own way, and also places the responsibility for doing so with him.

[2] This unusual technique for recording the counseling situation appears to be readily accepted.

Mary Jane: No—that would be all right. *(From this point on the interview is recorded.)*

C.R.: Now just forget that's there and you'll be all right. You used to get high grades and you used to—

Mary Jane: I got them, but I think I just must have memorized books. I know I just studied all the time. I didn't go out with anybody. I sorta shut myself away because I was hurt so much. So I—

C.R.: You said that you were hurt so much?[3]

Mary Jane: Yes, because when I was with people I just didn't feel comfortable. I felt so left out of social things and things of that sort. And well, I guess I just sorta—when I studied it was sort of an escape for me and I tried to forget. But I didn't study—I guess I didn't study with the right attitude to learn so I could get out of my dilemma. I sort of made it like it was a different world, my studying. I sort of secluded myself. You know what I mean? So that my studying wasn't something that could lead me to normality and to being with other people, and to having something in common with them.

C.R.: Your studying and your good grades and all you felt was just something sort of separate from the rest of your life and didn't help you very much.

Mary Jane: M-hm. That's right. And I—and that wasn't the right attitude, I know it wasn't. Because it was supposed to integrate you with life but it didn't—I guess I just made it an escape.

C.R.: You feel your studying and work was a way of getting away from things?

Mary Jane: That's right. And everybody else wondered why I liked to do homework and I just enjoyed it—I seemed to enjoy it—and, well it gave me something—it sort of stood me up a little but I don't seem to have learned very much from it—because—well—my memory doesn't seem to be good at all now. It's all so mixed up. I mean, I've been mulling it over and over in my mind and trying to get at the bottom of it. *(Pause)* But I just don't seem to be able to. And then when I think that it's such an effort for me to just go around living and just thinking these things I would think that something would have to be done. It isn't right and it isn't normal. It's an effort for me to walk down the street sometimes. It's a crazy thing, really.

---

[3] Here we find a direct lead which the counselor uses to follow up an expression of feeling the client has made. This allows the client to go further in her discussion of her unhappy childhood.

C.R.: Even just little things—just ordinary things, give you a lot of trouble.[4]

Mary Jane: M-hm, that's right. And I don't seem to be able to conquer it. I mean it just—every day seems to be over and over again the same little things that shouldn't matter.

C.R.: So, instead of making progress, things don't really get any better at all.

Mary Jane: That's right. And I just seem to have lost faith in everything—I don't know, I can see good for other people, but I can't—I can't believe it's true when it happens to me. It's such a terrible thing. *(Laughs)* It's nice to be—to be able to believe in good but I think it's sort of a—I sort of persecute myself in a sort of a way—sort of self-condemnation all the way through. And it's been growing for a long time.

C.R.: So that you—condemn yourself and don't think much of yourself and that's gradually getting worse.

Mary Jane: That's right. M-hm. *(Pause)* I don't even like to attempt things—I mean—when I go on a job or something—I just—well—I feel like I am going to fail. It's a terrible thing, but—

C.R.: You feel that you're whipped before you start in.

Mary Jane: M-hm. It's when I come in contact with other people. I did hold a job selling because I thought I should get out and be with people. And as soon as I started to think of myself in relation to it, instead of being able to face it, you know, and get over the fear, as soon as I think of myself in it—why, it just scares me—and then I can't do anything, and, well, it just seems that other people, they react to things and seeing how they take them it makes me feel that I know that I am not reacting to things right. And it makes me feel that I am inferior and that I am not normal. That's what always gets me.

C.R.: Other people do things you just feel that you can't measure up to. You just don't stack up to the other girls.

Mary Jane: M-hm. It's sort of a comparison. It is. It's just when I compare myself to the other girls it seems—I don't feel at all up to it. And just lately I've sort of gotten concerned about it. My girl friends—well—I guess it's funny for me to say, but they are all getting married—and—well, it wasn't that I was jealous, it was the fact that they were ready

---

[4] This response recognizes the feeling of despair about the difficulties the client is having with her life-experiences. It might well have gone even farther in catching and reflecting the hopelessness and personal inadequacy she feels.

for it—and they seem to be so normal in everything they did and they were unfolding the way everybody should unfold in this world. And when I thought about myself, I thought, "Well, my gosh! I'm not even coming *near* it." And it was just such a blow that—I just started to realize that I wasn't coming along the way I should—I mean I just wasn't progressing.[5]

C.R.: It wasn't that you were jealous, but that you gradually realized that here they were ready for a new part of their life and you just weren't ready for it.

Mary Jane: M-hm. It's a terrible feeling. It's just that I should have been because everybody else was, so naturally I guess I should have been, too. I just don't.

C.R.: That made you feel more than ever that somehow you weren't progressing as you ought to.

Mary Jane: That's right. *(Pause)* I've tried looking at other people and sort of losing myself and trying to forget myself when I'm with them and it's all right when I am with somebody, but as soon as I start thinking about what *I* am, I have such a terrible conflict at what I am that it sort of *(laughs)*—it makes me feel awful. It's such a self-depreciation that I hope nobody ever knows it. It's a terrible feeling. And self-confidence is what everybody has to have to build on and I just don't have it.

C.R.: Self-confidence is what you have nothing of.

Mary Jane: Yes. *(Laughs)* Well, and people always accuse me of acting—because I don't act natural I guess. It's sort of I'm so scared and trying to find myself that—they always tell me that I just don't act natural. *(Pause)* And it's something that I can't help because I'm afraid to act natural, I guess. Because I just don't feel as though I like myself.

C.R.: You feel that you can't act natural and it disturbs you that people recognize that you're not acting natural.[6]

---

[5] This is a real self-evaluation that is both problem-stating and insightful. It is perhaps the only real indication that this girl gives during the first interview that she has any motivation to work through the problem. There appears to be here some indication of a force for positive growth, very tentative in character, in the implied regret she feels in not being able to go on to the richer aspect of living that she witnesses in the situation of her girl friends. This may be an example of the "positive drive for growth" that Rogers postulates for the basis on which therapy takes place, i.e., the force within the individual which leads him to change himself.

[6] This is a good recognition of the feeling rather than of the intellectual content of what the client has said.

Mary Jane: M-hm—deeper than that—it's just a conviction—it's such a dumb thing. In fact, it seems that I just can't cope with things. Well, it's a lack of intelligence I feel all the time.

C.R.: You feel that you haven't ability enough to do these things.

Mary Jane: M-hm, it's the intelligence behind it, that's right. I mean, I should be able to look above these things and sort of be able to reason with myself, but I don't seem to be able to.

C.R.: You can tell yourself what you ought to do, but you can't get it done, is that it?

Mary Jane: Yes—I seem to be going backward all the time. In fact, I don't see any reason why I should be living. Sometimes I think about committing suicide, too, because I can't find any justification in living the way I do. *(Pause)* It's very funny, I can see it for everybody else but I can't—I have enough confidence in other people's ability but I can't see it for myself.[7]

C.R.: You can understand why other people would want to live but for yourself you can see very little reason.

Mary Jane: That's right, I just don't seem to have any hope. When Mother tells me that it's going to pass and things like that I just don't see any way out, I just don't see how it can.

C.R.: People try to reassure you, but it doesn't help.

Mary Jane: No, it doesn't. *(Long pause)* And another thing that sort of bothers me. I try to say, "Well, if you don't feel as though you are ready to get married, then you won't get married." But then I say to myself, "That isn't right," I mean—everybody else does, so why shouldn't I? I have two sisters that are married, but I'm just so afraid that I won't measure up to things—even the slightest thing—it just doesn't work.[8]

C.R.: You'd like to convince yourself that it would be all right anyway, but you can't quite make yourself feel that that's all right. You just feel that you won't measure up.

Mary Jane: That's right. Because, you see, just building a wall around that one thing makes me different from everybody else right there. Because

[7] This client rather quickly comes to an expression of the depth of her feelings of helplessness or of worthlessness.

[8] The client's concern about the possibility of never marrying becomes apparent here. This problem is not an unusual complaint for young women of this age, although it is often not as complicated by other sources of concern as it is in this case.

it seems as though love seems to be the major—it seems to be the major thrill of life. I mean, everywhere you go, it just seems to be. And just building a wall around me—that alone makes me not like anybody else. *(Pause)* It's a very confused thing. It goes round and round in circles. But I know it isn't right.

C.R.: And evidently the question of whether or not you'll be able to measure up to love and marriage and so on—that's one of the things that makes it even more crucial at the present time.

Mary Jane: Well, that sort of brought it about more so because (pause), well, I'm going on twenty-one. When I was a child, I said, "Oh, well, sometime in the future I won't feel like this. Something will happen." But it just kept going on that way. And then when you find that you're a certain age, I mean, you don't feel that you're that certain age, but the world looks on you and thinks, "Well, she's twenty-one, she should be an adult now." And you're still filled with these childish thoughts. It isn't right.

C.R.: And that's what gets you down.[9]

Mary Jane: That's right. *(Pause)* Sometimes I think I must be crazy. And I sort of wonder whether I shouldn't be in a sanitarium or some place where I can be helped—instead of just going around and around in circles. It isn't right.

C.R.: You almost feel as though you must be really abnormal.[10]

Mary Jane: Oh, definitely I feel that I must be. It isn't a matter of feeling either—I mean I—sort of—I proved it to myself in a negative way, I mean I just don't seem to be able to take normal situations as they are. If something goes wrong, it just knocks me for a loop. And if something goes right—I can't—I don't take it as a victory. I just don't even think about it.

C.R.: So that all the—all the balances are on the negative side.

Mary Jane: Yes. *(Pause)* I don't know whether I like to think negatively—I—don't know how I can, but it looks as though I like to feel negative about things and it doesn't get me anywhere, it pulls me backward. *(Pause)* It's sort of like seeing life pass you by and you feel as though you're just looking on at everybody else. It's a terrible feeling.

---

[9] A good recognition of the depth of the client's feeling is given.

[10] Notice that the counselor makes no effort to reassure the client that she is not becoming a mental case, but recognizes the intensity of her feelings about this.

C.R.: That really sums up a lot of what you've been saying, doesn't it—that you feel that life is passing you by, and here you are not ready to take it.[11]

Mary Jane: M-hm. *(Pause)* I mean the things I read in books about ordinary situations and about people getting married and having children and everything—I guess they—I guess women have their doubts and men do, too, but they seem to just sort of take it and enjoy it, and just take it as a natural thing and I guess I just can't. It seems to be too big of an obstacle for me, every little thing.

C.R.: You feel that even the little things are too much for you.

Mary Jane: That's right. And I have a little sister, anyway—well, she's only fourteen, and she's just the opposite, I mean, she has so many friends and she just feels wonderful with them, and she enjoys them, and she sees them in the right light. I mean in a normal way. She enjoys friendships and she has—well—she pals around with boys, and she has dates and this and that and the other thing. And she takes things so beautifully, I mean she goes everywhere and does things, and enjoys them and I suppose she has things to work out, too, no doubt she has. But it just seems as though she can take life as it is. You know, the way you should take it. And here I am the big sister and sitting at home. It just seems so ridiculous.[12]

C.R.: You feel you should be more mature than she is and here actually she seems more able to take life than you are.

Mary Jane: M-hm. *(Very long pause)* It seems so silly to be telling my tale of woe—everything I say is just so awful—it's crazy. But that's just how I feel.

C.R.: You feel that you're giving a black picture but at least it's a true one.[13]

Mary Jane: That's right. *(Pause)* I just don't feel that I can take my place in society like everybody else.

C.R.: M-hm.

[She goes on to say that she feels that she has a real flaw in her character. She is afraid to be unselfish or to feel love for fear she will be hurt. She feels people have to feel right about themselves if they are to go on, and she does not have this feeling. When people tell

---

[11] This is a good example of clarifying feeling by the process of restating in simplified form the emotion the client expresses somewhat less clearly in her previous statement.

[12] The intensity of the client's feelings toward herself, and their basis in reality, show up in this comparison of herself with her sister.

[13] A good recognition of an ambivalent feeling is given here. Notice that again no effort is made to reassure the client about the desirability of speaking freely.

her she is intelligent, she thinks it is only because they do not really know her. She has tried to pretend she is superior, but it hasn't helped. Her older sister has made a good adjustment, and she has tried to be like her, only to be told that she was "putting on." Sometimes she thinks there must be something wrong with her brain, some actual damage. The interview continues.]

Mary Jane: There must be something somewhere to counteract all this. I mean, other people must be going through part of the things I've gone through or they all feel that they could. I don't know how they do it. I realize I am feeling something everybody must feel. Because I didn't just make them, they were here before I came, I suppose. But I don't know, I just don't seem to find a way out.

C.R.: You feel that other people must feel some of the same things you feel and that some way they handle them, but for you, you don't see the way it can be done.

Mary Jane: That's right. Because I know that I'm not smart enough to invent all these things. It's not something that *I* invented. It must be something everyone goes through to a certain extent. I read about it. That's all I know about it. People don't usually talk about it. So I just wonder what the next step should be. *(Pause–ten seconds.)*[14]

C.R.: Well, I might say just a word about the kind of thing that we do here, and the kind of thing that you are starting to try, I suppose, today, and that is if you come in to try to talk through these things that do bother you and concern you—there's a chance at least that you may be able to discover for yourself some of the things that you can do about the situation, and I think it's up to you whether or not you think it's worth trying—and all I can say is that a number of people have tried that sort of thing and have found that it helped, but you can't be guaranteed anything. It might help or it might not. I think you're wondering whether anything might help.

Mary Jane: M-hm. I suppose I want to know just what to do, but then maybe nobody could give me that.[15]

---

[14] At this point, the client says in effect: "The problem is beyond me; it's up to you to tell me what to do next." The counselor (in his response) explains what can be expected of the therapy situation. This is structuring. More important, the counselor also indicates that if a solution is achieved it is likely to come through the positive efforts which the client herself is willing to make. He also carefully disclaims any ability to guarantee that results are certain to occur.

[15] The client recognizes that there is no short answer to her problem, although how deeply she is convinced of this question remains a problem through several succeeding interviews.

C.R.: You realize that you are probably looking for immediate answers that nobody could give you.

Mary Jane: I just don't know. I don't know what I'm looking for. It's just that I wonder if I'm insane sometimes. I think I'm nuts.

C.R.: It just gives you concern that you're as far from the normal as you feel you are.[16]

Mary Jane: That's right. It's silly to tell me not to worry because I do worry. It's my life. What is the theory behind this sort of thing? Do you sort of find things for yourself? I don't know. I guess nobody can really help you, can they?

C.R.: We can help you go about working on your own problems, but a lot of what happens will be up to you.[17]

Mary Jane: Is it just the talking about things? I mean, is that the whole thing? You don't say a word? *(Laughs)* I mean you try to understand, but I mean you don't guide people in any way, do you?

C.R.: I won't be giving you a lot of answers, except to help you work through some of the answers that you would be satisfied with. It's just like you say—someone may say, "You're nuts" and some people may say, "No, you're normal." Well, I could tell you you're normal, somebody else could, somebody else could tell you you're nuts. There's no—the thing that really matters is how you really feel about yourself.

Mary Jane: Well, I don't know how I can change my concept of myself—because that's the way I feel.

C.R.: You feel very different from others and you don't see how you can fix that.

Mary Jane: I realize, of course, that it all began a long time ago—because

---

[16] As above, the counselor attempts to recognize and clarify the client's concern about her sanity, but does not attempt to reassure her on the point, feeling that the reassurance would only direct her farther away from understanding her problem and doing something to alleviate it. In this exchange, the client admits that the reassurance would not help her much, and goes on to face the problem of whether she can do anything to help herself.

[17] The counselor clarifies the counseling situation, showing the part that both he and the client must play. In this exchange, the client states clearly the quandary that many clients feel when faced with this new experience. The explanation is a very clear statement of the reasons for avoiding the giving of "guidance." Later evidence suggests that there has probably been no lack of "guidance" in this client's life, but, on the contrary, probably a great deal too much.

everything begins somewhere. I wasn't just—somehow or other something failed somewhere along the line. And I guess we sort of have to get at it, a sort of re-education. But I don't feel as though I can do it myself.[18]

C.R.: You realize that the roots must go a long way back, and that at some point you will have to start in reworking it, but you're not sure whether you can do it.

Mary Jane: That's right. *(Pause)* It's just the idea that I can see myself going through life this way, fifty, sixty, and seventy years old—still thinking these horrible thoughts. And it just doesn't seem worthwhile—I mean, it's so ridiculous. While everybody else is going their way and living life, I'm sort of at the edge, and looking on. It just isn't right.

C.R.: The future doesn't look very bright when you look at it that way.

Mary Jane: No. *(Long pause)* I know I'm lacking in courage, that's the big thing I'm lacking. That must be it, 'cause other people aren't swayed so easily. It's a funny thing, though—when I think of those—those qualities, I always think of them, I don't know, not as realities, but as something that's far off somewhere. It's a hard thing to explain these things. It's just as though—it's—it's true but I laugh at it in a way. Sort of a feeling that I am sort of sneering at it—but I know it must be true 'cause other people go around expressing those things. It's a very confused feeling.

C.R.: Logically, you realize that courage is one of your deficiencies, but inside yourself you find yourself laughing at that notion and feeling that it doesn't really have anything to do with you. Is that it?[19]

Mary Jane: That's right. I always sort of make myself different. That's it.

C.R.: M-hm. You sort of say that might apply to other people but it's not for you because you're different.

Mary Jane: I don't know whether that's exactly right or not. I can't put my finger on it. Sometimes I feel lonely and sometimes I feel another way. Do you have cases this bad?

C.R.: You really wonder whether anybody else could be—

Mary Jane: I think I'm worse than anybody that I know. That's just it. I feel

---

[18] Nothing could be more clearly stated than the client's grave doubts as to whether she has within herself the power to find a solution to this problem.

[19] These are excellent reflections of the client's feeling.

as though I am terribly, terribly low. It just does not seem worth—bothering with it, it doesn't seem worthwhile, that I can't get up there to first base.[20]

C.R.: You think about making the struggle, but it doesn't seem possible.

Mary Jane: That's right. I just wonder what other people do when they find problems and stuff. I just wonder whether they see it through or try to find out something else.

C.R.: You feel that you'd like to know how somebody else would handle it.

Mary Jane: That's right. And yet I—I go through situations and put myself there, and then *(few words lost)*. For instance, if I went to a dance or something—and then if I wasn't asked to dance, it would hurt me terribly, and immediately I would feel that I was just no good, and that that proved it. But then there were others there who went through the same thing, and they carry on. I mean—and then—I can think of other times when I was asked to dance and then other people weren't and yet it didn't do anything for me. I mean it didn't make me feel any more different about myself. I just accepted that sort of thing and it didn't add anything. The best you can say is that it wasn't bad.

C.R.: The highest peak you ever reach is just not to feel bad. And, on the other hand, if any little thing happens of a negative sort *that* throws you clear down—well, I see our time is up for today. Want to come back next week?[21]

Mary Jane: *(Laughs)* I guess so.

C.R.: You're really puzzled, aren't you, whether or not to come back?

Mary Jane: I don't know whether this would help me any. I mean I don't know whether anything would help me. *(Pause)* Have you ever had cases that were this bad? *(Laughs)* Or anywhere near this bad?

C.R.: You're coming back to that question again, aren't you—wondering—well, I could answer that question—yes.[22]

---

[20] Here, and again (a few sentences later), the client expresses the full depth of her hopelessness. It simply is not worth the struggle to try to find a way out. Rogers believes that in such situations the counselor relies upon one element only—the basic drive of the individual toward growth. Note that the counselor simply endeavors to show a deep and empathic understanding of the client's hopelessness.

[21] The counselor makes it quite clear that the client's coming must be because of a desire to do so, and not because the counselor is persuading her to.

[22] The question asked by the client is not unusual in rather difficult cases. The counselor points up the client's need to know whether she is the worst case he has seen, but he does give her a certain amount of reassurance in stating that he has seen other cases just as bad.

Mary Jane: Do they eventually go to the insane asylum? *(Laughs, and C.R. laughs)* Sounds crazy, doesn't it? I know it does, but that's just how I feel.

C.R.: Well, you say the word on whether or not you'd like to come back next week. *(Long pause)*

Mary Jane: All right, I'll come back. *(Very softly spoken)*[23]

C.R.: O.K. *(Time is set)*

Significant Feelings Expressed in the First Interview

1. Everything is wrong with me. I feel I'm abnormal.
2. I feel my studies were just an escape for me.
3. I can't do even the ordinary things of life.
4. I have lost faith in everything, especially myself.
5. I'm sure I will fail on anything I undertake. I'm inferior.
6. I'm realizing that other girls are growing normally into marriage, and I'm not even coming near this readiness.
7. I have absolutely no self-confidence.
8. I can't act natural because I don't like myself.
9. I think about suicide, because I can see no justification for living.
10. I'm childish, but people expect me to be adult.
11. I am abnormal.
12. Successes do not buoy me up; failures, even small ones, floor me.
13. I should be more mature than my sister, but I'm not.
14. I can't take my normal place in society.
15. I have a real flaw in my character.
16. I do not dare to be unselfish or outgoing for fear I will be hurt.
17. When I try to imitate successful people, I'm only acting.
18. I feel others can cope with the kind of problems I have, but I cannot.
19. I realize the roots of the problem go back a long way, and I do not feel that I can change the situation myself.
20. I can't go on like this.
21. I'm lacking in courage, but somehow I sneer at the idea.
22. I feel I'm worse than anyone I know.
23. I wonder if you can help me. I doubt it.
24. I guess I will come back.

---

[23] Although this statement is made in a whisper, and only after a long hesitation, it is the one indication, throughout the entire interview, of a positive or purposeful attitude. It represents the first positive step this client makes. She has come in because of her mother's urging, she sees her own situation as definitely hopeless, but when given an opportunity to act, she *acts* as though there were some hope. Rogers believes that this constructive force is present in every client.

SUMMARY OF THE SECOND INTERVIEW
October 14

Mary Jane starts the interview by exploring her relationships with people. She feels she is not capable of any depth in such relationships, and has never really "belonged." She has no interests, because she would be afraid she could not carry them through properly, so will not attempt anything. She fears others will find out how "dumb" she is, especially men. "I wonder if there is any answer. What can you do with a person who doesn't have any faith in the idea that he will arrive at an answer? You really can't do anything with that kind of person, can you?" She feels that she does not even measure up to a little child, but feels that she should be beyond these things. "Is there any solution for me?" The counselor structures the relationship in a fashion similar to that given in the first interview. Mary Jane replies that she has gone out and done things that were suggested in psychological books, but it has not helped. The interview ends as follows:

Mary Jane: The point is—I mean—I know that nobody can really help me—I mean—I guess they can point out the way partly—but they can't do my thinking for me.[24]

C.R.: You feel that other people can be of some help but you realize, too, that the essence of it has somehow got to be in you.

Mary Jane: That's right. *(Pause)* I—I'm really so mixed up that I don't know what I hope to accomplish, actually.

C.R.: You really aren't sure what—what you're aiming toward.

Mary Jane: That's right.

C.R.: Well, I see our time is about up. Want to come back next week?

Mary Jane: *(Laughs)* Do you really think you could help me in any way? I mean, do you feel as though you can?

C.R.: I think I would have to leave it that—a—it comes back to the question—do you feel you want to work on it? If you do, we'll save time next week. If you feel that it is so hopeless that nothing can be done—

---

[24] Here the client is giving a very clear statement of the concept on which the non-directive technique is based. It is still apparent, however, that she doubts whether she can be helped at all. She raises the same question again, later. The counselor skillfully restates his position, and this is accepted by the client. When the clear-cut choice is before her, either to give up and to continue in her maladjustment or to struggle to find the answers within herself, she chooses the latter.

Mary Jane: It's really all in my own attitude, isn't it? *(Pause)* O.K. Let's make it next week, then.

THIRD INTERVIEW
October 21

C.R.: Well—how do you want to use the time today?[25]

Mary Jane: Well—I don't quite know. A—. *(Long pause)* I was just wondering, I was reading a book the other day. It was called, uh—*Your Life as a Woman*, and in this book—and the subtitle was "How to make the most of it." In this book it showed different types of people and their work, and it didn't go into the causes of it or anything—but—uh—it showed how that person is not living a full life, and it sort of shows why—I mean, uh—it shows why there are different responses to people and it defines for you the reasons why people didn't like them—I mean, uh—it went into how, uh—they thought too much of themselves when they were in a group. They didn't give anything and it explains very carefully that that person was just lazy—and didn't make the effort to do those things. Well, I thought the book was very good, and it said that the person who doesn't grasp those things isn't necessarily crazy, he just hasn't made the effort to do those things, and it's a constant effort to improve—to change. Well, when I read it, it gave me a sort of clear insight into the thing. But still—I didn't know where to start. When I read it I realized that people do go through those things—I don't even know why I brought that up—it just seemed to be sort of a good start.[26]

C.R.: M-hm. You felt that you gained something from reading that book that indicated that not getting along with a group wasn't necessarily abnormal, but that it might be a constant effort to keep building an association with a group. Is that it? But it still leaves you feeling "where do I start?" Is that right?[27]

---

[25] This is a very good beginning for an interview. It emphasizes the idea that the client is free to make use of the time as she sees fit, and that it is not the counselor who will direct the interview.

[26] The client has been making an effort to learn something about behavior; although she is unsure about what she has learned, the sign of positive effort on her part is a good one.

[27] The counselor avoids evaluating the material read, responding instead to the feelings that the client has about what it has done for her. If he had criticized the book, as he might justifiably have done, an intellectual discussion of the book and probably a defense of it by the client would have ensued. Such a discussion would not have been very profitable in helping the client to a better understanding of her own feelings.

Mary Jane: That's right. *(Long pause)* Well, in the first place, if I were to take a job right now I don't think that it would be fair to the employer, I mean, I really don't think that it would be—when I'm in a rut like this. The point is, am I just raising that as a defense mechanism for not getting out? Or am I really thinking that it just wouldn't be fair? That's an important question to me.[28]

C.R.: You feel that it wouldn't be fair, and at the same time there rises in your mind a question, are you just putting that up to keep from undertaking what would be a hard thing to do.

Mary Jane: That's right. *(Pause, laughs)* You shake your head. Is that all?[29]

C.R.: You feel perhaps *I* should know the answers, then.

Mary Jane: That's right. Is it fair to an employer to go out and take a job that you feel, well, it may help you but it may not do very much for him? *(Pause)* Is it justifiable?

C.R.: You feel you might really be cheating the employer by doing that.

Mary Jane: That's right. I've said that before. I know we've covered that once before. Uhuh. *(Long pause, laughs)* Well, what's the answer? Am I supposed to get the answers?

C.R.: You are wondering that, too, aren't you, whether maybe the answer is in you?

Mary Jane: In other words, I'd have to make a radical change before I—I'm supposed to change in attitude, and change in everything.

C.R.: You realize that it would mean a pretty radical shift if—uh—if you tried some of those things.

Mary Jane: That's right. *(Long pause)* I suppose it would be better for me, I mean, I probably wouldn't like it at first, but then maybe it would help me, wouldn't it? It would sort of force me to do the things I don't want to do, I guess—[30]

---

[28] The client has shown some sophistication regarding psychological concepts; her question about whether her thinking is a defense mechanism gives some estimate of her fairly high level of intelligence, and her sophistication regarding behavioral mechanisms.

[29] The client attempts here to force the counselor to give her an answer to her questions. First, she asks, can she work this thing out by herself, and, secondly, why can't the counselor give her some suggestions such as telling her whether she is justified in not going to work. She alternates between a feeling that such a solution is not feasible and one that the counselor may be niggardly about the help he offers.

[30] Left to her own thinking, she is able to evaluate clearly the advantages a job would have.

C.R.: You think that maybe it would be a tough proposition, but maybe it would really have a lot in it for you.

Mary Jane: Yes, it would probably force me to do something. *(Pause)* But then where do you go from there? What's next?

C.R.: You realize that, even if you did that, there'd still be plenty of unanswered questions and plenty of difficulty still ahead.

Mary Jane: That's right. *(Pause)* Does reading books on that sort of thing really help, though, I mean—if you seemingly cannot find the answer, if you just don't seem to be able to cope with the situation—you can't find the answer, will reading books help? I mean isn't there something to—a feeling of not wanting to accept what you read, because you haven't thought of it before yourself or something?

C.R.: You feel that somehow you have to kind of go deeper than just face these things in a book.[31]

Mary Jane: Yeah. It just seems as though I should have thought of those things—even though I can't—it seems as though I should have. *(Long pause)* Should I have? *(Laughs)* And yet I guess that's what books are made for. They're made to help people. People write books so that they can help others. I just wonder why I find it so hard to accept them. Even though I know that they're right.

C.R.: In other words, you realize that you have come across many good ideas—probably sound ideas, and so on—but that doesn't always mean you can accept them.

Mary Jane: That's right. Well, the reason I feel that way is because when you get ideas out of books, well, in the first place, they don't seem to be related to your situation very much. It seems like ideas that are there—well, if you add that one idea it doesn't seem to benefit other situations. I mean, you take one idea and you apply it and then you think, well—and then it takes you somewhere—and you don't know what to do from then on. *(Laughs)*

C.R.: M-hm. If I get your feeling there—it's just sort of a patchwork thing—you might take one idea from a book and even use it—but then what? I mean it just doesn't—

---

[31] This interesting discussion concerning the use a client may make of the reading of books (bibliotherapy) may relate significantly to some questions frequently considered by psychotherapists.

Mary Jane: That's right. Well, is the rest supposed to come naturally from your own deduction? I mean—I guess it should normally.

C.R.: You feel probably that there's got to be something in the individual that goes on from that point.

Mary Jane: That's right. When people get ideas from books—or something, they just adopt them, instantly, they sort of incorporate them, I guess. But they start on from there too, they don't just rely on what they read. The point is, by practicing what you read—I guess it's a help, it isn't as bad as staying in one spot. Will that sort of set something else into the process? Sort of start things on your own?

C.R.: You're wondering if you put into effect some of the steps that look to you good from books and so on—would that really lead to knowing what to do next.

Mary Jane: That's right. *(Pause, laughs)* Well, what's the answer? *(Pause)* There's one thing that I can't quite make up my mind—I've tried to figure it out—well, what is it, when I get into a rut like this, what is it that I really want? And when I examine myself I can't figure out what I really want. It's only by looking at what other people want that I think, well, maybe that's what I want. It's a very odd thing, and I don't like it. That's what makes me feel—that it's—a—that I can't do what I want to do because I don't really know what I want.

C.R.: You feel that, so far, the best you have been able to achieve along that line is just to take a goal that seems to be good for somebody else. But that you don't feel that there's any real gain that you are sure you want.

Mary Jane: That's right. *(Very long pause)* That in itself is very odd, I guess because—I—think—it appears that every human being has desires—they really want things quite badly. And it seems to me that somewhere I should have those desires too. And yet I—when I sit down and try to think about it I can't.[32]

C.R.: You have tried to figure out what are the things you really want, and yet you can't think that there are any such things.

Mary Jane: Well, I want them—I want them at times, very much. For instance I want to be comfortable when I am with other people—to feel warmth, and yet when I sit down to think about it, it doesn't seem to

---

[32] Beginning with this speech, the client starts to discuss the very significant problem of motivation, both with regard to herself and to other people. This is probably germane to many problem situations where counseling is desirable.

be a great desire—I mean, it's rather mixed up. Well, I mean—aside from that, when I sit down and think—well, what is it I really want toward life, so that I sort of go toward that direction, I don't really know what I want.

C.R.: You know that you do have some desires, and sometimes they're—quite clear, but in general when you really try to figure out what you want, you're just not sure.

Mary Jane: That's right. I mean—aside from the fact that I feel uncomfortable at times—when I draw up against something—or when I sit down and think about it in fear, or something like that—well, that's different somehow. That's just a fear feeling, somehow, sort of. But actually if I—if I really knew what I wanted, I think maybe it would help.

C.R.: You feel that it would be quite a step forward if you were sure of the place you wanted to go.

Mary Jane: Not exactly a place.

C.R.: Well, I mean that in a general sense— (Mary Jane: M-hm.) Things you wanted to reach.

Mary Jane: That's right. What I really want out of life. *(Pause)* But then would it really help? *(Laughs)* Then I think, well, would it really help?

C.R.: In other words, sometimes you wonder, even if you could do that, would that help you.

Mary Jane: Well, the thing is, if I felt a strong desire for something, and it were really an honest and sincere desire, maybe other things would come along.

C.R.: If you had some really genuine goal, it might do a lot for some of these other things that trouble you too.

Mary Jane: That's right. *(Long pause)* Well, how do you find that goal?

C.R.: Wanted: one goal. Hmmm?

Mary Jane: That's right. Why does it seem that just a little thing—an ordinary everyday thing wouldn't be the answer? Why does it seem that just a job, or something, when you go about doing it—When I have been working, I forget about the time I was depressed and I wasn't even able to think about working. And then I get very discontented—and then I won't know whether it's time to look for something better. I mean, whether I really feel as though I should progress—or whether it's just a feeling—whether it's just one of those unstable feelings, I mean—that—well, it's just sort of a defense mechanism. And then I can't really search my heart and know whether—I don't have that sure feeling of what I should do next, and that in itself bothers me. Because that's sort of the essence of progress, I mean, you know that you've gained something, that it's the next step.[33]

C.R.: In other words, if you had a goal, even an immediate goal and you had reached it, you could feel your progress, but when your thinking about your goal keeps shifting, then—you just don't quite know where you are. Is that it?

Mary Jane: Well, yes, that's it in a sense. *(Pause)* The point is, if I wanted to do something great, or what I considered to be great—actually I don't have the qualifications for it because you have to build up to it. So that sort of—*(laughs)* well, of course I don't seem to be willing to do the first thing.

C.R.: You feel that you're not quite willing to set the lower intermediate goals and still you know you are not really equipped to reach some high-up or far-off goals. Is that it?

Mary Jane: That's right. *(Pause)* The point is that in my whole philosophy somehow or other I got the crazy idea that I just wouldn't progress—that things just don't grow better. I don't know how I ever got it—but it's—it's a crazy thing. I mean, I can go to shows and see people progressing and see people getting where they want to go and everything working out fine through consistent effort and everything like that—and yet I don't feel that I can see progress somehow or other.

C.R.: In yourself.

Mary Jane: That's right. *(Very long pause)* The point is, if I did not think so much about my troubles, or myself, or what I think are my troubles, and I did other things and I set my mind on other things, does it actually change your attitude toward things that count? Do you know what I mean?

C.R.: That is, you're wondering if you—picked some goal like a job or something that you could definitely work on, would that really change any of your basic thinking or would it just be a temporary distraction, kind of?

Mary Jane: That's right. In other words, if I ever stopped thinking about—the things that are bothering me—somehow or other I still don't think

---

[33] A fair beginning in achieving insight may be observed here; it is of a generalized sort, however, and not too specifically applicable to this client's special situation.

that just by not thinking about those things for a month or two months and trying to think about other things—still I don't feel as though it would have changed me much, basically.

C.R.: You feel that just putting it to one side or shoving it out of mind for a little bit, that isn't quite the thing you are looking for or what would really help.

Mary Jane: That's right. *(Pause)* Well, actually I don't see how it could help if I was just going back to think the same things over again. *(Pause)* So I suppose you just have to change your ideas—for better, I guess—I mean if something tells you one thing and then you say "No" you've got to think about it this way. Does that actually help, attacking each idea as it comes to you, I mean each thought about something?

C.R.: At least you are wondering whether you could really tackle what you feel is wrong with your ideas as well as what you do.

Mary Jane: *(Statement unintelligible)*

C.R.: You feel it must really be a petty way of thinking about the whole situation that distorts your thinking about others and their attitudes toward you.

Mary Jane: That's right. *(Long pause)* And then the next step is *(laughs)* what am I going to do about all this?

C.R.: You feel that that might be another forward march, hmmm?

Mary Jane: Yes. But the funny thing is that when we—when you do that then somebody will do you a dirty trick—you lose faith all over again—I mean it just doesn't seem to jibe, you think it a—well, most things just seem right and then they'll do you a dirty trick—and a—and you don't seem as though you're justified in thinking of them that way.

C.R.: If you try to put some trust in other people—and—be—to feel they're broadminded and tolerant—then you're pretty sure they'll "do you dirt" and disillusion you.

Mary Jane: Well, it's happened quite often. *(Pause)* Oh, I used to take things—you just take them. *(Pause)* I guess you have to figure that you do them, too, sometimes.

C.R.: You feel you have to figure that no one is perfect all the time, that you make some slips and they make some slips.

Mary Jane: I guess so. *(Long pause)* The point is, what does occupy people's thoughts—I mean, what are they thinking of? That's what keeps me wondering. It always puzzles me, I always wonder what they're thinking of. And when you're—is it just an obsession that I've built up, is that what I really want? To feel—to feel that I can do it just as good as they can or something. That's what I try to figure out—what is it that I want?[34]

C.R.: You feel that might be your real aim—simply to be able to do things as well as the next person—is that it?

Mary Jane: Yes, because when you think of it in that way, that's sort of a crazy sort of a goal because that fixes things according to what somebody else is doing—it's just coming back to that all over again.

C.R.: That's fastening your whole scheme outside of yourself again. Is that what you mean?

Mary Jane: That's right. (Pause) Why does that bother me so much? (Pause) And why is it that no matter what I do or how much I do, externally, I always come back to that internally, I'll always be thinking about that.

C.R.: You feel that no matter what you might do, always you would be judging yourself by what others think of you. Is that it?

Mary Jane: Well—that—that permits outside things to affect me more than they should, much more—than they should, because what they think of you is actually what you think of yourself and what you are, combined. The point is, I—I can look around and see other people making great strides, and people in my family have done things that—they're able to graduate from a university and they've done great things, and then—it just sort of makes me feel—why—it just sort of has a funny effect on me. Instead of being an incentive, I don't know what it does, but—it just knocks me out, sort of.

C.R.: It just floors you.[35]

Mary Jane: M-hm. That's right.

C.R.: It makes you shrink back rather than moving forward.

Mary Jane: That's right. Where it shouldn't have that effect on me. It should be an incentive, shouldn't it? (Long pause) What, actually, is introspection? I mean, do some people just get into a rut of just doing too much of it, and just keep on doing it, or do some people do it well—somewhat? I mean is everybody introspective to a certain extent?

---

[34] The client expresses and idea very basic in her thinking, the question of whether she is as capable or as intelligent as other people are.

[35] Successful attempts to put into figurative expressions the deeper feelings of the client are made here.

C.R.: You wonder whether there are different degrees of introspection?

Mary Jane: That's right.

C.R.: Yes, I think so.[36]

Mary Jane: I guess there must be a degree where it gets to be pretty morbid.

C.R.: You feel it can be overdone.

Mary Jane: Oh, definitely. The point is I guess it's supposed to help you but when it doesn't help you it's no good any more. *(Long pause)* I can't think of a thing to say—

C.R.: You've run out of things to talk about.

Mary Jane: Yeah. *(Very long pause)* Does anybody actually feel as though he's—he's reached his ideal of himself? I mean, certain goals that he's set in his mind. Does anybody actually feel as though he's sort of satisfied with himself? I mean—a sort of an assured feeling, about himself?

C.R.: You are puzzled to know whether anybody ever really gets up to the point of their ideals or the place where they have set their goals. Is that—

Mary Jane: Well, not exactly. I mean just in their own eyes—the way they've handled things or done things.

C.R.: Does anybody really feel satisfied that they have reached their own goals—satisfied with themselves.

Mary Jane: *(Pause)* See, that's just it, I—I—can do something, or I can go through an experience, and I feel, well, I haven't done so badly, and then the next minute, "Oh, no." Immediately something inside attacks me and tears me down. And it discourages me, discourages me to the point where I don't want to repeat it.

C.R.: In other words, your own evaluation of yourself fluctuates so that it's very discouraging.

Mary Jane: That's right. You just fluctuate—that's a good word for it.

C.R.: One minute you feel pretty good, and the next you'd sell yourself for a dime a dozen.

[36] Notice that on a minor technical point the counselor gives a tentative opinion rather than make an issue of the information-getting question.

Mary Jane: What causes that? I mean, I wonder if there is any—if anyone knows what causes it. Is that the devil? *(Both C.R. and Mary Jane laugh)*

C.R.: You feel as though maybe it's your devil anyway.

Mary Jane: Yes. The trouble is, why can't I answer it back and say, "Well, I have done all right." There's always that doubt, that I haven't. And why it should matter so much, I don't know, but it does.

C.R.: You just feel that gnaws away at you.[37]

Mary Jane: That's right. *(Pause)* It really seems ridiculous when you bring it out in the open, but I must think those things, because I am saying I do and I guess I do. *(Pause)* The point is, is it really important or is it just something I think is important. Is it just something that I'm always thinking about myself, or is it something that really counts. *(Pause)* yes—*(laughs)*—go on—*(trying to get answer from counselor)*.

C.R.: *(Seriously)* I—I'm just trying to understand that. In other words you're feeling that it is possibly because you are egotistical that this whole business matters so much, and causes so much difficulty.

Mary Jane: It's a funny thing when you can't—I've heard of people who've had inferiority complexes, but they've used it to overcome things and they've harnessed it. In other words, instead of making them go backwards they make themselves go forward with it. That's a very good thing. The point is, how do you get it—to keep it from destroying you.

C.R.: You feel that the same motive power that drives some people who've had inferiority complexes might really destroy somebody else because it wasn't turned in the right channel.

Mary Jane: That's right, M-hm. I mean instead of it getting you down, I suppose it should make me go forward instead of—thinking, well, I just botched that up. *(Very long pause)* The funny thing is that at times I can be so terribly depressed that I just don't want to attempt anything. And then when I get there—I just—it's so unstable, it's so funny that my ideas change—and well—I think that I'm too good for the job. It just turns that way on me—sometimes I—I just don't feel as though I can do it—and then at other times if I do something well—it's just something within me that—well—it's a terrible thing, really. It makes me feel as though—I shouldn't be satisfied with it—but it's a sort of smug feeling—and it isn't a—it's a funny feeling—I—I mean it's—it really doesn't make very much sense, actually.

---

[37] These last few responses are very good reflections of the client's feelings. The preceding response carefully skirts a religious question that might stimulate a time-consuming and profitless discussion.

C.R.: You feel that either you have that very depressed feeling of inadequacy, or you go clear to the other extreme which you don't like either—of a very smug feeling that this is beneath me—I'm too good for this activity.

Mary Jane: Yes, but somebody else—my neighbor or something might be going through the same thing and won't take it in that way—I mean— they won't feel—a—well it isn't exactly that I would be too good for it. It's just a sort of a feeling that—well—I can't explain it. *(Pause)* Sort of like—if I were like somebody else I wouldn't have to do that—or that somebody else might not have to take it—that they are too good to take it, or something like that. It's a little bit difficult to explain.

C.R.: M-hm.

Mary Jane: And yet I know that somebody else will be going through it, but their attitude—their attitude is so different toward it. I mean—they accept it as a matter of course. And I might want to and yet there's something that—some little devil that rears its head and says—something like that, and it's really so—it just seems to be so much a part of me.

C.R.: You feel that it's some little devil right in your own attitudes.

Mary Jane: That's right. *(Pause)* And then if I try to change my attitudes—I think, "Oh you're just being a sap—you're just feeling foolish." It's really very funny. I guess it's just a matter of conquering those suggestions that sort of come. I guess the more you get into them the stronger they grow. I think that's just it—that's what I've always felt, I have known that other people go through certain things and yet when I say I wanted to be like them I won't accept them in a way. *(Pause)* I just sort of think that I've just thought life was meant to be a bed of roses—and that if I don't have it that way it just isn't right or something—

C.R.: You feel that maybe way down deep you've sort of felt that things should be easy and perfect for you or else—you won't take them at all.

Mary Jane: Yeah, I guess that's it. *(Long pause)* I hadn't thought about that in that way before, but that's just the way it is. I guess I've always felt that it's sort of a shame—or sort of something to be ashamed of not to have things perfect or to be struggling with something. I don't know, I guess it's a snobbery in a way.

C.R.: You have felt that it wasn't quite, mm—proper to be in a situation where it was a real struggle to make—

Mary Jane: That's right. *(Pause)* That's just a big laziness! *(Both laugh)* That's what it is really. I've sort of—I think that's the way I've always been but I didn't really know it. *(Long pause)* Isn't that a silly attitude to take? That's just something that a—that's just one of those things that I've always had and not really known. That's really a prejudice, isn't it?

C.R.: You feel that's just something in yourself that you've always had but that you're not very proud of.

Mary Jane: That's right. And when I change it—I mean when I've tried to change it, I've always had a smug feeling about it, when it shouldn't be that way. And that I resent, too. *(Laughs)* I mean things that other people would just do because they take for granted, because that's the way it is. It's just the extremes all over again. It's just jumping from one place to another.

C.R.: You feel it's the kind of struggling in between that you have never quite been willing to face or to take.

Mary Jane: M-hm, yeah. *(Long pause)* I can just see it as an opera or something. It's a funny thing, but when I was in grammar school—that's where it all started—my sense of values—got off to a very funny start. I was a sort of—I was the teacher's pet—and a—I was also a lawyer's daughter and everybody sort of made me feel—or something made me feel—as though I was too good—or I couldn't—was better than somebody else—or that I wouldn't make the effort to be nice to somebody because I was—I didn't have to, because I was better. And that just grew and grew and grew, and then when I wanted to make an impression, I really did not know how to.

C.R.: You feel you can see those roots of it going—back into some of those experiences.

Mary Jane: That's right. It was a childish—it was a sort of a funny world I lived in. It wasn't a world of reality, really. And I think I really enjoyed it—I enjoyed that kind of a world. The point is—why didn't I do something about it? Why didn't something awaken me?

C.R.: You wonder why you accepted that kind of a world.

Mary Jane: That's right. *(Pause)*

C.R.: The sleeping princess just wasn't awakened.[38]

Mary Jane: No. Not at all. I really always expected—I expected to be getting things without working for them. That was just it.

---

[38] This is another use of a figure of speech as a means of expressing in clearer form the feeling of the client.

C.R.: You expected to reach the goal without the work or struggle that went in between.

Mary Jane: That's right. Oh, I worked hard for my marks as far as that went, but I mean socially and other things that determined my attitudes. I expected things to be a certain way. And I guess I just thought they were because I wanted to think it. I mean—a—if they did make a pet out of me, I enjoyed it, I mean I liked the idea. But yet it wasn't really right. It wasn't being like the rest.

C.R.: You enjoyed it, but I take it you felt that even then that wasn't quite what you wanted.[39]

Mary Jane: That's right.

C.R.: Well, I see our time's up.[40]

Mary Jane: M-hm. I guess it is.

C.R.: Next Monday?

Mary Jane: Well, I don't know whether the time is so good. *(Pause)* What other time could you suggest? What's the very latest that your office hours ever are?[41]

C.R.: Well, till five.

Mary Jane: Well, is it possible to call up?

C.R.: Yes.

Mary Jane: I mean, how far in advance would I have to call up?

C.R.: Well, I—it's hard to say, it all depends on how my schedule fills up. But if you want to, you could take one of those times and I would save it if you wanted to use it. Would you like to leave it that way, or would you rather call me and let me know when you want to come in?

---

[39] The ambivalence of the client's feeling is recognized.

[40] As is usually the case, the counselor takes the responsibility of terminating the session.

[41] In view of later developments, the most likely interpretation of these questions is that Mary Jane was contemplating the possibility of getting herself a job, which would make usual office hour appointments impossible. Actually, she did not have the courage to get a job until after the seventh interview.

It is quite possible that the insight achieved in the latter part of this interview, and the impulse toward getting a job (if this interpretation is correct) proved to be rather discouraging to Mary Jane when she got away from the interview. The realization that she was undertaking a difficult and painful process of self-understanding and action may well account for her "illness" of the following week.

Mary Jane: Well, let's put it this way, you save a certain time and then I'll call you and let you know for sure. How soon would I have to call you?

C.R.: Well, try and call me by Thursday or Friday if you can. O.K.?

Mary Jane: M-hm.

DEVELOPMENTS BETWEEN THE THIRD
AND FOURTH INTERVIEWS

On the day before Mary Jane's next appointment her mother telephoned to say that she was ill, and the appointment was postponed one week. On this later date, the mother telephoned shortly before the hour to say that Mary Jane was "reluctant to come. I've been urging her to come, but she's reluctant. I don't believe this is doing her much good. She feels better after an interview, but then she gets depressed, and goes to bed. I wonder if counseling is enough in a situation as bad as hers. Could you suggest a psychiatrist that she could go to?" The counselor replied that he would wish to think over that possibility and would make suggestions if Mary Jane felt she was not getting help. He thought, however, that he would first write a note to Mary Jane. The mother offered to have her come to the telephone but the counselor said this was not necessary.[42]

The letter was carefully written to give an expression of warmth and interest but to be as non-directive as possible. It was written as follows[43]:

[42] Several significant factors stand out regarding the technique used here. The counselor avoided allowing this relationship to become one between himself and the mother, but placed the decision with the girl herself. He also implied the question, "Is it you, the mother, or the client herself who is ready to admit defeat in the attempt to use this method?" The interpretation is inferred that, if the girl herself wants to change, the method still offers an answer. It is significant that this mother, who is later shown to be largely responsible for the overdependence that represents her daughter's maladjustment, is fulfilling her role here in a manner that could be predicted.

[43] The careful thinking which went into the preparation of this letter may not be apparent to the reader who is not too familiar with the non-directive technique. Every word in this letter is deliberately planned so as to imply one of the following ideas:

a. The decision of whether to return must be your own.
b. The counselor can understand the difficulty involved in making the decision.
c. If you decide not to come in, I will not be critical of you, but I am making it possible for you to continue coming.
d. You do not have to explain if you do not wish to come, or you do not need to feel too guilty if you do not explain.

It is significant that the next telephone call is from the girl herself, and not from her mother.

Dear Miss Tilden:

Your mother gave me your message about feeling reluctant to come in. I can understand that reluctance, and realize that you feel somewhat discouraged about your situation. I do not wish to urge you in any way, and if you prefer not to come in again, that will be perfectly all right.

However, I am going to take the liberty of holding an appointment next Tuesday at the usual time, until Friday of this week. I would appreciate it if you would please phone me to let me know whether or not you wish to keep it. If I do not hear from you on or before Friday I will know you do not wish to return. In any event you have my sincere best wishes.

Yours truly,

Mary Jane telephoned Friday afternoon saying she would keep the appointment.

SUMMARY OF THE FOURTH INTERVIEW

November 11

Mary Jane found it rather difficult to get started talking about her feelings and remarked on this fact. She told of a social gathering at her home, and said she felt that she had entered into it—had really forgotten to think so much about herself. She had done better. She had particularly learned from one of the girls present. In a rather intimate conversation with this girl she had realized that this young woman accepted herself as she was, did not feel jealous of her sister who was prettier, or of fellows who were brighter. "That's remarkable," was Mary Jane's comment.

Mary Jane recounted her experiences in various fields, showing how similar the pattern had been. In music, in sculpture, in dancing, she can do entirely satisfactory work as long as the teacher is directing and coaching her. Then when she is supposed to be at a level where she can go on for herself, she simply cannot go forward. "I was always afraid that I wouldn't just do it quite right or something—I was just afraid to take a chance."

Mary Jane was somewhat disgusted at the picture she had been painting of herself. "The point is, does just seeing it as ridiculous, does that change it? I mean—I guess it should, really." She realized that she believes that other people can be helped, but she cannot accept that fact for herself. She concluded that there are two forces in herself, and one of them is a very "arrogant force" which just doesn't want to accept things or be helped.

She talked about the problem of trying to be natural, but "I don't know when I'm natural." She discussed problems of marriage and the manner in which she thinks about all the ways it might fail. "You see, it's that old pattern, that same thing repeats itself, I mean that I want to be sure that

I'm going to be perfect. It's that fear that just keeps repeating itself." She wants especially to feel that she is not too different from others.

At no time during the interview did she mention her failure to come in the previous week, or refer to the letter. The counselor made no mention of this aspect. She wished to return, but wondered about a late afternoon or evening hour. She did not say why she wished to change the time.

FIFTH INTERVIEW

November 17

Mary Jane: Hello again.

C.R.: What's what today?

Mary Jane: I don't know what. Every time I come I think I don't know what to talk about. I just come. *(Pause)* The point is that I come and I talk but it doesn't seem to make too much of an impression on me, I mean, while I'm here I feel better. Then when I go away I just don't seem to be able to hold on to it.

C.R.: You feel you make certain progress in an interview but after that it kind of slips.

Mary Jane: Yes, what I mean is, I can see things clearly for the moment while I'm here but then I go home—I don't think any differently about things. That's what the funny part is, I'm sure of it—I don't.

C.R.: You feel that it doesn't quite carry over to life in between times.

Mary Jane: That's right. Well, I've gone out a little bit more than I had been going out—that is—visiting more—and I've been with people more, but I still basically feel the same. I mean, it doesn't seem to make too much difference whether I am with them or I am not. Well, maybe I sort of shrink back from being with them and then I stay off and I sort of feel guilty about that. And then when I do go out and mix with them, I guess I don't have the feeling that I'm lost somewhere by myself. But it still doesn't seem to help too much.

C.R.: As I get that, you've done some things about it, I mean like trying to mingle a little bit more with people, but it still leaves something to be desired.[44]

---

[44] The counselor recognizes the first tentative steps in the direction of the client's planning and taking action directed toward improving her situation, but also accepts her ambivalence about that progress.

Mary Jane: Yes, M-hm. *(Pause)* I enjoy listening to people, I mean, I—uh—it really is wonderful. I was over to my sister's house and they had some people over, and they talked about some very interesting things. And it was stimulating while I listened to it, it was lovely. I tried to see that they saw things from an impersonal viewpoint. They were perfectly normal people and yet it didn't help me—I tried to get it to help me—and yet it didn't really.

C.R.: You've enjoyed getting more of an understanding of other people, and even tried to apply some of that understanding to you, but without much effect.

Mary Jane: That's right. I can appreciate that there were different people there that I thought were really very charming, and I could appreciate them all right. But somehow it didn't add anything—to things the way I thought of them. When I went home I told Mother that it was very nice and that I enjoyed it, but I didn't feel as though I contributed very much. And she told me that it was all right just to be there and just to be a good listener. There have to be people to listen and people to talk, too, so here's a good listener. But that, uh—that isn't satisfactory because I see what's behind it. Maybe they can't, but I know what's behind it.

C.R.: Your mother tries to assure you that you are doing all right, but I take it that you feel that if you were really just being a good listener that would be one thing but actually the motivation behind listening is a little bit different.

Mary Jane: That's it exactly. M-hm. Because I didn't feel as though I was contributing. *(Pause)* In other words, I don't want to just feel what people think about me is all right, I want to know that it's justified and I don't seem to be able to find a justification. Do you see what I mean?

C.R.: I'm not sure, let me see if I do. That you want to really deserve inside some of the approval, etc., you might get from other people. Is that, uh—[45]

Mary Jane: That's right. *(Pause)* But I constantly have that feeling that I don't. That's just it. And yet it isn't just the feeling—it's almost a certainty—more or less, I mean. It's just a dead certainty, that's all.

---

[45] The counselor's gesture of tentativeness of response is probably a useful technique, at times, when the client may be expressing a feeling which may be somewhat hard for her to face too rapidly.

C.R.: There's plenty of proof that you don't deserve approval. Is that it?

Mary Jane: That's right. *(Long pause)* Sometimes I wonder whether this is quite the right track. I don't know. I mean I realize that this has been going on a long time and that I can't expect to effect a change right away, because it has been such a long time. But I just wonder whether—I mean—my reactions don't seem to be very much better—on the face of it. I can't really tell, I guess, maybe you can tell a little better. But, uh—

C.R.: At any rate, you can't help but feel a little bit disappointed, perhaps, in the lack of obvious change in you, even though, on the other hand, you realize that it probably is somewhat likely to be a slow process since the problem has been present for a long time.

Mary Jane: Yes, that's true. The only thing is that I can't help but feel that I work against myself. I mean it's just so obvious to me that I do work against myself. And it seems rather silly to be one minute trying to do something about it, and then it seems so certain that there's something present that doesn't want to do anything about it. *(Pause)* It's such a contrary thing—the whole problem is just—[46]

C.R.: So that the very time that one part of you is perhaps really taking hold of this whole situation, another part of you is just sabotaging the whole business.

Mary Jane: That's right. *(Pause)* The whole thing is that somehow or other along the trail I lost fortitude—I know I did, because I just—I don't feel it. If somebody else might say, "Oh, well, cheer up, just look at it from another angle"—I just—it's just like a big balloon that's just deflated.

C.R.: You realize that the courage that people normally need to meet life you just feel in yourself has been all deflated.

Mary Jane: That's right. M-hm. I mean if somebody said something or did something, or some circumstance presented itself and it wasn't favorable, instead of, well, bolstering myself I just thought, "Well, everything's all wrong, and I can't do anything about it." And that was just a big accumulation, I mean, that's the way I always look at things, I guess. *(Pause)* Instead of fighting against things the way I should have.

[46] The client begins to recognize the elemental conflict within herself between the urge to change and the "neurotic" urge which attempts to defeat the more healthy desire. The unhealthy goal has its own values which have caused the patient to cling to it in the past. The counselor effectively recognizes the conflict in his next responses.

C.R.: You experienced a long series of defeats and the notion of taking the offensive is pretty difficult.

Mary Jane: Yes, that's right. If I did do it, I still wouldn't be sure—the point—I really can't understand. *(Laughs)* I mean just taking it and doing something about it—I still think, well, maybe I'm not doing the right thing. I still wouldn't be sure that it is the right thing to do. *(Pause)* It becomes a sort of an obsession or something.

C.R.: No matter what you might strive to undertake you still feel as though it's a very risky gamble.

Mary Jane: M-hm. That's right. Well, actually when you put it that way, and when I talk about it, if somebody else heard about it they'd say, "Well, what's the difference, why not do it? What the heck! What are you losing?" See, that's just it. I can't—I just don't seem to be able to take that attitude. Everything is so serious. I don't know why it should be but it is.

C.R.: You realize you really might take more of a gambling attitude but you just find it necessary to take the possibility of loss very, very seriously.

Mary Jane: M-hm. I think it's because I'm always testing myself, I mean, in my own eyes. Everything is always a test for myself, and it shouldn't be. *(Pause)* It's really such a funny attitude that I can't imagine how it ever came to be. Why I should always have to be testing myself. Actually, it's so childish that it's silly.

C.R.: You feel that every experience is something you must measure up to.

Mary Jane: That's right. It's just as though nothing else has gone before, as though each situation is just like I have to prove something, completely, I mean it—

C.R.: You have to start from scratch.

Mary Jane: Yes, that's right. M-hm.

C.R.: You don't have any accumulated savings that you can bring along with you, but you must absolutely start fresh with each experience to prove it.

Mary Jane: It isn't that I—well, maybe I just feel that I have to. I always feel that way though—I mean, if I meet somebody, I feel as though I just have to prove something to them. It's crazy, but that's the way I feel.

(Pause) And that, of course, is not a normal attitude, and they feel it, I guess. They must.

C.R.: The necessity of proving something about yourself is always there.

Mary Jane: That's right. *(Pause)* The thing is that most people, if they set about doing something—they say, well, if I do it, O.K. Then I prove something to myself that I can do it and then I can go on from there, but the point was when I did something like that and maybe I did do it right, I still had doubts about it. I thought, well, "No, I probably didn't"—you see, that's always just it—there was always another part that always wanted to sabotage, as you said.

C.R.: In other words, in a sense, even when an experience does prove something about yourself, still you can't accept the proof. That is, you might do something well and you would have reason to say, "Well, I did a good job on that," but you couldn't even feel that way.

Mary Jane: Well, I—maybe I felt it on top, but then there would be doubts about it, and then I would really begin to wonder.

C.R.: Any acceptance of it would be just a surface acceptance.

Mary Jane: M-hm. Yeah. I guess that's about it. *(Pause)* I guess I was behind the door when all those nice little gifts were handed out. *(Both C.R. and Mary Jane laugh)* That's the way I feel about it though.

C.R.: M-hm.

The remaining portion of the interview may best be given by stating in summarized fashion the major attitudes expressed by Mary Jane.

1. I'm afraid to venture, because I'm afraid I will fail.
2. I built up a little confidence on a job I once had, but then that confidence was destroyed. It was a blow.
3. I feel that I can't size up any human situation in a normal fashion.
4. I set out to become friendly with a girl on this job, and then I was disillusioned.
5. I was frightened by my jealousy when she went with a boy in whom I was interested.
6. It made me afraid to trust my feelings.
7. I haven't learned from life-experiences. It's an unwillingness to learn.
8. I see all these things, but I can't do anything about them.
9. I've tried in the past to make progress, but I've always failed.

10. I know I just don't have the ability to cope with things.
11. I'm afraid I'm getting worse in those respects.

SUMMARY OF THE SIXTH INTERVIEW
November 24

This interview, like the others, starts with negative attitudes. Mary Jane says that she always has to fight the "solemn conviction that things just aren't going to change."[47] She feels that she does not have the basic material within herself to work with. "I guess the reason I come is that I have to do something." But she does not trust her own feelings and judgments about herself, and feels that if she does make a new choice it must be something rigid and unchangeable. But when she does carry through actions in this spirit, she is again only acting a part.

She is deeply afraid that people will find out what she is really like. She also feels she is not adult, that she had just carried on her childish concepts of herself. She feels she should have done something about it, but she has not. She has just drifted into a peculiar world of her own which is not very realistic. She realized gradually that she had no real relationship with others, but as time went by the prospect of doing something about it became more and more frightening. And then she came to the feeling, "I'm not normal now and I just never will be. . . . But that isn't the least satisfying either."

The interview comes to its conclusion on the note that she cannot possibly trust her own thinking, but is completely swayed by what others think. "I think the other person is right because I have the notion that they have grown in the right way. I just haven't."

CONDENSATION OF THE SEVENTH INTERVIEW
December 2

Mary Jane: Well, I have come to the point—I have come to another point, where I just—I'm just a little bit tired of thinking about things. I just don't want to think about them very much—and I have been seriously considering going to work. I mean even if I'm fired—if I'm fired, then I'm fired, that's all. But I just think I'm going to go to work—and that's

---

[47] It is possible that Mary Jane's "always having to fight" the conviction that she will fail is another indication of that "force for growth" which Rogers postulates. She gives stronger evidence of this when she says the reason for her coming is that she "must do something."

what I'm going to do. I don't think it's going to help anything else a great deal, but on the other hand what I am doing now isn't helping anything either.[48]

C.R.: So that in a sense—you have thought about this enough—and you want to put something into action. Is that, uh—

Mary Jane: Yes. Well, I don't know whether that's my idea so very much. I mean, the idea isn't that I want to do something about it so much, as that I just—well, I just want a change.

C.R.: I see. It's more that you're more or less disgusted with the present situation, and you don't have too much hope that getting a job would necessarily help but, by gosh, that's what you're going to do!

Mary Jane: Yeah, that's right.

C.R.: M-hm.

Mary Jane discusses her plan for work in a rather discouraged way, fearful that "something will turn up and I'll sort of lose faith all over again. And then I'll realize or think that I haven't progressed so very much. . . . My will power is just so weak that everything I do seems to be sort of shaky, and I can't count on things."

She feels that in the past when she has endeavored to do something it has only been by an enormous concentration of will power and thought which has made the whole thing too important, so that everything else "seems to sort of get out of perspective. Maybe I end up with that one thing, but it still isn't what I want."

She considers this difficulty and brings in the thought, "Possibly it's because if I say I'm going out and look for a job my mother immediately pricks up her ears and, you know, talks about it or something. And then as soon as she starts talking about it I lose interest.[49] I just don't want to do it any more."

It is silly, the client thinks, to be bothered by so many things. Thinking about them should get her somewhere, but it does not. She knows herself better than anyone else, but "it's just as though I choose to know a self that just doesn't want to get anywhere—it would be nice to know the right kind of self."

---

[48] The decision in the direction of taking some action seems now to be fairly clearly made. When, however, the counselor suggests this in his reflection in his next response, the client is not willing to accept the behavior in this sense.

[49] This seems to be the first criticism of the client's family, and the part they have played in the development of her maladjustment.

She debates the question as to whether some sort of shock may not be necessary to make her want to change. She would like to find an easy way in which "somebody's going to do something for you." She also wonders whether if they could look at her brain, they might not find that there is some organic defect there. Perhaps she is going insane.

Toward the end of the interview she puts rather vividly the struggle between the constructive and regressive forces within herself. She talks of her doubts about herself and adds:

Mary Jane: There's a very definite force that is negative all the time.

C.R.: It's almost that when you want to turn in a positive direction that an even stronger force within you throws up all kinds of doubt about it.

Mary Jane: Yes, that's right. (Pause) And then because it's so strong, I just accept it, I guess because it seems to be the bigger thing, so I guess I just accept it.

C.R.: You feel that your doubting force is definitely stronger than your constructive force.

Mary Jane: Yes. (Very long pause) That's just it. (Pause) I guess I've always believed the other one because I've built it up so high and then I believe that it's true because it's so big. (Very long pause) That's something I never thought about. (Very long pause) It seems that the more I ever try to drive it out, the louder it yells. Every time I want it to say no, it just yells louder. And then the more the other doubts came—I mean, it seemed so much more positive—so much more positive than the littler one—I just accepted it.[50]

C.R.: You just felt that the armies of doubt are definitely unbeatable armies.

Mary Jane: M-hm. Yeah.

C.R.: And that the other is a pretty weak and struggling thing.

Mary Jane: (Laughs) Yeah, that's right. (Very long pause) I guess that just puts the whole thing in the—that just about states the whole case in a nut-shell—that I have always been willing—in other words, I guess I just

---

[50] The client is now clearly facing the question of a conflict which she so tentatively recognized in an earlier interview. It is significant that the counselor permits long pauses to occur in the counseling process without interrupting the flow of the client's thinking, and that these pauses are closely associated with significant insight, as represented in the statement, "That's something I never thought about."

didn't want to fight—and I was always more willing to believe the other than to put up a big fight or something.

C.R.: You feel you kind of tossed in an unconditional surrender rather than—just because you believed the other forces were impossibly strong.

Mary Jane: That's right. *(Pause)* I mean instead of trying to remedy the situation or trying to do better, I just sort of shut it off. Like shutting off an avenue instead of going back to it and trying to overcome it, I just, well, I just believed that I couldn't do it and that I just shut it out.

C.R.: M-hm.

SUMMARY OF THE EIGHTH INTERVIEW

January 6

There was about a month's interval between this interview and the last. This interview, with its conflicting attitudes, may best be presented by stating the main themes of Mary Jane's attitude which were expressed.[51]

1. I am working now, I have a job.
2. My problem hasn't cleared up any more.
3. I do understand more, but I'm not willing to see how I can change.
4. I read psychological books and see I've done all the wrong things.
5. It's such an accumulation, such an obstacle, I can't do anything about it.
6. I'm getting better on the job, but I don't feel it's because of me.
7. I want to make friends, but I can't. It's all such a mess.
8. I suppose there is a little progress in being able to get a job, and carrying through with it, but there is still a wall of self-defense around me.
9. I do understand now why I haven't been a success before.
10. I still feel that I can't make real contacts with people.
11. It's all very well to realize how your parents influenced you, but there's so little you can do about it. *(Cries)*
12. It's awful to feel that of all the ways of living I take the lowest road. *(Cries)*

---

[51] This method of analyzing the main attitudes expressed in an interview forms a very helpful guide for the counselor in studying the progress being made. Where only abbreviated notes of an interview are being kept, the method is also a good one for recording the major shifts of attitude, and the improvement that occurs. When the nondirective method is being used little else is necessary for the notes to represent an adequate picture of the progress of the therapy.

13. The more I'm with people the more discouraged I become.
14. My attitudes don't seem to want to change—everything is very discouraging.
15. I feel better when I'm with somebody who isn't very superior.
16. I want to stay at my own level.
17. If I think of doing things, I know I'll fail.
18. Well, I have shrugged off those thoughts and gone ahead and done things.
19. I have no creativity—no force that keeps pushing me on.
20. Of everything I want to do, I feel that in comparison with what others would do, it will be no good.
21. I don't have any standards of my own.
22. If I could be sure of anything in myself, I wouldn't be so bothered.
23. It seems as though my brother and sister had more will power.
24. My father praised me when I shouldn't be praised. I lived for praise. That was all wrong.
25. How can I sweep away these deep habits?
26. It's like leaving a shelter when I try to do something else. I feel I'm lost when I get in with others with a normal adjustment.
27. I feel I've distrusted others, but you can't live like that.
28. My whole attitude toward men is that they're terribly superior to me. Women, too, but men especially.
29. I'm just getting what I deserve in life, but it isn't pleasant. I'm being punished for my past. (Cries)
30. I just can't build my self-esteem.
31. If I had the conviction that I could change, I could, but I don't have that conviction.

It is apparent that in this eighth interview many very significant insights occur in the thinking of the client. Compared with the second or third interviews, it is apparent that a great deal of change has been occurring in a case in which the feelings were predominantly hopeless at the beginning of counseling.

NINTH INTERVIEW

January 13

Mary Jane begins with her feeling that she is making no progress. "I keep coming in here and I don't seem to be getting anywhere, and I think that isn't right." She quickly adds, however, "Well, actually I guess I have gotten somewhere because I see things a little clearer. But I still have the same feelings about things." She voices the attitude that she is not too well connected with reality. She discusses this and realizes that many of her past problems lie within herself. "I guess I wasn't so willing to change. It never occurred to me that all this trouble was my own, I mean the way I looked at things."

"The actuality of it is that I never really knew what the real 'me' was—it was all covered over really, and I got to thinking it was me. And then when that 'me' didn't strike the bell anywhere, it was pretty hard." She goes on in regard to the struggle to discover her real self and adds, "I'm looking for what everybody's always looking for, and that's probably finding yourself."

She realizes that she is always dissatisfied with anything she does—her job or any other undertaking. Part of the reason for this is that she feels she never achieves more than a mediocre standard, and this she cannot accept, but "I've got to face it, it just was." She is convinced that whatever she might do, it just would not work out well. She is convinced she is a moron because she can follow a teacher, but can do nothing on her own initiative. She continues:

Mary Jane: I've either been afraid to trust my own ability and afraid to go out on my own or something. That's just a habit, that was just sort of a habit that I formed. I mean, relying on my teachers, really, just groping at meanings.

C.R.: As long as someone else was in charge, why, it was O.K., you got along, but when it came to a question of doing something on your own ability, in your own direction, to choose and manage, why you don't have any luck.

Mary Jane: That's right.

C.R.: It boils down again to what's come up in some other ways, doesn't it, that you just trust others *(she cries)* and believe in them, but belief in yourself, that's just impossible.

Mary Jane: Yes, that's just the idea. Don't you think that somewhere along the line something would happen—something might turn up that—it's a very funny situation.

C.R.: You feel that something should have turned up to give you that confidence in yourself.

Mary Jane: Yes. It should. I should have thought of it or something. *(Crying)* When you watch a little child he seems to—well, he seems to want to get out on his own, he seems to be happy when he can get out.[52]

---

[52] As the client approaches a problem very painful to her, i.e., her lack of initiative and independence, she breaks into tears. This is frequently a measure of the depth of feeling associated with ideas the client is expressing.

C.R.: You feel very deeply about it, that even a little child feels so much pleasure in standing on his own two feet.

Mary Jane: Well, possibly being—oh, dear, here comes the rainstorm. *(Cries)*

C.R.: They say the rain makes things grow.[53]

Mary Jane: Very aptly put. *(Long pause, crying)* Well, perhaps being at home has something to do with—I mean my mother has always been very good to me. She had a very miserable childhood, her parents never paid any attention to her, then she tried to make up for it, and that way it didn't affect the others because they didn't accept it, but I accepted what she did for me and I just took it for granted, and it made me more reliant on her, really.[54]

C.R.: You feel that because of some of her very real needs that—she did a great deal for you and you accepted it and depended on her.

Mary Jane: That's right.

C.R.: You stood on her two feet.[55]

Mary Jane: That's right. Now my little sister, she isn't that way, she's in the adolescent stage right now; she is branching out for herself, I mean she just doesn't like it. She wants to be consulted about everything that she does, and everything like that. Well, my sister isn't letting it affect her. I know she feels in her own heart that it's right, and I used to wonder about that, I mean every time that I did something I used to think, well, maybe she is right, maybe I should do the way she does, and then I switched over, and I wouldn't stand up on my own two feet.

C.R.: You watched your sister stand out against some of your mother's thinking, and some of your mother's requests, but when you were in that stage you couldn't—you didn't feel it was quite right to stand up against her on any of those issues.

Mary Jane: That's right. And if I did I used to feel guilty about it. And then—well, that sort of mixed me up. I didn't see why I should feel

---

[53] By this slightly interpretive analogy the counselor gives reassurance and encouragement when the client is feeling especially pained at facing her less acceptable characteristics of personality. The client seems to accept this interpretation when she remarks, "Very aptly put."

[54] The client expresses some positive feelings toward her mother along with the negative ones in recognizing the reason for her mother's overprotecting attitude.

[55] The simplicity of this recognition of feeling makes it almost epigrammatic in character; this clarity of recognition of feeling combined with originality and style of expression is acquired only through a rich clinical experience.

guilty about something I felt was the right thing to do, and then I thought, well, maybe it isn't right. That was the confusion all over again, because I didn't know my own mind, I didn't know what was really right.

C.R.: Those guilt feelings made you feel you couldn't trust yourself even though before you thought that you were right in standing up for something.

Mary Jane: That's right. I mean normally I guess a person would feel guilty, but not to the same extent. The point is I can see it now more clearly than I did before, but I still don't feel as though it can have a bearing on what I really do, I mean I still feel as though it's quite impossible and those things, those habits that I've formed are very strong.

C.R.: M-hm.

She is very discouraged by these thoughts, but feels that independence is "just a matter of practice, I guess." She has felt that she cannot guide herself, and that her only standards are the comparison she feels with others. "I guess my standard is what somebody else is doing, but actually that's the only thing I have to go by." There are long pauses and tears as she faces these thoughts about herself, and the interview ends with this discouraged theme.

Mary Jane: The point is, actually, can a person who has habits formed like that, can he, I mean can he do anything about it? It just seems so impossible to me. Is there anything you can do about it? I mean, it's fairly easy to read a book and everything else, and see what somebody else does and says, but if you can't feel it in yourself it just doesn't work.

C.R.: That's a very deep question you keep facing me with—whether a person who for twenty years has been guided by the thinking and standards of others could possibly feel that they could take the reins into their own hands.[56]

Mary Jane: That's right. The trouble with my answer is that the answer's always no. When I ask myself that question, the answer is always no.

She decided that from this time on she will come in every two weeks instead of every week.

---

[56] The counselor gives some reassurance when he implies that the question is a "very deep" one. It is as if he were saying, "I know it's difficult work facing these things."

TENTH INTERVIEW

January 28

At the beginning of the interview Mary Jane's statements show that more progress is being made, though her initial sentences still sound negative, as the first part of the interview will show.

C.R.: How goes it today?

Mary Jane: Well, this morning there's going to be no rain. I don't have any Kleenex, so there can't be any. *(Both laugh)*

C.R.: What is the weather like today?[57]

Mary Jane: Well, it's going to be overcast maybe, but it's not going to rain. There really isn't much change in my attitude; every time I come here I wonder what I'm going to say—actually there isn't much to say. That's how I feel. There's nothing for me to say.

C.R.: Before you come in, you feel there's just nothing.

Mary Jane: That's right. It seems to me I just repeat the same old story over and over again. I, well, I guess I have made some progress. I'm considering taking up millinery designing. I've always sort of wanted to do it, so I've decided I would, and I'm going to register this week. I don't expect what I used to expect from things, I mean I don't expect it to give me a lot of happiness or anything, I'm just going to take it because I want to. That's all.

C.R.: You feel that you've made progress, that you're doing something that you've wanted to do. Now that you decided to do it, you feel that you don't have any illusions about what will come from it, is that it?

Mary Jane: That's right. I mean, it just seems to me that it would be very interesting. It makes life more interesting for me if I have something like that. So—

C.R.: Sounds also as though that's something you decided for yourself—did by yourself.[58]

Mary Jane: That's right. And, of course, then mother starts taking that up as a crusade, I mean, she tries to help me along. Well, it still hasn't

---

[57] The counselor builds rapport by continuing in this humorous manner to accept the client's need to cry.

[58] The counselor here again tacitly implies approval in pointing out the fact that the client has demonstrated self-initiated activity in the direction of improvement.

squelched the desire to do it. I still resent her doing that. She's only trying to help me, I realize that. Still I resent it. Is that normal or natural, to resent it?

C.R.: It really gets you when she takes hold of something that you had started, and then tries to make a crusade of it or push it very hard.[59]

Mary Jane: That's right.

C.R.: You feel she's sort of taking it out of your hands—is that it?

Mary Jane: That's right. She doesn't mean to—I'm sure she doesn't mean it that way at all. She's just doing it because in the past I haven't stuck to anything. She just wants to help me along, that's about it. But, the thing is, when I get to a little independent stage, I resent it.

C.R.: M-hm.

She continues with a discussion of the fact that when she is feeling good she feels much more adventurous, and is now thinking of taking a very different and interesting job during the coming summer, with a girl with whom she has become friendly at work. She is sure her family would disapprove of the work, would think it beneath her, and this tends to make her waver. However, she looks back on the decisions they have made for her, and does not have much confidence in them. Of course, she does not have much confidence in herself either, but she begins to think better of her own choices. She indicates that she can understand her parents, but that now she knows she differs from their attitudes and standards. In expressing some of this feeling about her mother, she says:

Mary Jane: I realize lately that when my mother wants me to go out with her, I find that I'm not too happy to go with her, it's just her personality that I don't like. Now I realize that mine isn't what it should be but then I don't enjoy hers either, and it's sort of a guilty feeling, too.

C.R.: You feel that in some very real ways—you just don't like your mother particularly well, and it bothers you that you should feel that way.[60]

Mary Jane: That's right, because I know it's wrong, because I know she

---

[59] The counselor carefully avoids the reassurance requested here, but instead reflects the feeling of the client. The rule usually followed in the non-directive method is to avoid reassurance except when praising real progress that has been made, or to reassure by recognizing the intensity of the client's feeling, whatever it may be.

[60] The counselor responds to the ambivalence of the client's feeling.

has done so much for me, and yet—I think, well, maybe she hasn't done so much for me—she was trying to merge herself in her children—actually she did it too much, though. She was just escaping, I guess. She didn't want to face things. And then she complains that now it's all gone—I mean there's nothing left practically. Instead of developing her own interests. And yet she has a certain amount of happiness. It may be just a little but she's getting something.[61]

She speaks of the fact that she feels better recently, but adds:

Mary Jane: Although, of course, there's always still a little ghost that rides along with me.

C.R.: The minute you're out, the ghost is too.

Mary Jane: That's right. I still feel that when I go out with somebody, I mean, a man or a woman, I still feel as though I don't have anything to give.

C.R.: The old doubt that you could be worthwhile to anyone else. You still feel that your friendship doesn't offer very much to anyone else.

Mary Jane: *(Crying)* Here we go again. That always gets me.

C.R.: And the tears come because you don't feel as though you really are good for anything to anyone else.

Mary Jane: That's right. It's so silly.

C.R.: You think it's foolish to weep a little.

Mary Jane: That's right. Let's talk about something else.

C.R.: All right.

She asks for a book that she might read, and the title of Travis and Baruch, *Personal Problems of Everyday Life*, is given to her with the remark that she may find it helpful, and she may not.

She tells of a friend she has made, a very interesting girl, whom she rejected at first, but has now come to like. Her sister thinks this girl is inferior, and discourages the friendship. Mary Jane feels, however, that her sister has her crowd, a group which is suitable for her, but that she will make her own friends. She continues to discuss the family situation. Her

---

[61] Real insight is shown here in the client's being able to recognize the mother's weakness in assuming the attitude she has toward her children.

sister reacted to the family situation by getting away from it, but "me, well, it completely sunk me."

ELEVENTH INTERVIEW
February 10

(This interview is given in full from verbatim notes.)

Mary Jane: Well, I have been doing some very serious thinking this week. I got the book you suggested and I have been reading that. I've enjoyed it a lot. I've gotten a good many things from it.[62]

C.R.: You found that you have gained something from reading it.

Mary Jane: Yes, I have, and I also started the millinery course. I find it isn't a course in millinery design but more of a course in making hats, but I have been having a good time. You know I find myself holding myself back a little this time. I'm beginning to show real signs of benefit. I used to throw myself into any new thing and then tire of it very quickly. This time I'm going in it more naturally and calmly. I'm really changing.[63]

C.R.: You feel that you've really noticed that you're becoming a different kind of person.

Mary Jane: Yes, I haven't felt so up until recently, but now I begin to realize that's true. A girl I've been going with, a girl I've gotten to know—she's helped me a lot. You know my idea of what I should be is changing. I always had ideas that were too high. I've always had a definite feeling of the kind of person I should be and now some of those thoughts are changing.

---

[62] The use of the technique of suggesting reading when the client requests it is commented on in the case of Robert Winslow Smith. In the present case, it seems to be of some real help, as indicated in this interview. It is interesting that in her previous reading of books the client did not make very satisfactory use of the material she had read. Perhaps the reason she is able to now is that she is now prepared to assimilate the reading after having passed some of her emotional blockings. Of course, it must be admitted that the material read is different, too.

[63] In this and numerous subsequent statements, the insights and discussion of plans occur with amazing rapidity, showing that as the client begins to make progress in understanding herself the process picks up speed, each forward step apparently making the next one easier.

C.R.: You feel that where you used to be trying for something way up high now it is different.

Mary Jane: Yes. Well, in school I used to get good marks and all. Take for instance in Latin—I used to just memorize the Latin and got very good grades. The only ones that were as good as me were some of the boys, but they didn't memorize it, they really learned it. And it was all very confusing to me because I knew that I didn't know it nearly as well as they did.

C.R.: You feel that with you it was just something that you parroted, while with them it was something that they really had learned for themselves and knew in themselves.

Mary Jane: Yes. The thing I can't understand is that I have always given the impression of knowing things that I really don't know.

C.R.: You feel that you put up a good front but underneath you have not made the knowledge really yours.

Mary Jane: When I read a book like this, I find I'm like other people in some ways and I can really begin to see I'm not entirely different from everyone else and I feel some measure of happiness. I begin to realize that someone else has something in common with me.

C.R.: You feel that you're not entirely different from others and that you can get some measure of happiness for yourself.

Mary Jane: Yes. So I've made a decision that I wonder if it is right. When you're in a family where your brother has gone to college and everybody has a good mind, I wonder if it is right to see that I am as I am and I can't achieve such things. I've always tried to be what the others thought I should be, but now I'm wondering whether I shouldn't just see that I am what I am.

C.R.: You feel that in the past you lived by others' standards and you are not sure just what is the right thing to do, but you're beginning to feel that the best thing for you is simply to accept yourself as you are.

Mary Jane: Yes. *(Pause)* Of course, some people might say that that idea would block progress—that if you just accept yourself as you are, then you wouldn't get anywhere. Do you think that is right? *(Pause)* Still, I've tried the other thing and I know that doesn't work.

C.R.: You realize that some people might think your present attitude would keep you from moving ahead, but you know within yourself that you tried adopting standards that were not your own and that doesn't work.

Mary Jane: That's right. Maybe I ought to accept the fact that I'm a dumbbell and not try to be something that I'm not. Is that right, Doctor? *(Laughs)*

C.R.: You sound as though you had your mind pretty well made up yourself and that you had decided to try to accept yourself as you are.

Mary Jane: Well, I guess that is so. I don't see what it is that has changed me so much. Yes, I do. These talks have helped a lot, and then the books that I've read. Well, I've just noticed such a difference. I find that when I feel things, even when I feel hate, I don't care. I don't mind. I feel more free somehow. I don't feel guilty about things.

C.R.: You feel as though these talks and the thinking you've been doing have just changed you so you feel more comfortable with yourself.

Mary Jane: Yes. *(Pause)*

C.R.: You find that you can even feel hatred toward somebody and not be bothered about it.

Mary Jane: Yes. I just don't care. You know it's suddenly as though a big cloud has been lifted off. I feel so much more content. Up to now I hadn't been willing to admit that I have changed much, but I begin to feel that I have.

C.R.: You feel that all this has made a great deal of difference in your own comfort. I've noticed the changes, too, and have wondered when you would break through and realize that they have occurred.[64]

Mary Jane: Well, the friendship with this girl has helped me a lot too. She and her husband have really accepted me. They tell me I'm as bright as other people. Oh, of course, that is flattery, but it has helped me, and then just the fact that they really seem to like me, that has made a lot of difference.[65]

---

[64] This statement is frankly approving in character. The counselor's indication that he has seen the changes coming might not be too helpful to the client, however, who might be inclined to wonder, then, whether the counselor could not have said something to encourage her a little earlier.

[65] It should be recognized that outside situations can contribute to the client's adjustment process; in this case, the friendship with the married couple seems to have done so. Perhaps the more significant fact, however, is that the client reached the point of being able to make the effort to cultivate this friendship, and then to gain help from it. It is doubtful if this would have been possible before the treatment started.

C.R.: You have felt that you have built up a real relationship there and it has helped to have them like you.

Mary Jane: The thing is that I've always been striving to be what other people have wanted me to be—my family mostly. I couldn't be satisfied with what I might really be. I've always tried to live up to what others have wanted.

C.R.: The standards you have been trying to reach have always been out in other people, not something you have really believed in yourself.

Mary Jane: Part of the trouble is my parents. They have never really sat down to talk with me. I don't think they understand me. Of course, my father has always been proud of things I have done and when I would bring home a good mark he would praise me. Well, that's it. I've always just lived for his praise and that is why I've felt it awful if I fail to come up to what they expect. I guess that is the kind of relationship it has been with them.

C.R.: You feel that rather than any relationship of understanding, you've just lived for a pat on the back from your dad.

Mary Jane: Yes. I think that is what has been the matter. Of course, until I was seven I was the youngest and they, they made a lot of me, and then, of course, when my younger sister came along and I suppose I sort of lost out and they—well, I suppose that is why it meant too much to me to have them praise me. You know that you read about things like that in books but—(pause).

C.R.: Now you've come to understand that sort of situation in your own experience.

Mary Jane: Yes, that's it. (Pause) The thing is I've always had a feeling of looking down upon someone who is dumb. I've never wanted to be that kind and I never would look at anything in myself that contradicted the notion of being superior.

C.R.: It made you afraid of looking clearly at yourself.

Mary Jane: Yes. Now I have begun to think if there is one other person

[66] The client has decided to accept herself, rather than try to be someone different. The theoretical question might here be raised as to whether the client is as "dumb" as she thinks she is. Many of her responses in this treatment suggest that she has a fairly good mentality. The philosophy which motivates the non-directive method holds that it makes little difference regarding the real situation. The aspect that is important is the client's attitude toward her intelligence. Even very bright people frequently cannot be convinced of their superiority if they have emotionally satisfying reasons for believing themselves inferior.

like me in the world then I can get along. Other people get along without lots of ability. I have the right to exist, too.[66]

C.R.: You've come to believe that you can get along like others.

Mary Jane: Well, take like my sister—she is willing to admit that she is dumb. I talked to her about that. I said, "How can you go with somebody you know is brighter than you are and not feel badly about it?" And she said, "Well, in some ways I always think that I'm better than they are."

C.R.: You feel that she has come to accept the fact that, although the other person might be brighter, still she thinks, "I've got some good qualities, too."

Mary Jane: Yes. Well, she's comfortable and content so she gets along well with other people.

C.R.: Looking at herself that way makes it easier for her to adjust to others. *(Pause)*

Mary Jane: So you see I've come a long way. I've faced some of these things. I've realized I'm not so bright, but I begin to think I can get along anyway.

C.R.: Yes, you have come a long way and you really have faced some of these things pretty deeply.[67]

Mary Jane: You know I've come to accept the idea of marriage, too. I have the idea—well, I read it in a book somewhere and I agree with it—I've read that if a person's basic needs are not met in marriage, that is what spoils the marriage, and I think, well, if I can find a man who meets some of the needs that I have and if he can feel that I meet the needs that he has, then O.K., and if I can't find such a person then I just won't get married.

C.R.: You're comfortable about the fact that if you can find a mutually congenial partnership, well, then, you will get married. If not, you think you can live without it. *(Pause)*

Mary Jane: So that is my story. *(Laughs)* You know, I've gone bowling and I've gone out with the girls. I've been much more active than I used to be.[68]

---

[67] Here again is frank counselor approval. Rogers feels it is probably satisfying to the counselor rather than helpful to the client.

[68] The client is making numerous efforts to improve her adjustment; this is the action-taking aspect of the treatment which indicates that real progress is being made.

C.R.: You really have been making friendships and taking yourself out into social activities.

Mary Jane: Yes. Well, there is one girl—she lived with her grandmother when she was young and her grandmother wouldn't let her play with friends, so until she was older she didn't have any chance for mixing. She tells me that just lately she has been able to mix a little with people. And you know, being with her—that has helped. I feel somehow that we can sort of do it together.

C.R.: You feel that both of you are facing similar situations and that makes it easier.

Mary Jane: Yes. There is one other thing I have to face. Now take like the fact that she is in commercial art and she is good at it. Well, with all these people, I feel that in some ways they are like me, but she is good in something. I still have that terrible feeling down inside that I'm not good at anything. There isn't anything that I can do well.

C.R.: You still have that terrible feeling that there isn't anything that you can point to—any solid achievement that you have had.

Mary Jane: No, I wouldn't need to point to it if I had the feeling inside of myself. *(Pause)* Of course, it helps to understand why I haven't had any real achievement. I begin to see why all this has happened the way it has.

C.R.: Even though you would like the achievement, it helps to understand the basis for the lack of it.

Mary Jane: Yes. I've also met a woman in my millinery class. She is a silly person. She doesn't seem to have much ability, but everyone accepts her and she told how her boy came home—she is a married woman—and told her he had to write a paper on the atomic bomb and wanted her to help him. She laughed and said, "I told him I couldn't help him. I'm dumb. He has a smart father. He should get his father to help him." You know, that made me feel good. She could face it and accept it and laugh about it. I thought that was really good.[69]

C.R.: You really respected the fact that she could realize the limitations of her own ability.

---

[69] No counselor could put more clearly the need which this client felt that her own statement does when she describes her friend as being able to "face it and accept it and laugh about it," referring, of course, to her own inferiority. In the next statement, she brings up the deeper aspect of her problem, that is, could any husband accept her lower ability?

Mary Jane: Yes, but how can her husband accept her? Can a man accept a woman who is a lot lower than he is in ability? What do you think?

C.R.: I expect we all see examples of that.[70]

Mary Jane: Well, yes, I suppose so. I think her husband could accept it perhaps and probably feel good about being superior to her. But then can he go with her and meet friends with her and not feel ashamed of her?

C.R.: You feel that the discrepancy might be so great that it would really make him ashamed of her and unhappy in that way.

Mary Jane: Yes. Of course, when I ask that question, I'm asking for myself. I tell myself that it is O.K. for you to accept yourself. I am what I am. And even with my friends, I can see how they can accept me better if I am more natural, but in something more permanent and intimate like marriage, could a person accept you if you didn't have a good mind?

C.R.: You feel that being your real self makes you more comfortable, and makes your friends comfortable in accepting you, but could it work in a permanent relationship?

Mary Jane: That's right. *(Pause)* On the other hand, I suppose you can balance it off. The other person might be very intelligent but might have a serious fault that would make it hard for him to get along with people. That would sort of balance it off perhaps.

C.R.: You feel that the husband might have real flaws in his personality which would sort of make up for a slight lack of ability on your part.

Mary Jane: You say it is a slight lack; it seems very great to me. I don't think I'll ever get over what I wanted to be. Of course, though, I suppose everybody wants better things, but I don't know whether I'll really get over not being able to reach the standards that I've always thought about.[71]

---

[70] In reply to a direct question the counselor here gives a reassuring answer. While this may be helpful to the client, it is interesting to note that she merely comes back with some expression of doubt and a more insistent request for reassurance. When, however, her need of reassurance is reflected, she seems somewhat more ready to accept the idea that she could be acceptable. It takes some more reflection on her part, however, before she seems greatly convinced. But in her next statement she starts to recognize that intelligence may not be the only attribute a person may bring into marriage, and that she might be able to make up for the deficiency of the partner in some respects.

[71] The client does not intend to let the counselor minimize in any way the severity of her shortcomings; she is quite convinced that they exist. In her next statement, the client herself describes the signs of improvement.

C.R.: Your deficiency seems pretty great to you and you wonder if you really ever will give up the heights you used to want.

Mary Jane: Well, I certainly am better. Yesterday I could go to a meeting and not wonder what all the others were thinking about me. And then I went to a dance and danced without thinking all about myself. There is improvement.

C.R.: You recognize that there is really a big change in yourself.

Mary Jane: Yes. My, you are getting a lot written down there.

C.R.: You've said a lot.[72]

Mary Jane: Well, that's one thing, too. It is very easy for me to talk now. I don't think so much about what I'm saying. You know you read books and it tells you to build up the other person when you are talking to him and to think of something that will establish a common bond. Well, I did it very consciously and when I start thinking too deeply about something like that it just makes me anxious and it doesn't work. Is that natural?

C.R.: I suppose it is. You found, at any rate, when you work so planfully at it, it just didn't get across and now you feel more comfortable with yourself and less anxious about the whole thing.

Mary Jane: Well, right now I feel I'm using instinct more than I ever did before. Remember what I said at first about how some people could go by their natural feelings and I always had to think what I did? Now I find that I can just act natural.

C.R.: You feel that you're being guided more by the real feelings within yourself than you used to be.

Mary Jane: Yes. I'm much more comfortable, too, with the people I'm working with. I think that it is partly because I have been there now for awhile. It takes me awhile to build up any feeling of confidence. You know I'm finding that by taking an interest in the customers, everything goes much better. Instead of thinking about myself or making a sale, I just get interested in them and really try to help them. It takes longer to deal with a customer that way, but I like it better.

C.R.: You're putting out more of your interest in them.

Mary Jane: Yes, and the customers thank me for it. That helps me build

---

[72] Here again the counselor, apparently feeling that the client is well along the way to self-understanding, gives reassurance in this unique fashion.

up my confidence. You know, I really help them think through what they really like. (*She tells of an incident in which she felt particularly good about a sale.*) I guess it is even more profitable that way, because the customers come back to me.

C.R.: You're finding that forgetting yourself and forgetting sales is really good business in the long run.

Mary Jane: Yes. That's right, so—actually, if I failed I'd be down in the dumps, failed in my job I mean, but I've been told that I'm doing nicely and that I'm getting along well. So being more interested in them has helped me.

C.R.: You're really getting a feeling of success out of that job.

Mary Jane: Well, I find people more responsive to me now. They think better of me and they talk to me more easily. I'm more friendly and I guess they sense it.

C.R.: You feel that being more natural yourself has made people respond to you.

Mary Jane: Yes. (*Pause*) Though even as I say this, I have a fear that it may not be permanent. I want to be honest about it, and I just don't know if this can really last.

C.R.: You're sure that these things have happened, but still it seems to you that it might be too good to be true, that you might slump again.

Mary Jane: Yes, I've had times before when I've been up.

C.R.: You feel this might be just another temporary wave of encouragement.

Mary Jane: Well, I doubt it. I think I know now if there is a down or slump, it is because I'm impatient with myself. You know, that is always a part of my trouble. I just can't wait to get there and if I should get discouraged it would be because of that.[73]

C.R.: You feel if you do get discouraged it will be primarily because you're impatient about getting somewhere in too much of a hurry.

Mary Jane: That's right. And then I wonder—I get afraid that maybe I'll get tired of myself this way. That's what always happened to me before. You know I told you I would try to be a different kind of person but then I'd get tired of it.

---

[73] Although the client herself wonders whether her new feelings are going to remain with her permanently, she herself seems to believe that there is not too much question about their doing so.

C.R.: You think that you have a new self now, but that you might not like it in time.

Mary Jane: Well, I see other people and some of them seem to be quite boring people, and they don't seem to get tired of themselves. Maybe I won't either. The point is I feel I've made a real start. I no longer want to be superior. I just want to feel equal to people. In fact, if I'm like the least person it is O.K.

C.R.: You feel that that is very important, that you no longer desire to be above everybody but if you can even be equal to some of them you can then live with yourself and feel it will be all right.

Mary Jane: Well, I've made myself realize that I can't be a certain type of person. If I didn't accept that idea, I would be very unhappy. You know I've always felt that—well, you know bright girls can go to college, they can make a name for themselves and all, and I've always tried so hard to be that kind of girl but I can't. I've just got to realize that I'm not that sort of person. And then the fact that most of my relatives are that kind of people, it has made it hard, do you see what I mean?

C.R.: You've always respected and looked up to that intellectual group and now it comes kind of hard to accept the fact that perhaps you don't belong there but in another group.

Mary Jane: Yes, that's just it.

C.R.: I see our time is up. Will you be wanting to come back or not?

Mary Jane: Well, I think I would like to leave it this way—I'll call you and let you know. You know, I felt this wouldn't do any good, but it has. But I don't want to get out of touch with you. I don't feel quite steady yet. I think that probably I would like to come in in three weeks, but I'll call you.

C.R.: All right. You call the office and they'll give you an appointment even if I'm not in. You really have come a long way in your thinking, haven't you?

Mary Jane: Good-bye—and thanks.

C.R.: Good-bye.

Significant Feelings Expressed in the Eleventh Interview

1. I am taking a new course of my own choosing.
2. I am really changing.
3. I have had too high ideals for myself, but those are changing.
4. I have always tried to live up to a false front which wasn't genuine.

5. I realize I am actually like other people.
6. I wonder if I should be what I am instead of what others think I should be.
7. I believe that is what I want to do.
8. I have changed a great deal.
9. I am no longer afraid or guilty about my feelings.
10. I feel more free.
11. I feel more content.
12. I haven't been willing to admit that I have changed, but I have.
13. I have been helped by these talks, by books, by a friendship I have made.
14. I understand how my family relationships made me what I was.
15. I've come to realize that I'm not so bright, but I can get along anyway.
16. I can accept marriage, if it comes, or accept the lack of it.
17. I've been out much more with friends and enjoy it.
18. I find it easier to make social adjustments with another girl who has had similar difficulties.
19. I still feel that I'm not good at anything specific.
20. I admire people who can accept their limitations.
21. I wonder if a husband could accept a wife who lacked ability.
22. I guess I could balance that lack with other positive qualities.
23. I no longer think so much about myself.
24. I talk more freely than I used to.
25. I find I can just act natural, be guided by my real feelings.
26. I'm much more comfortable with people.
27. I'm getting a feeling of success out of my job.
28. I'm fearful this may not last, but I think it will.
29. I'm afraid I may tire of my new self, but I don't think I will.
30. It's really hard for me to accept abilities as not being superior, but I am doing it.
31. I feel this has really helped.
32. I don't feel quite steady yet, and would like to feel that I can come for more help if I need it.

FOLLOW-UP INFORMATION

Following the conclusion of the counseling interviews Mary Jane continued to hold her position. She engaged more actively in social life. Also, she went with her family on a trip and here, too, was much more socially active. In general her improvement seemed to be beyond question in the ten months following the conclusion of the counseling interviews.

Shortly after a year had elapsed Mary Jane was invited to come in for a follow-up interview. At that time she reported that until recently things had been going much better for her but that within the past two months many of the old feelings of futility had returned. She reported that she had recently given up her job. Some of her conversation in talking about herself sounded very much like a repetition of the first interviews. She also raised the question of whether perhaps something "stronger" was needed to help her. She wondered if she ought to go to a psychiatrist. The counselor expressed willingness to help her find such a resource or to have her return for further counseling, but left the decision up to her. She stated she would telephone for an appointment or information if she desired it. She did not call. The only intimation she gave for the cause of her slump was that a boy friend with whom she had been going had seemed to her to look down upon her as a person of little ability. She felt this had tended to destroy her confidence.

Some weeks later a telephone conversation with her mother indicated that Mary Jane was getting along more satisfactorily. She had another job with a relative and seemed again more cheerful and better adjusted.

It will be seen that the evaluation of final outcome in this case remains somewhat in doubt. There can be no question that the eleven counseling hours were followed by a period of improved adjustment. Whether the recent regression is temporary remains to be seen.

CLIENT-CENTERED THERAPY AND UNDIVIDED ATTENTION

The Case of Mary Jane Tilden

Robert E. Dingman

And always there is this struggle to reach a state where there is no pain, where there is no disorder. But the very attempt to bring about order seems to increase disorder, or bring about other problems.

—J. Krishnamurti, *Krishnamurti to Himself* (1987), p. 54

The organization of personality is, like a good golf stroke, not always best achieved by focusing consciously on it.

—Carl R. Rogers, *Client-Centered Therapy* (1951a), p. 100

To strive toward a particular form, image, or model of what one *should be*, is to deepen division and chaos within the self, to be cut off from the reality of experience. Such an effort, whether by counselor or client, will necessarily fail to resolve conflict. Such patterning imposed upon immediate experience implies suppression and subjugation, a denial of unacknowledged and unorganized attitudes and feelings. In October 1946, 20-year-old Mary Jane Tilden seemed exhausted from just such an effort, the fight to embody the attitudes and behaviors she thought appropriate for someone her age. She envied her younger sister's easy give and take with friends. She felt abnormal, left behind, flawed, as she compared herself to others approaching marriage and autonomy. Living at home with her parents, Mary Jane felt excluded from life, an onlooker, a spectator. She longed to "be natural," to be herself, only to be accused of acting when she tried. Mary Jane, vacillating between enormous desire to "fix" herself and

200

certainty that she never would, compared herself brutally to those around her and concluded that there was something dreadfully wrong with her.

In her first interview with Rogers, Mary Jane rapidly catalogued her strategies for change that had failed. She had done battle with herself, tried to reason with and convince herself, tried to learn from books, and tried to imitate and practice what others did—and always within her something would not be changed:

Mary Jane: And I don't seem to be able to conquer it. I mean it just—every day seems to be over and over again the same little things that shouldn't matter.

Mary Jane: I should be able to look above these things and sort of be able to reason with myself, but I don't seem to be able to.

Willpower, effort, ambition—none of these produced change in Mary Jane, or assisted her to feel "natural" and at ease. Instead, they only deepened the conflict within her:

Mary Jane: I still don't think that just by not thinking about those things for a month or two months and trying to think about other things—still I don't feel as though it would have changed me much.

She wanted desperately to be different, to move out of the stagnant waters in which she lived. Yet no amount of judgment or self-reproach, of viewing herself with contempt, could transform her into the young woman she envisioned. Mary Jane, even early in her therapy, sensed the futility of this severe evaluation: "The point is, does just seeing it as ridiculous, does that change it?"

Mary Jane wanted relief from the heavy weight of self, from thinking ceaselessly about herself. She did not measure up, feared that the best in life—love and marriage—would pass her by. Aware that she was divided, Mary Jane could not escape the thought that "what I am" is far from "what I should be":

Mary Jane: I've tried looking at other people and sort of losing myself and trying to forget myself when I'm with them . . . but as soon as I start thinking about what I am, I have such a terrible conflict at what I am that it sort of (Laughs)—it makes me feel awful.

"What I am" seemed ugly and repulsive, not possibly of value. Pushing away hard, Mary Jane's heroic efforts to change only bound her more to a regressive, deteriorating path. She could not bear the thought:

Mary Jane: I seem to be going backward all the time. In fact, I don't see any reason why I should be living. Sometimes I think about committing suicide, too, because I can't find any justification in living the way I do.

Mary Jane asked repeatedly for answers from Rogers, for new strategies to change herself. Rogers consistently chose not to do this, despite her insistence and frustration. As Mary Jane strained to conform to the values and behavior she thought appropriate for someone her age, Rogers refrained from advising or guiding. He refrained from explaining her problems or the process of therapy, from setting up yet another external standard to be met, against which Mary Jane might have compared and measured herself. Rogers chose instead to remain empathically present, to understand her frustration and confusion without prescription for change. He simply would not undermine Mary Jane's movement toward encountering fully the "what I am" by providing "answers." Rogers spoke forcefully to the consequences of such a counselor choice:

> It is possible to explain a person to himself, to prescribe steps which should lead him forward, to train him in knowledge about a more satisfying mode of life. But such methods are, in my experience, futile and inconsequential. The most they can accomplish is some temporary change, which soon disappears, leaving the individual more than ever convinced of his inadequacy. (Rogers, 1963, p. 33)

More than an experience about self, client-centered therapy is an experiencing *of* self. (Rogers, 1951a, p. 108) And thus, within the empathic enclosure that Rogers provided, Mary Jane's introspective, intellectual interest in self shifted slowly to more primary experiencing. Gradually, Mary Jane abandoned her desperate search to be repaired, or to fix herself, and instead she focused her attention increasingly, though tentatively at first, on her ongoing perceptions of herself, her actual sensory and visceral reactions. She began by considering what she truly wanted and encountered a void:

Mary Jane: There's one thing that I can't quite make up my mind—I've tried to figure it out—well, what is it, when I get into a rut like this, what is it that I really want? And when I examine myself I can't figure out what I really want. It's only by looking at what other people want that I think, well, maybe that's what I want.

Here, instead of the tactical planning about how to change, an exploring quality emerged, a simple observing of the "what I am" that only a short time ago was unapproachable. Mary Jane looked inward, fearfully, and realized that she could find no solid ground upon which to build:

Mary Jane: Every human being has desires—they really want things quite badly. And it seems to me that somewhere I should have those desires too. And yet I—when I sit down and try to think about it I can't.

She wondered if some desire authentically her own might possibly provide the guidance she craved:

Mary Jane: If I felt a strong desire for something, and it were really an honest and sincere desire, maybe other things would come along. . . . I don't have that sure feeling of what I should do next, and that in itself bothers me.

As Rogers listened, Mary Jane slowly expressed the deeper, more disrupting divisions within her. She spoke of having believed since childhood that she was somehow special, and of how this attitude was contradicted by the poor standard she attained. She had been the teacher's pet, and she was a lawyer's daughter, conditioned to believe she was better than other children. She was often praised for mediocre efforts. Mary Jane spoke of her terrible uncertainty about her own abilities and the values that this had left her with, the unrealistic belief that she would or should not have to struggle. Late in the third interview, Mary Jane, ridden with shame, confronted this attitude:

Mary Jane: I guess I've always felt that it's sort of a shame—or sort of something to be ashamed of not to have things perfect or to be struggling with something. . . . I think that's the way I've always been but I didn't really know it. *(Long pause)* . . . That's just something . . . I've always had and not really known.

Later, Mary Jane brought up with Rogers a central conflict—her battle with the part of her that resisted change, the powerful doubting part. It was a dark, negative presence: "There's a very definite force that is negative all the time."

Rogers did not interfere with Mary Jane's exploration of this dangerous, uncharted territory. He continued his empathic listening, without attempting to redirect or influence Mary Jane's experience, a practice that is extremely difficult without a deep belief in the forward-moving tendencies of the human organism:

C.R.: It's almost that when you want to turn in a positive direction that an even stronger force within you throws up all kinds of doubt about it.

Mary Jane: Yes, that's right. *(Pause)* And then because it's so strong, I just accept it, I guess because it seems to be the bigger thing, so I guess I just accept it.

C.R.: You feel that your doubting force is definitely stronger than your constructive force.

Mary Jane: Yes. *(Very long pause)* That's just it. *(Pause)* I guess I've always believed the other one because I've built it up so high and then I believe that it's true because it's so big. *(Very long pause)* That's something I've never thought about. *(Very long pause)* It seems that the more I ever try to drive it out, the louder it yells.

Here a new insight emerged: the discovery that her resistance, her battle to drive out the presence, to divorce herself from an unwanted portion of self, had deepened the division. In response, Rogers made no effort to diminish Mary Jane's feeling of powerlessness, to give her something to fight with, to bolster her defenses against an occupying, overwhelming force. The empathic union continued:

C.R.: You just felt that the armies of doubt are definitely unbeatable armies.

Mary Jane: M-hm. Yeah.

C.R.: And that the other is a pretty weak and struggling thing.

Mary Jane: *(Laughs)* Yeah, that's right. *(Very long pause)* . . . That just about states the whole thing in a nut-shell—that I have always been willing—in other words, I guess I just didn't want to fight—and I was always more willing to believe the other than to put up a big fight or something.

These statements from Mary Jane had a new, objective tone. The attitudes expressed seem free of harsh judgment, the thick crust of self-condemnation that marked so much of her earlier therapy. In these statements she simply *was* the beaten, defeated child who could no longer resist, who came to believe she could never be free of doubt or shame:

C.R.: You feel you kind of tossed in an unconditional surrender rather than—just because you believed the other forces were impossibly strong.

Mary Jane: That's right. *(Pause)* I mean instead of trying to remedy the situation or trying to do better, I just sort of shut it off.

The very long pauses contained in these moments, the weeping later to come, seem important to the unified perception, the undivided attention, and immediate un-self-conscious contact with primary visceral data so central to Mary Jane's healing. These indeed were perhaps the very moments of assimilation of denied experience into a new and living Gestalt. Although language—Mary Jane's verbal self-exploration, and Rogers' verbal empathic support of her—brought her to the doorstep of this unified perception, the use of language also implies the most basic division of subject and object, of experience and experiencer, and must be relinquished for an unmediated contact to occur. In Mary Jane's silence, in her weeping, even this division was extinguished.

Far from having arranged this new pattern, Mary Jane simply was discovering that she was changing. Her attitudes about her self clearer and more acceptable, her anger and resentment over her parents' treatment of her finding expression, Mary Jane's emerging perceptions of self were abstracted from, and grounded in, her own basic experience "rather than being a formulation or structure which is imposed upon experience" (Rogers, 1951b, p. 323). Long after having worked with Mary Jane, Rogers (1951a) quoted this stunning articulation, by a different client, of this strangely effortless falling-into-place of experience:

> You know, it seems as if all the energy that went into holding the arbitrary pattern together was quite unnecessary—a waste. You think you have to make the pattern yourself; but there are so many pieces, and it's so hard to see where they fit. Sometimes you put them in the wrong place, and the more pieces mis-fitted, the more effort it takes to hold them in place, until at last you are so tired that even that awful confusion is better than holding on any longer. Then you discover that left to themselves the jumbled pieces fall quite naturally into their own places, and a living pattern emerges without any effort at all on your part. Your job is just to discover it, and in the course of that, you will find yourself and your own place. (p. 97)

That this discovery of longed-for change was occurring on its own late in Mary Jane's sessions with Rogers, outside of her direct awareness and curiously without effort, seems clear. Although her process was neither smooth nor linear, late in her therapy many of Mary Jane's jumbled, disordered pieces came together quickly.

Mary Jane's behavior seemed to change and be modified in accordance with her changing self-concept, often with little awareness on her part. Following the pivotal third interview—the first horrifying look inside—after missing two appointments and nearly dropping the therapy, Mary Jane reported attending a social gathering at home after weeks of isolation. Here she felt she had really forgotten to think so much about herself. A few weeks later, while arguing that she only felt worse, she related to Rogers that she had gone out to her sister's home, had spoken with others, and had been influenced positively by a young woman.

Many of Mary Jane's significant behavioral changes seemed, astonishingly, to accompany her gnawing hopelessness, her certainty that she would never be different from the way she was. In the sixth interview Mary Jane stated not only her deep conviction that she would never change but also her fear that people would find out what she was really like. One week later she indicated that she was seriously considering going back to work, and the next week she began a new job. A month later, while complaining that therapy seemed like just going over and over the same territory, Mary Jane related her growing interest in a millinery class but saw this as only a modest gain. Later still she entered the class and spoke of meeting a girl with whom she felt comfortable. She went bowling. She attended a party. She danced without thinking about herself.

These changes in behavior, "neither as painful nor as difficult as the changes in self-structure" (Rogers, 1951b, p. 325), were barely noticed by Mary Jane until much later. In her last interview, when the significance of such changes began to flood her awareness, Mary Jane described with joy an experience she could previously neither will nor feign—being natural, comfortable with herself among others:

Mary Jane: Remember what I said at first about how some people could go by their natural feelings and I always had to think what I did? Now I find that I can just act natural.

An additional, paradoxical aspect of Mary Jane's therapy was that as more and more of her organismic experiences were available to awareness, her "self" as an object of awareness tended to disappear. How odd to consider that this most excruciating examination and experiencing of self should eventuate in less rather than more self-consciousness. In her final session Mary Jane expressed the wonderful freedom this entailed:

Mary Jane: Yesterday I could go to a meeting and not wonder what all the others were thinking about me. And then I went to a dance and danced without thinking at all about myself.

Mary Jane: It is very easy for me to talk now. I don't think so much about what I'm saying.

Mary Jane: Right now I feel I'm using instinct more than I ever did before.

Mary Jane: You know I'm finding that by taking an interest in the customers, everything goes much better. Instead of thinking about myself or making a sale, I just get interested in them and really try to help them. It takes longer to deal with a customer that way, but I like it better.

Years after counseling Mary Jane, Rogers quoted from a session with her, and then interpreted the heavy, somber preoccupation with self of the maladjusted person:

> Frequently a client at the beginning of therapy expresses real fear that others might discover [her] real self. "As soon as I start thinking about what I am, I have such terrible conflict at what I am that it makes me feel awful. . . I'm afraid to act natural, I guess, because I just don't feel as though I like myself." In this frame of mind behavior must always be guarded, cautious, self-conscious. But when this same client has come to accept deeply the fact that "I am what I am," then she can be spontaneous and can lose her self-consciousness. (Rogers, 1951a, p. 515)

Although only 11 sessions occurred between Rogers and Mary Jane, although the conclusion of therapy seems stunning, perhaps difficult to believe, Mary Jane demonstrated through many of her statements a growing understanding of the process of change, a growing acceptance and prizing of self. Near the end, Mary Jane realized that her desire to sweep away "what I am," her ongoing undercurrent of experience, her desire to replace it with an imposed structure, is what originally caused her so much pain. She would be wary of the return of that desire:

Mary Jane: I think I know now if there is a down or slump, it is because I'm impatient with myself. You know, that is always a part of my trouble. I just can't wait to get there and if I should get discouraged it would be because of that.

Mary Jane: I've made myself realize that I can't be a certain type of person. If I didn't accept that idea, I would be very unhappy.

By February of 1947, after only 4 months of therapy, Mary Jane experienced the beginnings of a freedom she had longed for but could not force, the freedom to simply be her experience without judgment:

Mary Jane: I find that when I feel things, even when I feel hate, I don't care. I don't mind. I feel more free somehow. I don't feel guilty about things.

By the end of their relationship the deep, enveloping acceptance that Mary Jane experienced from Rogers characterized more and more the attitude she took toward herself. More comfortable with the "what I am," Mary Jane no longer sought "what should be":

Mary Jane: I've always tried to be what the others thought I should be, but now I'm wondering whether I shouldn't just see that I am what I am.

Mary Jane: I've always been striving to be what other people have wanted me to be—my family mostly. I couldn't be satisfied with what I might really be.

Mary Jane: The actuality of it is that I never really knew what the real 'me' was—it was all covered over really, and I got to thinking it was me.

Movement toward adjustment, for Mary Jane, involved surrender of all structures imposed upon experience, of her preoccupation with *becoming* a specific kind of person with specific qualities and abilities. The healing of division, the reorganization of self to include deeply denied aspects of experience, occurred precisely when in a prizing and empathic relationship Mary Jane's resistance to the "what I am" ceased. Evaluation, comparison, analysis, the longing to be what one is not—all this somehow had to die for the new "living pattern" to emerge. Client-centered therapy, perhaps uniquely among all therapies, acknowledges these obstructions to immediate, undistorted perception, and seeks to avoid them. It seeks not to reinforce what the client must dissolve: the resistance to a simple, undivided attention to the ongoing flow of current experience.

A counselor or client wish for some other state of affairs in the relationship, for a more acceptable self or a quickened process, precludes this quality of attention, and it creates a barrier that must somehow be relinquished for the direct contact that Rogers believed was so healing to occur.

Willpower, on the part of counselor or client, is not the factor of change. Mary Jane demonstrated abundantly that straining to be "herself" only deepened her isolation and conflict. Rogers carefully avoided the numerous subtle contaminants to this friction-free listening, and he staked the entire outcome of Mary Jane's therapy on an absorption of himself into her attitudes and perceptions, to see Mary Jane as she saw herself, without resistance or comparison to others:

> We have come to recognize that if we can provide understanding of the way the client seems to himself at this moment, he can do the rest. The therapist must lay aside his preoccupation with diagnosis and diagnostic shrewdness, must discard his tendency to make professional evaluations, must cease his endeavors to formulate an accurate prognosis, must give up the temptation subtly to guide the individual, and must concentrate on one purpose only; that of providing deep understanding and acceptance of the attitudes consciously held at this moment by the client as he explores step by step into the dangerous areas which he has been denying to consciousness. (Rogers, 1951a, p. 30)

In Mary Jane's moments of deepest pain, any reassurance, reframing, or explanation would have been to resist, to have communicated that such raw experiencing is not trustworthy, that it cannot possibly lead to order. To make contact with Mary Jane, to receive her unconditionally, required of Rogers a personal understanding that order flows from the basic experiencing of the human organism and cannot be imposed. As he facilitated, through steadfast acceptance and accurate empathy, a loosening of the patterns fastened to Mary Jane's experience, so did Rogers extend to himself this same freedom, to *be* his experience in the relationship. The result, he states, is potent:

> Yet the paradoxical aspect of my experience is that the more I am simply willing to be myself, in all this complexity of life, and the more I am willing to understand and accept the realities in myself and in the other person, the more change seems to be stirred up. It is a very paradoxical thing—that to the degree that each one of us is willing to be himself, then he finds not only himself changing; but he finds that other people to whom he relates are also changing. (Rogers, 1963, p. 22)

Rogers came to see this congruence as central among all the conditions he postulated for a helping relationship (Rogers, 1986, p. 131). Late in his life he described one of those rare moments when, with friction between "what I am" and "what I should be" suspended, with perhaps no awareness of "self" apparent in either counselor or client, a profound, unpremeditated congruence emerges that is suprarational and exquisitely facilitative:

> Then simply my *presence* is releasing and helpful. There is nothing I can do to force this experience, but when I can relax and be close to the transcendental core of me, then I may behave in strange and impulsive ways in the relationship, ways which I cannot justify rationally, which have nothing to do with my thought processes. But these strange behaviors turn out to be right in some odd way. . . . Profound growth and healing and energy are present. (Rogers, 1986, p. 130)

Rogers believed that only as he could offer what is real in himself could clients like Mary Jane search for the real in themselves. Just as it was impossible for Mary Jane to *try* to be herself through the imposition of some structure alien to her real experience, so did Rogers assert that to be effective, client-centered therapy must likewise be genuine. It cannot be a trick or a tool. It cannot be imposed upon the personality of the therapist. (Rogers, 1951a, p. 30). Rogers consequently came to a harsh and stunning conclusion about the foundations of many therapies:

It has gradually been driven home to me that I cannot be of help to this troubled person by means of any intellectual or training procedure. No approach which relies upon knowledge, upon training, upon the acceptance of something that is taught, is of any use. (Rogers, 1963, p. 32)

It is a strange, compelling land into which Mary Jane wandered with Rogers so many years ago, where maps and guides are curiously unhelpful, the landmarks fluid and elusive. No less strange is the prospect that Rogers' warning applies as well to his own method, that as long as client-centered therapy is merely an intellectual or training procedure, grounded merely in something *taught*, it will not be useful.

Rogers' approach, for clients and therapists alike, is not for the faint-hearted. I believe that Mary Jane Tilden might have agreed, when, with no one to rescue her, or shield her from her pain, she stopped her flight and turned without resistance to face the darkness within her. Mary Jane could not will herself into the form she had chosen; this only separated her further from the peace for which she longed. Similarly, for therapists, the effort to become "client-centered," to train oneself after this fashion, to imitate or emulate, is a contradiction of the way of being and the process Rogers described. As long as this facilitative quality of being remains a goal to be attained, one can no more embody what it means to be client-centered than could Mary Jane unfold herself as she thought a young woman *should*. This, more than anything, is what I have learned through considering Mary Jane's experience with Rogers: I am required to journey as she did so many years ago, to abdicate my notions of a client-centered ideal to which I *should* conform, and to explore the landscape directly, to make it my own. It is a paradoxical task, indeed, this giving up in order to acquire, this grieving over the loss of what I have wished to become, so that I may be present, alive, and useful to others like Mary Jane, who have lost their way.

REFERENCES

Krishnamurti, J. (1987). *Krishnamurti to himself: His last journal.* New York: HarperCollins.

Rogers, C. R. (1951a). *Client-centered therapy: Its current practice, implications and theory.* Boston: Houghton Mifflin.

Rogers, C. R. (1951b). Perceptual reorganization in client-centered therapy. In R. R. Blake & G. V. Ramsey (Eds.), *Perception: An approach to personality* (pp. 323–325). New York: Ronald Press.

Rogers, C. R. (1963). *On becoming a person: A therapist's view of psychotherapy.* Boston: Houghton Mifflin.

Rogers, C. R. (1986). Rogers, Kohut, and Erickson: A personal perspective on some similarities and differences. *Person-Centered Review, 1,* 125–140.

A CONTEMPORARY PSYCHOANALYTIC PERSPECTIVE

Rogers' Brief Psychotherapy
with Mary Jane Tilden

Jesse D. Geller
Edith Gould

The pioneering work of Carl Rogers occupies a special place in the history of psychotherapy. Rogers was the first major theorist to make what he actually did with "clients" available for public scrutiny and scientific study. Included in his legacy is a detailed transcript of a brief psychotherapy conducted in 1946 with a young woman to whom the pseudonym "Mary Jane Tilden" was given. In this chapter we will examine this case from a contemporary psychoanalytic perspective. Particular attention will be given to exploring the therapeutic possibilities and limitations of the theoretical principles that guided Rogers' work at the time of this case.

Like Freud, Rogers was willing to revise and refine his theoretical framework in the light of continued study. In the mid-1940s, according to Zimring and Raskin (1992), the following hypothesis stood at the center of Rogers' theorizing: "If the therapist accepts, recognizes, and clarifies the feelings expressed by the client, there will be movement from negative feelings to positive ones, followed by insight and positive actions" (p. 634).

We believe that then, as now, the psychotherapeutic situation and the process of therapy itself must be considered in relation to the sociocultural

211

context and the circumstances in which they are occurring. Forms of psychotherapy, and the problems clients bring to therapy, are a product of both a time and a place. We will therefore begin our discussion with a brief overview of what is currently included under the rubric of psychoanalysis and with some comments on the lives of women in post-World War II America.

PSYCHOANALYTIC THERAPY: AN OVERVIEW

With respect to matters of technique and the question of how therapeutic change comes about, psychoanalytic theorizing is far more varied today than it was in 1946. In 1992, Sandler concluded that "we cannot speak of any single theory of technique held in common by all analysts" (p. 190). Up until the 1950s, however, there was a general consensus among psychoanalysts that fostering and interpreting a "transference neurosis" in order to uncover and work through repressed infantile conflicts was the defining feature of psychoanalysis (Wallerstein, 1989). The basic components of psychoanalytic technique were free association, the use of the couch, dream interpretation, and relative neutrality and inactivity on the part of the analyst.

In the late 1940s, when Rogers was treating Mary Jane, psychoanalysts were also committed to the idea that it was possible to distinguish clearly between psychoanalysis and psychoanalytic therapy. Rogers himself had not yet differentiated between "counseling" and "psychotherapy" (Rogers, 1951). At present, psychoanalysis and psychoanalytic therapy are considered as overlapping rather than as sharply distinct and different forms of treatment. The utility of a narrowly conceived notion of the transference neurosis has, moreover, been called into question and reformulated (Cooper, 1987), as have other hallowed concepts such as penis envy (Grossman & Stewart, 1976) and feminine masochism (Person, 1990). A far broader concept of transference (e.g., Gill, 1982) and the complementary notion of resistance (e.g., Schafer, 1976) remain, on the other hand, at the center of psychoanalytic theory, as does the concept of the dynamic unconscious and its disguised elaborations in mental contents, symptoms, and behavior.

In current practice, the primary aim and direction of psychoanalytic treatment continues to be the establishment of a therapeutic relationship. Within this relationship, client and therapist share the goal of identifying and resolving maladaptive patterns and their symptomatic manifestations through mutual scrutiny and interpretation of the origins, meanings, and consequences of their problematic manifestations, most particularly as they are revealed within the therapeutic relationship itself (Eagle, 1984).

"UNITY WITHIN MULTIPLICITY"

During the late 1940s classically trained analysts regarded emotionally intensified understanding of unconscious processes, including the forgotten past, as solely responsible for bringing about psychoanalytic change. The origin of this exclusive emphasis on insight can be traced to Freud's efforts to distinguish psychoanalysis from those therapies that rely on suggestion and persuasion. Today, however, the majority opinion is that the search for a single mechanism of change is doomed to failure. Some psychoanalysts consider the reconstruction of the past to play only a minor and optional role in bringing about therapeutic change (Gill, 1982). Many contemporary theorists take the position, and we concur, that the quality of the relationship between client and analyst is as important as insight in producing change (e.g., Eagle, 1984). In recent years there has, furthermore, been a renewed emphasis on the hypothesis that the internalization of benignly influential aspects of the therapeutic relationship makes an independent positive contribution to bringing about positive analytic change and to the maintenance of treatment gains following termination (e.g., Dorpat, 1974; Geller, 1988; Kohut, 1971; Stolorow & Lachmann, 1980).

In a phrase, psychoanalysis is moving in the direction of "unity within multiplicity" (Loewald, 1978). According to Pine (1988), psychoanalysts have actually produced four conceptually separable perspectives on the functioning of the human mind, which he terms the "psychologies of drive, ego, object relations, and self" (p. 571). Each of these perspectives offers a somewhat unique vantage point from which to listen, observe, and organize clinical material. During successive phases of therapy, psychoanalytic work with different clients is guided, in varying degrees, by these alternate points of view. In the pages that follow we will illustrate how our reading of the case of Mary Jane was shaped by these four perspectives.

What emerged from multiple readings of the text were two overarching conclusions. First, we were impressed by the centrality of Mary Jane's struggle to establish a positive feminine sense of self. Secondly, we believe that Mary Jane's efforts to discover her "truer self" (Winnicott, 1960) were being thwarted by the interaction between her relationship with her mother and the sociocultural conditions that were in existence when she entered psychotherapy with Rogers.

FEMALE ROLES AND IMAGES: 1946

Cultural norms regarding women, and psychoanalytic perspectives on female psychology, are now quite different from what they were in 1946.

Statistical information, sociological studies, and content analyses of the mass media indicate that the end of World War II ushered in a domesticity boom in the United States and a resurgence of disparaging attitudes toward women who dared to have professional careers. Marriage license bureaus did more business in 1946 than in any year in American history, before or since (U.S. Bureau of the Census, 1946). According to the social historian Filene (1974), this "marital fever" continued throughout the next 10 years, expanding the married proportion of the population to unprecedented size, pushing the average age of marriage to an unprecedented low, and was most pronounced among urban, white women in their 20s, especially those who were college graduates. A popular phrase among college women during this era was "I'm here to get my MRS degree." The birth rate also soared to historic heights in the era following World War II. In 1945, 31% of white women thought the ideal number of children was four (Filene, 1974). Moreover, child care authorities, most notably Dr. Benjamin Spock (1946), were urging women to stay at home and take care of their babies.

When World War II finally ended, an unprecedented number of women were employed, especially married women (Faludi, 1989). However, despite the large female influx into the labor market, most of the newly employed, like women of previous generations, did not take on careers, but merely jobs. Most young women regarded work as essentially a way-station on the path toward domesticity and/or as a means to raise one's family's standard of living toward upper-middle-class abundance, as opposed to a means of pursuing their interests and developing their talents to the fullest. Concurrently, so-called "career women" were being portrayed in fiction (Faludi, 1989) and films (Haskell, 1974) as more unfeminine, unattractive, and unhealthy than at any time since the turn of the century. Reinforcing this trend, advice experts filled books with warnings that education and jobs strip women of their femininity, deny them marriage and motherhood, and that the employment of women gives rise to "mental instability" (Faludi, 1989).

Paralleling or mirroring these cultural norms, psychoanalytic theorizing about female development, during this period, emphasized the roles of penis envy and masochism (Deutsch, 1944–1945). The vaginal orgasm was viewed as the sine qua non of feminine adaptation and mental health. Since penis envy was a theoretical given, the only solution for the "castrated" girl was to hope to acquire the idealized penis symbolically through marriage and babies. Contemporary psychoanalysts have pointed out that psychoanalytic therapy during the 1940s and throughout the 1950s was implicitly biased toward these ends and thus supported cultural sanctions against women who did not confine themselves to motherhood and domesticity (Eichenbaum & Orbach, 1982; Person, 1990).

In sum, at the moment that Mary Jane was making the transition from adolescence to adulthood, the culture provided her with few viable role models other than wife and mother. In retrospect, a good deal of this client's predicament can be interpreted as foreshadowing the efforts of subsequent generations of postadolescent women to emancipate themselves from narrowly defined gender roles.

ON BEGINNING THE THERAPY

Mary Jane Tilden, a high school graduate and the fourth of five children from an upper-middle-class family, was brought by her mother to the University of Chicago Counseling Center that Rogers created in 1945. Mary Jane's mother described her as "staying in too much" and "acting strange." "She sleeps all the time . . . broods and introspects and is harder to get on with." Obviously concerned and displeased by what she saw as her deviance, Mary Jane's mother told Rogers that her daughter needed "to be set straight on some matters." Was this a disguised plea to save her daughter from becoming an "old maid"?

By contemporary diagnostic standards, Mary Jane would be regarded as suffering from a major depression. The presence of suicidal ideation, strong self-critical attitudes, low self-esteem, vegetative symptoms, lack of motivation, and social isolation are all defining features of depression. Rogers did not become alarmed, however, nor did he conduct a systematic diagnostic interview. Perhaps he was impressed, as we were, by Mary Jane's overall level of ego functioning, which included an insightfulness and willingness to engage in self-exploration. Had the initial interview(s) been conducted by a psychoanalytic therapist in 1946, he or she would have included an investigation of the nature, onset, and vicissitudes of Mary Jane's symptomatic history. A psychoanalytically oriented therapist would, moreover, have elicited remembrances of her childhood and adolescent development, and would have developed a dynamic formulation with a view toward assessing her suitability for treatment.

From the opening moments of the first interview, Rogers revealed a consistent emphasis on the here and now, attempting to establish as quickly as possible an investigatory or exploratory atmosphere. He began with a standard open-ended question, asking Mary Jane, politely, if she would like to tell him why she has come in now. Her response was "It is a long story. I can't find myself. Everything I do seems to be wrong. I can't get on with people. If there is any criticism or anyone says anything about me I just can't take it. When I had a job, if anyone said anything critical, it just crumpled me."

In response to Rogers' clarification of what she had just said, she continued by saying, "It goes way back. In grammar school I never felt I belonged. Oh, sometimes I would try to feel superior, but then I'd be way down. I used to be the teacher's pet, but that didn't help with the other girls." These statements are informative, relevant, and coherent. They reveal that Mary Jane is articulate, psychologically available, capable of participating in cooperative exchanges, and able to take a developmental perspective on the origins of her presenting complaints. These attributes suggest that she would have been regarded as a suitable candidate for psychoanalytic therapy.

STYLES OF EXERCISING AUTHORITY

It is important to note that Rogers began the third, seventh, and tenth sessions with questions: "Well—how do you want to use the time today?" "What is what today?" and "How goes it today?" Questions, even open-ended ones such as these, limit the way any answer, right or wrong, may be given. Nevertheless, they are far less directive than requiring clients to free associate. Psychoanalytic technique, proper, came into being when Freud (1913) "instructed" his patients to say without censoring whatever entered their minds.

Rogers' opening gambits are one of many manifestations of what can be understood as his own value-based modification of the psychoanalytic style of exercising authority. He adopted an "egalitarian" style of exercising authority and downplayed his expertise. He did not tell Mary Jane explicitly how to communicate, nor what she was to talk about. Instead, he gently encouraged her to take responsibility for the course of her interviews. Throughout the therapy he provided her with repeated opportunities to assert her preferences, to select what would be talked about, and to terminate the discussion of a theme. By consistently allowing Mary Jane to lead the way, we believe Rogers succeeded in strengthening her capacities for autonomy and mutuality.

Psychoanalytic therapists similarly try to move their clients toward experiencing themselves as full and equal partners in the realization of the goals of therapy. Psychoanalytic efforts in this direction are, however, based on the assumption that in order to fully experience themselves as working closely together with their therapists in a collaborative endeavor, some clients must first struggle with, and come to understand, their more childlike and conflictual patterns of relating to "authority figures." For example, helping the highly dependent client entails helping him or her to move beyond the experiencing of self as merely the recipient of the therapist's warmth, support, and helpfulness. Others come to feel that they share the responsibility for realizing the goals of therapy only after they have worked through their need to defy authority.

With respect to Mary Jane, we believe that powerful forces emanating from her passive, compliant, approval-seeking relationship with both her parents impeded the full development of a therapeutic alliance. We assume, furthermore, that a therapy relationship between a 20-year-old unemployed female high school graduate and a middle-aged male doctor, in 1946, could not have been truly egalitarian.

THE THERAPEUTIC ALLIANCE

In the 1940s, psychoanalysts had not made a systematic distinction between the transferential aspects of the therapeutic relationship and what has come to be variously called the "therapeutic alliance" (Zetzel, 1956) or "working alliance" (Greenson, 1967). Most broadly defined, transference reactions are patterns of wishes, hopes, and fears that are mobilized in response to situations that are perceived as resembling the original childhood scenarios that gave rise to them (Basch, 1980).

Today, there appears to be an evolving consensus to the effect that the therapeutic alliance consists of at least two components (Luborsky & Crits-Christoph, 1990). The first depends upon the client experiencing the therapist as warm, helpful, and supportive with himself or herself as recipient of that warmth, and so on. The second is based upon the sense of working together in a joint struggle against what is impeding the client. The emphasis here is on shared responsibility for realizing the goals of therapy. When an alliance of the first type is in ascendancy, a client may feel changed by treatment and believe that the therapeutic process is helping him or her to overcome problems without experiencing his or her own efforts and abilities as having contributed significantly to bringing about change.

According to our theoretical perspective, once an alliance of the first type (i.e., one based on warmth, caring, and support) has been established, it becomes possible to explore both the client's style of resisting the obligation to be absolutely honest and his or her conflictual reactions to the power differentials and status inequalities that separate the client and therapist in their relationship. This work gradually democratizes the therapeutic relationship, and facilitates the emergence of an alliance of the second type—one based upon joint effort and accountability for the work.

At present, the establishment of a therapeutic alliance is regarded as an essential prerequisite for the effectiveness of any therapeutic intervention; it is also generally assumed that a consistent focus on threats to, and ruptures of, the alliance is essential to the success of the enterprise. This emphasis upon constantly monitoring the quality of the alliance and on intervening promptly when disruptions in the alliance occur is particularly apparent among advocates of short-term forms of psychodynamic psycho-therapy (e.g., Davanloo, 1980; Malan, 1976; Sifneos, 1979).

Although Rogers never labeled it as such, he did attempt to lay the groundwork for the establishment of a therapeutic alliance. For example, midway through the first interview, he makes the attempt to educate Mary Jane about his form of psychotherapy. He conveys to her the notion that a certain amount of deprivation and pain must be tolerated in the interest of achieving therapeutic goals, and he provides her with a rationale for the relevance of his techniques to her difficulties. While he offers her no guarantees regarding the success of psychotherapy, he does conduct himself in a manner suggestive of confidence in his own approach. For example, Rogers says to Mary Jane, "a number of people have tried that sort of thing and have found that it helped, but you can't be guaranteed anything. It might help or it might not." And later on in the interview, he observes, "I won't be giving you a lot of answers, except to help you work through some of the answers that you would be satisfied with." All these remarks are made in an uncharacteristically verbose and clumsy manner.

Moreover, a careful review of these interviews leads us to believe that Rogers and Mary Jane never did achieve full agreement about the goals of treatment, their relative responsibilities, or the kind of attachment or relationship required to do the work of therapy. Mary Jane's absences, cancellations, repeated threats of termination, and directly and indirectly expressed disappointments with the therapy are all diagnostic of an alliance in need of repair. Because of the theoretical advances noted above, we believe that if Rogers were working today, he would have monitored and clarified, in an ongoing fashion, Mary Jane's ambivalent involvement in therapy.

LISTENING THERAPEUTICALLY

Almost everything that clients tell us about themselves, others and their relations with others, is open to multiple interpretations. Variations among so-called schools or theories of therapy highlight different facets of the multiple meanings inherent in clients' communications. Consequently, one would expect that the focusing power of the four theoretical perspectives identified by Pine would alert clinicians to different facets of the same clinical material.

For example, when listening from the object relations perspective, a clinician would be likely to pay less attention to Mary Jane's conflicts regarding sexual and aggressive issues, and correspondingly greater attention to separation–individuation conflicts, than if he or she were listening from the perspective of the importance of instinctual drives and their derivatives. In our reading of the text, we were most impressed with the extent to which Mary Jane's efforts to create an independent and valued sense of self were being thwarted by her failure to master the developmental tasks of late adolescence (e.g., the consolidation of an initial adult identity and the development of the ability to enter into intimate relationships while maintaining continuing access to the distinction between self and nonself).

Every theory of therapy suggests not only what to listen for but how to listen. To counteract the restrictive and biasing influence of the theory itself, Freud (1913) advised psychoanalysts to listen to what the patient had to say with "evenly suspended attention." What this special form of listening requires is a continuous rhythmic shifting between focused and unfocused modes of allocating attention, or, as Pine (1988) put it, "the task of analytic listening remains that of suspension between knowledge of human functioning and open-ended ignorance of how a particular hour with a particular patient will come to be best understood" (p. 578).

Rogers' style of listening can best be described as patient, attentive, interested, nonintrusive, goal-directed, and empathic. Although he remained alert to the multiple connotations of what Mary Jane said, his listening cannot be characterized as "evenly suspended" in nature. Today's psychoanalytic models of optimal listening are based on the assumption that to be effective a therapist's listening should be empathically attuned to a client's needs, feelings, views, as well as "pandirectional" in nature (Schwaber, 1983; Spence, 1982). It was not until 1951 that Rogers placed empathic listening, rather than clarification of feelings, at the center of his own theory of therapy. Nevertheless, there is abundant evidence that Rogers did attempt to see the world from Mary Jane's point of view, which is of course the essence of empathic listening. He retained the ability to remain open-minded, nonjudgmental, and he joined in her private, perceptual world on a moment-to-moment basis. Moreover, in anticipation of Kohut, Rogers was the first theorist to regard empathy not merely as a tool of observation but as a healing agent in and of itself (Kahn, 1985).

In the ordinary conduct of therapy, even the most experienced and well-educated therapists sometimes fail to provide their clients with empathic understandings or they retreat defensively from the pursuit of such understandings. Rogers' technique can, in part, be understood as an attempt to deal with the fact that a therapist's capacity to understand is always incomplete and imperfect. Extending upon this realization, Kohut (1971) sensitized clinicians to the therapeutic possibilities of the sequence of empathy, failures of empathy, and their reparation. According to Kohut, repeated interventions that empathically address clients' negative reactions to feeling misunderstood and unaffirmed gradually promote the activation of "transmuting internalizations" and the structuralization of the sense of self. That Rogers intuitively prefigured Kohut's hypothesis regarding the therapeutic action of empathy, disruption, and repair cycles can be inferred from the following sequence of events.

Throughout the early sessions, Mary Jane ruminated obsessively about and provided Rogers with abundant examples of her inhibitions regarding self assertion, searing doubts and feelings of inadequacy regarding her feminine self, conflicts about taking responsibility for self-direction, difficulties with self-regulation, fears of revealing her "real self," as well as her difficulties differentiating, defining, and articulating aspects of herself, such as what it is she desires.

On the other hand, Mary Jane remained rather secretive about her self-aggrandizing and exhibitionistic dispositions, as well as her virtues and talents. A notable exception occurred toward the end of the third interview. At this juncture, the client courageously revealed some of the narcissistic components of her self image—"I was the teacher's pet—and a—I was also a lawyer's daughter and everybody sort of made me feel, or something made me feel—as though I was too good—or I couldn't—was better than somebody else—or that I wouldn't make the effort to be nice to somebody because I was—I didn't have to, because I was better."

We believe that Mary Jane felt more shame about her "grandiose self" (Kohut, 1971), than about her failures to live up to her "search for glory" (Horney, 1950) and that she felt humiliated by having revealed to the therapist her sense of superiority over others. Lewis (1980) has alerted us to the importance of recognizing and accepting the shaming consequences of self-disclosure. We hypothesize that Rogers' theory-driven inattentiveness to Mary Jane's unexpressed shame may have been experienced by her as an empathic failure and that her subsequent withdrawal from Rogers was an attempt to shore up her self esteem and prevent further narcissistic injury.

It is important to note that after the third session Mary Jane's mother called to cancel her daughter's next appointment because "she was ill." The following week, a second call from Mary Jane's mother informed Rogers that her daughter was "reluctant to come" and that the therapy was not doing her much good. Clearly there had been a rupture in the treatment relationship. There were, moreover, intimations of Mary Jane's "reluctance" at the end of the third interview when she seemed to hedge about the next week's appointment time.

At this juncture Rogers reached out to Mary Jane by writing her a letter. In it he expressed warmth, interest, and understanding of her discouragement, but he left the decision about returning to therapy up to her. We believe that this letter repaired the rupture of the therapeutic alliance that had occurred in the third interview, and it enabled Mary Jane to return to therapy.

CLARIFICATION, CONFRONTATION, AND INTERPRETATION

In accord with his own theoretical stance, Rogers did listen with a refined sensitivity to the verbal manifestations of Mary Jane's feelings. Although, at this phase of his career, he regarded the clarification of feelings as akin to insight, Rogers did not attempt to clarify or interpret the conscious or unconscious thematic content of Mary Jane's self-disclosures—two radical departures from contemporary psychodynamic approaches to brief (e.g., Luborsky, 1984; Strupp & Binder, 1984) as well as long term psychotherapy.

Interpretations are essentially explanations; they present new meanings and provide reasons for behavior. Interpretations take various forms, but they are all designed to help the client comprehend him- or herself in a new way or to form a new perspective. In traditional psychoanalytic practice, all other interventions, including clarifications and confrontations, have always been regarded as merely laying the groundwork for the making of transference interpretations and the resultant creation of insights.

Today, many analysts continue to emphasize this sequence of interpretations leading to insight, thus furthering the development of a more conscious life. Others stress the relationship-transforming power of accurate interpretations, including their capacity to promote constructive identification with representations of the therapist's "analytic attitude" (Schafer, 1983). Moreover, psychoanalytic therapists today rely on interpretations not only to link the meanings of present behavior to affectively significant events in the past but to establish connections between seemingly isolated statements or events occurring in the session. In this way, latent themes are highlighted and clients are familiarized with their resistances.

In standard technique, the resistant client is viewed as an adversary who is "hiding" or attempting to "defy" the analyst in order to preserve his or her innocence or ignorance. A more affirmative reformulation of the concept of resistance highlights, however, what resisting attempts to accomplish, and it expresses an empathic appreciation of the client's fears of retraumatization (Schafer, 1976).

We conceptualize and use the notion of resistance in both of the above ways, but neither of these perspectives is manifested in Rogers' approach. The adversarial perspective on resistance would, for instance, suggest the following kinds of questions: What was Mary Jane avoiding when she canceled her sessions? Why did Mary Jane not talk more about her father, or her brother? The affirmative perspective, on the other hand, generates a different set of questions, such as, What goal was Mary Jane pursuing when she canceled her sessions? Were her frequent requests to change the time of her appointments attempts to assert her autonomy rather than attempts to challenge Rogers' authority?

Both of these perspectives are relevant to Mary Jane's abrupt termination of therapy. Her sudden and unilateral departure, on the one hand, can be interpreted as an attempt to avoid separation guilt in relation to her mother; on the other hand, it can be viewed as a positive sign of her desire and increased capacity to function independently. In our experience, the failure to interpret the nature of clients' resistances, whatever their meanings, frequently eventuates in premature terminations.

In contrast to interpretations, clarifications are intended to put into words the client's experience—as viewed by the client, not the therapist. Clarifications essentially paraphrase, reflect, or summarize what a client has been communicating, either verbally or nonverbally. Providing clients with clarifying descriptions of their inner states, or of their conflicts, has always played a vital role in psychoanalytic therapy. Even simple repetition of what a client has said may bring about a noticeable effect because, as Horowitz, Marmar, Krupnick, Wilner, and Wallerstein (1984) have observed, "the patient hears meanings quite differently when they are echoed by the therapist" (p. 74). Calmly putting into words that which the client has feared is too dangerous to fully express divests words and meanings of their anxiety-producing potential and encourages clients to broach threatening topics more courageously.

It seemed to be tacitly understood by Rogers and Mary Jane that he would not require her to provide details or reconstruct the temporal or causal sequences of events that led to her problematic states of mind. For example, when Mary Jane expressed highly charged "core conflictual themes" (Luborsky, 1984) such as "I was hurt so much," "somebody will do you a dirty trick," and, from the summarized comments from the seventh session, "I was frightened by my jealousy when she [her coworker] went with a boy in whom I was interested," Rogers continued to limit himself to clarifications of her feelings rather than asking her to elaborate more fully on these experiences. We believe this self-imposed restriction had an inhibitory influence on the immediacy and depth of Mary Jane's functioning during her therapy sessions.

What Loewald (1978) referred to as "active mirroring" blurs the boundaries between clarifications and interpretations. According to Loewald, such interventions state in more precise, vivid, comprehensive, and emotionally differentiated fashion what the client has said. Rogers was disinclined to use clarifications that went beyond Mary Jane's expressed thoughts and feelings. By putting into words Mary Jane's experiences as she viewed them, not as he viewed them, Rogers succeeded in reinforcing her sense of feeling understood, accepted, and respected. We believe, however, that by *not* paraphrasing or translating the content of what she had been communicating, either verbally or nonverbally, into words that were more specific, concrete, personal, or intimate, he limited the depth of her self-explorations regarding the what, when, how, and why of the more troublesome aspects of her life.

Rogers' technique at this stage of his career also proscribed his use of confrontation. Confrontations bring to clients' conscious awareness those phenomena that the therapist deems in need of exploration (Greenson, 1967). For example, confrontations are used to help clients become aware of discrepancies between their words and their behavior, or between two statements they have made. In contemporary psychoanalytic practice, how clients say things—and what they say or do not say—are recognized, in principle, as equally important sources of "therapeutic material" (Shapiro, 1989). In other words, the advent of the study of the ego brought into sharper focus the "styles" (Shapiro, 1965) with which clients resist the emergence of infantile wishes, fantasy-linked associations, and memories into consciousness.

A working clinical hypothesis is that a client's expressive style reveals, on the one hand, his or her attitudes about what is being discussed and, on the other hand, his or her transference-based attitudes toward the therapist. For example, the stylistic imprint of hysterical trends can be discerned in the frequency with which Mary Jane uses the term "it" and other ambiguous referents to refer to conflictual matters. In contemporary psychoanalytic therapies when clients are vague, therapists ask them to be more specific and concrete, or confront them with their vagueness. Rogers missed crucial opportunities to confront Mary Jane with striking discrepancies between *what* she was saying and *how* she was saying it. For example, in the first interview Mary Jane *laughs* after saying, "And I just seem to have lost faith in everything. . . . It's such a terrible thing." Later in the session, she again *laughs* while saying, "I have such a terrible conflict at what I am that it sort of—it makes me feel awful." Proponents of brief forms of psychoanalytic psychotherapy (e.g., Sifneos, 1979; Strupp & Binder, 1984) have stressed the importance of consistently making clients aware of the meanings and consequences of such discrepancies.

THE GOALS OF PSYCHOTHERAPY

There are many ways of describing the goals or aims of psychoanalysis or of psychoanalytic psychotherapy. Viewed from the perspective of classical drive theory, the primary aim remains the creation of insight, as does the basic operating premise that replacing unconscious defenses with conscious choices occurs indirectly by means of the gradual elimination of resistances to consciousness and verbalization. In several important respects, a heightened capacity for insight is synonymous with, and presupposes, the fostering of ego development. Loewald (1978) has written that whatever else is conveyed by consciousness and ego, these terms mean "taking responsibility for one's history, the history that one has lived and the history in the making" (p. 34). Alternatively stated, the goal of brief psychoanalytic psychotherapy is to bring about an "enlarged appreciation of activity in apparent passivity" (Schafer, 1973, p. 138).

Rogers' therapeutic efforts were clearly directed toward helping the client appropriate or take ownership of her subjective experiences, including her more ignoble reactions to others and her disappointments in therapy and in Rogers. Rogers' style of working can be viewed as essentially directed toward helping Mary Jane forge a cohesive sense of self, capable of individuation. Indeed, throughout his career and in anticipation of self psychology, Rogers' primary aim was to support the development of the client's unique individuality and expressiveness.

We believe that Roger's technique, as well as his willingness to intermittently depart from it, set in motion a variety of intrapsychic and interpersonal processes that relieved Mary Jane's pain and promoted therapeutic change. First of all, he consistently provided Mary Jane with empathic responsiveness tempered by optimal frustration. Like most analytically trained therapists, Rogers refrained from providing her with advice, guidance, reassurance; he was neither indulgent nor critical. By not gratifying her frequent requests for "answers," Rogers enabled his client to take increasing responsibility for her own life.

Second, by departing from his noninterpretive stance on several occasions Rogers was able to convey to Mary Jane his deep understanding of her feelings, needs, and views. The ninth interview contains two examples of such departures. Mary Jane, beginning to cry, says, "oh dear, here comes the rainstorm." Rogers responds with "They say the rain makes things grow." Moments later Mary Jane speaks of her dependence on her mother. Here Rogers makes the interpretation "You stood on her two feet."

It is clearly true, moreover, that by allowing Mary Jane to fully experience and articulate her criticisms of his approach, Rogers was able to help her to take fuller responsibility for her own authentic emotional reactions. By departing from his commitment to nondirectivity on several important occasions, Rogers conveyed to Mary Jane his willingness to provide her with "corrective emotional experiences" (Alexander & French, 1946). During the tenth interview, for example, Rogers gave Mary Jane "permission" to be angry at her mother, to have a mind of her own, and to erect a firm line of demarcation between her opinions and those of her mother. By sanctioning her aggressive feelings he enabled her to feel more natural and calmer.

Psychoanalysts Alexander and French (1946) coined the term "corrective emotional experience" when experimenting with a method of brief psychotherapy that challenged the importance of genetic understandings. But where Alexander and French advocated the use of manipulation and control to provide clients with corrective emotional experiences, Rogers' efforts seemed to derive from his deeply felt political and philosophical values.

IDENTITY FORMATION AND SEXUALITY

We believe that Rogers was at his weakest therapeutically with respect to his handling of issues related to gender and sexuality, and their accompanying transference manifestations. For example, throughout the sessions, Mary Jane made numerous references to marriage. In the first interview she told Rogers that she has two married sisters, but she is "afraid" she "won't measure up to things". In the fourth interview she talked about the problem of trying to be "natural" and all the ways in which marriages might fail. The client went on to say "I want to be sure that I'm going to be perfect. It's that fear that just keeps repeating itself." From our perspective Mary Jane appears to have been alluding, among other things, to the subject of sex and her fears of sexuality, but Rogers did not pick up on this underlying theme. She expressed a wish to be "natural," that is, sexual, but issues outside of her awareness interfered with this.

In the course of working with Rogers, Mary Jane became aware of the stranglehold her mother had upon her. In an impressive demonstration of her insight and psychological-mindedness, she described her mother as living vicariously, "trying to merge herself in her children" because "she didn't want to face things." Mary Jane was caught up in a powerful conflict. Her own "developmentally imperative self-differentiation processes" (Stolorow, Brandchaft, & Atwood, 1987, p. 50), which include the need to become an autonomous and sexual woman, are at odds with equally pressing needs to sustain and perpetuate vital ties to her mother, which oppose her self-differentiation. To marry and be sexual would be to abandon her mother, who desperately required her daughter's dependence upon her.

For Mary Jane, sexuality was unconsciously equated with separation from her mother. Was she searching, in veiled ways, for Rogers' sanction for these vitally important motivations to separate and differentiate herself from her mother, become a sexual person, and achieve intimacy with a man? Rogers did support and encourage her to stand on her own two feet, but he avoided specific references to the young woman's fears and concerns about her sexuality. His nondirective theoretical stance required that he stay, as close by as possible, to the manifest utterances of his client.

Mary Jane did not, of course, refer to sex directly, and Rogers did not bring it up himself. By thus failing to explore Mary Jane's feelings about marriage in depth, Rogers implicitly colluded with her conviction that marriage is a woman's badge of success. (What modern-day analyst would concur with a 20-year-old's self-evaluation that she is a failure because she is unmarried?)

Does Rogers' avoidance of the theme of sexuality in his treatment of Mary Jane represent an unconsciously held bias in relation to women? It is true that in 1946, despite the fact that the country was gripped by marital fever, women's sexuality, for the most part, was unacknowledged and unsanctioned. The prevailing media image of a woman was that of a desexualized, apron-clad mother, a mother blissfully working away in the kitchen. The dichotomy between the madonna and the whore held sway in the culture. Perhaps the client's turning to various self-help books such as *Your Life as a Woman* was an attempt to gain the sexual enlightenment she had not received from her mother and was not acquiring from Rogers.

Rogers, unlike many psychoanalysts, has never been accused of supporting gender stereotypes about women's nature and abilities. Nevertheless, he did nothing whatsoever to help Mary Jane call into question, let alone transcend, the rigidly prescribed female roles that were available to her. This young person talked a great deal about feeling inferior to, and envious of the intelligence, beauty, and spontaneity of both men and women. At other times, however, she acknowledged that she felt superior to others and described herself as "arrogant" and "smug," especially in regard to other females. "[In school] the only ones that were as good as me were some of the boys." She seemed to be asking Rogers for permission to place her own, what she felt to be selfish, ambitions before the needs of others. She also criticized herself for wanting to do something great, not "ordinary."

In the fourth interview Mary Jane fantasized that it would be unfair to an employer if she took a job at this time. Rogers might have taken this as an opportunity to mirror her "narcissistic" aspirations. Instead he merely reflected back to her, "You feel it wouldn't be fair." Although Mary Jane apparently was an excellent student, with interests in art, sculpture, and dance, she either belittled these talents and interests or invited Rogers to collude with her in viewing them as essentially defensive. Even in the first interview, she told Rogers how she created a "different world" with her studying, a world that gave her something and "stood (me) up a little." From our perspective, the client was describing a self-enhancing capacity and the sense of pleasure she derived from solitary, intellectual activity. Studying made her feel that she was a person of substance rather than a nonentity. Although it does become apparent that Mary Jane's narcissistic grandiosity was unmodulated, and therefore rendered her vulnerable to severe deflations of self-esteem, Rogers neglected to recast these qualities as strengths rather than weaknesses. We believe that, during the course of therapy, her grandiosity was replaced by a more realistic ego-ideal. However, there is also reason to believe that, even at the conclusion of treatment, Mary Jane regarded her efforts to become successful and ambitious as essentially masculine aspirations that were therefore to be shunned. Contemporary psychoanalytically oriented therapists would challenge this view as a distorted belief about gender roles and expectations.

Finally, there are suggestions in the text that Mary Jane was recapitulating, in her relationship with Rogers, the core conflictual themes that organized the narratives that she had recounted about her interactions with her mother and her father. With her mother, Mary Jane was compliant. She talked about how she had remained overly available for complementing her mother's weaknesses and limitations. In order to enhance, strengthen, and insure the psychological survival of her mother, she had sacrificed herself.

Mary Jane's own avoidance of sexual themes may have represented her heightened alertness and sensitivity to Rogers' discomfort with such themes. This unconscious collusion on her part can be understood as a reversion to her compliant, self-sacrificing stance with her mother. Moreover, her continuous affirmations of Rogers' interventions (note how frequently she tells him, "that's right") may have been designed to provide him with the praise that she so desperately longed for, for herself, from her father. These unconsciously reenacted transference paradigms were never analyzed. Because of their direct relevance to the client's efforts to establish an increasingly differentiated, stable, realistic, and essentially positive sense of self, we believe they should have been made a central focus of inquiry.

Our overall judgment about Rogers' efforts on behalf of Mary Jane is captured by the following anecdote. The jazz musician John La Porta reportedly told one of his pupils: "I have good news and bad news about your playing. The good news is: You've got a lot of technique. The bad news is: You've got a lot of technique" (Crow, 1990, p. 45).

CONCLUSION

Any consideration of the aims or goals of psychotherapy inevitably leads to the issue of the limits of what psychotherapy can achieve. Mary Jane began therapy feeling intensely self-critical, hopeless, inhibited, fearful of disapproval, bereft of a sense of purpose, lonely, and alienated from the affectionate regard of her peers. As the end of therapy approached, she had become increasingly self-accepting. Her fears of failure and of success were muted. She was moving toward greater clarity regarding major life choices. She had revised her view of marriage, and she could imagine herself as a wife. She was experiencing less separation guilt and was increasingly able to form and sustain friendships, especially with women. Thus, Carl Rogers demonstrated, 20 years before the current popularity of short-term psychodynamic psychotherapy, that it was possible to achieve ambitious therapeutic goals within a relatively short period of time.

The epilogue to the case is the following: a year after her treatment with Rogers ended Mary Jane was invited to come in for a follow-up interview. At this time she reported that she was experiencing a resurgence of the old feelings of worthlessness, doubt of her own ability, and feelings of futility. Did this regression represent a transient reaction to her boyfriend's condescending attitude toward her or did it represent her need to return for further psychotherapy? Rogers' own doubts about the final outcome of the case leave us with a number of questions of our own. Can any course of psychotherapy inoculate a client sufficiently against the inevitable frustrations and deprivations inherent in an average, expectable environment? Could Mary Jane's therapeutic gains be interpreted as having been a transference cure? In other words, was her improvement temporary because it may have been based on an unanalyzed compliant transference to Rogers? Would her gains have been more enduring if, as we have suggested, Rogers had addressed Mary Jane's unconscious conflicts related to sexuality, aggression, and separation–individuation issues more specifically? Yet another possibility is that Mary Jane did not fully internalize the benignly influential aspects of her relationship with Rogers. For example, she could not continue the psychological work of therapy in the absence of her therapist. Nevertheless, we believe that Mary Jane's initiative in seeking psychotherapy suggests that she did create some enduring internalized representations of Roger's warmth, support, and helpfulness.

REFERENCES

Alexander, F., & French, T. (1946). *Psychoanalytic therapy: Principles and applications.* New York: Ronald Press.

Basch, M. F. (1980). *Doing psychotherapy.* New York: Basic Books.

Cooper, A. M. (1987). The transference neurosis: A concept ready for retirement. *Psychoanalytic Inquiry, 7,* 569–585.

Crow, B. (1990). *Jazz anecdotes.* New York: Oxford University Press.

Davanloo, H. (1980). *Short term dynamic psychotherapy.* New York: Jason Aronson.

Deutsch, H. (1944–1945). *The psychology of women* (2 vols.). New York: Grune & Stratton.

Dorpat, T. L. (1974). Internalization of the patient–analyst relationship in patients with narcissistic disorders. *International Journal of Psycho-Analysis, 55,* 183–191.

Eagle, M. N. (1984). *Recent developments in psychoanalysis.* New York: McGraw-Hill.

Eichenbaum, L., & Orbach, S. (1982). *Understanding women: A feminist psychoanalytic approach.* New York: Basic Books.

Faludi, S. (1989). *Backlash: The undeclared war against women.* New York: Crown.

Filene, P. G. (1974). *Him/her self: Sex roles in modern America.* New York: Harcourt Brace Jovanovich.

Freud, S. (1913). On beginning the treatment: Further recommendations on the technique of psychoanalysis. In J. Strachey (Ed. and Trans.), *The standard edition of the complete psychological works of Sigmund Freud* (Vol. 12). London: Hogarth Press.

Geller, J. D. (1987). The process of psychotherapy: Separation and the complex interplay among empathy, insight, and internalization. In J. Bloom-Feshbach & S. Bloom-Feshbach (Eds.), *The psychology of separation through the life span* (pp. 459–514). San Francisco: Jossey-Bass.

Gill, M. (1982). *Analysis of transference* (Vol. I). New York: International Universities Press.

Greenberg, J., & Mitchell, S. (1983). *Object relations in psychoanalytic theory.* Cambridge, MA: Harvard University Press.

Greenson, R. (1967). *The technique and practice of psychoanalysis* (Vol. I). New York: International Universities Press.

Grossman, W. I., & Stewart, W. A. (1976). Penis envy: From childhood wish to developmental metaphor. *Journal of the American Psychoanalytic Association, 24,* 193–212.

Haskell, M. (1974). *From reverence to rape.* New York: Holt, Rinehart & Winston.

Horney, K. (1950). *Neurosis and human growth.* New York: W. W. Norton.

Horowitz, M., Marmar, C., Krupnick, J., Wilner, N., & Wallerstein, R. (1984). *Personality styles in brief psychotherapy.* New York: Basic Books.

Kahn, E. (1985). Heinz Kohut and Carl Rogers: A timely comparison. *American Psychologist, 40,* 893–905.

Kohut, H. (1971). *The analysis of the self.* New York: International Universities Press.

Lewis, H. B. (1980). *Shame and guilt in the neuroses.* New York: Wiley.

Loewald, H. (1978). *Psychoanalysis and the history of the individual.* New Haven: Yale University Press.

Luborsky, L. (1984). *Principles of psychoanalytic psychotherapy: A manual of supportive–expressive treatment.* New York: Basic Books.

Luborsky, L., & Crits-Christoph, P. (1990). *Understanding transference.* New York: Basic Books.

Malan, D. (1976). *Frontiers of brief psychotherapy.* New York: Plenum.

Person, E. S. (1990). The influence of values in psychoanalysis: The case of female psychology. In C. Zanardi (Ed.), *Essential papers on the psychology of women* (pp. 305–331). New York: International Universities Press.

Pine, F. (1988). The four psychologies of psychoanalysis and their place in clinical work. *Journal of the American Psychoanalytic Association, 36,* 571–597.

Rogers, C. R. (1951). *Client-centered therapy.* Boston: Houghton Mifflin.

Sandler, J. (1992). Reflections on developments in the theory of psychoanalytic technique. *International Journal of Psycho-Analysis, 73,* 189–198.

Schafer, R. (1973). The termination of brief psychoanalytic psychotherapy. *International Journal of Psychoanalytic Psychotherapy, 2,* 135–148.

Schafer, R. (1976). *A new language for psychoanalysis.* New Haven: Yale University Press.

Schafer, R. (1983). *The analytic attitude.* New York: Basic Books.

Schwaber, E. A. (1983). Psychoanalytic listening and psychic reality. *International Review of Psycho-Analysis, 10,* 379–392.

Shapiro, D. (1965). *Neurotic styles.* New York: Basic Books.

Shapiro, D. (1989). *Psychotherapy of neurotic character.* New York: Basic Books.

Sifneos, P. (1979). *Short-term dynamic psychotherapy.* New York: Plenum.

Spence, D. P. (1982). *Narrative truth and historical truth.* New York: W. W. Norton.

Spock, B. (1946). *Common sense book of baby and child care.* New York: Duell, Sloan and Pierce.

Stolorow, R. D., Brandchaft, B., & Atwood, G. E. (1987). *Psychoanalytic treatment: An intersubjective approach.* Hillsdale, NJ: Analytic Press.

Stolorow, R. D., & Lachmann, F. M. (1980). *Psychoanalysis of developmental arrests: Theory and treatment.* New York: International Universities Press.

Strupp, H. H., & Binder, J. L. (1984). *Psychotherapy in a new key: A guide to time-limited dynamic psychotherapy.* New York: Basic Books.

U.S. Bureau of the Census. (1946). Marital status and family status. *Current Population Reports Series* (p. 20). Washington, DC: U.S. Government Printing Office.

Wallerstein, R. (1989). Psychoanalysis and psychotherapy: An historical perspective. *International Journal of Psycho-Analysis, 70,* 563–593.

Winnicott, D. W. (1960). *The maturational processes and the facilitating environment.* New York: International Universities Press.

Zetzel, E. R. (1956). Current concepts of transference. *International Journal of Psycho-Analysis, 37,* 369–376.

Zimring, F. M., & Raskin, N. J. (1992). Carl Rogers and client/person-centered therapy. In D. K. Freedheim (Ed.), *History of psychotherapy* (pp. 629–657). Washington, DC: American Psychological Association.

CHAPTER 7

THE CASE OF JIM BROWN (1962)

TRANSCRIPT

Tuesday

Carl Rogers (C.R.): I see there are some cigarettes here in the drawer. Hmm? Yeah, it is hot out. *(Silence of 25 seconds)*

C.R.: Do you look kind of angry this morning, or is that my imagination? *(Jim shakes his head slightly.)* Not angry, huh? *(Silence of 1 minute, 26 seconds)*

C.R.: Feel like letting me in on whatever is going on? *(Silence of 12 minutes, 52 seconds)*

C.R.: *(Softly)* I kind of feel like saying that if it would be of any help at all I'd like to come in. One the other hand, if it's something you'd rather—if you just feel more like being within yourself, feeling whatever you're feeling within yourself, why that's OK too—I guess another thing I'm saying, really, in saying that is, "I do care. I'm not just sitting here like a stick." *(Silence of 1 minute, 11 seconds)*

C.R.: And I guess your silence is saying to me that either you don't want to or can't come out right now and that's OK. So I won't pester you but I just want you to know, I'm here. *(Silence of 17 minutes, 41 seconds)*

C.R.: I see I'm going to have to stop in a few minutes.[1] *(Silence of 20 seconds)*

---

[1] Long experience had shown me that it was very difficult for Jim to leave. Hence I had gradually adopted the practice of letting him know, 10 or 12 minutes before the conclusion of the hour, that "our time is nearly up." This enabled us to work through the leaving process without my feeling hurried.

C.R.: It's hard for me to know how you've been feeling, but it looks as though part of the time maybe you'd rather I didn't know how you were feeling. Anyway it looks as though part of the time it just feels very good to let down and—relax the tension. But as I say I don't really know—how you feel. It's just the way it looks to me. Have things been pretty bad lately? *(Silence of 45 seconds)*

C.R.: Maybe this morning you just wish I'd shut up—and maybe I should, but I just keep feeling I'd like to—I don't know, be in touch with you in some way. *(Silence of 2 minutes, 21 seconds) (Jim yawns.)*

C.R.: Sounds discouraged or tired. *(Silence of 41 seconds)*

Jim: No. Just lousy.

C.R.: Everything's lousy, huh? You feel lousy? *(Silence of 39 seconds)*

C.R.: Want to come in Friday at 12 at the usual time?

Jim: *(Yawns and mutters something unintelligible.) (Silence of 48 seconds)*

C.R.: Just kind of feel sunk way down deep in these lousy, lousy feelings, hmm?—Is that something like it?

Jim: No.

C.R.: No? *(Silence of 20 seconds)*

Jim: No. I just ain't no good to nobody, never was, and never will be.

C.R.: Feeling that now, hmm? That you're just no good to yourself, no good to anybody. Never will be any good to anybody. Just that you're completely worthless, huh? Those really are lousy feelings. Just feel that you're no good at all, hmm?

Jim: Yeah. *(Muttering in low, discouraged voice)* That's what this guy I went to town with just the other day told me.

C.R.: This guy that you went to town with really told you that you were no good? Is that what you're saying? Did I get that right?

Jim: M-hm.

C.R.: I guess the meaning of that if I get it right is that here's somebody that—meant something to you and what does he think of you? Why, he's told you that he thinks you're no good at all. And that just really knocks the props out from under you. *(Jim weeps quietly.)* It just brings the tears. *(Silence of 20 seconds)*

Jim: *(Rather defiantly)* I don't care though.

C.R.: You tell yourself you don't care at all, but somehow I guess some part of you cares because some part of you weeps over it. *(Silence of 19 seconds)*

C.R.: I guess some part of you just feels, "Here I am hit with another blow, as if I hadn't had enough blows like this during my life when I feel that people don't like me. Here's someone I've begun to feel attached to and now he doesn't like me. And I'll say I don't care. I won't let it make any difference to me—But just the same the tears run down my cheeks."

Jim: *(Muttering)* I guess I always knew it.

C.R.: Hmm?

Jim: I guess I always knew it.

C.R.: If I'm getting that right, it is that what makes it hurt worst of all is that when he tells you you're no good, well shucks, that's what you've always felt about yourself. Is that—the meaning of that you're saying? *(Jim nods slightly, indicating agreement.)* M-hm. So you feel as though he's just confirming what—you've already known. He's confirming what you've already felt in some way. *(Silence of 23 seconds)*

C.R.: So that between his saying so and your perhaps feeling it underneath, you just feel about as no good as anybody could feel. *(Silence of 2 minutes, 1 second)*

C.R.: *(Thoughtfully)* As I sort of let it soak in and try to feel what you must be feeling—it comes up sorta this way in me and I don't know—but as though here was someone you'd made a contact with, someone you'd really done things for and done things with. Somebody that had some meaning to you. Now, wow! He slaps you in the face by telling you you're just no good. And this really cuts so deep, you can hardly stand it. *(Silence of 30 seconds)*

C.R.: I've got to call it quits for today, Jim. *(Silence of 1 minute, 18 seconds)*

C.R.: It really hurts, doesn't it? *(This is in response to his quiet tears.)* *(Silence of 26 seconds)*

C.R.: I guess if the feelings came out you'd just weep and weep and weep. *(Silence of 1 minute, 3 seconds)*

C.R.: Help yourself to some Kleenex if you'd like—Can you go now? *(Silence of 23 seconds)*

C.R.: I guess you really hate to, but I've got to see somebody else. *(Silence of 20 seconds)*

C.R.: It's really bad, isn't it? *(Silence of 22 seconds)*

C.R.: Let me ask you one question and say one thing. Do you still have that piece of paper with my phone numbers on it and instructions, and so on? *(Jim nods.)* OK. And if things get bad, so that you feel real down, you have them call me. 'Cause that's what I'm here for, to try to be of some help when you need it. If you need it, you have them call me.[2]

Jim: I think I'm beyond help.

C.R.: Huh? Feel as though you're beyond help. I know. You feel just completely hopeless about yourself. I can understand that. I don't feel hopeless, but I can realize that you do. Just feel as though nobody can help you and you're really beyond help.[3] *(Silence of 2 minutes, 1 second)*

C.R.: I guess you just feel so, so down that—it's awful. *(Silence of 2 minutes)*

C.R.: I guess there's one other thing too. I, I'm going to be busy here this afternoon 'til 4 o'clock and maybe a little after. But if you should want to see me again this afternoon, you can drop in around about 4 o'clock. OK?—Otherwise, I'll see you Friday noon. Unless I get a call from you. If you—if you're kind of concerned for fear anybody would see that you've been weeping a little, you can go out and sit for a while where you waited for me. Do just as you wish on that. Or go down and sit in the waiting room there and read magazines—I guess you'll really have to go.

Jim: Don't want to go back to work.

C.R.: You don't want to go back to work, hmm?

This is the end of the interview. Later in the day the therapist saw Jim Brown on the hospital grounds. He seemed much more cheerful and said that he thought he could get a ride into town that afternoon.

The next time the therapist saw Jim Brown was 3 days later, on Friday. This interview follows.

[2] Two words of explanation are needed here. He seemed so depressed that I was concerned that he might be feeling suicidal. I wanted to be available to him if he felt desperate. Since no patient was allowed to phone without permission, I had given him a note that would permit a staff member or Jim himself to phone me at any time he wished to contact me, and with both my office and home phone numbers.

[3] This is an example of the greater willingness I have developed to express my own feelings of the moment, at the same time accepting the client's right to possess his feelings, no matter how different from mine.

Friday

C.R.: I brought a few magazines you can take with you if you want.[4] *(Silence of 47 seconds)*

C.R.: I didn't hear from you since last time. Were you able to go to town that day?

Jim: Yeah. I went in with a kid driving the truck.

C.R.: M-hm. *(Voices from next office are heard in background.)* *(Silence of 2 minutes)*

C.R.: Excuse me just a minute. *(Goes to stop noise.)* *(Silence of 2 minutes, 20 seconds)*

C.R.: I don't know why, but I realize that somehow it makes me feel good that today you don't have your hand up to your face so that I can somehow kind of see you more. I was wondering why I felt as though you were a little more here than you are sometimes and then I realized well, it's because—I don't feel as though you're hiding behind your hand, or something. *(Silence of 50 seconds)*

C.R.: And I think I sense, though I could be mistaken, I think I do sense that today, just like some other days when you come in here, it's just as though you let yourself sink down into feelings that run very deep in you. Sometimes they're very bad feelings like the last time and sometimes probably they're not so bad, though they're sort of—I think I understand that somehow when you come in here, it's as though you do let yourself down into those feelings. And now—

Jim: I'm gonna take off.

C.R.: Huh?

Jim: I'm gonna take off.[5]

C.R.: You're going to take off? Really run away from here? Is that what you mean? Must be some—what's the—what's the background of that? Can you tell me? Or I guess what I mean more accurately is I know you don't

---

[4] I had, on several occasions, given magazines and small amounts of money to Jim Brown, and I loaned him books. There was no special rationale behind this. The hospital environment was impoverished for a man of Jim Brown's sort, and I felt like giving him things that would relieve the monotony.

[5] Clearly my empathic guessing in the two previous responses was completely erroneous. This was not troublesome to me, nor, I believe, to him. There is no doubt, however, that my surprise shows.

like the place but it must be that something special came up or something?

Jim: I just want to run away and die.

C.R.: M-hm, m-hm, m-hm. It isn't even that you want to get away from here to something. You just want to leave here and go away and die in a corner, m-hm. *(Silence of 30 seconds)*

C.R.: I guess as I let that soak in I really do sense how, how deep that feeling sounds, that you—I guess the image that comes to my mind is sort of a, a wounded animal that wants to crawl away and die. It sounds as though that's kind of the way you feel that you just want to get away from here and, and vanish. Perish. Not exist. *(Silence of 1 minute)*

Jim: *(Almost inaudibly)* All day yesterday and all morning I wished I were dead. I even prayed last night that I could die.

C.R.: I think I caught all of that, that—for a couple of days now you've just wished you could be dead and you've even prayed for that—I guess that—One way this strikes me is that to live is such an awful thing to you, you just wish you could die, and not live. *(Silence of 1 minute, 12 seconds)*

C.R.: So that you've been just wishing and wishing that you were not living. You wish that life would pass away from you. *(Silence of 30 seconds)*

Jim: I wish it more'n anything else I've ever wished around here.

C.R.: M-hm, m-hm, m-hm. I guess you've wished for lots of things but boy! It seems as though this wish to not live is deeper and stronger than anything you ever wished before. *(Silence of 1 minute, 36 seconds)*

C.R.: Can't help but wonder whether it's still true that some things this friend said to you—are those still part of the thing that makes you feel so awful?

Jim: In general, yes.

C.R.: M-hm. *(Silence of 47 seconds)*

C.R.: The way I'm understanding that is that in a general way the fact that he felt you were no good has just set off a whole flood of feeling in you that makes you really wish, wish you weren't alive. Is that—somewhere near it?

Jim: I ain't no good to nobody, or I ain't no good for nothin', so what's the use of living?

C.R.: M-hm. You feel, "I'm not any good to another living person, so—why should I go on living?" *(Silence of 21 seconds)*

C.R.: And I guess a part of that is that—here I'm kind of guessing and you can set me straight, I guess a part of that is that you felt, "I tried to be good for something as far as he was concerned. I really tried. And now—if I'm no good to him, if he feels I'm no good, then that proves I'm just no good to anybody." Is that, uh—anywhere near it?

Jim: Oh, well, other people have told me that too.

C.R.: Yeah. M-hm. I see. So you feel if, if you go by what others—what several others have said, then, then you are no good. No good to anybody. *(Silence of 3 minutes, 40 seconds)*

C.R.: I don't know whether this will help or not, but I would just like to say that—I think I can understand pretty well—what it's like to feel that you're just no damn good to anybody, because there was a time when—I felt that way about myself. And I know it can be really rough.[6] *(Silence of 13 minutes)*

C.R.: I see we've only got a few more minutes left. *(Silence of 2 minutes, 51 seconds)*

C.R.: Shall we make it next Tuesday at 11, the usual time? *(Silence of 1 minute, 35 seconds)*

C.R.: If you gave me any answer, I really didn't get it. Do you want to see me next Tuesday at 11?

Jim: Don't know.

C.R.: "I just don't know." *(Silence of 34 seconds)*

C.R.: Right at this point you just don't know—whether you want to say "yes" to that or not, hmm?—I guess you feel so down and so—awful that you just don't know whether you can—can see that far ahead. Hmm? *(Silence of 1 minute, 5 seconds)*

C.R.: I'm going to give you an appointment at that time because I'd sure like to see you then. *(Writing out appointment slip.)* *(Silence of 50 seconds)*

C.R.: And another thing I would say is that—if things continue to stay so rough for you, don't hesitate to have them call me. And if you should decide to take off, I would very much appreciate it if you would have

---

[6] This is a most unusual kind of response for me to make. I simply felt that I wanted to share my experiences with him—to let him know he was not alone.

them call me and—so I could see you first. I wouldn't try to dissuade you. I'd just want to see you.

Jim: I might go today. Where, I don't know, but I don't care.

C.R.: Just feel that your mind is made up and that you're going to leave. You're not going *to* anywhere. You're just—just going to leave, hmm? *(Silence of 53 seconds)*

Jim: *(Muttering in discouraged tone)* That's why I want to go, 'cause I don't care what happens.

C.R.: Huh?

Jim: That's why I want to go, 'cause I don't care what happens.

C.R.: M-hm, m-hm. That's why you want to go, because you really don't care about yourself. You just don't care what happens. And I guess I'd just like to say—I care about you. And I care what happens.[7] *(Silence of 30 seconds) (Jim bursts into tears and unintelligible sobs.)*

C.R.: *(Tenderly)* Somehow that just—makes all the feelings pour out. *(Silence of 35 seconds)*

C.R.: And you just weep and weep and weep. And feel so badly. *(Jim continues to sob, then blows nose and breathes in great gasps.)*

C.R.: I do get some sense of how awful you feel inside—You just sob and sob. *(Jim puts his head on desk, bursting out in great gulping, gasping sobs.)*

C.R.: I guess all the pent-up feelings you've been feeling the last few days just—just come rolling out. *(Silence of 32 seconds, while Jim continues to sob.)*

C.R.: There's some Kleenex there, if you'd like it—M-hm. *(Sympathetically)* You just feel kind of torn to pieces inside. *(Silence of 1 minute, 56 seconds)*

Jim: I wish I could die. *(Sobbing)*

C.R.: You just wish you could die, don't you? M-hm. You just feel so awful, you wish you could perish. *(Therapist laid his hand gently on Jim's arm during this period. Jim showed no definite response. However, the storm subsides somewhat. Very heavy breathing.) (Silence of 1 minute, 10 seconds)*

C.R.: You just feel so awful and so torn apart inside that, that it just makes you wish could pass out. *(Silence of 3 minutes, 29 seconds)*

---

[7] This was the spontaneous feeling that welled up in me, and that I expressed. It was certainly not planned, and I had no idea it would bring such an explosive response.

C.R.: I guess life is so tough, isn't it? You just feel you could weep and sob your heart away and wish you could die.[8] *(Heavy breathing continues.)* *(Silence of 6 minutes, 14 seconds)*

C.R.: I don't want to rush you, and I'll stay as long as you really need me, but I do have another appointment, that I'm really late for.

Jim: Yeah. *(Silence of 17 minutes)*

C.R.: Certainly been through something, haven't you? *(Silence of 1 minute, 18 seconds)*

C.R.: May I see you Tuesday?

Jim: *(Inaudible response)*

C.R.: Hmm?

Jim: Don't know. *(Almost unintelligible)*

C.R.: "I just don't know." M-hm. You know all the things I said before, I mean very much. I want to see you Tuesday, and I want to see you before then if you want to see me. So, if you need me, don't hesitate to call me. *(Silence of 1 minute)*

C.R.: It's really rough, isn't it? *(Silence of 24 seconds)*

Jim: Yes.

C.R.: Sure is. *(Jim slowly gets up to go.)* *(Silence of 29 seconds)*

C.R.: Want to take that too? *(Jim takes appointment slip.)* *(Silence of 20 seconds)*

C.R.: There's a washroom right down the hall where you can wash your face. *(Jim opens door; noise and voices are heard from corridor.)* *(Silence of 18 seconds)* *(Jim turns back into the room.)*

Jim: You don't have a cigarette, do you? *(Therapist finds one.)*

C.R.: There's just one. I looked in the package but—I don't know. I haven't any idea how old it is, but it looks sort of old.

Jim: I'll see you. *(Hardly audible)*

C.R.: OK. I'll be looking for you Tuesday, Jim.

---

[8] As I have listened to the recording of this interview, I wish I had responded to the relief he must have been experiencing in letting his despair pour out, as well as to the despair itself.

A SILENT YOUNG MAN
The Case of Jim Brown

Jerold D. Bozarth

The case of Jim Brown consists of 166 sessions of Carl Rogers with an individual diagnosed as having "schizophrenic reaction, simple type." Jim was one of the participants in a research study (Rogers, Gendlin, Kiesler, & Truax, 1967) examining the effectiveness of client-centered therapy with hospitalized patients diagnosed as schizophrenic. The two transcribed sessions presented in this volume were, according to Rogers (1967), "two significant and I believe crucial interviews in the therapy with James Brown" (p. 401).

Rogers' work with Jim is important for several reasons. One is that the case represents one of the few examples of client-centered psychotherapy (or any other psychotherapeutic approach) with hospitalized psychotic clients. Also, in addition to the two full sessions reprinted in this book, 15 4-minute segments from Jim's 166 sessions with Rogers were selected (approximately one every 11 sessions), and included in the published description of the research study (Rogers et al., 1967). In the same volume, this representative sampling was commented upon by six notable, experienced therapists (O. Spurgeon English, William C. Lewis, Rollo May, William Alanson White, Julius Seeman, and Carl A. Whitaker; see Truax & Commentators, 1967). I discuss this sampling and the commentaries on it later.

My strategy in this commentary is to focus on two questions of theoretical importance: (1) in these sessions, is Rogers consistent with his theoretical and therapeutic intent? and (2) what does Rogers *do* within these two sessions?

ROGERS' THERAPEUTIC INTENT

Rogers (1951, 1957, 1959, 1986) was clear about his therapeutic intent. His goal was to create the atmosphere that he trusted would promote the actualizing tendency of the other individual. As Brodley and I (Bozarth & Brodley, 1991) explain: "Rather than intervening and thereby assuming therapeutic expertise about the client, the client-centered therapist trusts the client to move forward in a constructive direction. The constructive forward movement of the client is propelled by the sole and inherent motivation in human beings; that is, the actualizing tendency" (p. 3).

To Rogers, the whole purpose of therapy from a functional standpoint was "to hear and accept and recognize the feelings that the client is having" (quoted in Baldwin, 1987, p. 47). He considered it effective for the therapist's goals to be limited to the process of therapy and not to its outcome. As he stated: "I think that if the therapist feels 'I want to be as present to this person as possible. I want to really listen to what is going on. I want to be real in this relationship,' then these are suitable goals for the therapist" (quoted in Baldwin, 1987, p. 47).

Rogers' (1957) hypothesis regarding the "necessary and sufficient conditions" for constructive personality change has enormously influenced the whole field of psychotherapy. Change, according to this formulation, occurs when:

1. Two persons are in psychological contact.
2. The first, whom we shall term the client, is in a state of incongruence, being vulnerable or anxious.
3. The second person, whom we shall term the therapist, is congruent or integrated in the relationship.
4. The therapist *experiences* unconditional positive regard for the client.
5. The therapist *experiences* an empathic understanding of the client's internal frame of reference and *endeavors* to communicate this experience to the client.
6. The communication to the client of the *therapist's empathic understanding and unconditional positive regard* is to a minimal degree achieved. (p. 96, emphasis added)

According to Rogers, no other conditions are necessary. If these six conditions exist, and continue over a period of time, this is sufficient. The process of constructive personality change will follow.

Note that of the three therapist conditions that create the climate to promote the client's actualizing process, unconditional positive regard and empathic understanding are postulated as needing to be *experienced* by the therapist who endeavors to communicate them to the client. The therapist's congruence can exist without being communicated to the client.

Rogers later indicated that he might have overemphasized the three basic conditions: "Perhaps it is something around the edges of those conditions that is really the most important element of therapy—when my self is very clearly, obviously present" (quoted in Baldwin, 1987, p. 45). This statement is important in relation to his work with Jim because the "crucial" aspect of this case clearly involves Rogers' use of self.

My analysis (Bozarth, 1990a) of the evolution of Rogers as a therapist has led me to conclude that over a time span of 30 years his preponderant response efforts were clearly geared to the understanding of his clients' world—whether in 1955, 1965, 1975, or 1985. A more inclusive review (Bozarth, 1990b) led me to conclude that the essence of client/person-centered therapy is the therapist's dedication to going with the client's direction, at the client's pace, and in accordance with the client's unique way of being.

Overall, then, we can assume that Rogers' intent with Jim was solely to create a facilitative climate. According to his tenets, Rogers expected to accomplish this by experiencing unconditional positive regard and empathic understanding toward Jim and by successfully communicating these attitudes to him. Concomitantly, his intention would be to feel congruent in the relationship—to be "fully" himself and "fully" present to his client. He would, following the essence of the therapy, be dedicated to going with Jim's direction, at Jim's pace, and in accordance with Jim's unique way of being.

THE CASE OF JIM BROWN: AN OVERVIEW

According to Rogers (1967), Jim Brown was 28 years old when Rogers first saw him (twice a week) as part of the research project. It was his third hospitalization (the first had been a 3-month stay when Jim was 25). At the time Rogers began to see him Jim had been in the hospital for 19 months, and these interviews were recorded 11 months after that. (The therapeutic encounter between Jim and Rogers lasted for a total of 2½ years.) Rogers points out that Jim had a high-school education and had taken some college courses.

These two sessions seem to me to be significantly different from the 15 segments selected in a different portion of the research project (Truax & Commentators, 1967). In that selection, the 15 randomly drawn 4-minute segments depicted response patterns that were more similar to the response patterns characteristic of other therapy demonstrations by Rogers. That is, there was, for the most part, a clear pattern of client response followed by a therapist response; in addition, there were few silences in the sampled segments. By contrast, silences were a prominent aspect of the sessions with Jim: "He [Jim] was never articulate, and the silences were often prolonged, although when he was expressing bitterness and anger he could talk a bit more freely" (Rogers, 1967, p. 408). In the two sessions in this book it is clear that there was a relationship that involved more than therapeutic interactions. For example, Rogers loaned money to Jim and periodically gave him cigarettes. In short, there seemed to be less intensity and less of an internal struggle for Jim in the 15 selected segments than in the two sessions being reviewed here.

The comments of the six experienced therapists about the 15 segments of typical interactions between Rogers and Jim may prove helpful in reviewing the two sessions in this book. Their initial responses were to the question, "What movement, if any, occurs?" Four of the therapists identified some degree of movement while two did not. Their rationale for progress or lack of progress was related to the subsequent questions: "What is the therapist doing that is helpful?" and "What is the therapist doing that is not helpful?" For those who did not discern progress, the failure was due to what they saw as "the essential ineffectiveness of the therapist's attempts toward reflection of feeling" (Truax & Commentators, 1967, p. 446). Those who discerned progress identified two aspects of the therapy that they felt were present either alone or in combination: "(1) the therapist's effective reflection of feelings and communication of understanding and (2) an attitudinal quality involving especially the therapist's warm and personal dedication" (p. 446). Based on my reading of the 15 segments, I agree with the assessment of the commentators who saw progress. In addition, I feel Rogers stayed close to his theoretical and therapeutic intent in these segments.

The two sessions selected by Rogers and reviewed in this book, I believe, represent a more poignant example of his relationship and interactions with Jim. It is also clear from data provided by Rogers (see below) that he perceived there to be progress over the course of this therapy. The degree to which Jim's progress was due to Rogers' actions is, of course, hard to determine, as in all such evaluation. However, it is reasonable to me to think that Rogers had some role in fostering Jim's considerable progress.

Jim wrote a letter to Rogers (quoted in Rogers, 1967) after they had discontinued therapy and Jim had been released from the hospital. A quote from this letter offers an insightful reflection of his progress: "All in all things couldn't be too much better for me, compared to what they have been. It sure feels good to be able to say, 'To hell with it' when things bother me" (p. 415). Rogers perceived the progress more generally in the following ways:

> The progress he made appeared to grow primarily out of the qualities of the relationship. It appeared to have very little to do with fresh insights, or new and conscious self-perceptions. He *became* a new person in many ways, but he talked about it very little. Perhaps it is more accurate to say that he lived himself, and used himself, in many new ways. In some fundamental characteristics he is still very much the same person. As of this writing he is completely on his own, functioning well, with friends of both sexes, entirely out of touch with the personnel of the hospital or the research group. (p. 416)

It would appear that by reasonable assessment Jim indeed made progress. Moreover, it would appear that Rogers' work with him in these two sessions was consistent with his theoretical and therapeutic intent. He did "a great deal of empathic guessing" (p. 403), and he felt assured that Jim would let him know when his guesses were wrong. Rogers also indicated that he tried "to be" his feelings in relationship with Jim. He thought that these feelings "were largely those of interest, gentleness, compassion, desire to understand, desire to share something of myself, eagerness to stand with him in his despairing experiences" (p. 403).

THE TWO SESSIONS

What, then, did Rogers actually *do* in these two sessions? An examination of them depicts a pattern of silences. The first session has over 50 minutes of silence (with about 50 words uttered by Jim), and the second session, 3 days later, contains about 52 minutes of silence.

The First Session

Rogers makes about five "empathic guess" responses interspersed in the 50 minutes of silence; he makes two personal statements; and he makes 11 responses that can be classified as reflections with the intent of checking Jim's meanings. Most of the "empathic guess" responses appear early in the session. These responses range from "Do you look kind of angry this morning, or is that my imagination?" to "Sounds discouraged or tired." For the most part, Jim Brown corrects Rogers when the therapeutic responses are not accurate. For example, when Rogers says, "Sounds discouraged or tired," Jim after a period of silence, responds with, "No.

Just lousy." Jim then generally continues in silence or gradually proceeds on his own, in his own direction. The major personal expression in this session occurs early on when Rogers indicates that he cares and is "not just sitting here like a stick." Rogers also expresses himself to some extent in the latter part of the session by indicating that he is there "to try to be of some help."

Of the reflective responses, two might be considered "pushing" for meaning. The first of these occurs following Rogers' relatively long reflection on how hurt Jim feels by an acquaintance's statement that he (Jim) is "no good." Jim, responding *defiantly* to what appears to have been an accurate reflection by Rogers, says, "I don't care though." Rogers then responds with the statement: "You tell yourself you don't care at all, but somehow I guess some part of you cares because some part of you weeps over it." After a 19-second silence, Rogers continues: "I guess some part of you feels, 'Here I am hit with another blow, as if I haven't had enough blows like this during my life when I feel that people don't like me. Here's someone I've begun to feel attached to and now he doesn't like me. . . . But just the same the tears run down my cheeks.' " The second "pushing" reflection occurs a few minutes later when Rogers again responds to Jim's tears: "It really hurts, doesn't it?" and after a 26-second silence adds: "I guess if the feelings came out you'd just weep and weep and weep." It seems clear that Rogers is focusing on the feeling of hurt that he sees Jim expressing. This focus appears to have emerged from the point at which Jim corrected one of Rogers' empathic guesses about his mood by saying, "No. Just lousy." Following the client's "lousy feelings" is of course, consistent with Rogers' theoretical intent. Occasionally then, this pursuit of a client's meaning extends to a more active attempt to understand the deeper feelings beyond the client's actual words. For the most part, though, Rogers' reflective responses in this session stay close to the client's actual words. For example, when Jim declares, "I think I'm beyond help," Rogers responds, "Feel as though you're beyond help. . . . You feel just completely hopeless about yourself."

The Second Session

This session contains approximately 52 minutes of silence. Of Rogers' 49 statements in this session, 19 can be considered reflections. He seems to experience Jim's intensity and incorporates the edge of this intensity in his reflections. In addition, there are several significant empathic guesses during the session. For example, Rogers at one point guesses that Jim allows himself during the sessions to "sink down into feelings that run very deep in you." Jim appears to ignore these remarks, noting instead: "I'm gonna take off." Rogers reflects, "You're going to take off? Really run away from here?" but also asks for the background of that feeling. As Jim continues in his own direction, Rogers responds to the intensity of Jim's feelings by using the metaphor of "a wounded animal that wants to crawl away and die." Then, as part of this dialogue, Rogers again resorts to an empathic guess: "Can't help but wonder whether it's still true that some things this friend said to you—are those still part of the thing that makes you feel so awful?" This statement seems accurate since Brown responds affirmatively (albeit with a qualification) saying: "In general, yes."

Rogers also has three clear personal expressions scattered throughout the session. One of these is the statement to Jim that "it makes me feel good that today you don't have your hand up to your face so that I can somehow kind of see you more. . . . I don't feel as though you're hiding behind your hand, or something." Later in the session, Rogers makes this personal expression: "I think I can understand pretty well what it's like to feel that you're just no damn good to anybody." Then he adds: "because there was a time when—I felt that way about myself. And I know it can be really rough." In a footnote accompanying this passage, Rogers acknowledges that this was a most unusual response for him. He felt he wanted to share his experience with Jim, "to let him know he was not alone." Rogers' next personal moment followed an attempt to clarify Jim's meaning. This was the response: "M-hm, m-hm. That's why you want to go, because you really don't care about yourself. You just don't care what happens. And I guess I'd just like to say—I care about you. And I care what happens." Jim burst into tears and unintelligible sobs after this statement, and within 10 to 15 minutes of silence, Rogers attempted to reflect the feelings that were coming forth.

In a footnote Rogers explained this personal expression as a spontaneous feeling that "welled up" in him without any plan. He not only viewed this statement as the "crucial turning point" (see quote below) in the therapy but came to regard it as one that helped him realize the importance of using his "presence" of self in therapy. As he recalled:

> I recognize that when I am intensely focused on a client, just my presence seems to be healing and I think this is probably true of any good therapist. I recall once I was working with a schizophrenic man in Wisconsin whom I had dealt with over a period of a year or two and there were many long pauses. The crucial turning point was when he had given up, did not care whether he lived or died, and was going to run away from the institution. And I said: "I realize that you don't care about yourself, but I want you to know that I care about you, and I care about what happens to you." He broke into sobs for ten or fifteen minutes. That was the turning point of the therapy. I had responded to his feelings and accepted them but it was when I came to him as a person and expressed my feelings for him that it really got to him. (quoted in Baldwin, 1987, p. 45)

SUMMARY

Rogers believed these two sessions constituted especially significant aspects of Jim's psychotherapy; he also believed that these sessions were representative of the use of the self of a therapist in therapy. These sessions may also be viewed from the vantage point of the questions asked of the experienced therapists who reviewed segments of the active therapy: "What movement, if any, occurred?" "What was the therapist doing that was helpful?" "What was the therapist doing that was unhelpful?"

Movement occurred with Jim on two levels. First, he moved toward greater self-sufficiency and independence, enabling him to leave the hospital, to function at a reasonable level of competence, to be reasonably happy, and to be involved with friends. Second, Rogers (1967) thought that Jim's view of himself "as stubborn, bitter, mistreated, worthless, useless, hopeless, unloved, unlovable" was altered to a view of himself as a softer person who no longer experienced himself as "the shell of hardness and bitterness, the stranger to tenderness" (p. 411). In regard to the other two issues: Rogers' helpfulness was primarily that of "caring" and, perhaps, communicating that caring to the client. The erroneous guesses of Rogers did not seem to matter.

The two questions considered in the present commentary were:

1. Is Rogers consistent with his theoretical and therapeutic intent?
2. What does he do within these two "crucial" sessions?

As noted earlier, the consistency of Rogers' theoretical and therapeutic intent in this session is apparent to me. He was consistently striving to experience the client's frame of reference and to communicate this as well as his unconditional positive regard to the client. Rogers doggedly strove to understand this man within the confines of long silences and negativistic responses. He showed a general dedication to the client as a fellow human being by even loaning money to him. Although Rogers appears occasionally to push for Jim to express his more intense feelings, in general, he maintained the theoretical stance of following the client's direction and going with the client's unique way of being. In addition, Rogers' experience with this particular person was no different from what would be predicted from the general theoretical and therapeutic stance that he espoused. Consistent with the value he placed on congruence, Rogers felt he "was simply trying to be my feeling in relationship with him" (p. 403). Similarly, Rogers preferred to relate to Jim Brown "in the relationship, as he was a person at this moment" (p. 402).

Finally, what Rogers did in these two "crucial interviews" can be summarized in his own words: "I felt a warm and spontaneous caring for him as a person, which found expression in several ways—but most deeply at the moment when he was despairing. . . . We were relating as two real and genuine persons" (p. 411).

A PERSONAL REACTION

I was pleased to have the opportunity to review and comment upon Rogers' sessions with Jim because of my early experience working with chronic long-term hospitalized clients. I learned client-centered therapy working with such clients during the late 1950s and early 1960s. I was a psychiatric rehabilitation counselor who began one of the first "vocational/therapeutic" programs for the incarcerated mentally ill in Illinois. I did individual and group therapy with the "patients" and also provided resources and opportunities for them to leave the hospital. The patients I worked with were considered "impossible." However, they achieved an incredibly high discharge and "improvement" rate and low recidivism record. Most of these individuals had been in the hospital for 20 or 30 years. I do not remember any "moments of change" or "crucial turning points," but I do remember over 100 patients who changed their behaviors and attitudes in ways that enabled them to get out of the hospital or, at least, to get out of locked wards. Their major therapeutic contact was with me, which sometimes consisted of primarily talking about jobs or training possibilities.

Rogers' review of Jim's sessions reminds me of sessions that I had with one young man. I had over 50 that were predominantly silent. I experienced him as exuding anger to the point that I was often uneasy being with him and would occasionally express my feelings toward him without ever getting a response. Yet, I learned many years later that he had married, obtained a graduate degree, and was a successful professional.

I was struck by the fact that Rogers had 166 hours of therapy with this client without intervening or judging or interfering with the client's way of being. The client could choose! He did not need to be threatened by conditions of worth put on him. Rogers stuck to the foundation of his theory, that is, the actualizing tendency of the individual. Rogers, true to his theory, trusted the client as the best authority of his own life. I wonder if it is what one does not do as a therapist that is just as important as what one does. I was also struck with Rogers' dedication to this client; he searched for cigarettes for him, was concerned about his next appointments, looked for magazines to give him, and even loaned him money. All of these actions seem to me to be very human acts of caring and interest toward a person.

In addition, Rogers was tenacious in his determination to understand Jim's experiences, to understand the experiential world of the other. I view this intent as the primary reason for his "pushing" for Jim's intense feelings.

I get the feeling that it might have even been difficult for Rogers to allow the client to redirect the focus away from these intense feelings. Nevertheless, Rogers seemed able to return to the client's world even when he probably felt the intensity of Jim's sobs should be dealt with. I wonder, too, if it would have made a difference in the direction of the therapy if Rogers had concentrated on Jim's statements of defiance in addition to his sobs and self-discounting.

I also wonder whether Rogers' willingness to look for a cigarette for Jim may have been a significant factor in Jim's progress as the one moment Rogers believed to be crucial. I fantasize Jim saying, "Doc always found me a cigarette and that's what I needed to help me through all those bad times." *Is there a crucial moment of change in therapy?* There was in Rogers' perception of this case.

Finally, I am personally most struck by Jim's stamina for going in his own direction and in his own way. He was defiant and remained defiant even after the "crucial turning point" of deep and "irreversible" experiencing of feelings. Even in his letter to Rogers, Jim noted that it felt good to be able to say "To hell with it" when things bothered him.

In sum, I find these two sessions to be meaningful representations of Rogers' theoretical and therapeutic intent. They represent Rogers' consistent intent to experience and communicate accurate empathy and unconditional positive regard while being a congruent therapist. These sessions are of special interest because they are not typical of other demonstrations by Rogers. I believe they reveal the nature of long-term sessions with individuals labeled psychotic and the need to address the individuality of those with whom we work. I am mostly reminded, however, of the remarkable resiliency of human beings when they are given adequate opportunity to grow.

REFERENCES

Baldwin, M. (1987). Interview with Carl Rogers on the use of self in therapy. In M. Baldwin & V. Satir (Eds.), *The use of self in therapy*. New York: Haworth Press.

Bozarth, J. D. (1990a). The essence of client-centered and person-centered therapy. In G. Lietaer, J. Rombauts, & R. VanBalen (Eds.), *Client-centered and experiential psychotherapy: Towards the nineties* (pp. 88–99). Leuven: Katholieke Universiteit te Leuven.

Bozarth, J. D. (1990b). The evolution of Carl R. Rogers as a therapist. *Person-Centered Review, 5*(4), 390–398.

Bozarth, J. D., & Brodley, B. T. (1991). Actualization: A functional concept in client-centered therapy. *Journal of Social and Behavioral Change, 6*(5), 45–59.

Rogers, C. R. (1951). *Client-centered therapy.* Boston: Houghton Mifflin.

Rogers, C. R. (1957). The necessary and sufficient conditions of therapeutic personality change. *Journal of Consulting Psychology, 21,* 95–103.

Rogers, C. R. (1959). A theory of therapy, personality, and interpersonal relationships, as developed in the client-centered framework. In S. Koch (Ed.), *Psychology: A study of a science: Study 1. Conceptual and systematic. Vol. 3. Formulation of the person and the social context* (pp. 184–256). New York: McGraw Hill.

Rogers, C. R. (1967). A silent young man. In C. R. Rogers, E. T. Gendlin, D. J. Kiesler, & C. B. Truax (Eds.), *The therapeutic relationship with schizophrenics* (pp. 184–256). Madison: University of Wisconsin Press.

Rogers, C. R. (1986). Client-centered approach to therapy. In I. L. Kutash & A. Wolf (Eds.), *Psychotherapist's casebook: Theory and technique in practice* (pp. 197–208). San Fransisco: Jossey Bass.

Rogers, C. R., Gendlin, E. T., Kiesler, D. J., & Truax, C. B. (Eds.). (1967). *The therapeutic relationship with schizophrenics.* Madison: University of Wisconsin Press.

Truax, C. B., & Commentators. (1967). The client-centered process as viewed by other therapists. In C. R. Rogers, E. T. Gendlin, D. J. Kiesler, & C. B. Truax (Eds.), *The therapeutic relationship with schizophrenics* (pp. 419–506). Madison: University of Wisconsin Press.

THE POWER OF EMPATHIC EXPLORATION

A Process-Experiential/Gestalt Perspective on the Case of Jim Brown

Leslie S. Greenberg

These two sessions of Rogers', which deal with Jim Brown's deep sense of woundedness and vulnerability, provide us with a compelling example of the power of empathy and caring in psychotherapy. Jim, after what appears to be many years of being hurt by others close to him, has withdrawn from the possibility of being hurt. Rogers' acceptance and caring opens him again to his hurt and his tenderness and to the possibility of again being in-relation to another.

Rogers' (1959) formal statement of his theory suggests that the therapist's primary role is to enter the client's frame of reference and provide an atmosphere of empathy, unconditional positive regard (prizing), and congruence. The theory states that establishing these conditions in therapy will tap the vast resources for self-understanding and growth that individuals have within themselves. Rogers proposed that these conditions would release an inherent directional tendency toward the constructive fulfillment of possibilities. In these sessions, Rogers clearly provides these conditions, and he demonstrates his faith in Jim's organismic capacity for growth.

In this commentary I discuss a number of important features of the therapeutic process demonstrated in these sessions and highlight my agreements and disagreements with aspects of client-centered theory and practice. I agree with Rogers and client-centered theory about the nature and importance of the overall relationship conditions in therapy, but I believe Rogers is intentional in his behavior over and above the provision of these conditions. I disagree with Rogers and client-centered theory with regard to the inborn nature of the actualizing tendency and what it is in therapy that releases the growth capacity.

The most striking initial feature of Rogers' sessions with Jim is that the relationship is not one centered on the transference but is rather a true encounter between two human beings attempting to make contact in a helping context. The relationship is much more a real, caring relationship between two people than it is an analysis of the client by a therapist that focuses on the client's past experiences projected into the present. The relationship manifests qualities of presence, immediacy, inclusion, confirmation, and nonexploitativeness that characterize the I–thou relationship (Buber, 1958). Rogers' caring presence, in fact, appears to be central in breaking through Jim's defensive shell. The primary conditions of the client-centered relationship can be seen in these two sessions in all their power. The prizing of one human being by another and the experience of acceptance and nonmanipulative caring for another's inner pain, without any direct attempt to change it, has a tremendously nourishing effect. Rogers' empathy and prizing help Jim reestablish contact with his inner vulnerable self-organization (Greenberg, Elliott, & Foerster, 1991; Greenberg, Rice, & Elliott, 1993), allowing it to emerge from under its protective cover, and facilitating its participation in regenerative contact with the human environment. In essence, the relationship encourages Jim to risk living again.

Rogers' acceptance of his client's despair in this therapy is one of the important demonstrations of his method. We see how the acceptance of "what is" leads to the acknowledgment of the avoided or obscured inner self-organization (Greenberg, 1995). This allowing and accepting of pain in the often hidden and vulnerable self-organization is a crucial therapeutic movement—a real moment of change. However, by emphasizing this core aspect of therapy, I think client-centered practitioners and theorists have mistakenly seen what may indeed be the essence of the therapeutic encounter as if it were the entirety of what successful therapy requires. They have created a general framework and a total method based on this essence, thereby overlooking other important aspects of the process. That is, Rogers developed a method that applied the principles of empathy, prizing, and congruence to all aspects of the therapeutic encounter when they alone are the best approach only at particular times in therapy. Seeking these as the core conditions is crucial to being able to respond to inner experience and the most vulnerable self-organizations. However, one has not always reached such a point in therapy, and the therapist who responds in this manner throughout is likely to miss opportunities for more rapidly overcoming blocks and deepening the process in other ways. It seems to me that Rogers himself did different things at different times, and that his actions—especially at certain key moments in therapy—were not always intended purely as the provision of understanding and relational acceptance, as important as these conditions are.

In my view, Rogers does more in this case than is implied by the triad of conditions mentioned above or by notions of nondirectiveness. I am not suggesting here that I disagree with the importance of the three conditions or with what Rogers says and does in this session but rather that the elements of his formal theory do not fully explain the curative elements of the process that he and other experientially oriented therapists make possible. Rogers, I suggest, is intentional and directed in his own process. The foci he chooses to take at different times within the general provision of his conditions is highly important in understanding how change occurs.

Specifically, Rogers, in accordance with his theory of the importance of empathically responding to feelings, is highly selective in what feelings he attends to; indeed, at times in these sessions he attends to deep unexpressed feelings. In the first session, he accurately senses and responds to Jim's inner hurt and then later focuses on Jim's thwarted human desire to break through his walled-off state, to get past his defiant "I don't care about anything" attitude. Rogers intentionally and selectively guides Jim to focus inward on the deeper painful emotions that lie behind his defiance. Rogers is *directive* in the process, providing a gentle consistent pressure on Jim to focus on his internal experience and to focus on particular feelings at particular times—those that seem to come from his inner core.

Near the beginning of these sessions, when Jim states that he "ain't no good to nobody, never was, and never will be," Rogers first responds with empathic understanding of this feeling: "Feeling that now, hmm? That you're just no good to yourself, no good to anybody." This focus on feeling is accompanied by the very real prizing of the client in the statement, "Those really are lousy feelings." Jim begins to weep quietly but claims not to care. Even only reading the transcript, one can feel Jim's hurt defiance. Rogers then responds strongly and with a particular focus: "You tell yourself you don't care at all, but somehow I guess some part of you cares because some part of you weeps over it," and following a silence says, "I guess some part of you just feels, 'Here I am hit with another blow, as if I hadn't had enough blows.' "

With these responses Rogers senses deeply beyond what the client has said. This is not simple reflection. Rogers essentially picks up on a duality in the client's experience, a split between organismic experience and the self-concept, or between the real self and false self (Greenberg, 1979, 1984). This type of split functioning can also be viewed profitably in terms of a distinction between primary and secondary emotion (Greenberg & Safran,

1987, 1989), in which the secondary emotion (defiance) is viewed as reactive, or secondary, to the underlying more primary experience, the hurt. The task of the therapist, in this situation, is to focus on bringing out or acknowledging primary emotion, as Rogers does here, and not to emphasize the secondary emotional responses. Rogers thus does not reflect Jim's secondary defiance but rather selectively focuses on and directs his attention to Jim's more primary tears and sense of hurt. Throughout this first session Rogers continues empathically to explore his client's inner world, continually pointing Jim toward his deepest feelings with comments such as "cuts so deep, you can hardly stand it," and "if the feelings came out you'd just weep and weep and weep."

Another outstanding characteristic of these sessions is, of course, the long periods of silence, and Rogers' patience and ability to accept them. Clearly, Rogers' capacity to sit with a client and remain attentive without exerting too much pressure to be a particular way is a great communication of prizing and sensitivity to the client's inner being. However, the way Rogers does respond to the silence with empathic conjectures (Greenberg & Goldman, 1988)—he refers to this as empathic guessing—about what the client might be experiencing also reveals very clearly an important technical aspect of Rogers' functioning. He consistently attempts to access and deepen the client's internal experience.

Thus, I am claiming that in these sessions Rogers does far more than provide an accepting relationship (although he does this also). It is more accurate to say that he empathically explores, and conjectures about, what the client might be experiencing at the edges of his awareness. Empathically exploring involves engaging the client in a search for new information by focusing on the leading edge of the client's experience, while empathically conjecturing involves guessing about what the client may be feeling but not yet articulating (Greenberg & Goldman, 1988; Greenberg et al., 1993). Use of these types of interventions implies that Rogers is engaged in inducing the client to search experientially for something more, rather than simply mirroring back what is being said. Thus the therapy contains a directional tendency, a striving toward symbolization and experiencing by Jim of his not fully articulated primary feelings and idiosyncratic meanings. This process direction is always balanced with an understanding and acceptance of what *is* by empathic reflections of what the client is saying and a prizing of the client's whole being.

The important issue is that the therapy involves a form of process directiveness that points the client consistently inward toward what is most strongly felt and toward a process of making meaning and explicating what lies within. For example, in the first session after establishing contact with Jim, Rogers responds to his statement that "this guy I went to town with . . . told me [I was no good]" by conjecturing the meaning Jim gave to this:

"here's somebody that—meant something to you and . . . he's told you that he thinks you're no good at all" and "that just really knocks the props out from under you." This exploration of implicit meaning is central to Rogers' endeavors.

Explication of feeling and meaning is done, however, without invalidating or contradicting what the client explicitly says. Rogers achieves this, for example, in the statement, "but somehow I guess some part of you cares because some part of you weeps." He uses a tentative, exploratory style and alludes to another part of the self. Here the client is not being confronted or contradicted but encouraged to explore another aspect of experience. In addition, the selective focus introduced by Rogers does not come from the position of a dominant, distant expert ("What you are really feeling is . . . ") but rather is offered as his attempt at understanding what the client feels. His interpersonal stance would be rated on a therapy coding system such as the Structural Analysis of Social Behavior (SASB; Benjamin, 1993) as low on dominance and high on affiliation, as opposed to an expert stance that would be rated higher on dominance and lower on affiliation.

Another point of importance in understanding Rogers' selectivity and process directiveness relates not to his aim, but to his timing. This speaks to the point that my colleagues and I have made elsewhere (Greenberg, 1986; Greenberg et al., 1993; Rice & Greenberg, 1984)—that psychotherapy should not be construed as a uniform, singular process but rather a highly complex and differentiated one that can be understood best by breaking it down into different events and units. Thus, Rogers does different things at different times. Sometimes he is silent in response to a client's silence; at other times, when the client appears to be experiencing something but is not saying what it is, Rogers conjectures about the silence. At times, moved by his own inner experience, Rogers discloses. When the client presents a more defensive self-concept organization, he specifically focuses on the unarticulated and attempts to articulate it. So when Jim speaks from his "defensive shell," Rogers focuses on what is beyond. That is, he recognizes the shell as defensive and searches for what is more primary behind the shell. Thus, although providing relationship conditions is primary, Rogers' moment-by-moment process is not uniform in nature. Rather, his specific aims seem subtly different at different moments depending on what he regards as most facilitative at a given time.

Yet another feature of these sessions that seems important to note is that therapeutic improvement does not take place in a fashion fully captured by the classical client-centered theory of change. This theory suggests that facilitative conditions allow the client's experience to be incorporated into his or her self-concept through a relaxation of conditions of self-worth (Rogers, 1959). This view does not fully capture the truly dialogical, interpersonal nature of the change process in Rogers' therapy.

In this therapy it is Rogers' caring for and prizing of Jim, communicated first by his empathic way of being, but later explicitly by his statement of caring, that gets through to Jim. Rather than change occurring by a relaxation of Jim's conditions of worth so that some previously unaccept-able aspect of Jim's organismic experience could break through into awareness and be accepted by his self-concept, change seems to have occurred as a result of Rogers' caring. This helps Jim fully experience pain and despair he had avoided. It is facing the avoided rather than relaxing the conditions of worth that led to change.

Feeling cared for by another allows one to face previously disowned pain and despair, perhaps because it contradicts a pathogenic belief (Weiss, Sampson, & the Mount Zion Psychotherapy Research Group, 1986) such as "No one ever cares about me." In my view, this pain is not organismic experience that is blocked because it is incongruent with the self-concept or certain internalized conditions of worth, but rather it reflects a pool of experience filled with anxiety, fear, and sadness that comes from a history associated with unmet needs and the experiences involved in attempts at satisfying these needs. The experience is dreaded or avoided because the pain and fear are not easily tolerated and the person feels hopeless about ever getting his or her needs met. The change process in my view involved his interpersonal experience with Rogers—an experience of feeling truly cared for that provided the interpersonal support, hope, and courage he needed to face the disorganizing impact of the pain. This demonstrates how affirmation of the client by the therapist and the encouragement that comes from interpersonal caring, and from communication of faith in and respect for the client's value and resources, are important ingredients of therapy. It is thus the therapist's positive regard, a dialogical process, that is change-producing and leads to the facing of pain, rather than the release of healthy organismic experience that had been denied by a negative self-concept. I believe that Jim could let down and let his hurt break through because he felt cared for by Rogers and trusted that Rogers was "there for him." What happened here was that the client had a corrective emotional experience in which the presence and actions of the therapist helped disconfirm certain core dysfunctional beliefs about how others will re-spond to needs and experience. This was not a relaxing of conditions of worth but a new experience and interpersonal learning. In this view, as the source of change, the dialogue is privileged over the actualizing tendency.

Given the above perspective on the importance of interpersonal learning in therapy, I believe that the growth tendency also needs to be re-conceptualized in more interactive terms. In part, it was Rogers' ability to *see and communicate* his trust in Jim that helped Jim have faith in his own experience. How one person sees another has an effect on how that person develops. For example, when teachers see a child as bright, the child's performance improves. Similarly, therapists' belief in their clients' potential for growth, and their communication of this belief by manner, focus, and framing, facilitate the growth tendency of clients. Thus, the growth tendency needs to be understood as coming into existence in a dialogue, in a context of empathic attunement. The growth tendency does not exist exclusively within the organism as a genetic blueprint independent of the environment. Rather it is a product of interaction. We know children show a failure to thrive if not given sufficient contact/comfort. Thus, survival and growth are potentials that are social as well as biological. Analogously, the growth tendency comes into being in an environment that appreciates it and confirms its existence. Growth does not occur in any environment, rather it is the empathic environment of human dialogue that helps the person to *become* "growthful."

One view of this therapy, thus, is that it involves countering discouragement with interpersonal caring. Rogers in these sessions, in his manner and content, was a powerfully confirming agent in the client's environment. When one exposes oneself (as Jim did) in all one's vulnerability and the messiness of one's experience, or view of oneself as ugly, to another, and discovers that the other does not flinch or reject but empathically prizes and understands, the experience is overwhelmingly affirming (Greenberg et al., 1993). It provides a significant boost to one's ability to accept oneself and grow. When the struggling seedling of growth is bathed in the light of acknowledgment, it gains strength and struggles toward the light. The tendency toward growth is thus better conceptualized as an interpersonal field event than a purely biological tendency within an individual.

In my view, conceptualizations of change in client-centered therapy that depart from the conflict–denial theory (conflict between organismic experience and self-concept) and rather emphasize experiential unfolding (Gendlin, 1962, 1974) more adequately capture the role of interactiveness in experience and the change process. It is important, however, in attempting to understand the true nature of the growth or actualizing tendency in the psychological realm to emphasize how important it is that the therapist "sees" the client as having the capacity for growth. Thus, therapists must not only try to focus clients on their inner experience but also communicate faith in clients' organismic wisdom and capacity for growth, both implicitly and explicitly. This communication facilitates the capacity to become a helpful guiding force.

One of the most interesting but least clearly understood aspects of the process of experiential growth concerns the ways in which therapists use language, framing their clients' experience so as to reflect a growth process, either explicitly in terms of the potential for growth or implicitly in terms of possibility, hope, a struggle toward something, a new process, or the future. This framing of potential, paradoxically, occurs in the context of accepting what is. That is, the therapist does not push the client to be where he or she is not but rather recognizes the moment of the client's desire to change or grow, which is paradoxically an acceptance of where he or she is.

The skill involved in being able to accept the client while simultaneously being attuned to the presence of the directional tendency is the hallmark of good experiential therapy. A reflection that misses the desire to grow misses a crucial aspect of experience. Thus, if someone is in great despair, the therapist's first task is to acknowledge it. It is crucial, however, to focus on this tendency whenever it is there, for it is the recognition of this growth edge, by both client and therapist, that impels the process forward. A constant frame that growth is possible, even though it may not be operative now or is currently lost, creates possibility.

Saying that one *feels* worthless is different from saying that one *is* worthless. Rogers' reflection adds a sense of perspective—the perspective that there is an agent apart from the experience of the bad feeling, that there is a "me" apart from the feeling. Although this is a subtle distinction, it is an important one. It symbolizes a way to see oneself as apart from the referent and creates a place to stand and view it. It can give one a sense of a broader self and the possibility of process and change. This is especially true when the reflection includes a time perspective, for in reflecting that I feel this way "now," it suggests I might feel another way later.

In the second session, Jim expresses a wish to die, and Rogers confirms how awful he feels. But then Rogers brings out the situation that might be responsible for this feeling, conjecturing that it was something Jim's friend had said that made him feel so awful. Finding what set off this flood of feelings contextualizes it as a response to a particular event; again this creates a sense of possibility. Rogers is communicating to Jim that the feeling is in response to something specific rather than being pervasive. From there Rogers proceeds to frame the client's experience in an interesting fashion. He reflects back to Jim what Ellis would term an irrational belief, " 'If he feels I'm no good, then that proves I'm just no good to anybody' " and "If you go by what others . . . have said, then . . . you are no good." This presents the alternative idea that Jim can still think of himself as good. Possibility again is created.

Later Rogers discloses that there was a time when he felt the same way Jim does about himself. In addition to letting Jim know he is not alone, this response implies that it is possible to survive or change. Rogers also emphasizes time and process with "Right *at this point* you just don't know—whether you want to say yes" (emphasis added). Thus, even in this therapy with a schizophrenic patient, in which caring is the major ingredient and the relationship supersedes any technical aspect, the focus on the growth tendency and on possibility is evident in a variety of his responses. In addition, intervention involves more than empathy or checking of understanding alone. Rather Rogers' responses are guided by many varied intentions that help clients deepen their experience and engage in a variety of process enhancing cognitive/emotional processes.

In my view, Rogers, in his use of client-centered therapy, functioned by selectively attending to and emphasizing particular aspects of functioning. Thus, he favored feelings, felt meanings, and primary emotions over thoughts, conceptualizations, and secondary emotions. The growth possibilities, rather than being strictly in the self, arise interpersonally in a dialogue, and interpersonal caring and valuing affirm the other as worthwhile and provide a corrective emotional experience. This is a highly active process, with particular experiences being responded to in particular ways with particular intentions. The principles governing these selections and aims need to be fully articulated. Here lies the growth edge in client-centered therapy that needs to be attended to and developed.

REFERENCES

Benjamin, L. S. (1993). *Interpersonal diagnosis and treatment of personality disorders.* New York: Guilford Press.

Buber, M. (1958). *I and thou.* New York: Scribner's.

Gendlin, E. T. (1962). *Experiencing and the creation of meaning: A philosophical and psychological approach to the subjective.* New York: Free Press.

Gendlin, E. T. (1974). Client-centered and experiential psychotherapy. In D. A. Wexler & L. N. Rice (Eds.), *Innovations in client-centered therapy* (pp. 211–246). New York: Wiley.

Greenberg, L. S. (1979). Resolving splits: The two-chair technique. *Psychotherapy: Theory, Research and Practice, 16,* 310–318.

Greenberg, L. S. (1984). A task-analysis of intrapersonal conflict resolution. In L. N. Rice & L. S. Greenberg (Eds.), *Patterns of change: Intensive analysis of psychotherapy process* (pp. 67–123). New York: Guilford Press.

Greenberg, L. S. (1986). Change process research. *Journal of Consulting and Clinical Psychology, 54,* 4–9.

Greenberg, L. S. (1995). Experiential approaches to acceptance. In S. Hayes, N. Jacobson, V. Follette, & M. Dougher (Eds.), *Acceptance and change.* Reno, NV: Context Press.

Greenberg, L. S., Elliott, R., & Foerster, F. S. (1991). Experiential processes in the psychotherapeutic treatment of depression. In D. McCann & N. Endler (Eds.), *Depression: Developments in theory, research and practice.* Toronto: Thompson.

Greenberg, L. S., & Goldman, R. (1988). Training in experiential psychotherapy. *Journal of Consulting and Clinical Psychology, 56,* 696–702.

Greenberg, L. S., Rice, L. N., & Elliott, R. (1993). *Facilitating emotional change: The moment-by-moment process.* New York: Guilford Press.

Greenberg, L. S., & Safran, J. D. (1987). *Emotion in psychotherapy.* New York: Guilford Press.

Greenberg, L. S., & Safran, J. D. (1989). Emotion in psychotherapy. *American Psychologist, 44,* 19–29.

Rice, L. N., & Greenberg, L. S. (Eds.). (1984). *Patterns of change: Intensive analysis of psychotherapy process.* New York: Guilford Press.

Rogers, C. R. (1959). A theory of therapy, personality, and interpersonal relationships, as developed in the client-centered framework. In S. Koch (Ed.), *Psychology: A study of a science: Study 1. Conceptual and systematic. Vol. III. Formulations of the person and the social context* (pp. 184–256). New York: McGraw Hill.

Weiss, J., Sampson, H., & the Mount Zion Psychotherapy Research Group. (1986). *The psychoanalytic process: Theory, clinical observations, and empirical research.* New York. Guilford Press.

CHAPTER 8

THE CASE OF SYLVIA (1976)

TRANSCRIPT

Commentaries are in brackets to distinguish them from the actual interview.

Carl Rogers (C.R.): Well, where would you like to start this morning?

[This is my fifth interview with Sylvia. The fourth interview had been held on the previous day. Prior to that there had been the three interviews a year earlier. The interview will be shown as it was recorded, but with comments both from Sylvia and from myself at points where we felt we wished to clarify what was going on or to make some comment about what was going on.]

Sylvia: Well, uh, I want to tell you about something that I've been thinking about and that it's a, a sharing more than telling you a problem.

C.R.: M-hm, m-hm.

[So often clients and counselors get the feeling that the relationship is one which must be filled only with problems. Sylvia gives a little indication of that, this is just a sharing, it's not a problem.]

Sylvia: And that is, I just recently noticed in myself that I've been learning. (C.R.: M-hm.) And that's a big deal. Uh, I hear people say all the time, "Oh, I've learned so much, I learned this, and I learned that, and that was such a learning experience." And I, all these years that I've been growing up, I haven't felt any learning, and I feel, "Well, what did you learn and how did you know that you learned it?" And it was a mystery to me. (C.R.: Uh-huh.) And just the last few weeks, or, actually I've been realizing the last year, mainly, is that I learned some things, and I know

261

I've learned them, and I know that, OK, that I'm at this point and with a certain situation or idea, and that 6 months ago or 3 months ago it was different. (C.R.: Uh-huh.) And so I'm feeling my learning, and that's really exciting.

C.R.: It's the awareness of it that's new. (Sylvia: Uh-huh.) That you're beginning to realize, "Hey, I am different in this respect, I've learned something."

[A relationship should be one in which good feelings have just as much place as bad feelings, and here she's bringing out some very positive feelings about herself, which is a healthy and valid part of a counseling relationship. It's always exciting to me to hear a client telling of positive steps which he or she has been taking, and here Sylvia sounds confident 'cause she's doing something that she has decided to do in her own way, not necessarily following all the books, but doing what she feels and experiences is right.]

Sylvia: I've changed. (C.R.: Uh-huh.) And I can see the difference and feel the difference. (C.R.: Uh-huh.) Yeah.

C.R.: What are some of those differences?

Sylvia: Well *(small laugh)*, um, I, I've made a decision to be more strict with my children and to, uh, to listen to them but decide that I'm their mother and I know many things they don't, and that I will make many more decisions than I've made in the past. And uh—

C.R.: M-hm, m-hm. Sounds as though you feel a bit stronger that way.

Sylvia: Yes. And, and I've been trying it. (C.R.: Uh, m-hm.) Trying being the more strict person and it's working beautifully. (C.R.: Uh-huh.) Uh, they at first they, you know have their little resistance or whatever it is, but then we go on with the program, which is my program more, and I feel a lot better about that as being, uh, uh, helping children to adjust to the world.

C.R.: Sounds, sounds as though you feel more like a grown-up mother.

Sylvia: M-hm. Capable. (C.R.: M-hm.) Of making appropriate decisions. (C.R.: M-hm.) For them. And another area is sex. And, uh, and I, I've done a lot of things in the past year, in the past mainly year that I haven't done before. That is, I've had intercourse with a few different men and put myself in situations where before I was absolutely unwilling to do because of my fears and, and I've learned some things about myself, like I know a lot more right now today about what kind of sexual relationship, what kind of intimate relationships that I want to have with men and that feels good. (C.R.: M-hm, m-hm.) Beca—, and, um, and it only came through, uh, risking, I mean there was no, it only came through trying things out, there was no amount— (C.R.: Uh-huh, Uh-huh.) There was no amount of therapy or reading or thinking or talking that helped me to learn those things, but it was feeling strong enough within myself that I could take chances.

C.R.: So risking has been the road to learning in the sexual area.

Sylvia: Yes. Uh-huh. (C.R.: M-hm.) And it is with my children, and it is with relating to people in many ways, not just sexually. (C.R.: M-hm.) Other ways too.

C.R.: M-hm.

[Sylvia is showing a lot of risking behavior. She's risking a good deal to talk about things like this on film. But what's more important is that she has come to the point in her own life where she realizes that her own experience is the best guide for her. Not books, not therapy, not anything outside of herself. It is her own experience from which she can learn, and here she is learning in a very sensitive and personal area and is willing to share that with us.]

Sylvia: Reaching out to people and approaching strangers and uh—

C.R.: Taking all kinds of risks that you hadn't before.

Sylvia: Some. More, which, I mean I, I don't know about all kinds.

C.R.: Yeah.

Sylvia: Quite a few, and it's been exciting and hard.

C.R.: And I guess that leads to a, um, a deeper kind of learning, at any rate a learning that you feel more sure of. I get, I get a sense of assurance in what you're talking about. Assurance in you.

[One thing that has been true with Sylvia in every interview we have had is that she thinks carefully about what she says, she thinks carefully about what I say, and when what I say is not correct, doesn't match her experience, she's quite willing to correct me. She is very precise in both describing her own feelings and also in making sure that my response to them is accurate.]

Sylvia: Well, yes. Yes and no. And I, I feel more im—, like I was saying before, I feel more mature and more and I'm more aware of my immaturity. (C.R.: M-hm.) They're both, uh, a part of each other. (C.R.: M-hm.) And uh, does that make—does that, I guess I'm thinking that it just sounds crazy.

C.R.: No, I don't—

Sylvia: To say that I feel more mature because I know I'm how, I know more about how immature I am.

C.R.: Uh-huh. No, that makes a lot of sense to me.

[Sylvia: I was surprised that what I said made sense to him. I think that I thought that it made sense to me, but that doesn't necessarily mean it would make sense to other people. I mean, it made sense in my own system. It felt good that he could understand me, and he knew I valued that it made sense to him too.]

[C.R.: It's important to Sylvia to make sure that she's accurately understood. Can anyone understand how she can be more mature by being aware of her immaturity? Well, to me, that's quite understandable, but it's clear that she wants to make certain that my understanding extends to that degree.]

Sylvia: It does.

C.R.: Uh-huh. Because you're, you're, uh, more aware of all aspects of yourself, and it sounds more acceptant of them too. "Yes, I'm mature in certain ways and here's some ways I know I'm immature."

Sylvia: M-hm. And I didn't know that before, or I, I knew I felt uncomfortable that I didn't understand it. (C.R.: M-hm.) But that's related to something I've been thinking about, I think, about being here with you and, uh, and telling myself two things. One is, "Oh, you're just a," I'm just a dependent personality, you know, Carl Rogers or blah-blah-blah-blah, don't, I don't run my own life. I go for help a lot. And then I tell myself I'm always being so strong and so together and having everything so worked out in my head that I don't allow myself to be, to be helpless in a situation where it might be good for me. Like right here now with you, I would like to be more helpless, which to me means open, I think. (C.R.: M-hm, m-hm.) To what to us, and, uh, and I see myself being, uh, together and not being helpless.

[I think at that point I was feeling concern that I was just gonna go to another session of being, oh, in control of things and rattling on and on. I probably made a conscious decision that I have to do something to, to break that and, uh, which was talk about it, talk about my fear. My fear was a concern that I wouldn't learn anything.]

C.R.: M-hm. Sounds as though you, you voice that as a conflict, but it sounds as though really you're more on the, on the side of the second aspect that, uh, uh, to be open and, and in that sense helpless and vulnerable, I guess might be a possible term too, uh, is something you, you really believe that's what you are, rather than that you're a totally dependent person and really helpless and have to, have to run for help. I sort of get the feeling you like this aspect of you that is able to be with me in a way that is, uh, more open, more vulnerable perhaps.

Sylvia: Well, I like it, and I also scold myself for being dependent, so there's—

C.R.: There are the two sides, uh-huh.

Sylvia: There's something missing in the middle to connect, and I, it seems like you might have been talking about that and I still didn't hear it.

C.R.: M-hm. So really to get it more accurately, you scold yourself for, for being dependent, for, for wanting to be here, for example, with me, and yet at the same time you, you feel, uh, well, that's good, I, I really like that, but where's the, where's the integration of those two, uh, points of view.

Sylvia: M-hm.

[That seemed to me like a very excellent, uh, not paraphrase, but when he, you know, tells me back what he thinks I meant. It, um, solidified what I expressed in the previous comment about that there was something missing. It made more sense to me.]

That's right. *(Small laugh)* May I hold your hands again?

C.R.: Sure. M-hm.

Sylvia: We feel an old feeling.

C.R.: OK.

[Sylvia: When we did the filming in A_____, we held each other's hands the whole time, and I imagine it occurred to me that it might be good to do that again. I feel good. At that time, I, I wanted to get away from being in my head so completely the whole time, experiencing.]

[C.R.: I felt very comfortable during this holding of hands. Uh, I'm reminded of a friend of mine who said that he did eye therapy and, uh, in a sense that's what this was. Our eyes were very much in contact, and, uh, I think as much was going on at a nonverbal way as in a verbal way. It was a close relationship, and we both experienced it that way.]

Sylvia: *(Clears throat)* I would like to be less, uh, less strong right now. I would like to give myself the gift of not having to be sensible and reasonable and— (C.R.: M-hm, m-hm.) Also the protection, protect, protect myself.

C.R.: M-hm, m-hm, m-hm. Really would be giving yourself a gift if you could just kind of let go and not, uh, not be so competent and able—

[It seems clear that the reason she wants to hold my hands is that she wants to experience something that is very frightening to her, namely to drop her competent, reasonable, strong self and let herself be some of the weakness and vulnerability that she is.]

Sylvia: M-hm, m-hm. And I think it helps to touch you, to, to, to let go of the should, of my shoulds. *(Small laugh)*

C.R.: M-hm, m-hm. And you feel some contact and maybe you can say, "Well, maybe I don't have to be so strong, so—" (Sylvia: M-hm.) "Maybe I can just let go more."

Sylvia: Yes. *(Small laugh) (20-second pause)* I want to get away from all, um, my rationalizing right now this minute, and I don't know how to do that except to shut up. (C.R.: M-hm, m-hm.) And, so it's not like I have so much a desire to sit and not talk and look in your eyes as I have a desire to not be the way I am all the time. (C.R.: M-hm.) And I don't know yet what else to do.

C.R.: You have to be kind of silent, to let go of that rational and rationalizing part of you.

[In the interviews that we held a year ago, the silences were very long and Sylvia found a great deal of security and, uh, seemed to profit a great deal from holding my hands during the interview, and here she returns to the pattern of a year ago. It's another indication of the fact that these interviews with her perhaps rest more solidly on just the fact of the relationship than they do even on the content of what she's saying and talking about.]

Sylvia: M-hm. *(20-second pause)* It feels easier to focus on, uh, in this position that I'm in now with you, I feel more focused, yeah.

C.R.: M-hm. Are there any things that sort of come bubbling up?

Sylvia: Yeah, I know it's something I want to talk about.

C.R.: OK. M-hm. *(10-second pause)* But it's not easy, huh.

Sylvia: No, it's not easy, and I'm enjoying the richness of feeling— (C.R.: M-hm.) Your hands this way and letting go of some more of, of the camera business and the— (C.R.: M-hm, m-hm.) And, uh, and the fear about bringing up something that *(laughs) (clears throat)* and knowing that in about 15 minutes, it'll all seem, um, I don't know, not quite as serious.

[It just had to take its own time for me to get to where I could feel like I could say the words that I needed to say. It was almost like waiting and just like, uh, you know, what else is new while I'm waiting? For something that took a natural process that it had to take.]

C.R.: M-hm.

[If anyone has a doubt about the value of silences, it should be removed by this interchange. Sylvia's saying, "I'm doing more work when I'm silent than I am when I'm talking."]

[Sylvia: His specific comments or the content of his comments is not necessarily helpful as opposed to not helpful. But what it does do that is valuable is that it gives me something to bounce against. It's a stimulation to better focus myself.]

Sylvia: There's something I've been wanting to talk over with you.

C.R.: OK.

Sylia: It's, I'm real attracted to black people. (C.R.: M-hm.) And, uh, that's about the craziest part of me, um, I'm ashamed. (C.R.: M-hm.) Um, I'm embarrassed, not right now this minute, but when I'm out walking around.

C.R.: When it happens, m-hm.

Sylvia: And living my life.

C.R.: You feel what an awful thing it is that "I'm attracted to black people."

[I think that from the time that she first wanted to hold my hands, I felt that she probably was going to make use of that closer relationship to get to something that she hadn't been able to express before, and now she's taking really a great risk in talking about something very private, very personal.]

Sylvia: M-hm. Not, not all black people I see, but a lot. (C.R.: M-hm, m-hm.) And, like the black people that I talked it over with, it seems, it doesn't seem like any problem at all, they understand perfectly. (C.R.: M-hm.) And, but my family, I think it's a real painful situation for them when I have as many black friends as I do. (C.R.: M-hm, m-hm.) And—

C.R.: That sounds like not only your family looks down on it or something but that you scold yourself for it too.

Sylvia: Uh-huh, right, I, I think there's something wrong with me.

C.R.: Yeah, that's it.

Sylvia: M-hm. But it doesn't—

C.R.: "What kind of a crazy person am I that I feel attracted to so many blacks?"

Sylvia: I'm sick, sick, I think—

C.R.: Sick, that's—

Sylvia: And ne—, neurotic, um— (C.R.: Hmm.) Strange. (C.R.: M-hm.) *(Clears throat)*

C.R.: You really feel that there's something sick in you that causes you to have so many black friends.

Sylvia: Well, I keep looking for a reasonable explanation, and there is none.

C.R.: So there isn't any reason except that you feel that way.

Sylvia: M-hm. And I—

C.R.: And that isn't good enough.

Sylvia: Well, I, I, I've been struggling so long to accept that in myself, and I'm still fighting. It's like I'm fighting to accept that in myself and, and letting go rather than thinking it's a terrible thing and, and that I can't let other people know. (C.R.: M-hm, m-hm, m-hm.) And, uh—

C.R.: "It's that I should not feel that way. I shouldn't be that way. It's sick."

[I think by that response I was trying to exaggerate her feelings in order to assist her in becoming more accepting of them, but as I listen to it, I think I might have responded more powerfully by responding to her struggle to accept herself as a person who is attracted to blacks.]

Sylvia: Like when I, wh—, I, imagine when I meet a black person that I am attracted to that that person will know, and I always wonder if they can tell.

C.R.: M-hm, see if it shows. (Sylvia: Uh-huh.) M-hm, m-hm.

Sylvia: And that they'll think I'm strange. (C.R.: M-hm.) M-hm. And it has something to do with all the black–white sex stuff that goes on, like, um, black women and white men, which is very foreign to me. I have very little thinking or, um, concern about that. But the black men–white women thing, um, and I'm attracted to a lot of black men. (C.R.: M-hm.) Yeah.

C.R.: It has something to do with the sexual attraction.

Sylvia: I know, yeah, it does, I know it does. (C.R.: M-hm.) But it's not just that, it's also— (C.R.: M-hm.) Children and, and women and lifestyle— (C.R.: M-hm.) And as I see it through my tunnel vision, which I do. (C.R.: M-hm.) *(Clears throat)*

C.R.: So I guess you're saying, um, yeah, there's a sexual element in it, but I'm also attracted to their way of living.

Sylvia: M-hm. That I see.

C.R.: Yeah.

Sylvia: And I, but I think what I see isn't what is.

C.R.: That it's partly your fantasy or something.

Sylvia: Maybe putting that, that, this on this film will help me to *(laughs)* stand on the ground and be who I am. (C.R.: M-hm, m-hm.) And not be so ashamed, so embarrassed and so— (C.R.: M-hm.) Um, uncomfortable.

C.R.: In a way you're saying it out loud and really in a wa—, in a sense, publicly, may help you to feel, "I don't need to be so ashamed of that."

[I've filmed a number of interviews, but I never had a client knowingly make use of the filming to try to gain more acceptance of self, and clearly that's what Sylvia is doing in this interchange. By putting herself clearly on record, she feels perhaps then she will feel less ashamed, less sick, more uh, truly acceptant of the person that she is and the experiences that she has.]

Sylvia: M-hm. And I tell myself I should be joyful, I mean, *(small laugh)*, why, why negative? (C.R.: M-hm, m-hm.) And I, I guess you know, the culture or I don't know, I— *(sighs)*

C.R.: But you feel disapproved of probably, certainly by your family and maybe by the culture in this respect.

Sylvia: My friends don't understand. (C.R.: M-hm.) My white friends. *(Pause)*

C.R.: M-hm. Makes you feel different. (Sylvia: M-hm.) Set apart or something like that.

Sylvia: Well, sometimes I feel different, but I know a lot of other people, I believe a lot of other people, feel the same way, (C.R.: M-hm.) and I know a lot of other white women are attracted to black men. So I believe that's common.

C.R.: So that somewhere you know you're not alone in this.

[Here's another example of the fact that expressing all the negative attitudes she has toward her own attraction to blacks leads her to realize this really is not so bad after all; there are positive sides of it, other people, other women feel the same way.]

Sylvia: But it seems like the strength of my feelings and, uh, the ongo- ingness and my de–, my desire to identify with the black culture and– (C.R.: M-hm, m-hm) Um, is, is what seems out of proportion to me. That I feel out of proportion about it.

C.R.: M-hm. So OK, other women feel the same way but not to the degree that you do, you think. (Sylvia: M-hm.) That's kind of out of– (Sylvia: M-hm.) Out of scale.

Sylvia: Or in general to the degree too, not just man–woman, but people. *(15-second pause)* Maybe I, it'll *(small laugh)* just come with time, accept- ing that part of myself.

C.R.: Maybe someday you won't be ashamed of yourself for that.

Sylvia: M-hm. Maybe someday I can be proud of myself. (C.R.: M-hm, m-hm.) And for what I believe and feel. (C.R.: M-hm.) I'm gradually learning to do that.

C.R.: Uh-huh, Uh-huh. So perhaps what you are and what you feel will be something you can take real satisfaction in instead of feeling– (Sylvia: M-hm.) "How shameful."

Sylvia: M-hm. And to me it's, it's, a sign of my growth is being able to do what I'm doing with you now, you'll make a film *(laughs)*. (C.R.: M-hm, m-hm, m-hm, m-hm, m-hm.) It's a brazen thing to do.

C.R.: Yeah. (Sylvia: M-hm.) Feel this is a risk. (Sylvia: M-hm.) And that's a sign of learning and of growth.

Sylvia: M-hm. Well, also it somehow it's a little different from a risk in the sense of some of my friends say, "A film? Wh–, what do you want to do that for?" I mean, there's suspiciousness about it and–

C.R.: M-hm, m-hm. So that's seen as another strange part of you.

Sylvia: Well, not so much, I mean, that's not a–

C.R.: Not so.

Sylvia: It doesn't bother me. *(Clears throat)* Sometimes I, well, right now, *(laughs)* sometimes I have the sense of talking away what we were talking about, and I'm wondering, if I went away, if I withdraw from the subject, uh, what's your perspective? It seems like we were talking about my attraction to black people, and now we're not. And I'm, I don't know, did we finish talking about it or did I withdraw?

[My sense is that I was feeling confused about what was going on.]

[C.R.: I think this is a sample of Sylvia's sharp awareness of her own experiencing. I don't believe that in content we had left the subject of her attraction to blacks. But she realizes in herself that somehow she has withdrawn from that. She's, as she says, talked away from it. Obviously, that's because it has been a frightening subject to her. Perhaps also because she feels she's gone as far as she can do with it at the present time.]

Sylvia: Um—

C.R.: It's more of your analyzing it, isn't it? Trying to think about what's happening. "Did I run away from it? Or was I finished with it?" Or continue think about it?

Sylvia: Analyze it (*small laugh*).

C.R.: Instead of asking, "Do I feel as though I'm finished with it?" (Sylvia: M-hm.) "Do I feel as though I'm escaping from it?"

Sylvia: I like that. I like your, your questions, or comments. (C.R.: M-hm.) Do I feel finished? No, I don't, I don't feel, I don't know about escaping and feeling finished, it's—

C.R.: The feeling is one of uncertainty.

Sylvia: M-hm. (*35-second pause*) Well I, I feel like I want to go back and listen to what we just talked about, that I didn't hear it very well. (C.R.: M-hm, m-hm, m-hm, m-hm, m-hm.) And—

[C.R.: This is one of the commonest experiences when a person delves into areas that are sensitive, where they've exposed themselves in ways that make them very vulnerable. Sylvia, like many other clients, hardly knows what she has said because it has come so close to her inner feelings, because it's just a delicate experience. Incidentally, this is one point where a wrong response on the part of the counselor can be very frightening and very threatening because her inner self is really very exposed at this point. This inability to remember is the defense of the self against being changed too rapidly. It probably would be very good for her to hear this later and to begin to accept more fully what she's just been expressing.]

C.R.: "What did I say?" "What did I feel?" You'd like to have a rerun of it and it—

Sylvia: M-hm. Like I just went jabber-jabber-jabber-jabber. (C.R.: M-hm.) And then all that. (C.R.: M-hm.) And so—

C.R.: Sounds like you scold yourself for that, as though, "Oh, I just talk-talk-talk." (Sylvia: M-hm.) It didn't sound like just talk-talk-talk to me.

Sylvia: It didn't? *(Laughs)*

C.R.: No.

[Throughout these interviews, my own feelings have been largely empathic and caring ones. Here's the first time that I express some other feeling of my own. I simply couldn't permit her to scold herself for what she's been doing, and so I said, "It doesn't sound like just talk-talk-talk to me," which was a very real feeling on my part at that moment.]

[Sylvia: At that time I had the feeling that Carl was really asking me something that he wanted to know. Genuinely interested and concerned about that.]

Sylvia: Well, I would like to hear it again, and it has and, and slowed down somehow, and I now *(small laugh)*, I could see like taking your hand and looking at you and slowing down. (C.R.: M-hm.) And then when I'm slowing—and that's what I want to do. (C.R.: M-hm.) But while I'm doing it, I'm scolding myself, like, "What are you doing this for?"

C.R.: Let me give you a very brief rerun of part of it. You were saying, "I'm ashamed of myself for being attracted to black men. Uh, I know many other women have some of the same feeling, but it seems to me I have that feeling disproportionately strong, and, uh, my family is critical of that, the culture is critical. Um, I'd like to be able to accept those feelings in myself. Maybe I'm making a little bit of progress along that line, but still there does seem a need to be a, a strange part of me that I don't understand."

Sylvia: That's right.

C.R.: "And part of that attraction is sexual but I'm also attracted to their children, to the way they live, to a lot of things about them."

[Sometimes when I show what an accurate listener I am, I feel proud of myself, and I do in this moment.]

Sylvia: M-hm. And what I, what you said that strikes me the most is it's the part of me I don't understand, it's a part of me I don't understand.

C.R.: It just is, but you can't quite, uh, can't quite get at the reasons for it. You have to have the reasons.

Sylvia: *(Laughs)* And I don't know why I have to have the reasons, m-hm. I don't have to explain to anybody. (C.R.: M-hm.) So it seems like I don't have to have a reason.

C.R.: M-hm. *(20-second pause)* So maybe the intellectual understanding isn't as important as you thought it was.

Sylvia: I think the acceptance is what's most important, my acceptance.

[C.R.: As she has shown throughout the interview, as she says, she analyzes and analyzes. She has to see the reasons for all of her behavior, and now she's taking a little bit lighter look at that, and realizing, "I don't have to have a reason for every bit of my behavior, I don't have to understand all of it. I can simply accept it. Perhaps I can simply accept it." I admire Sylvia's courage in being willing to voice the very intimate feelings she has on film. I believe that both the expression of those feelings will be constructive for her and that the willingness to share them with a wider audience will also have a positive effect in her life.]

C.R.: M-hm, m-hm. "If I could accept it, I wouldn't have to understand in the sense of knowing the reasons."

Sylvia: Or explain to anybody. (C.R.: M-hm, m-hm, m-hm.) M-hm.

C.R.: Sounds like that's what you're doing in imagination a lot, trying to explain it to somebody.

Sylvia: M-hm. *(25-second pause)* It seems like I'll probably never understand it. So I can make life a lot easier for myself by not trying.

C.R.: M-hm. It may be one of those things that if you can accept it, you wouldn't need to have all the explanations.

Sylvia: Wonder what *(sighs, clears throat)* what keeps me, um, feeling like I need to justify myself. (C.R.: M-hm.) Like that's a more basic—

C.R.: M-hm. It's a broader statement of it.

Sylvia: Than about a particular view, you know, accepting myself about this and about that.

C.R.: M-hm. You would in general feel, "I have to justify myself with proper reasons."

Sylvia: M-hm. *(20-second pause)* Well, do you do that? Do you—

C.R.: I suspect we all do, some.

Sylvia: Yeah.

C.R.: M-hm.

Sylvia: So there's nobody that just *(laughs)* floats along on their intuition. That's not it either. So what I need is more balance really. (C.R.: M-hm.) Not that I'm wrong to justify it, but that I can be more, justify it less and feel more, and feel comfortable.

[This experience that I had with Carl is, uh, real special to me and, uh, one of the things about it that feels real close to me is the emotional safety I felt with him. That there was somehow a boundary or a fence or a something that, uh, separated the space that I was in with Carl from the rest of the world. And inside that space I was very safe, and I would not be hurt. I didn't have to have any fear that I would be hurt no matter what I said or did, and the focus of my thinking was how very safe that felt. Another thing I felt from him that I think has affected me some over this time is that I felt, uh, like support from him to be myself, to listen to myself and to respond for myself and to care about, to put myself first. I think about how my life might have been changed by my experiences with Carl. I think Carl's caring for me in the way that he did, his, uh, modeling, helping me to learn to care for myself, where like maybe my most important resource would be myself. So it seems to me that in his style of relating there's a lot of support to do that, a lot of encouragement and influence to listen to myself.]

C.R.: M-hm, m-hm, m-hm.

ROGERS AND SYLVIA
An Intimate and Affirming Encounter

David J. Cain

Sylvia is an exceptional person who had an extraordinary therapeutic encounter with Carl Rogers. It was the kind of therapeutic experience that has an indelible effect on both client and therapist. Sylvia and Rogers touched each other in a way that was mutually enriching, gratifying, and enhancing. As in all therapy sessions I have witnessed, there were points at which one could question the therapist's response. But despite this encounter's few imperfections, it offers practitioners of client-centered therapy and other schools of thought a good deal on which to reflect, especially regarding client and therapist factors that may facilitate or impair growth.

Sylvia was an attractive woman who appeared to be in her mid-30s. She was a mother of at least two children whose ages we do not know. Her marital status is unclear and she makes no reference to a partner. Little else is known about her background. This was her fifth interview with Rogers. She had had three interviews the previous year, presumably during a workshop, and one prior to this during the same workshop. At the time this interview was filmed, Rogers was in his mid-70s. The film was released in 1980. It should also be noted that both Sylvia and Rogers reviewed the session after its completion and made several comments on their experiences that were then incorporated into the final version of the film. Thus, at several points, the viewer sees and hears Sylvia's and Rogers' reactions to various aspects of their session.

SYLVIA AND ROGERS' INTERACTIONS

Sylvia was intensely involved with Rogers throughout their session. She was extremely receptive to her experiences and to Rogers. Two of the most striking features about their encounter were the constant and strong eye contact she kept and the fact that they held hands, on her request, throughout much of the interview. Sylvia gazed at Rogers in an open-faced manner that conveyed a deep sense of engagement, captivation, and possibly even awe and adoration. One woman who saw the film described Sylvia as "melting," though without any sexual connotation. Rogers met Sylvia's gaze with strong eye contact that communicated his intense interest, presence, and full immersion in her and her experience. Rogers and Sylvia seemed to be in an almost impenetrable bubble in which the rest of the world, including cameras, lights, and the filmmakers, faded into the background.

Rogers listened intently to whatever Sylvia had to say and responded frequently with short acknowledgments (e.g., "m-hm, m-hm" or "uh-huh"). The majority of his responses might be described as empathic since he clearly wished to understand or clarify his understanding of Sylvia's intended meaning and experience. Accordingly, Rogers usually followed Sylvia's lead, but, on a number of occasions, he followed his inclinations and asked or answered questions or interjected his perceptions and beliefs. Throughout the interview, it is obvious that Rogers was pleased with his relationship with Sylvia and her growth.

SIGNIFICANT MOMENTS AND ISSUES:
A SEQUENTIAL ANALYSIS

Therapy as Learning

Sylvia begins the session by expressing pride that recently she has been learning. She comments: "I've been realizing the last year . . . that I learned some things, and I know I've learned them. . . . I'm feeling my learning, and that's really exciting. . . . I've changed. . . . I can see the difference and feel the difference."

Though it may seem obvious, the main purpose of therapy is to assist another to learn and to transform that learning into effective and satisfying living. Therapy is, after all, a relationship with a purpose. I emphasize this point because some client-centered therapists, in their emphasis on the importance of the therapeutic relationship, tend to deny or minimize an interest in their clients' learning or personal growth. Not only does Sylvia express satisfaction in what she is learning but she experiences it as *self-affirming*. She now knows that she is a person who *can learn* and who *has learned.* Sylvia also tells us *how* she has learned: "There was no amount of therapy or reading or thinking or talking that helped me to learn those things, but it was feeling strong enough within myself that I could take chances."

Clients learn in different ways, though the manner in which they learn often is not acknowledged either by themselves or their therapists. It is significant that Sylvia articulates that she learns best by taking risks. As Rogers notes, she has also learned to trust the experience that comes with her risk-taking.

Beyond Empathy

Rogers makes a number of responses throughout the session that I would describe as *inferential empathy.* That is, in an attempt to sharpen his understanding, he makes inferences about what Sylvia means rather than staying close to her actual statement. For example, within the first few minutes of the session, when Sylvia says that she has "made a decision to be more strict" with her children and that she will "make many more decisions" than she has in the past, Rogers goes beyond Sylvia's statement, inferring something about her underlying feeling state: "Sounds as though you feel a bit stronger that way."

When Rogers responds inferentially, or when his response does not seem right, Sylvia carefully considers his words to determine if they fit her experience. I believe that when therapists trust and encourage their clients to assess critically both their experience and the therapist's view of it, as Roger does here, it is unlikely that clients will adopt the beliefs of their therapists' that are incompatible with their own. Under such conditions, it is unlikely that clients will be "manipulated" by therapists, even inadvertently.

Within the span of about two minutes, Rogers makes two empathic responses that are slightly off target, judging from Sylvia's reaction (e.g., "Well, yes. Yes and no"). Then she shares an experience that does not yet make sense to her: "I feel more mature because I know . . . more about how immature I am." Rogers simply comments: "That makes a lot of sense to me" and then communicates this understanding with an extremely accurate reflection of Sylvia's meaning. When she reviews this segment of the session, she expresses surprise and satisfaction that Rogers could and does understand this very significant personal learning.

This segment raises an interesting question about the importance of the therapist's empathic response. When Rogers makes responses that are slightly off, Sylvia simply uses them as a reference point to clarify her meaning. According to Sylvia, "His specific comments or the content of his comments is not necessarily helpful as opposed to not helpful. But what it does do that is valuable is that it gives me something to bounce against.

It's a stimulation to better focus myself." Thus, clients with a strong enough sense of themselves, like Sylvia, can often move forward even when their therapists' empathic responses are not entirely accurate. Indeed, it may be that slightly inaccurate responses are sometimes facilitative, providing the client with a gentle push toward greater clarity. On the other hand, with fragile clients, or even with strong clients who are struggling with something of vital importance, the therapist's accurate understanding may be more crucial and more potent in its impact. A failure to demonstrate accurate understanding with such patients, or at such moments, may have a more adverse effect on the relationship. My point is that we do not yet know enough about how variations in the accuracy of a therapist's understanding may affect different clients at specific moments. This underscores, for me, the importance of remaining sensitive to our moment-to-moment impact on the client as well as to individual differences in clients.

Holding On—Letting Go

Early in the session, Sylvia says that she learns by risking. She then says she would like to be more of her helpless, dependent, and open self. She is aware of her conflict between avoiding dependence and allowing herself to be dependent. Sylvia experiences a gap (incongruence) in these states that she wishes to close (integrate). She requests to hold Rogers' hands as she had in a previous session. He accepts. Sylvia then states: "I would like to be, less, uh, less strong right now. I would like to give myself the gift of not having to be sensible and reasonable and . . . also . . . protect myself." Upon holding Rogers' hands, Sylvia identifies this contact as a factor that helps her use therapy more effectively: "in this position that I'm in now with you I feel more focused."

This "touching" moment beautifully illustrates and affirms the importance of safety and support when the client is approaching or confronting a deeply personal and potentially threatening aspect of self. Once again, I am impressed with Sylvia's capacity to know and articulate what she needs for growth—an opportunity to risk in a context of personal contact and safety. Rogers was at his best at these crucial moments. He was deeply and accurately empathic, receptive, supportive, and fully present and engaged with Sylvia. Clear evidence is provided that the nature and quality of the therapist–client relationship are crucial variables in facilitating the potential for therapeutic change.

Search for Understanding: Struggle for Self-Acceptance

After a long silence to prepare herself, Sylvia addresses a puzzling and disturbing aspect of her life—her sexual attraction to black men and her general attraction to black people. She comments: "I'm real attracted to black people. . . . And, uh, that's about the craziest part of me, um, I'm ashamed. . . . I think there's something wrong with me, . . . sick, . . . neurotic, . . . strange." Rogers reflected her feeling about this attraction: "You really feel that there's something sick in you that causes you to have so many black friends."

Sylvia is trying to make sense of her experience: "I keep looking for a reasonable explanation, and there is none." Rogers, partly by the tone of his voice and partly by the way he "reframes" Sylvia's dilemma, seems to be working toward helping Sylvia accept, rather than understand, her feelings. He responds: "So there isn't any reason except that you feel that way" and "And that isn't good enough." Rogers seems to be struggling here with his apparent inclination to help Sylvia to accept *and* make sense of her experience, but he is more focused on acceptance.

As this phase of the session progresses, Sylvia struggles with the discrepancy between how she thinks she should feel and how she does feel: "I tell myself I should be joyful. . . . But . . . the strength of my feelings and . . . my desire to identify with the black culture . . . is what seems out of proportion to me. . . . Maybe someday I can be proud of myself." She then identifies her willingness and desire to state her feelings on film as a sign of her growth in this conflicted area of her life but then starts to feel confused about whether she has begun to move away from her feelings. She asks Rogers for his perspective. He does not answer directly, but his reflections in question form (" 'Did I run away from it? Or was I finished with it?' "), help her grapple with her uncertainty about what she is experiencing in the moment.

Sylvia seems to have lost her bearings. She knows she has expressed something important but cannot quite recall or take it in. My understanding of her experience is that she is in a fog—a state in which she cannot comprehend her experience. She seems to be too immersed in a threatening experience to be able to stand apart from it and see it clearly. Rogers eloquently comments on this experience as follows: "Sylvia, like many other clients, hardly knows what she has said because it has come so close to her inner feelings. . . . This inability to remember is the defense of the self against being changed too rapidly."

As Sylvia struggles with her confusion, Rogers makes a comment that is clearly intended to help her see that she is not just speaking intellectually or avoiding herself: "It didn't sound like just talk-talk-talk to me." Sylvia is still not so sure and says, "It didn't?" In the preceding response, Rogers' heart was in the right place, as usual. He commented after viewing the tape that: "I simply couldn't permit her to scold herself for what she's been doing." Depending on one's perspective, this response could be viewed as either overly protective (and not respectful of her confused state) or genuinely caring and supportive. Whether it was a "mistake" in terms of facilitating Sylvia's capacity to emerge from her self-doubt and confusion is worthy of our consideration. If Rogers had focused on Sylvia's confusion about what was going on, she might have clarified things for herself. Had she done so, it is more likely that she could have increased her confidence in her ability to assess her reality more effectively.

Is Acceptance Sufficient?

At one point Sylvia notes the following: "What you said that strikes me the most is . . . it's a part of me I don't understand." Rogers then responds: "It just is, but you can't quite . . . get at the reasons for it. You have to have the reasons."

In my view, Rogers' bias in this case has clearly emerged. He tries to acknowledge Sylvia's desire to understand herself but believes that it is more important, and probably more therapeutic, to accept than to understand. He gently dissuades her from being as concerned as she is with understanding herself intellectually. I believe Sylvia's need to make sense of her attraction to blacks was powerful and persisted beyond this interview. Without some explanation that is satisfactory to her, she would be unlikely to come to terms fully with this area of her life.

After Rogers gently chides her about having to "have the reasons," Sylvia laughs and responds: "I don't know why I have to have the reasons. . . . I don't have to explain to anybody." Sylvia is now expressing ambivalence about the importance of knowing the reasons for her behavior, perhaps because Rogers has discouraged her from pursuing an intellectual understanding of it. Her next statement continues to reflect this ambivalence: "So it seems like I don't have to have a reason." Rogers' bias emerges even more strongly with his next response: "So maybe the intellectual understanding isn't as important as you thought it was." By a subtle recasting of Sylvia's message, Rogers has communicated his belief that acceptance is more important than understanding. Sylvia then says: "I think the acceptance is what's most important, my acceptance." Rogers reflects: " 'If I could accept it, I would not have to understand in the sense of knowing the reasons.' "

Sylvia, to be sure, recognizes that simply accepting herself is desirable. Yet, she also wishes to understand. Rogers has emphasized acceptance rather than acknowledging the importance, *to Sylvia*, of understanding and acceptance. Obviously, even a master therapist like Rogers will at times fall prey to his personal beliefs when they conflict with the client's needs or beliefs. In my personal contact with Rogers, I observed a disinclination to be self-analytic; he seemed to be content to simply acknowledge and accept some aspect of his behavior rather than understand it. More specifically, he seemed to downplay the importance of rational, intellectual, cognitive explanations regarding individuals' motivations or behaviors. Not surprisingly, he demonstrated this position in his work with Sylvia. Rogers' belief may, of course, be correct for some clients, as it was for him. But for other persons, having an explanation for a troubling or puzzling behavior may be more therapeutic or as therapeutic as simply accepting the behavior. My point is that clients vary in how they learn and in what they need to learn in order to change and grow. In this case, Sylvia seemed to need both intellectual understanding and self-acceptance.

After a long pause, Sylvia continues to address the issue of her understanding her behavior: "It seems like I'll probably never understand it. So I can make life a lot easier for myself by not trying." Rogers follows with: "It may be one of those things that if you can accept it, you wouldn't need to have all the explanations." She then concludes the session by saying: "So what I need is more balance really. Not that I'm wrong to justify it, but that I can . . . justify it less and feel more . . . comfortable."

Sylvia's last statements suggest that she has concluded that she needs a balance between her self-understanding and self-acceptance. She has not given up her desire to make sense of her attraction to black people, but seems to have reached a tentative conclusion that an increase in self-acceptance would be helpful in easing the tension she experiences when she feels a need to justify or explain her behavior. Although I believe Rogers' bias led him to emphasize self-acceptance, I also feel that the safety and trust he offered Sylvia enabled her to reach a position that represented a blend of her beliefs and his. Without follow-up, it is impossible, of course, to know whether this synthesis of beliefs was ultimately integrated in a harmonious manner, or if Sylvia continued to wish for greater cognitive understanding and continued to feel troubled by her behavior.

FACTORS FACILITATING LEARNING AND GROWTH

Rogers' basic hypothesis regarding the necessary and sufficient conditions for therapeutic personality change remained virtually unchanged after he first articulated it in 1957. It can be stated as follows: If an incongruent client is in contact with a therapist who is perceived as unconditional in positive regard, empathic and congruent, then constructive change will occur in the client. Although I do not disagree in any basic way with Rogers' hypothesis, I view it as incomplete. From the viewpoints of research, theory, and clinical evidence, it seems indefensible to suggest that three therapist qualities (or conditions or behaviors) could possibly account for the range and complexity of factors, interacting together, that affect constructive change in a given client. A major limitation of Rogers' hypothesis is that it focuses almost entirely on therapist factors to account for change, thereby diminishing the importance of the client's contribution to the success (or failure) of therapy. The challenge faced by client-centered practitioners and theorists is to see and hear freshly the variety and nuance of factors at play in the therapeutic interaction. To the degree that client-centered therapists remain wedded to Rogers' theory, they are likely to continue to see only what the theory suggests is true.

Sylvia's session with Rogers is a good illustration of the intricate composite of client and therapist factors that affect session outcome. This session also suggests that the therapeutic potential for constructive learning and growth is enhanced when there is mutuality in the therapist–client interaction. In this regard, Sylvia was an exceptionally receptive person— both to her experiences and to Rogers' responses to them. Receptivity is defined as an openness to internal and external experience and information. In a receptive state, the client takes in experience for reflection in a nonevaluative and nondefensive manner. Thus, Sylvia's receptivity and reflection, combined with her risk-taking, were prime contributors to her learning and growth.

For Rogers' part, in addition to his having been congruent, accepting, and empathic, he displayed a high level of *presence* in his contact with Sylvia. Presence is defined as a manner of being in which the therapist is fully attentive to and immersed in the client and the client's experience. Throughout the interview, Rogers was centered in himself and highly focused on Sylvia. In addition, Rogers was also highly *affirming* of Sylvia. That is, he not only acknowledged and accepted Sylvia's experiences but validated them as well. Rogers' affirmation of Sylvia also supported and encouraged her self-affirmation.

Rogers and Sylvia were mutually *engaged* with each other within the therapeutic process. Engagement goes beyond the concept of contact described by Rogers in his "necessary and sufficient conditions" hypothesis. As conceived here, engagement means a mutual experiencing of the other as personally involved in a collaborative relationship whose purpose is to facilitate learning and growth in the client. As was evident throughout the session, Rogers and Sylvia were closely bonded in a manner that provided an enormous amount of support, safety, and trust for Sylvia to explore and be herself. As Sylvia commented about the interview: "There was somehow a boundary or fence . . . that separated the space that I was in with Carl from the rest of the world. And inside that space. . . . I didn't have to have any fear that I would be hurt no matter what I said or did. . . . Another thing I felt from him that I think has affected me some . . . is that I felt . . . support from him to be myself, to listen to myself . . . and to care about, to put myself first."

CONCLUDING THOUGHTS

After having reviewed the videotape and transcript of this session on numerous occasions, I find myself reaching a few simple and basic conclusions. The nature and quality of the relationship between Sylvia and Rogers was the primary therapeutic force behind its constructive impact on Sylvia. The intensity, closeness, safety, and personal involvement in this encounter were factors that transcended the content of the issues Sylvia discussed or the quality of Rogers' responses, some of which were exceptional. What made this encounter so powerful was its collaborative nature, the mutuality of client and therapist working in a partnership in which each brought to bear his or her personal resources for learning and growth. Both Rogers and Sylvia fully immersed themselves in a process that facilitated Sylvia's risk-taking and learning. In her assessment, Sylvia indicated that she *learned* to "be myself," "care for myself," "listen to myself," and to realize that "maybe my most important resource would be myself." As I understand Sylvia, she discovered that she was learning how to learn and to draw from her resources to take care of herself. She was becoming her own therapist. In my view, that is an optimal outcome for all clients and their therapists.

ROGERS AND SYLVIA
A Feminist Analysis

Maureen O'Hara

Psychoanalysis is the creation of a male genius, and almost all those
who have developed his ideas have been men. It is only right and reasonable that they should evolve more easily a masculine psychology and
understand more the development of men than of women.

—Karen Horney (1926), p. 324

All through the time I worked closely with Carl Rogers, first as a graduate
student, later as a colleague and friend, I had the profoundest love and
respect for both the man and his work. This respect deepened over the
years as I saw him, in countless and varied situations, apply in the flesh the
same principles he had outlined theoretically in his writings. Over those
same years, my own developing intellectual work took me into arenas of
thought and practice that constantly challenged me to examine and reflect
upon the ideas I held about human nature, the process of therapy and
growth, and my own place in the world. I acquired my own set of lenses,
filters, and frames of reference with which to "read" or "listen" to Rogers'
approach to facilitating the growth process of others, whether as a therapist, teacher, group facilitator, parent, friend or colleague.

From the beginning, our relationship was yeasty and passionate. We
had innumerable discussions, dialogues, and plain old fights about our
different frames of reference and different "constructions of reality"—although we would not have known to name it such in those days. Our
differences were very often productive for both of us, sometimes cutting
through each other's ossified conceptualizations with the analytic precision
of the diamond cutter's knife. Other times reformulations of conceptual

schemas or "truths" came about gradually, more like the way the florist creates a bouquet from the assortment of flowers and foliage at hand.

Rogers was always open to new ideas and new ways of looking at things. We read many of the same books, admired many of the same people, worked harmoniously side by side, saw eye-to-eye on many of the social, political, and spiritual issues of the times. On many occasions our discussions would result in both of us seeing things anew; seeming differences were vigorously explored only to dissolve in a greater shared perspective.

But, as the years went on, it became clearer that our most fundamental and troubling differences come not from intellectual disagreement over such things as theories of personality, techniques of therapy, or even commitment to person-centered therapies. No, the genesis of our differ-ence had to do with the position in the universe each of us occupied. There were times when not even the empathic genius of Carl Rogers could bridge the gap and reconcile the fundamental differences in "world view," "per-ceptive sensibility," "construction of reality," "knowledge claims," "knowl-edge interests," "ways of knowing," or "paradigm," between Rogers—a famous, powerful, successful, upper-middle-class, white American male—and myself—a young, unknown, immigrant, working-class, white English female. It was maddening to want desperately to arrive at a consensus or agreement and discover that the deeper we dug the further away from each other we got. It was all the more frustrating because both of us at the time were laboring under the Enlightenment belief that, if we talked long enough, somewhere beneath our misunderstanding we would find a more fundamental truth that would be true for both of us. Thoroughly accultur-ated, as we both were, in the Western scientific tradition, neither of us was ready for a poststructuralist world!

Not surprisingly the gap between us was most obvious when it came to relational issues such as power, authority, inclusion and exclusion, and political realities such as sexism and racism. On the one hand, I did (and still do) see client-centered and person-centered approaches, both theoreti-cally and in practice, as providing support for an ideal of "full personhood" and empowerment for each and every individual. I have written elsewhere about what I see as the profoundly emancipatory aims of person-centered therapies (O'Hara, 1989). I saw, both in his writings and in his practice, Rogers' deep-felt belief in the essential worth of all people. It was for this above all else that I valued person-centered therapies and based my own work as a therapist on them. On the other hand, though, as the years have elapsed and my consciousness as a woman has evolved through my own experience in the world, in dialogue with feminist and nonfeminist women, disenfranchised peoples of color, lesbian women and gay men, men and women of oppressed classes in Latin America, and the working class of

Northern England, I have begun to see another side to the story of person-centered approaches.

Despite the powerful emancipatory promise in person-centered therapy, there are aspects of it that, whether consciously or unconsciously, serve to preserve, maintain, and protect the interests of the Eurocentric, patriarchal, Judeo-Christian world. Illustrating the principle that Karl Mannheim (1936/1954) described, "If one were to trace in detail . . . the origin and . . . diffusion of a certain thought-model, one would discover the . . . affinity it has to the social position of given groups and their manner of interpreting the world" (p. 276), Rogers' own place in the world was firmly embodied in his theories. In the same way that Freudian psychoanalytic theory and method both challenged and reproduced the conditions of 19th-century Vienna (Showalter, 1985), Rogerian person-centered therapies both critiqued and perpetuated the conditions of mid-20th-century North American culture. Although certainly not entirely or exclusively, that culture was and to some degree still is sexist and racist.

In this discussion I want to take up these points and, by reference to the session with Sylvia as text, reflect on both the content and the process of the interview with a view to gaining a greater understanding of some of both the power and limitations of person-centered therapy as an emancipatory strategy.

It should be noted that my reflections will also illustrate Mannheim's thesis. A similar interpretative analysis of *my* reflections reveal the biases and particularities of my place in the universe. I will be satisfied if the following permits a deeper appreciation and understanding of Rogers' contribution to our ongoing search to understand ourselves and our relationships.

ANALYSIS

Self as Knower

At the outset of the exchange Sylvia says she wants to share. Her choice of the word "share" is interesting. "Share" is a word that tells us both about the activity—something is to be distributed—and the relationship between the parties to act. With this use of the word "share" she signifies that she sees the process as one of mutuality and that she does not want to take a subordinate position in the exchange. This seems to foreshadow what will become a major theme in the session—her growing sense of personal empowerment as a woman. She goes on to discuss her experience of herself as a learner and the sense of achievement she feels about that. "That's a big deal!" she tells Rogers.

In their work on women's development, Belenky and her colleagues

(Belenky, Clinchy, Goldberger, & Tarule, 1986) identified as a major developmental turning point the moment when a woman's view of herself shifts from seeing herself as part of the world of the ignorant to seeing herself as part of the world of the "knowers." When a woman who has been disenfranchised and silenced first discovers she is capable of learning, her consciousness of herself as an active agent in her own life makes a quantum leap. Sylvia, who had always felt herself outside the community of learners, now discovers herself a member. Importantly, Carl seems to recognize that the moment is significant, marking it by stepping out of a purely reflective empathic stance and directively asking Sylvia to go further along the path to a new order of mind by saying more about herself as a learner.

Self as Mother

It is illuminating from a women's development standpoint that the sphere of knowledge that Sylvia claims first is her mothering. This was also true for many of the women in the Belenky et al. (1986) study. Sylvia tells Rogers that she has become stricter with her children. She has taken charge of them, where before, we gather, she had not. And even in the face of her children's resistance, she has the confidence, the sense of "knowing better," to insist on her parenting program. She has reclaimed her authority as a mother.

Critical scholars have long argued that one of the most oppressive aspects of the Eurocentric or androcentric world-view is the way it marginalizes, devalues, and even pathologizes the knowledge of subordinated groups (Weedon, 1987; Weisstein, 1971). Their experiential knowing is not seen as a valid "other perspective" but instead is seen as trivial, erroneous, seditious, or not seen at all. Mothering[1] is a complex, dense web of skills, knowledge, ways of responding, acting speaking, and feeling that has evolved through the concrete experience of raising children in a particular context. The real authorities on maternal knowledge are the people who do the mothering (Ruddick, 1980). The problem is that in a world where only women take care of children and where women's work is seen as trivial and "natural," that is, not real "expertise," the knowledge a woman acquires in the course of her work is devalued by her society and therefore by her. Without cultural validation, she cannot use it, say, as an attorney might, to strengthen her sense of herself as a person who has valuable knowledge. When Sylvia reclaims her maternal knowledge she gains a sense of herself as knower, and, with that, power and self-esteem.

Rogers' response to this is interesting and revealing. He interprets Sylvia's experience as feeling more "grown-up." The implication here is that he ("grown-up" is Rogers' word, not Sylvia's) sees Sylvia's previous sense of incompetence as immature. In this choice of image, Rogers appears to fall into the tendency of members of dominant groups to see dominated groups as "children" and their behavior as immature.

Rogers could have used any number of other words or concepts. He could have suggested Sylvia had become more "empowered," "authorita-tive," "emancipated," "secure," and so on. Such language would have left open the possibility that Sylvia's lack of confidence was not a dispositional problem but was situational, that is, a consequence of living in a world that systematically devalues women's knowledge. By making it a personal development issue that she could "grow" out of, Rogers' language obscures the possibility of social origins of Sylvia's psychological experience. In other words, it blames the victim.

Sylvia goes on next to describe her increasing sense of empowerment with regard to her sexuality, not coincidentally perhaps, another area of women's lives where the weight of societal expectations come down heavily. Women's sexuality has always been subjected to restrictions, taboos, controls, and prohibitions. Until very recently and even now, in all but a small segment of contemporary society, women's sexuality was/is the exclusive property of men. The idea that a woman can express her sexuality for her own satisfaction has been universally condemned by patriarchal institutions as "sinful," "unfeminine," "unnatural," "pathological," and at worst the work of Satanic forces.

Sylvia says that she is no longer looking to therapists, books, or other people for wisdom about her sexual life. She has stopped looking for knowledge "out there" and has begun consulting her own lived experience as a guide to what pleases her. She has begun to base her sexual reality on an experiential, body-based knowledge, rather than on theoretical or abstract constructs. Her use of the word "risk" in this context, however, suggests that she sees her desire to be sexually authentic as problematic.

What does she mean here by the use of the word "risk"? Clearly she is not talking about the risk of pregnancy or disease. She suggests that it is her own fear that has been a barrier to her authenticity. Her language is that of individual pathology rather than societal oppression. She too (as do most of us raised in this culture) appears to subscribe to an androcentric view of female sexuality, even her own. My interpretation is that she is referring to feelings of anxiety she encounters when she wants to act spontaneously on her sexual feelings. It is not her sexuality per se that is "risky" but it becomes so in a world where sexuality, especially female sexuality, is subject to social control. In attributing her sexual reticence to her own fears, without acknowledging or understanding why she experi-ences fear at being sexual, I believe Sylvia mislocates the origin of the problem.

Rogers also picks up and focuses on the word "risk" and goes on to reiterate this concept several times. By doing so, both he and Sylvia create a shared belief that her previous sexual experience had been limited because of her own unwillingness to take risks—once again a dispositional or intrapsychic explanation.

Reframing this situation from an emancipatory feminist perspective might include exploration of where the sense of danger that Sylvia experiences comes from, what kind of danger she envisions, and so on. This might have served to shift the sense of danger away from her own sexual inclinations, which could then be accepted as authentic and whole, and onto patriarchy's social interest in the control of female sexuality. Instead of seeing her own impulses as dangerous, she might have come to a better understanding of the dialogical relationship between her culture's view of female sexuality and her own lived experience—an altogether different reality.[2]

In the commentary, Rogers also uses "risk" to describe several of Sylvia's recent behaviors. How much more empowering would it have been, one wonders, if he had seen not "a lot of risking behavior" but a lot of self-assertiveness, self-confidence, authenticity, or politically revolutionary behavior?

Gaining a Voice

There is a strong theme in Sylvia's description of her process of what Belenky et al. (1986) have termed "gaining a voice." Her insistence on "sharing" rather than seeking help is the first clue to this. She then goes on to tell Rogers that she is gaining her voice as a mother. She is gaining new self-significance in her role of raising children who are acceptable to the world, and she is now willing to give voice to her knowledge.

Sylvia also demonstrates a keen sense of the important relationship between gaining a voice and the development of self. She explicitly acknowledges that speaking out loud, in the form of making the film, serves to give weight and importance to her growth. It makes both her progress and her self more real. Clinchy and Belenky (1987), in their work with poor rural women, used tape recorders in a similar way to enable women who have previously felt silenced to learn from their own and others' stories. As they note, for the women in the study the simple act of recording their words, and playing them back so others may learn from them, gave both the words and the speakers greater significance. Sylvia, too, recognizes that the power of words is in making them public.

Separateness or Connection: Conflicting Views of Maturity

After a whole series of statements from Sylvia about her growing sense of autonomy and empowerment, Rogers reflects what he has heard, saying that he feels her to be more "self-assured." Interestingly, Sylvia seems to resist this idea. She responds by backing away from this view of herself. She begins at once to talk about her "immaturity." She seems confused about whether she is immature or mature. As she says more about this, we get the idea that to Sylvia maturity means independence, separateness, self-sufficiency, and not needing any help from anyone.

In the past 25 years it has become clear that this view of maturity is an essentially Anglo-Saxon and masculine view. In the field of psychology it is derived from developmental research using predominantly middle-class white male subjects. When the development of other cultural groups (Shweder & Bourne, 1982) and the development of women and girls are examined (Gilligan, 1982), we find a somewhat different pattern. The work of feminist psychologists and others has revealed that in the lives of women, connection and relatedness are essential aspects of maturity (Belenky et al., 1986; Gilligan, 1982; Jordan, Kaplan, Miller, Stiver, & Surrey, 1991). Only when compared against models of maturity based on maps of white male development would Sylvia's wish for connection, support, and nurturance from Rogers be seen as signs of pathology or "dependent personality" as Sylvia herself labels it. Sylvia, like so many women who have been exposed to a traditionally modernist psychology, has internalized its individualist myths and is now using them against herself.

Here we see a clear illustration of the way Sylvia's own sense of herself has become "pathologized" as a consequence of the introjected values of an androcentric view of development. Sylvia believes that there are only two possible positions for her in relation to Rogers. She can either be "mature" and strong, in which case she must be self-sufficient, or she can be "immature," helpless, not in control, in which case she can receive something from her connection to Rogers. The dilemma here is obvious—strength is equated with separateness, closeness with loss of control and helplessness. Sylvia feels she must choose between a version of empowerment that severs her connections or a connectedness that renders her powerless.[3]

At this point, one of the limitations of a strictly reflective, empathic therapy emerges. Rogers' response here is to support Sylvia's view of her predicament. He does try to reframe her self-label "dependent" by the use of the word "vulnerable," but her core belief that in order to learn she must give up power and control goes unchallenged. This means that subsequent concepts will be built on this erroneous conceptual "foundation," locking her into a disempowering view of the learning process.

A more actively dialogical therapy would have permitted Sylvia's potentially self-defeating conceptual schema to be challenged. A feminist therapist for instance, might have pointed to Sylvia's own earlier statements as a way to draw new awareness from her own experience. She had told

Rogers that she was "learning" as a mother and about her sexuality, not through therapy but as a consequence of her own empowered action in the world. She might have come to see how her belief that she must surrender power to male authority in order to gain from the relationship is perhaps driven more by cultural mythology than her own experience. She might also have come to realize that in relationships that are free from the exploitative elements of sexism, closeness and mutuality do not come at the expense of one's personal power but are enrichments of it.

As it happens, Sylvia's actions are more self-assertive than her beliefs. She does not, in fact, surrender to Rogers but actively reaches out to make the kind of contact she wants. She takes hold of his hands. And in yet another demonstration of the importance of connection and mutuality in the growth and therapy of women, it is in the context of this closer connection that more conflictual feelings emerge.

Internalization of Culture: The Socially Constructed "Self"

As the session proceeds Sylvia's struggle for authentic identity becomes the dominant theme. After establishing a physical connection with Rogers, she confesses to him that she is attracted to black people and she feels ashamed and embarrassed about it. Using harshly evaluative language she labels herself "crazy," "neurotic," and "sick." She experiences the conflict on multiple levels. At the intrapsychic level she experiences shame; interpersonally, she suffers her family's and friend's disapproval; and, at the societal level, she confronts a racist culture.

In their exploration of her experience, once again both Rogers and Sylvia are trapped by their Eurocentric–androcentric ways of thinking. Sylvia looks for a psychological explanation of her attraction. Interestingly she does not seek to explain her embarrassment! Neither she nor Rogers addresses the societal issues of racism and sexism. Both deal with the problem as an intrapsychic issue.[4] But, we should ask, where do her feelings that a white woman's attraction to blacks is sick or crazy originate? Once again Sylvia might be mislocating her problem. It is possible that she is so thoroughly psychologically "colonized" by a culture of racism, that, even in her own inner psychological world, she has made a complete inversion.

Here we glimpse the way social, cultural, and linguistic habits construct inner psychological reality. French deconstructionist feminists such as Julia Kristeva and Luce Irigaray have attempted to demonstrate that even at the level of desire—let us say sexual desire for a particular person—we learn from birth the expectations, interests, taboos, and values of our culture, such that all future psychic reality will be experienced, interpreted, and constructed in terms of these primary elements. Established in the body, before the development of language (and later symbolized by it), the embodied attractions, revulsions, and antipathies feel "natural."[5] We feel no need to explain desires that are consistent with this felt natural sense. In this way the culture is carried in the "selves" it creates and is reproduced by raising children in its own image.[6] Only when there is absence of desire in the "right" direction, or presence of desire in the "wrong" direction, do we experience anxiety and look for "reasons" (Toril, 1987). Without following Kristeva or Irigaray into the labyrinth of Lacanian–Marxist–deconstructionist assumptions about the presence or absence of a phallus as the primary psychic organizer, we can nonetheless use these ideas in order to examine the way Sylvia has perhaps mislocated the pathology.

Sylvia experiences desires at odds with the interests of white racist society and its ideas of "normalcy," so she feels anxious. Her desires are not mirrored by either the microculture of her family or the culture at large, and she labels her feelings pathological.

As I said, it is not her anxiety that puzzles her but her attraction. (She misses the importance of her own observation that her black friends see nothing to be explained in her attraction.) Despite the fact that her embarrassment and her critical self-judgment might be considered a form of internalized racism, in fact, from an emancipatory therapy perspective at least, Sylvia's desire system must already be more "color-blind" or emancipated than that of most whites, for Sylvia actually experiences her fascination. Most of us are not as open as Sylvia. Her anxiety has not been sufficient to actually extinguish the fascination but only to burden it with shame—the introjected censure of white racist society.

What Sylvia does here psychologically reveals the enormous potency of cultural attitudes like racism and sexism. She turns upon herself and labels her pain as her own pathology. She is blind to the way in which her inner psychological process serves not her own authentic interests but those of the cultural mandates of the dominant class. In the private recesses of her own mind, she has become an agent of racist society in the service of her own oppression. But with the focus so resolutely intrapsychic none of this can emerge from the dialogue between Sylvia and Rogers. On the contrary, Carl participates in keeping the focus personal.

Sylvia seems to conceive of her task as one of gaining a stronger sense of individual identity. She also seems aware that if her identity is too deviant, too out of step with her community, it will be hard to maintain her sense of authority. Once more linking voice with self, she makes active use of the medium of making a film with Carl Rogers as a way to amplify her own voice and counteract the critical voices of her society. It is probably also true that Rogers' nonjudgmental position and her search for "other women who feel the same way" can all be seen as attempts to minimize the discomfort she experiences in the tension between being and belonging. As we shall see, even these, apparently, are not enough.

Being or Belonging: The Struggle for Authentic Relationship

What happens next is interesting and even more revealing of how essentially conservative consciousness often is. After exploring her "deviant" desire system, Sylvia begins to disconnect from her own words. She has a sense of "talking away" her feelings. And she wants to go back over what she has said because she "didn't hear it very well." Rogers' interpretation is that the disconnection is a defense against changing too fast.

We may ask, "What is the danger in changing too fast?" To answer this we need to ask two more questions: the first, "What change would her new awareness bring about?" and the second, "What are the perceived consequences of such a change?" The answers to both questions are given in the text.

Sylvia moves from seeing herself as voiceless and powerless, with attractions that are shameful, to seeing herself as empowered, "envoiced" and willing to own her attraction even if it means the disapproval of her society. By working toward an understanding of her authentic knowledge and inclinations, she has become involved in a personal revolution against her culture. At this point in her journey toward a fuller humanness, Sylvia encounters in her own psychological defensive process the existential conflict between freedom and connection, between being and belonging. As Sylvia sees it, she is in a lose–lose situation. Authenticity brings freedom but it also brings rejection and isolation; societal conformity brings guilt and shame. She is in a state of cognitive dissonance in which a coherent sense of self is at odds with her sense of social integration. This predicament is especially anxiety provoking for women. As noted above, the work of feminist researchers suggests that, for most women, identity development is inseparable from their sense of embeddedness and connection in mutually affirming relationships. If Sylvia were to openly acknowledge to herself the reality emerging from her exploration with Rogers, she would have to face the prospect of losing her social connections with friends, family, and culture. Should the anxiety (in this case we might call it existential anxiety) become overwhelming, she could either defend herself by ignoring her new awareness (by dissociation and denial) or expand her map of reality and reach some new level of cognitive (and emotional) development that could support her new self-concept.

It seems that Sylvia's first inclination is to "deny" her experience—to not "hear" her own words, to discount them as "jabber-jabber-jabber" and to turn upon herself once again. This time Rogers does not follow her into the intrapsychic battleground but instead assertively disagrees with her self-assessment. Paradoxically, he counters Sylvia's self-discounting by discounting her reality! In his exquisite interpretation of her words, Rogers gives real weight to them, making denial more difficult and advancement of consciousness more possible. The emancipatory potential for the client of deep, empathic listening by the therapist—the sine qua non of person-centered therapies—is clearly demonstrated by the way Rogers' reiteration helps Sylvia listen deeply to her self and in so doing take her own words more seriously.

Rogers' willingness to listen carefully and to enter the relationship in a real way (by disagreeing with Sylvia) also serves to show Sylvia that there is an alternative to her lose–lose scenario. His attention and focus on her words offer her a new connection—with him and people who have the values he does. She may become alienated from groups who reject her new identity, but she may discover new connections with people who are willing to listen to her with respect and to enter into mutually affirming contact. The possibility exists that she will not have to choose between being and belonging. As she realizes this, she relaxes and reengages with the learning process.

Retreat from Reason: The Personal, Not the Political

Discussions as to whether or not person-centered therapies are apolitical have been a long-standing tradition. Within the ranks of those who call themselves client- or person-centered therapists, there is a general acceptance of the view that these approaches are profoundly political. Indeed, much of Rogers' later work was in the public, political arena, working as he did in South Africa, South America, Eastern Europe, and the Soviet Union. On the other hand, critics such as feminist Miriam Greenspan (1983) have argued that in their focus on the intrapsychic levels of reality and in the emphasis on feelings over thoughts and analysis, client-centered and other humanistic therapies actually keep the oppressed from an adequate understanding of the social sources of their pain and in so doing become part of the problem rather than the solution. I have also discussed this issue elsewhere (O'Hara, 1989). An examination of the final interchange between Sylvia and Rogers points up some of the difficulties with client-centered therapy as an emancipatory therapy.

After Rogers' reiteration of her words, what strikes Sylvia is her realization that there is a part of herself she simply does not understand. Rogers adds to her statement, "You have to have reasons." He seems to imply from his tone of voice here that perhaps reasons are not necessary. Sylvia picks this up and says, "So it seems like I don't have to have a reason." Rogers supports this by stating, "So maybe the intellectual understanding isn't as important as you thought it was." Sylvia concludes, "I think the acceptance is what's most important, my acceptance." In the commentary on this idea, Rogers makes it even clearer that he sees Sylvia's analyzing as unnecessary. Following this in the transcript, speaking from her point of view, he says, " 'If I could accept it, I wouldn't have to understand in the sense of knowing the reasons.' "

I think this passage makes it clear that Rogers was looking at Sylvia's struggle from a strictly psychological point of view, and a very narrow, intrapsychic, emotional version of psychology at that. By creating a false dichotomy between reason and acceptance, he implied that acceptance could never come from intellectual understanding. Here he returned to the position he held throughout his career that interpretation and insight are of limited usefulness in therapy. I believe there would have been something important to gain, both politically and psychologically, if Rogers had been able to help Sylvia explore the connection between understanding and acceptance. A powerful illustration of the way analytical, intellectual knowledge supports the psychological can be seen, for example, in work with women who have been molested or raped. In addition to the pain of their trauma, these women are often wracked with guilt because of internalized societal myths that their conduct somehow caused what happened. Understanding the way sexist society sets up women—all women—for such trespass on their bodies is frequently the most significant therapeutic intervention, permitting self-acceptance and self-comforting to occur.

Beyond the obvious problem of Rogers' false dichotomy, there is another, perhaps more serious problem in the interaction. Sylvia asserts that she would not have to "explain to anybody," and Rogers suggests that in her imagination she *is* trying to explain it to someone. Sylvia then sits for 25 seconds in silence and then says it seems she will "never understand it. So [she] can make life a lot easier for [herself] by not trying." In this interaction Sylvia is being supported by Rogers in seeing her struggle both as an entirely personal issue and one that is not worth the trouble to figure out. His support of her defeat and the suggestion that it is not so important for her to understand as to accept, has to me a ring of "don't worry your little head about this." The two of them agree to reduce or at least limit the whole struggle for her emergence as a woman to an intrapsychic struggle for self-acceptance. They tacitly agree to ignore entirely the therapeutic potential for Sylvia, not to mention the transformative potential for the whole society if Sylvia were able to understand and explain, not only to herself but to others, her predicament, its origins, and her successes in the direction of her liberation. What if Rogers had asked her, in the directive way he had asked her questions about her learnings, "To whom do you want to explain?" or "Who do you think could benefit from your experiences if you were able to explain them?" and so on? Had Rogers done this it might have become clear to both of them that in exactly the same way that Sylvia's inhibited self bore the traces of her development in a racist and sexist world, sharing her emancipation from those cultural introjections with others could be part of a revolutionary cocreation of a new, less sexist and less racist, culture. By reducing her work to the private sphere, Rogers kept Sylvia politically impotent. When she asked Rogers if he ever looks for reasons to justify himself, his answer, "I suspect we all do," is strangely coy for a man who has had a major transformative impact on his culture by doing just that!

CONCLUSION

In comparing person-centered approaches to therapy to the pedagogical strategies outlined by Paulo Freire in his *Pedagogy of the Oppressed,* I enumerated the significant ways I considered person-centered approaches to be emancipatory in the broadest sense.

> The work is . . . aimed directly at the uneven balance of power . . . the disparity, between the individual and . . . family, community, culture. . . . The work involves re-examination of introjection and the way the individual is diminished and limited in expression of full humanness. (O'Hara, 1989, p. 17)

In affirming the dignity and worth of his clients, and by extension the worth of every individual, in the theory and practice of person-centered approaches, Rogers' ideas take their place alongside the great ideas of the Western liberal humanist tradition. That this humanism is emancipatory when compared to other views of the human condition, such as totalitarianism, fascism, feudalism, and other ideologies of subjugation, cannot be disputed. But for all that the interview with Sylvia shows us, there are serious limitations, both theoretical and practical, that must be addressed if the full potential of person-centered therapies as emancipatory strategies for the disenfranchised can be realized.

Perhaps the most important limitation is due to the historical fact that the approach was formulated prior to the emergence of what is now variously called the constructivist, poststructuralist, or deconstructionist movements in epistemology.[7] Rogers lived his life in a world which believed in a unitary reality. He believed that it was possible for the therapist to arrive at a level of understanding in which she or he could accurately know the world of the client. He stated that the therapist must assume

> the internal reference of the client, to perceive the world as the client sees it, to perceive the client himself as he is seen by himself, to lay aside all perceptions from the external frame of reference while doing so, and to communicate something of this empathic understanding to the client. (Rogers, 1951, p. 29)

Postmodern thinking puts the therapist in an entirely different relationship with the client. If we accept the postmodern proposition that the knower is inseparable from what is known, that perception and meaning making are active and creative processes, then we must also admit that empathy as described by Rogers in the above quotation is not possible. It is not possible for us to set aside our own subjectivity in this way. Without it we would have no way to make sense of what we hear. Furthermore, any claim that we have done so blinds us, more than our own subjectivity ever could, to the ways in which our own biases and interests are inevitably embodied in all our understandings of the world, in all our expressions of our own world, and in all our questions.

Postmodern epistemologies make it necessary for us to reconsider what we mean when we speak of empathy. Such epistemologies would see dialogue, like that between Sylvia and Rogers, as an intersubjective mutually transforming conversation in which Sylvia explored her inner and outer reality and the world in which that reality was forged, while Rogers allowed himself to be involved, touched, and moved by her story. Empathy becomes a term for how one person's life can be touched, illuminated, affected in connection with another's. Like a hermeneutic reading of a sacred text, we understand another's world by way of, not despite, our own subjectivity.

Rogers demonstrated, here in this interview, and on many occasions, what an extraordinary "reader" he was. And over the years I worked with him he got ever better. This is not because he was better able to put his own subjectivity aside but rather the reverse. He had, by his countless deep readings of others' lives, expanded his own inner landscape so that, in somewhat the same way that someone who knows many languages has a better chance of decoding an ancient scroll than someone who does not, Rogers' enormous wealth of experience enhanced his ability to understand the meanings offered in the expressions of his clients.

Not less self then, but more. This brings us to the issue of blind spots and biases, which leads us back to Mannheim. We must admit that Rogers did not achieve his stated ideal of laying aside any outside frame of reference. Nor could he, for in order to hear others we must already have a language to hear them in. With that language come myriad cultural associations and meanings that describe and define the way of life of those who share the language. As I have illustrated, the language and values of client-centered therapy are those of its creators—white middle-class mostly North American males. It could not be other, and there is nothing inherently disempowering in that situation. The problem comes in the failure to recognize the inevitability of bias. By denying that all "listening" implies interpretation, that we hear what we expect to hear, that what we are aware of and what we say reveals our own construction of reality, client-centered therapists run the risk of engaging in covert "reality making" for clients. That this goes unacknowledged makes it all the more insidious and potentially oppressive, as in my view we have seen in Sylvia's interview. On the one hand, realities that are very important for her and for women in general were missed, misunderstood, minimized, or distorted possibly due to Rogers' own biases and blind spots; on the other hand, he offered (entirely unknowingly) subtle pressure to conform to a Eurocentric, androcentric status quo.

Perhaps if Rogers had not been such an extraordinarily open man, so flexible in point of view in comparison to most other men of his age and class, his biases would have been seen more clearly earlier. Perhaps if he had not been such an exquisite therapist, the structural and theoretical limitations of client-centered therapy might have been more obvious. Until feminists and others began to elaborate a postmodern critique, there had been no language with which to adequately discuss these problems. If client-centered therapy is to survive and thrive in this new postmodern pluralistic world, it will need to incorporate these multiple "other ways of knowing."

NOTES

1. "Mothering" here is used to mean childbirth and nursing, which are exclusive to women, and nurturance and care of children, which are also overwhelmingly, although not exclusively, done in our culture by women.

2. I was made aware of this kind of conceptual "mislocation" of the source of danger when a woman client of mine reacted to my use of the terms "risk" and "courage" in her decision to separate from a misogynistic partner. As we explored her reaction, it became clear that the "risk" or "courage" was in remaining in an abusive situation for the sake of the two children. Packing up her kids and leaving was an act of nurturance and self-assertion. By accurately locating the source of danger, her actions on her own behalf felt, as she put it, "more like rolling down hill than pushing up hill." This conceptualization constructs an image of authenticity as far less grueling than is created by the use of words like "risk."

3. She may, in fact, be correct in her assumption. In traditional patriarchal societies male–female relationships are situations in which connection means subordination. Patriarchal concepts of masculinity see men as "protectors" and "providers" and women as "dependents."

4. This is not to say that Rogers, when confronted consciously with relationships between people who are assigned to different race categories in Eurocentric thought, would have been disapproving or unsupportive. Rogers' long history of work toward ending sectarian and racial violence and injustice is well known. The bias I am referring to here is at the deepest tacit levels of the structure of thought,

conceptual habits, and linguistic constructions, much of which are usually beyond conscious awareness.

5. I am deliberately sidestepping the issue of "first causes" here—the religious determinist versus free will arguments as to whether or not our interests are biologically determined, reincarnated from previous lives, or created in toto from our experiences in the world. What matters from a therapeutic point of view is that phenomenologically, we can experience what we call our "authentic self" and that this can change during our lifetime. What may have felt "not me" 2 years ago may feel like "me" today, and what I would have sworn by before I now reject.

6. For a community to be stable, it must be able to reproduce itself in each succeeding generation. Mores, values, "reality stories" must seem "natural" and as "the way things are." To the extent that its values are life-enhancing, this process may drive healthy communities and to the extent that they are life-negating they may drive cultures of oppression. The goal of emancipatory therapies (or philosophies, pedagogies, or politics) is to identify the unconscious internalized values that dehumanize, and to replace "unconscious" patterns of life with conscious "fully human" processes. The ultimate (admittedly utopian) goal is the gradual cocreation of a world in which one group's (or person's) well-being does not come at the expense of another's.

7. In its insistence on unconditional acceptance of the client's internal frame of reference, in other words its openness to radical subjectivity, person-centered approaches verge on being postmodern, although the implications of this for the theory have yet to be elaborated.

REFERENCES

Belenky, M. F., Clinchy, B. M., Goldberger, N. R., & Tarule, J. M. (1986). *Women's ways of knowing: Development of self, voice, and mind.* New York: Basic Books.

Clinchy, B. M., & Belenky, M. F. (1987, August). *Women's ways of knowing: A theory and an intervention.* Paper presented to Smith College School of Social Work, Northampton, MA.

Gilligan, C. (1982). *In a different voice: Psychological theory and women's development.* Cambridge: Harvard University Press.

Greenspan, M. (1983). *A new approach to women and therapy: How psychotherapy fails women and what they can do about it.* New York: McGraw-Hill.

Horney, K. (1926). The flight from womanhood. *International Journal of Psycho-Analysis, 7,* 324–339.

Jordan, J. V., Kaplan, A. G., Miller, J. B., Stiver, I. P., & Surrey, J. L. (1991). *Women's growth in connection: Writings from the Stone Center.* New York: Guilford Press.

Mannheim, K. (1936, 1954). *Ideology and utopia: An introduction to the sociology of knowledge.* New York: Harcourt Brace.

O'Hara, M. (1989). Person-centered approach as conscientização: The works of Carl Rogers and Paulo Freire. *Journal of Humanistic Psychology, 29*(1), 11–35.

Rogers, C. R. (1951). *Client-centered therapy.* Boston: Houghton Mifflin.

Ruddick, S. (1980). Maternal thinking. *Feminist Studies, 6,* 342–367.

Showalter, E. (1985). *The female malady.* New York: Pantheon.

Shweder, R. A., & Bourne, E. (1982). Does the concept of the person vary cross-culturally? In A. J. Marsela & G. White (Eds.), *Cultural concepts of mental health and therapy* (pp. 97–137). Boston: Reidel.

Toril, M. (Ed.). (1987). *French feminist thought: A reader.* London: Blackwell.

Weedon, C. (1987). *Feminist practice and poststructural theory.* Oxford: Basil Blackwell.

Weisstein, N. (1971). Psychology constructs the female. In V. Gornick & K. B. Moran (Eds.), *Women in sexist society* (pp. 133–146). New York: Basic Books.

CHAPTER 9

THE CASE OF "ANGER AND HURT" (1977)

SUMMARY BY DEBORA C. BRINK
AND DEBRA ROSENZWEIG

Before this 1977 interview began, Carl Rogers explained to the audience that it was the second session with a man who had leukemia, but it was in a state of remission. He described that, in the first interview, one of the client's important realizations was that at the age of 7 he valued himself but that he had lost that valuing of self as a result of conforming to social expectations. During the first interview, the client had begun to feel angry about the loss, but he had not yet expressed his anger.

Because permission to publish the verbatim transcript of the second session was not granted a summary of it is included here. The videotaped case, "Carl Rogers Counsels an Individual on Anger and Hurt" (Whitely, 1977), may be obtained by mental health professionals through the auspices of the American Personnel and Guidance Association. The reader should be aware that this summary cannot convey the full emotional impact of this often moving and sometimes frustrating session. The client (who is nameless throughout this session) speaks for the most part in a groping manner (see example below), as if in a thick fog; Rogers often changes the tone and intensity of his voice in what seem to be attempts to be either empathic or encouraging of the client's struggles to express his feelings.

Rogers asks the client where he wants to start, and the client replies that he has thought a great deal about their earlier talk of anger:

Client: I'm not sure that, uh, I really don't want to be angry, you know, and I'm not sure if anger, being angry now, is a part of the process and

I've got to do that, but I'd like to. I guess my mind, uh, academically or something, you know, and something, that emotion or whatever, would like to tell that, uh, I'd like to, uh, not be angry and skip over that part, if that's part of the process, you know? But I'm not sure I can do that *(small laugh)*, you know.

C.R.: Your mind says sort of, "Oh, cool it, don't get into, uh, some strong emotion."

The client agrees with Rogers, then says it seems to him that he feels pulled into such traps by whatever environment he is in. Rogers responds that his mind is now speaking for the system, telling him to "do the proper thing," while another part of him is saying, "Yeah, but there's some anger there."

The client affirms Rogers' statement and then says that in this country there seem to be only two positions possible with regard to race—being racist or antiracist. He no longer wants to be the latter, nor does he want to be a reflection of the larger society. Rogers responds that he (the client) seems to want to connect with his own inner reality. Agreeing, the client acknowledges that he can more easily trust his own experiences than external circumstances. He realizes, he adds, that the things they discussed in the first session were, strangely, worse than the leukemia—that the suffering caused him by people was worse than that of the disease. For, if he had died, he would have had no awareness of past or present, but now he is too well aware of what is currently happening in his life. The bodily deterioration due to the disease, he says, "is the same thing that happened to my mind." Rogers suggests that society has given him "a cancer of the mind." The client agrees with Rogers' restatement of his words and adds that he really does want to say those words but that a part of him, his culture, says that he should not be angry because militancy is disapproved of. He adds that, traditionally, blacks became militant when angry.

He cannot find anyone who can be blamed for starting what is happening in the culture; it would be better, he thinks, if he could blame someone and try to "do that person in." Rogers understands this to mean that he thinks identifying that one person might justify his rage, and the client then wonders how one can blame another who is sick—for those who are responsible for racism are really sick. At the same time, he questions whether he is being forgiving or trying to accept their sickness; he also states that he has not had the opportunity of anyone accepting his own sickness. Rogers hypothesizes that the client has so many reasons for not venting his anger that he would like to discuss them all.

The client says, with a small laugh, that some day he just might be angry and feel better for it, adding that when he is smiling "there's a lot of anger there . . . but it's not in my nature to be angry." Groping, he arrives at not knowing "how you'd be angry in a productive way." He says that before, when people gave him double messages, he tried to avoid giving offense, but now he says, "Hey, that's a bunch of crap." He now rejects negative nonverbal messages that contradict positive ones. Rogers interjects, "I get what you're saying, and I also feel quite strongly that I want to say it's OK with me if you're angry here." After a pause, the client replies that he is not sure how to be angry, that it is hard for him. Rogers reassures him that anger is not demanded of him, it's simply OK for him to be angry if he feels angry.

Client: You really believe that?

C.R.: Damn right.

After a 27-second pause and a sigh, the client says that he does not know how to respond because part of the anger is the hurt. Maybe if he really vented his anger he would be face to face with his hurt. That realization comes as a revelation to him, and he doubts that he wants to risk getting angry. For him, his anger means an open admission that he is hurt, and that is more frightening than facing death and its symptoms. "And for God's sake, . . . having to show somebody . . . that I'm hurt, . . . how can I trust that to somebody?" He wishes he could justify his fear ("I'd like just to say it's my conditioning"), but he finds this unacceptable. He explains by putting his hand on his chest, stating that he can express the hurt with words but that he always "keeps something down here."

The client then talks about not knowing how to fully express his feelings and that he does not want to have the kind of emotional experience that would represent, implying that he does not drink alcohol because of his fear of losing control and experiencing too much. He realizes that during his last session with Rogers he would have liked to have been able to say, "Yeah. I was screwed over and I got hurt and everything else like that, or whatever, but it's almost an admission, in a way, on another level, of saying that they got the best of me, . . . they beat the hell out of me." He has no regrets about caring or loving, but in a way too he is "a kid" who also wants to be loved. So he is going to start expecting some in return. He agrees strongly with Rogers' statement: "You want love to be mutual" and adds that he does not want his present situation—fear of letting anyone see his hurt—ever to recur. The client says that his dread has to do with being a man, with "the race thing," with a relationship that failed, and with being an absentee father. It adds up to his feeling like a victim, and unable to let it out.

After a pause of 18 seconds, he says he does not know at all how to get those feelings up and then laughs. Every time he comes close to it, he says, he takes a drink of water (he laughs as he says this) and wonders if that serves to keep things down. Maybe "exorcism" can free him, he says, because it feels "like there's something there," sometimes a big lump in his throat. Not believing in cookbook answers, he nevertheless wishes someone could tell him what to do to get rid of the hurt and be left in peace. He wonders if Rogers is holding something back from him, then realizes that he is holding out on himself.

Roger suggests that if the client could let out his hurt, it would be "the voice of the victim." In response, the client wonders whether he has "any control" over the victim inside him. He relates that one time he saw the effects of culture in another's intellectualizing, and he "really wanted to just . . . deck him," a reaction not in his "nature." A friend who was present at the time cautioned him that one day he might really "lose it." The client explains that he wants to free himself of what was done to him, or at least find the skills to cope with it constructively. When he sees the things done to him now being done to others it makes him angry, and he has started to strike out on their behalf. Yet, he is not sure what he has ever done to protect himself. If only he could cry and have things be all right—but crying is a "trip." Maybe, suggests the client, if he went to a tear-jerker movie he would have an excuse to cry. However, he doubts that crying for himself can be "constructive." Rogers then offers what seems to be an interpretation: "Hmm. You say you're not sure whether crying for yourself is constructive. I feel also you're afraid of crying for yourself." Agreeing, the client says he was conditioned from the time he was a little boy to believe that men should not cry; he remembers crying but doing so alone. Laughing, he adds that a mere two or three people in the world have ever seen him cry. He describes his ex-wife's frequent crying as most likely "healthier" than his own way, which is to work hard and not think about it. Rogers says that the client tried to be too busy to have these sad thoughts, but that the sorrow was still there.

Asked by Rogers what he would cry for if he did cry, the client describes the very long hours away from his family. He says that all of his time working, missing seeing his children grow, even his leukemia, might have been worthwhile if at least someone had benefited from it. He also wants to cry for his father-in-law who was killed 6 months before the onset of the client's leukemia, and to tell him that he loved him very much. Despite their sharp differences, including the fact that they were of different races, they really loved each other, went fishing together. His father-in-law encouraged him to free himself from "that stuff" and to do what he really wants. A week after he had agreed to help the client finance his own restaurant, he died in a hunting accident.

The client considers his father-in-law to have been "straighter" with him than many people. With his father-in-law's death about 8 months earlier, all communication ceased with his ex-wife's family. He says that even they, his own family, had begun to "take on the attitudes of the culture." Recently he has come to see his relationship with them as lacking: "It wasn't real. . . . I wasn't getting any nourishment back . . . smiles and polite kisses. . . . That is part of the hurt." He would have preferred blunt honesty to false niceness. He wishes he could have been outspoken about how he was hurt. Still, he believes that saying they were racist or terrible does not really express his feelings. And they would not understand his hurt because they see black people as not being human. In response to Rogers' statement that he (the client) would get some satisfaction out of expressing to his family how hurt he had been, even if they failed to get the message, the client remarks that he cannot trust them enough to state his true feelings because then he would get "squashed."

Rogers' remark that the client has opened up to him elicits agreement. The client says, "You know that I'm a person, and I don't really want that denied to me . . . ever again." The client adds that he does not want to love anyone again the way he had loved his father-in-law. That love was nourishing and then taken away. No more in-laws for him, of whatever color: "It's crazy to love. It's just like loving a pet rock or something." He doubts that telling his in-laws he was hurt would make a difference; he does not think they can understand. It had taken 6 or 7 months from the time he left her for his wife (of 7 years) to understand that he had felt hurt and desperate. He might as well try to get understanding from Dick Nixon. Nixon could not relate to his situation; he is as remote from the client's reality as "that family" was. It seems "insane"; in one way he feels all right for having loved them but not all right about any further sharing with them.

The client then describes his belief that his body must have gone through changes that have made it impossible for him to let out his locked up feelings. Despite knowing all the reasons for letting them out, he cannot work up the strength to get them out. Still, he says, talking to Rogers really helps: "It's incredible. . . . This is the first time that I've talked to anybody. . . . that I haven't been in control. . . . I've given up a lot of control to you." Agreeing with Rogers that letting feelings loose is a new experience for him, the client says he wants to work to be able to feel and not fear crying. He says that, if he could, he would have doctors cut him open and "get that out." Rogers laughs while saying, "Hmm. Probably it'd be simpler to have an operation." The client agrees and sighs. He says he really does want to tell Rogers how hurt he is, but that he cannot. Rogers replies, "I understand that. . . . It visualizes in my mind you're walking all around the edge of that pit, but you're not really letting yourself go down into it, so you're letting me know all about it, but not it." The client agrees with Rogers' vision of his experience and adds, "[I] don't know how to do that."

Rogers says that what he hears the client saying is that he really does want to get to it, but it has to be at his own pace. The client agrees. He feels that it is a sick part of him: "That's really the cancer, you know. . . . If I could eliminate it, I could eliminate all the cancer from my body." He goes on to blame his illness on his lifestyle, on stress, and on racism. He wants to give, but not like before.

The client then mentions that, on his way to the session, he thought of yelling but now he has doubts about it. Encouraged by Rogers to give it a try, he laughs, saying it would not be "cultured." If he were to express his anger it might come out in obscenity, calling someone a bad name. He does not know what effect it would have, but he would really like to do that:

C.R.: You'd like to just tell off the bastard.

Client: Yeah, right, right, right. For sure. *(Laughs)* Oh my goodness! *(Laughs)*

C.R.: You can't even do that.

Client: *(Sighs)* Oh, it's incredible. I don't know. Phew! I'm getting warm!

The client then talks about how he used to use words like "bastard" and "goddamit" with his wife but not with his teachers, his family, or his colleagues. He indicates that he does not think he wants to speak that way to them: "I was raised properly." Still, he knows that, for himself, he needs to get those feelings out in the open. He feels rotten, really screwed. Rogers reflects this sentiment: " 'The bastards really screwed me.' " The client concurs and tries to describe what had been done to him: "To describe that hell to somebody is just the hardest thing. . . It's like somebody knocking you down . . . stomping on you and spitting on you . . . and feeling like garbage." And although his friends would say that he has everything, he feels that this is not true. He states, "I didn't have everything, certainly didn't have that respect as a person."

The client then says he will not allow himself to be treated with scorn again, because he is weary of fighting. He does not know what will happen in terms of his getting out his feelings; he does not want to say he is "hurt" because that does not sufficiently describe his experience. Rogers restates these thoughts: "Yeah, to say a word like that or several of the words you've used just isn't at all the same as feeling those feelings inside and really feeling them fully." The client agrees, then likens his inner feelings to the green slime that the girl spewed up in the movie *The Exorcist.* The feelings are now part of him and his body wants to get rid of them, but he fears looking "horrible" if he were to express that kind of hurt and anger. However, at the moment his overriding concern is not with expressing his feelings but with maintaining control for fear of getting sick again. Laughing, he says he knows his fear to be illogical. Then he sighs.

After a 20-second pause the client says he feels beaten "right now," not knowing why. He has things to say and thinks he will feel better—but maybe he will not. He says he is talking in circles. Rogers suggests that if "only something could come out, you wouldn't feel beaten." After another pause the client says that what he has been through has almost turned him into something inhuman. "It damn near made an animal out of you," Rogers replies. The client follows this up with another emphatic statement: He never again wants a repetition of what has happened to him. No one, he says, has the right to do that to anyone, neither teacher nor spouse, "just like somebody took a big goddamned tree and just rammed it u—, ooh, so you know? *(Sighs)* Hard to describe, you know?" Rogers then asks, "Took a great big stick and rammed it up your ass—is that what you're saying?" The client responds, laughingly, that he never said that. Rogers, though, asks him if that was what he meant to say. The client admits that it was, and Rogers responds, "OK. That's what I want to know, whether I was catching your meaning correctly."

The client states that such a thing would probably be very painful but that he still does not know how to tell Rogers how badly he has been hurt. Rogers says, "Goes beyond words"; then, a moment later, clearly being empathic, he adds, "You're feeling some of that hurt now." The client agrees and tells Rogers about how he was thinking of a wino on the street who continues to drink and does not have anywhere to go, but he thinks that "there may be some reasons." He says that he himself has become more sensitive to such people because of what he has been through. Rogers tells the client that it seems to him that he (the client) knows what it is like to feel desperation and that he knows to what depths it can bring someone. The client agrees and says that his heart goes out to people like that. He says that he used to have a lot of money, but it is all gone and he is happier now. He is uncertain about where to go next, except for not wanting his old kind of life again. He wants to give, to help, to talk to people, but first he wants to get his own thing together, part of which may be the admission of being hurt and expressing it, to "reaffirm the fact that I'm a person." After the client speaks a bit more about how he needs to keep his hurt inside and how he manages to convince himself that nothing hurts and that he is fine, Rogers, somewhat uncharacteristically, but in an apparent attempt to be empathic, says, "That's a lot of bullshit. Yeah, that's right, hmm. And just for a moment there, I felt you really were experiencing that too, really feeling that stick shoved up your ass." The client, after appearing a bit flustered, declares that his natural reaction when he has "felt stuff like that" has been to put it out of his mind by bringing it down to a "safe level."

When the client asks whether it is all right to blame one's problems on others, he and Rogers both laugh. Rogers then suggests that the client feels others are to blame but that his mind holds on to the sense that he probably has a share in it too. The client then says he let himself be hurt by giving too much most times, by sharing and loving in a total way.

Client: But . . . I've never really been this beaten . . . and if I show you how much I've been beaten . . . I'd probably become nothing in this chair. *(20-second pause)* Really too much for me.

Rogers and the client agree that he has gone about as far as he can. Rogers summarizes: "You've walked around that pit of hurt and pain and beaten-ness, and you've felt some of it, and perhaps that's as far as you can go right at this moment. . . . Even though you know there's more there, you know that you're keeping some of it down, and to know those things may be helpful too." The client begins to explain how he can talk about his leukemia, but Rogers interrupts him, pointing out that it is easier for him to discuss his cancer than to talk about all the hurt he has suffered. The client, sighing, says: "Whew, oh, I really . . . I have to stop. OK?" Rogers reaffirms that he has gone as far as he can go, and that they should "call it quits."

In his postsession commentary, Rogers reviewed the session: "Here is an armor-plated man. He's been sufficiently hurt but he hides his real feelings very deeply. But in this relationship, the armor begins to crack—just begins to crack. . . . We find the upper layer is anger, but further down in the slime are the unspeakable hurts." Rogers went on to say that he did not regret that the client held back. He regarded it as a demonstration of the wisdom of the client. It is the client who knows where his most tender places are, what he is capable of, and what pace to go at.

Rogers noted that he was fascinated by certain intellectual and theoretical aspects of the interview, for example, the extent to which the client's introjected self was his "cultured" self. In addition, Rogers spoke about the client's fantasy that if he let his feelings out, it would make him sick again. He noted, too, that when he repeated the client's own words, the client realized how ridiculous this assumption was. Another theoretical aspect of the interview Rogers discussed was the client's reaction to being given permission to be as angry as he wished. Rogers explained that this permission stopped him from feeling angry and helped him realize that it was not his anger but the hurting and vulnerable part of him that he feared most. Finally, he described how the client gained from speaking about his love for his father-in-law, as he had never before been able to express those loving, mournful feelings.

Rogers ended his commentary by providing his own feelings about the client, the interview, and what others could gain from it. He stated: "Finally, he [the client] makes it very clear that for him, there are many more frightening aspects of his life than the prospect of death. Somehow this seems to contain a message for all of us. As for me, I felt very present in the relationship—an understanding companion on this trip of exploration which seems so potentially dangerous to him. I think it's a good example of how I work with an articulate client."

REFERENCE

Whitely, J. M. (Producer). (1977). *Carl Rogers counsels an individual on anger and hurt* [Film]. American Personnel and Guidance Association.

UNCHARACTERISTIC DIRECTIVENESS

Rogers and the "Anger and Hurt" Client

Barbara Temaner Brodley

In 1977 Carl Rogers conducted two one-hour therapy sessions on consecutive days with a volunteer client. The sessions had been arranged in order to produce films demonstrating his way of working within the client-centered framework.[1] There was no audience for these demonstrations other than the film crew, and the resulting films reproduce the complete sessions. The film of the first session was titled "The Right to Be Desperate" (Whitely, 1977a). The film of the second session, the more famous of the two, was titled "Carl Rogers Counsels an Individual on Anger and Hurt" (Whitely, 1977b). It is the second of the two sessions that is summarized in this book and is the focus of this analysis.

Rogers never gave the client a pseudonym, and he has come to be known simply as "the client from the film of Anger and Hurt." Rogers had not met the client until the start of the first session. At their first meeting Rogers said to the client that he had been told only "a few things" about him, "all good things," and "that you have leukemia but that you're in a stage of remission."

The client, a young black man who appeared to be in late 20s, was attractive, articulate, and expressive. He exhibited a great range of emotions as he interacted with Rogers. This made him compelling to watch as his expressions changed from moment to moment. The entire session is rich and intense full of the client's forays into his pain and Rogers' highly focused empathic responsiveness.

While Rogers' style of therapy evolved in some respects over the years, he never changed his basic assumption nor his basic theory as expressed in terms of the necessary and sufficient conditions for therapeutic change (Rogers, 1957, 1959, 1986a). Rogers' long-held basic assumption was expressed in 1986 as "the person-centered approach is built on a basic trust in the person. . . . [It] depends on the actualizing tendency present in every living organism. . . . [It] trusts the constructive directional flow of the human being" (Rogers, 1986a, p. 198). Rogers' axiom, the actualizing tendency, and its corollaries of trust in and respect for individual persons, dictate the distinctive client-centered, nondirective attitude (Raskin, 1947) toward the client and the therapy process.

This nondirective attitude is implied throughout Rogers' presentations of therapeutic theory and practice, and it is expressed in his conception of the therapist's goals as "limited to the process of therapy not the outcome" (Rogers, quoted in Baldwin, 1987, p. 47). He meant by this that the client-centered therapist's goals are exclusively to engender in him- or herself the therapeutic attitudes of congruence, unconditional positive regard, and empathic understanding in relation to the client.

According to Rogers, one way a therapist can help keep these goals for him- or herself appropriately limited and focused is by asking the question, "Am I really with this person in the moment?" (Baldwin, 1987, p. 48). Thus, the client-centered therapist does not have specific objectives for the client and consequently does not direct the client. Instead, the therapist attempts to provide attitudinal conditions that support and facilitate the client's inherent actualizing tendency toward constructive change. The actualizing tendency is thought to be activated when the therapeutic attitudes are presented by the therapist and perceived by the client.

Accordingly, in Rogers' session with the "Anger and Hurt" client, we would expect to observe him behaving in ways that consistently implement his therapeutic attitudes, exhibiting trust and respect for the client with a nondirectiveness that allows the client his own pace, direction, sense of importance of things, and perceived reality. We would also expect Rogers' therapeutic attitudes to pervade the form of his empathic responses, any references to himself, and his responses to explicit questions. We would expect him to be sensitive and adaptive to the issues and vulnerabilities that appear in the client. And, in fact, we do observe all of these expected elements in Rogers' session with this client; but we also find some unexpected elements.

Before sitting down to write this commentary, I had viewed the "Anger and Hurt" film many times with my students. While I perceived the client-centered qualities and behaviors from Rogers I expected, it also appeared to me that he was, at times in the session, attempting to influence the client in a systematically directive way. Consequently, the session seems very different from other sessions of Rogers' that I have experienced.

In these other sessions, Rogers either behaved strictly empathically or he met Raskin's (1988) criteria of "a freely functioning client/person-centered therapist."[2] In this session, however, Rogers seemed to have specific objectives for the client, instead of the nondirective goals he espoused, of experiencing and implementing the therapeutic attitudes.

Because I felt Rogers was functioning differently in the "Anger and Hurt" interview, I compared his behavior in this session with his behavior in relation to nine other clients he worked with at different points over a 40-year period. The research (Brodley & Brody, 1990; Brody, 1991), from which I drew the comparison, analyzed 10 of Rogers' sessions, including this one. Brody and I classified the total number of Rogers' substantive verbal responses in the 10 sessions into two categories: "empathic following responses" and "responses from the therapist's frame of reference" (see Table 9.1). The first consists of Rogers' responses that were intended to check[3] with the client whether or not Rogers accurately understood the client's immediate internal frame of reference. The second category consists of responses from Rogers' own frame of reference. (In Table 9.1, these are further divided into four subcategories.)

The study shows that while 4.2% of the total number of Rogers' responses in the nine other sessions were from his own frame of reference, 22% of his responses in the "Anger and Hurt" interview were from his own frame of reference. It is likely that such a high frequency of responses from the therapist's frame of reference is the result of attempts to implement specific objectives for the client. It is, however, not only the frequency of such responses that may reveal directiveness. The definitive test of directiveness is whether or not responses from the therapist's frame of reference systematically implement a directive intention or attitude in relation to the client. In short, does the therapist consistently express some specific objectives for the client in his responses? If so, that behavior is directive and inconsistent with client/person-centered principles.

Not only does Rogers' session with the "Anger and Hurt" client have a higher frequency of responses from the therapist's own frame of reference compared with the other nine sessions in the sample, but many of these responses seem to reveal that Rogers had specific goals for the client at times during the session. Several sequences of interaction in the session reveal this uncharacteristic behavior in which Rogers manifests a directive attitude in the pursuit of an objective he has for the client. The first sequence that reveals systematic directiveness begins at the point of the client's 29th statement in the transcript.

Table 9.1. Category System for Rogers' Articulate Verbal Responses in Therapy, with Some Examples from This Case

Category	Examples
Empathic following responses	"Your mind says sort of 'oh cool it, don't get into such strong emotion.' "
	"Just like to have socked him!"
	"You wonder about that—whether if you, let out all the—all the hell that you've experienced inside, it might, uh, it might bring back your illness."
	"It damn near made an animal out of you."
Responses from the therapist's frame of reference	
Therapist comment/ observation	"I've thought a lot about what you had to say about that."
Therapist interpretation/ explanation	"You say you're not sure crying for yourself is constructive. I feel also you're afraid of crying for yourself."
Therapist agreement	"Yeah, maybe you haven't given it to them."
Leading question	"If you cry, what would some of the themes of that crying be?"

Note. Vocal gestures such as "M-hm" are not counted in this system although they contribute to the therapist's communication and to the client's perception that the therapist is attentive and following.

Client: I don't know if I'm sounding confused or whatever, maybe, you know, but trying to accept their sickness, you know. (C.R.: M-hm.) And at the same time, I really haven't had the opportunity of letting anybody accept mine. (C.R.: M-hm.) Or maybe I haven't given it to them.

C.R.: Yeah, maybe you haven't given it to them.

Client: Right.

C.R.: That's what I sense is going on now—that you feel, "there's so many reasons why I really shouldn't express my anger. I'll, I'll talk about all those reasons."

Client: Yeah *(small laugh)*, for sure . . . I don't know really, you know. Maybe I'll just be angry one day *(small laugh)* and maybe I'll really feel better or whatever, you know, and, . . . and I—when I, when I smile, I—I'm, uh, you know, I'm smiling but there's a lot of—and I'm sure you know that—there's a lot of anger there. (C.R.: M-hm.) You know, but it's not my nature to be angry. (C.R.: M-hm.) It's not my nature to be angry, but I feel angry.

C.R.: Yeah, um, and, uh, so I hear you explaining and explaining that uh, uh, "that's not my nature to be angry. It's just that I am angry right now."

Client: For sure *(slight laugh)*, for sure.

In Rogers' first response above, he asserts the client's idea that he may not have let his needs be known to others. In his second response Rogers uses this to reinforce his *own* idea that the client is avoiding the expression of his angry feelings. This is an interpretation of Rogers' that implies that the client *should be* expressing his anger. It is also notable, and unusual for Rogers, that he states his interpretation in the assertive mode when he says, "That's what I sense is going on now."

The client appears to have been uncomfortable in reaction to Rogers' interpretation and eases himself away from the pressure in Rogers' statement saying, "Maybe I'll just be angry one day." Immediately following this statement, the client continues in a somewhat hesitant and ambiguous fashion: "and maybe I'll really feel better or whatever, you know, and, . . . and I—when I, when I smile, I—I'm, uh, you know, I'm smiling but there's a lot of—and I'm sure you know that—there's a lot of anger there." It is not clear whether the client was complying with Rogers' implicit direction to express anger when the client commented that his smile covered angry feelings, or if the was revealing some anger toward Rogers in reaction to the interpretation.

In any case, Rogers does *not* give an empathic response that acknowledges that the client feels he has been provoked to feel angry and, consequently, has become angry. Instead, Rogers reiterates his interpretation that the client avoids anger by "explaining and explaining." Ironically, it seems that Rogers has been so strongly goal directed in his attitude at this point that he bypasses the fact that the client has said that he is angry right at that moment.

Rogers' goal, for the client to be immediately angry, is explicit in Rogers' comment within the interaction following the one above.

Client: I don't know how you'd be angry in a productive way, you know, in terms of . . . It's like now when I, when I respond to people, if, if when you encounter people, whether it's in the street, whether it's in a professional situation or whatever, if people send out certain messages and, no matter what they're saying, there are certain kinds of messages that I'm getting. They're saying, "hey," you know, "that isn't for me" kind of thing. And that's before. . . . I'd like to work with that and ride it, like to try to communicate without alienating— (C.R.: M-hm.) People or whatever. But now I'm ending up saying, like, "hey, that's a bunch of crap." (C.R.: M-hm.) You know. "Don't tell me about the way I should do it or give me all that nonverbal stuff about, um, saying that I'm OK, but by nonverbally saying 'hey,' you know, 'you're really not OK.' " And I don't want to hear that kind of stuff anymore.

C.R.: I get what you're saying and I also feel quite strongly that I want to say, "It's OK with me if you're angry here."

Client: *(Pause)* But I don't, you know, it's hard to know how to be angry, you know, hard to—

C.R.: Sure, sure, I'm not saying you have to be.

Client: Sure.

C.R.: I'm just saying it's OK with me. (Client: M-hm.) If you feel like being angry you can be angry.

Client: You really believe that?

C.R.: Damn right!

The client's response to Rogers' statement of permission indicates that he interprets the permission as an encouragement. Although Rogers denies that he meant to imply that the client *should* get angry, the vehemence of Rogers' reassurance probably communicated the advocacy of anger to the client. In addition, Rogers sacrifices an opportunity for an empathic response and, in the process, again overlooks, and distracts the client from, the feelings he was immediately experiencing.

From here, Rogers responds nondirectively and empathically for many interactions. Then Rogers makes a comment that implies encouragement for another immediate feeling.

Client: When I see other people doing it to other people, it grinds me, it makes me angry, you know? And I would think that in those situations, I've begun to kind of strike out, you know, or like, protecting somebody else or fighting for somebody else or whatever. *(Pause)* And, if I could cry and have it be all right—

C.R.: That's what I was thinking.

Client: That would be—

C.R.: I was just thinking, if you could only cry.

Here, Rogers interrupts the client twice to state his own idea that it would be good for the client to cry. Even though Rogers supports the client's idea, he asserts it as his own thought. Again the encouraging response overlooks the client's ownership of the idea that immediate feeling and expression (crying) are desirable. After this, Rogers follows empathically for several interactions and then makes an interpretation.

Client: I can cry, you know and have an excuse to cry. But crying for myself, I'm not sure that's going to be constructive, you know *(laughs)*.

C.R.: M-hm, you say you're not sure whether crying for yourself is constructive. I feel also you're afraid of crying for yourself.

This interpretation does not accept the client's doubt that crying for himself would be constructive. The interpretation carries the message that the client *should* cry, that he would be better off crying, and that the real experience the client is having is the latent one of crying. Rogers gives additional evidence of his directive attitude with respect to crying in his next response to the client when Rogers says, "Probably your 7-year-old could cry."

In this response, Rogers is referring to the client as a child, mentioned earlier in the session, who, lonely as he was, had an authentic self before he reacted to the falsifying pressures of culture. Rogers' statement implies that the client would be more authentic if he could cry for himself.

Rogers empathically follows during the next four interactions until he breaks the empathic process with a leading question.

Client: I really don't know how to de—, and I *really* don't know how to deal with that. I really don't. I really don't *(sighs)*. You know, just really giving so much of yourself, and it's just really crazy. Too much *(sighs)*.

C.R.: If you did cry, what would some of the themes of that crying be?

Here, again, Rogers overlooks and deflects an immediate feeling in his apparent effort to move the client toward immediacy and expression of feelings. The client *is* feeling his sadness. His words, sighs, and appearance indicate it very clearly. But Rogers' question redirects the client to draw out information and explanations, which distracts the client from the feelings he was experiencing before the question.

By the midpoint of the session, Rogers has already encouraged the client to feel angry and to cry in the session. Then he encourages the client to express another emotion, one of intense hurt or anguish.

Client: I just don't want to get caught up into that anymore, and I want to continue to give, but I don't, I'm just not going to do it the way I did before. May—, yelling, you know, one of those long, big long, you know. But I'm not sure I want to do that *(smiles).*

C.R.: You could try it.

Rogers' encouragements and permissions, his pressure on the client to express anger, to cry, and to yell out his pain, subvert in each instance, if only briefly, the client's actual immediate feelings. This type of deflection is characteristic of directive therapies (psychodynamic, Gestalt, family systems, etc.) but rare in client-centered work. Although a directive therapy may consider the immediate expression of feeling as desirable, the directive behavior often results in the therapist's overlooking and deflecting spontaneous feelings in the client. In contrast, the client-centered therapist's usual empathic attention and responsiveness leave the client free to experience a feeling or shift away from it according to his or her inner leanings. The deflections that appear in this session are unusual, possibly unique, in available examples of Rogers doing therapy. As if he were aware of this, each time Rogers' directiveness interferes with the client's immediacy, Rogers resumes empathic responding and, as a consequence, the client's feelings are reestablished and a productive client-centered process is reinstated.

There is an additional way, other than through interpretations and encouragements, that Rogers conveys a directive attitude in relation to this client. In two instances in the session, Rogers conveys a directive attitude by expressly introducing a profanity into an otherwise empathic understanding response, as a means to press the client to express intense feelings. In the first instance, this stimulates embarrassment in the client.

C.R.: You'd like to just tell off the bastard.

Client: Yeah, right, right, right. For sure. *(Laughs)* Oh, my goodness! *(Laughs)*

The client's embarrassment about having profanity attributed to him (although he acknowledges that the sentiment is correct) may be caused by his awareness that the session is being filmed, or his beliefs about the correct manner of speech in therapy, or the fact or the fact that he is speaking to Rogers, an elder and a professional person. In any case, he is obviously uncomfortable with the attribution.

In the second instance of Rogers' modeling of profanity, the client had been talking about his resolve and determination that he would no longer allow other people to degrade or dehumanize him as had been done to him in the past. He speaks with strong emotion evident in his words and his manner.

Client: I don't think anybody has a right to do that to anybody. *Nobody,* teacher, wife, husband, whatever. Uh, uh, you know, and it, and it really wasn't my fault either, and I'm not the blameless, I mean, I'm not without any blame or whatever, but you know, you know, just like somebody took a big goddamned tree and just rammed it u–, ooh, so you know? *(Sighs)* Hard to describe, you know, you know?

C.R.: Took a great big stick and rammed it up your ass—is that what you're saying?

Client: *(Laughs)* I, I didn't say that.

Rogers' response—one that refers to an emotionally charged situation and that focuses on a metaphor with a compelling emotional meaning—is a type that Rogers used often in his empathic responding. But in this instance he seems to have been pushing the explicit profanity that the client communicated quite well while avoiding the phrase "up my ass." And, as might be expected, given his previous embarrassed response to Rogers' use of the word "bastard," the client reacts with nervous laughter and denies he used the phrase. The focus on stating the profanity deflects him from the strong emotion he appeared to be experiencing when he used his own metaphor but omitted the profanity. (An empathic response that Rogers could have made that would have respected the client's reserve in the session about profanity but also communicated the intensity of his feelings might be: "Nobody has the right to *violate* you, or anybody, the way you've been violated, degraded and hurt.")

In these interactions and others, Rogers seemed to be working from an idea that the client would benefit from intensely and immediately vocalizing his feelings. It seems, paradoxically, that this idea led Rogers to make responses that, at times, inhibited or undermined that very goal.

The client resumes contact with his strong feelings after several more interactions with Rogers. That such a recovery is possible seems to be the consequence of the activeness and intensity of the client's feelings and of Rogers' powerful nondirective empathy that, aside from moments of directiveness, predominates in the session. (Seventy-eight percent of Rogers' responses were empathic following responses.)

Near the middle of the session, the client makes an observation that expresses my perception that Rogers' oscillations between directiveness and his characteristic empathic, acceptant, nondirective attitude resulted in Rogers exerting control over the client in the session. The client says, "It's incredible, you know. This is the first time I haven't really been in control. To some extent I've really given up a lot of control, uh, to you." Clients of client-centered therapists often give up excessive controlling tendencies as a consequence of the relationship. But the client's muted words "to you" express his sense that Rogers is in control—a different matter. The client's words speak to my perception that Rogers was trying to influence the client toward specific objectives—to immediately and intensely experience anger, sadness, and hurt feelings.

The question naturally arises as to why Rogers wavered in this session between an uncharacteristic, theoretically inconsistent directiveness and his usual, theoretically consistent nondirectiveness. I do not know and would rather not speculate. The purpose of my commentary has been to demonstrate Rogers' uncharacteristic directiveness in this session, not to explain it. For those who are inclined to speculate there are rumors which, if true, might support certain explanations.

One rumor has it that Rogers felt some reluctance to make the films, but that he responded to pressure from a colleague and went ahead with the project. Mixed feelings about the filming situation may have made him in some way impatient with the client's reserve, which may have caused him to lose his nondirective discipline with the client. Another rumor has it that the client misrepresented critical information about himself, for example that he suffered from leukemia; and although Rogers had no knowledge of this at the time the sessions took place, he may have sensed something in the client that threw him off of his usual congruent state in the relationship.

The peculiar, and disturbing, uncharacteristic quality of Rogers' work with this client was echoed in another way at the very end of the film. In the final minutes of the session, Rogers is purely empathic, expressing acceptant and accurate understanding of the client and, as a result the client became very emotional. Tears came to his eyes and he requested that the interview be ended because he felt too emotional to continue. As the session closed, Rogers leaned toward the client and tenderly touched his knee in a gesture of support and care.

Then, immediately after this moving sequence of events, in his post-session comments (not in the client's presence), Rogers began his remarks by describing the client as an "armor-plated man." This metaphoric description is strangely and disturbingly at odds with the viewer's experience of the man who had been talking emotionally with Rogers during the hour. It was also an uncharacteristically harsh statement for Rogers to make about a client, and it seems contradictory to the caring attitude Rogers conveyed at the end of the session. This contrast supports other evidence that Rogers was not entirely himself in the session with this client.

Therapists often function in an imperfect manner with their clients, both in general, with respect to the ideal of their own theories, and more specifically for client-centered therapists, with respect to Rogers' conception of the necessary and sufficient conditions for therapeutic change. Nevertheless, clients feel and report progress and can be objectively assessed to show progress. Rogers' (1957) statement of his therapeutic theory makes it very clear that a therapist need not function with absolute consistency nor always provide the highest levels of the therapeutic attitudes in order to foster therapeutic change. Even so, during my examination of many sessions conducted by Rogers (Brodley, 1994), I have found that he often achieved an absolute level of therapeutic presence, but not with the "Anger and Hurt" client.

NOTES

1. Also referred to as the person-centered framework or approach.

2. According to Raskin (1988), the "freely functioning client/person-centered therapist" is one "who not only responds empathically but who may also offer reactions, make suggestions, ask questions, try to help the client experience feelings, etc.—in a spontaneous and non-systematic way while maintaining a basic and continuing respect for the client as the architect of the process" (pp. 2–3).

3. Rogers (1986b) asserted that his empathic responses were not intended to reflect the client's feelings, but rather to check the accuracy of his own understandings.

REFERENCES

Baldwin, M. (1987). Interview with Carl Rogers on the use of the self in therapy. In M. Baldwin & V. Satir (Eds.), *The use of the self in therapy* (pp. 45–52). New York: Haworth Press.

Brodley, B. T. (1991). Some observations of Carl Rogers' behavior in therapy interviews. *Person-Centered Journal, 1*(2), 37–48.

Brodley, B. T., & Brody, A. F. (1990, August). *Understanding client-centered therapy through the study of ten interviews conducted by Carl Rogers.* Paper presented at the Annual Conference of the American Psychological Association, Boston, MA.

Brody, A. F. (1991). *Understanding client-centered therapy through interviews conducted by Carl Rogers.* Clinical Research Paper submitted in partial fulfillment of requirements for Doctor of Psychology in Clinical Psychology, Illinois School of Professional Psychology.

Raskin, N. J. (1947). *The non-directive attitude.* Unpublished manuscript.

Raskin, N. J. (1988). Responses to person-centered vs. client-centered? *Renaissance, 5*(3 & 4), 2–3.

Rogers, C. R. (1957). The necessary and sufficient conditions of therapeutic personality change. *Journal of Consulting Psychology, 21*, 95–103.

Rogers, C. R. (1959). A theory of therapy, personality and interpersonal relationships, as developed in the client-centered framework. In S. Koch (Ed.),

Psychology: A study of a science: Vol. III. Formulations of the person and the social context (pp. 184–256). New York: McGraw-Hill.

Rogers, C. R. (1986a). Client-centered therapy. In I. L. Kutash & A. Wolf (Eds.), *Psychotherapist's casebook* (pp. 197–208). San Francisco: Jossey-Bass.

Rogers, C. R. (1986b). Reflection of feelings. *Person-Centered Review, 1*(4), 357–377.

Whitely, J. M. (Producer). (1977a). *The right to be desperate* [Film]. American Personnel and Guidance Association.

Whitely, J. M. (Producer). (1977b). *Carl Rogers counsels an individual on anger and hurt* [Film]. American Personnel and Guidance Association.

THE CASE OF "ANGER AND HURT"

Rogers and the Development of a Spiritual Psychotherapy

Samuel E. Menahem

Carl Rogers was perhaps the foremost figure in the development of humanistic, or third-force, psychology. His contributions, which have been extensively documented elsewhere, guarantee him an esteemed place in the development of the field of psychotherapy. The point of view in this chapter is that at least one of Rogers' accomplishments has been largely unrecognized: his contributions to the emerging development of "fourth-force," or transpersonal, psychology.

Unlike those who have viewed Rogers' work from within, I am not primarily concerned with how well Rogers followed his own theory or technique in the case of "Anger and Hurt." Instead, I will be using the case as a means to examine Rogers' role in the development of both third- and fourth-force psychology. The basis of both approaches to psychology is Rogers' contention that "goodness" and self-actualization are likely outcomes when individuals are provided the necessary and sufficient therapeutic conditions of unconditional positive regard, empathy, and, especially, genuineness and emotional congruence.

THE CASE OF "ANGER AND HURT"

The actual title of the filmed interview, "Carl Rogers Counsels an Individual on Anger and Hurt," suggests that Rogers thought that dealing with these emotions is necessary for people to grow and to become connected with their underlying goodness. Throughout the interview we can see that Rogers is urging the client to feel and express his anger and hurt, so that the client can return to the more positive emotions that lie beneath the hurt.

The session begins with the client telling Rogers how much mental pain he is in. The client knows he is angry but fears expressing and experiencing the anger. He fears anger so much that he would like to "skip over" it. Here is a man who has been diagnosed with leukemia, yet he feels that the emotional pain is worse than the physical pain of his cancer. In fact, he states that his mind is as deteriorated as his body. He feels that anger is not *in his nature*, yet his experiences have led him to be very angry. The problem is that he has been taught that anger is an emotion that should be controlled and not expressed. The pain of this wellspring of unexpressed anger is so great that the client fears it more than the possibility of a premature death.

This part of the session is directly in line with Rogers' feeling that immediacy of *experience* is most important. The client feels trapped between his current desire to express anger at a racist, hypocritical society and his parents' message that he should deny his perceptions, pretend that everything is all right, and not express the anger. This is the situation in many dysfunctional families and has been well documented by the Swiss psychologist Alice Miller (1981, 1990), among others.

Rogers' behavior and reactions—his consistent encouragement of the client to fully express his pain and anger—imply that he is quite concerned with this highly toxic situation. To the extent that Rogers was in touch with a spiritual or transpersonal dimension of existence, we might speculate that he considered the client's cancer to have been caused (or at least exacerbated) by his great emotional pain. Regardless, Rogers' intuitive responses to the client were more directive than usual for him. He stated explicitly that it is all right to be angry in the session. This statement, which seems genuine and empathic, takes the client by surprise and provokes what (Milton) Ericksonian therapists call an "unconscious search." After three pauses, the client achieves his first major insight—the anger is really hurt.

My view of this uncharacteristically directive intervention is that it came out of Rogers' genuine caring and concern for this man. Perhaps he knew he did not have much time with the client due to the situation or the illness. At any rate, Rogers trusted his intuitive response, and the result was rapid insight on his client's part.

The next stage of the interview is an exploration of the hurt. It seems that experiencing the hurt is more painful than the anger. It also leads to the client's realizing that he *fears* showing anyone that he is hurt because it would make him appear weak, dependent, or vulnerable. He does not trust that being open to others will lead to a loving response. Here he alludes to his marriage, where he did his best, felt that he loved his wife, and still ended up getting hurt. He views the failed marriage as someone "getting the best" of him.

To summarize the interview so far, we have the following situation: One perceptive remark by Rogers leads the client to an insight (that anger is actually hurt) consistent with Rogers' theory, part of which is that beneath angry–hurt feelings, people are basically good. Thus, the client is seen as a good person who was hurt. The hurt is made doubly painful by the client's shame that he foolishly trusted his wife and expressed love. This has made him vulnerable to the hurt of feeling not "good enough." His view is that his ex-wife got the best of him because he was vulnerable, and showed her his vulnerability. His solution is to suppress the anger, hurt, and shame, and try to appear invulnerable so nobody can "get the best of him" again. This suppression of powerful emotions leads to psychic, and perhaps even physical, suffering. The client really feels like a victim and is very much afraid of *experiencing* his feelings completely. Experiencing and expressing vulnerability is too much at odds with his ideas of how a man should behave in a relationship. Thus, he jokingly asks Rogers to exorcise his painful feelings.

After a number of empathic statements by Rogers, the client reaches a point at which he says he would like to be able to cry but feels it would not be "productive." Rogers challenges this reasoning, suggesting that the client is afraid to cry. Again, this is unusually directive for Rogers. As the client explains that he avoids crying, Rogers again directs him by asking a leading question: "If you did cry, what would some of the themes of that crying be?" Although this is rare for a client-centered therapist, again, it quickly leads to a fertile area. The client wishes that he could cry for the loss of his father-in-law, who really loved him. He wishes that he had told his father-in-law that he loved him before he died. Rogers reiterates the importance of expressing this love and even adds the possibility of a spiritual dimension (an unseen spiritual realm) by stating, "So you're telling me in place of telling him and maybe even speak to him, I don't know." These unusual responses (direct questions, positing an unseen world), along with his more usual genuine empathic responses, seem to indicate the deep trust Rogers had in his intuitive responses at this point in his career. It does appear that he strongly encourages the client to feel and express his feelings. On the surface, this is contrary to the Rogerian spirit of allowing clients to come to their own conclusions at their own pace. Yet each time Rogers makes one of these uncharacteristic responses, the client goes deeper into his own experience, his own emotional reality.

It appears that, in his heart, the client wants to be able to love and be loved. Yet his experience tells him that he would not be loved or understood but rather hurt and abandoned. First, his wife failed to understand how hurt he was until months after they had parted. Then, his father-in-law died suddenly and left him. Then, his ex-wife's family treated him like a nonperson by hypocritically asking how he was in a way that showed they did not care about his feelings. He concludes, from this, "I have been hurt, and I really don't want to get involved anymore in terms of with people that can't return love and can't accept people. . . . I'm sick and tired, sick of it."

At this point, the client goes so far as to blame his cancer on stress caused by racism and all the blockages of love just described. Rogers accepts this statement and encourages yelling and profanity, to no avail. Apparently, the client is not going to go all the way into his feelings in this interview. In fact, he slips two times and states that he cannot express feelings or his cancer might recur. When Rogers repeats the client's statement, the client laughs and says he knows that he has it backwards. It would seem that the client's body is very reactive to emotion. His body reacted to the profanity expressed by Rogers by getting warm, but as usual, he controlled the sensation. It was threatening for him to get in touch with and express his anger and hurt. He feels he must control his powerful emotions.

Later in the interview, the client uses two evocative metaphors, "vomiting up green slime" and "somebody took a big goddamned tree and just rammed it u—." It seems from this that he does connect with his feelings, at least in part. Importantly, he expresses compassion for anyone who is feeling as overwhelmed by life as he is. He notes that even winos have reasons for the painful, humiliating kind of life they lead. He remarks that he wants to "give . . . help . . . and talk to people." Such statements suggest greater comfort with his own feelings and, perhaps, too, an awakening of spirituality. Yet there is also restraint, a limit to these feelings. As the client states, "the overriding thing is that I want to keep at least the control." Similarly, he notes that when he starts feeling hurt he has to "put it all out" of his mind, "bring it down to a different level."

In response to this last statement, Rogers essentially accepts the client's decision to stop "close to the pit." Therefore, despite the fact that the client did not go as deeply into his pain as Rogers appears to have wanted, he felt the client gained something from the experience. The client was not ready to feel the depth of his pain, but he was ready to see that his anger was really hurt. He also admitted that the hurt had led him to mistrust people and made him reluctant to show his vulnerability. He had not quite yet realized that happiness requires the vulnerability of giving and receiving love. The client's reluctance to work through the hurt so he could again have a chance at love was his stuck point. He felt defeated and beaten. He felt damned if he did and damned if he did not (express love). Thus, the interview ends with the client's need to stop being respected and the hope that, at some future point, he could connect more closely with the feelings and once again take the risk of loving.

ROGERS AND THE FOUR
FORCES OF PSYCHOLOGY

The field of psychology has undergone rapid development in the past 100 years. There is some disagreement as to whether behaviorism or psycho-analysis is the "first force" of psychology. Kreutzer (1984) calls behaviorism the first force, whereas Lueger and Sheikh (1989) consider psychoanalysis the first force. Behaviorism appeared first and established the scientific validity of psychology by measuring observable human behavior. Never-theless, psychoanalysis probed deeper into human behavior by stressing the importance of unconscious phenomena and motivation. These two forces dominated psychology until Rogers' influence began to be felt in the 1940s.

Beginning with observations of his therapy "clients," Rogers devel-oped his then-unique theory that people are basically good and are able to heal themselves when given the proper therapeutic conditions. In effect, he took the best of behaviorism (scientific rigor, measurable observations) and psychoanalysis (healing through a therapeutic relationship) to form a new humanistic psychology. Moreover, he set out to examine just how effective he and his colleagues were. He was a pioneer in psychotherapy research, one of the first to engage in controlled studies of psychotherapy using audiotape.

Humanistic psychology, the third force, did not deny the unconscious as radical behaviorism did, but it also did not elevate it to central impor-tance as psychoanalysis did. Rather, this new movement was designed to liberate human potential by providing in adulthood the warmth, integrity, genuineness, and unconditional positive regard that may well have been lacking in individuals' previous relationships. In Rogers' style of humanistic psychotherapy, people's reports of experiences are considered existentially real. Unconscious motivation is less important than immediate experience. The primary emphasis of the treatment is on helping people explore themselves and open up to their experience. The ultimate goals of treat-ment go beyond reconditioning or removal of pathology. Rather, the emphasis is on self-actualization, and the promotion of health, creativity, self-regard, and openness to experience.

Rogers (1977) pointed out that one of the by-products of third-force psychology had been that it reduced the therapist's power a great deal.

Instead of being the expert who knows how to heal, the therapist becomes a catalyst for and facilitator of the growth potential within each person. One might expect that this "reduction" of the therapist's role would have led to much resistance on the part of the establishment, and it did. Yet, with the publication of *On Becoming a Person* in 1961, Rogers, his theory, and his "technique" became the vanguard of the 1960s "human potential movement."

ROGERS AND FOURTH-FORCE PSYCHOLOGY

Nobody would deny the importance of Rogers in the development of third-force psychology. However, there is a good deal of debate about his interest in and influence upon the fourth force, transpersonal psychology. The remainder of this chapter will examine the place of transpersonal psychology in Rogers' life and work, and its manifestations in this particular case.

There are as many as 40 definitions of transpersonal psychology (Lajoie & Shapiro, 1992). Illustrative of these ideas is Grof's (1985) notion that transpersonal psychology is "a model of the human psyche that recognizes the importance of the spiritual or cosmic dimensions and the potential for consciousness evolution" (p. 97). Similarly, Hutchins (1987) states that "the simplest definition of transpersonal psychology is spiritual psychology. . . . It recognizes that humanity has both drives toward sex and aggression *and* drives toward wholeness, toward connecting with and experiencing the divine" (pp. 9, 12). Finally, Hoffmann (1988) contends that transpersonal psychology is "an approach founded and introduced within *humanistic* psychology by Abraham Maslow in the 1960s, which seeks to incorporate human spirituality into a comprehensive model of human nature and its potential" (p. 342).

We can see from the above definitions that there is extensive overlap between humanistic and transpersonal psychology. The most important difference, however, is the humanistic emphasis on the person and the transpersonal emphasis on the spirit. As is discussed below, Rogers had a lifelong interest in spiritual matters; he studied for the ministry before obtaining his doctorate in psychology. Although he dabbled in arcane spirituality toward the end of his life (once attending a seance to contact his deceased wife), his spiritual development was more in the direction of one human spirit touching another, leading to transformation and transcendence.

It is my view that Rogers saw the human being as the meeting point for psyche and spirit. At a 1986 workshop with his daughter and granddaughter (both therapists), Rogers (Rogers, Rogers, & Fuchs, 1986) spoke to this point. He said that the universe is run by certain fundamental principles. When people align themselves with these principles, "transcendental feelings" sometimes result. He was unsure if these feelings were "spiritual," but they were beyond his ordinary experience, and he was open to the possibility that they were connected to spirituality.

His difficulty in being definite in this area may have been related to his early religious training. He spent 2 years in a seminary, where spirituality implied a God separate from human beings. Later, he developed a humanistic philosophy that never ruled out divinity but was unclear as to its role in human life. Spirituality, especially its transcendent aspects, seemed to become more salient to Rogers in his later years. Indeed, in his essay on growing older (Rogers, 1980), he wrote that he was "impressed by some of the reports of reincarnation," "interested in the work of Elisabeth Kubler-Ross," and he found "definitely appealing the views of Arthur Koestler that individual consciousness is but a fragment of a cosmic consciousness" (p. 88). And, in this same essay, he speculated about the nature of death: "So I consider death with an openness to the experience. It will be what it will be, and I trust that I can accept it as either an end to, or a continuation of life" (p. 88). Moreover, he noted that there were a series of experiences, including meetings with an "honest medium" and events surrounding his wife's death (e.g., her visions and dreams of family members), that changed his "thoughts and feelings about dying and the continuation of the human spirit" (p. 90). "I now consider it possible," wrote Rogers, "that each of us is a continuing spiritual essence lasting over time, and occasionally incarnated in a human body" (p. 92). The development and convergence of psychotherapy and spirituality in Rogers' life will now be examined.

ROGERS AND SPIRITUALITY

It is important at this point to look at Rogers' family background. Even a casual inspection suggests that he would be a good candidate for interest in spirituality. He was raised in an "almost fundamentalist" (Thorne, 1992) Christian family, with a traditional theology. God was seen as external and superior to humankind. The Church was the intermediary between humankind and God, and standards of behavior were high. Rogers' parents were highly educated for that era. His father was a college graduate who became an engineer and later a farmer because he wanted to protect his children from the temptations of city life. His mother had 2 years of college. The family had the attitude that they were the "elect" and were therefore required to live by higher standards than the outside world. The emotional atmosphere in the household was attentive but strict. For example, simple amusements like theater or cards were forbidden. The family of eight was close knit with a strong emphasis on hard work and fundamentalist theology.

During his adolescence, Rogers attended a 6-month Christian student conference in China during which he radically changed his theological views. He came to feel a personal, intimate relationship with Christ. This experience could be seen as a forerunner to the later development of a psychology stressing intimacy and personal relationships. Upon his return to the United States, he pursued his bachelor's degree, with a major in history, and decided to become a minister. He spent 2 years at the liberal Union Theological Seminary. Here, he discovered that he could not devote himself to any set of dogmas, even liberal ones. He became more and more interested in psychology and eventually entered Teachers College, Columbia University, to study psychology. Teachers College at that time was dominated by behaviorists. Rogers even set out to raise his first son by Watsonian methods (though his wife soon talked him out of it). After his graduation and training from a "first-force" university, he received training in "second-force" psychoanalysis from the Institute of Child Guidance in Rochester, New York. He was then ready for the career that led to the development of third- and fourth-force psychology.

Rogers' consuming interest throughout most of his life was the development of an effective client-centered psychotherapy. His theological views, expressed later, seemed to emanate from his views of humankind. He noted early on that people who underwent successful psychotherapy often became more interested in spiritual matters than they had been before (Rogers, 1961). In this matter he followed Jung, who thought that all problems in the second half of life were essentially spiritual, and preceded Wilber (1986), who theorized a psychospiritual spectrum of development. In Wilber's theory, spiritual development proceeds in an orderly fashion out of earlier psychological development. This position parallels Rogers' observation of increased spiritual interest in those in the process of solving their psychological problems.

Rogers' emphasis on personal growth and interpersonal intimacy has traditionally been associated with a spiritual understanding of reality. According to Thorne (1992), the experience of participating in person-centered groups had the effect on some individuals of opening "a channel into spiritual terrain" that had "previously remained unexplored and whose very existence has been denied" (p. 105). Further, Thorne believed that "Rogers' earlier experiences, however perverse the theology underpinning them, ensured that his understanding of subjective phenomena and of interpersonal relationships could not in the end fail to embrace what, in his own words, he described as the transcendent, the indescribable, the spiritual" (p. 105). Thorne concludes with the conviction that, 50 years from now, it is likely that Rogers will be remembered primarily as a psychologist whose work made it possible for men and women to apprehend spiritual reality at a time when conventional religion had lost its power to capture the minds and imaginations of most people.

It is apparent, then, that Rogers can be viewed as an important influence in the development of transpersonal psychology. The valuing of spirit is the clear differentiation between third- and fourth-force psychologists. Thus, whereas Maslow might also be considered influential in the development of the fourth force, others such as Fritz Perls or Rollo May could not. In fact, May (1988), in a letter to the *APA Monitor,* argued that there is no room in the American Psychological Association for transpersonal psychology. He asserted that psychologists need to study individuals and not some mystical connection among all human beings.

Rogers, on the other hand, with his lifelong interest in theology, contributed to the spiritualizing of psychology. The theology that connects third- and fourth-force psychology would necessarily be pantheistic. Pantheism asserts that God is in all things, which are then necessarily good. Rogers, in perceiving the essential goodness and divinity in man, was not denying human pain or misdeeds. Rather, he was affirming the divine within each human being and in humanity as a whole. This pantheistic idea, though threatening to traditional theologians and mainstream psychologists, forms the foundation for a spiritual psychology.

According to Kreutzer (1984) distinctions between humanistic–existential (third force) and transpersonal (fourth force) therapy are subtle (p. 869). Rogers certainly did not set out to develop a spiritual psychology. However, his humanistic attitude, stressing the importance of love, unconditional positive regard, genuineness, and congruence often seemed to set the stage for spiritual longings and feelings to emerge (Rogers, 1961). Thus, although it cannot be said that his client-centered approach was a spiritual "technique," it was a humanistic technique that often opened the door to spiritual issues. In *On Becoming a Person,* Rogers noted that this could occur with or without specific mention of spiritual issues and conflicts.

Ajaya (1984) considers all psychotherapeutic approaches amenable to the ultimate goal of transpersonal psychotherapy, which is enlightenment. Wilber (1986) agrees and suggests that the type of psychotherapeutic intervention should be determined by the developmental level of the client and the nature of the issues being dealt with. Thus, Rogers' use of his third-force, client-centered technique is appropriate for psychological healing and possibly (though not necessarily) may lead to discussion of spiritual (enlightenment) issues. The view of transpersonal psychology is that the pursuit of enlightenment underlies psychotherapy, although this might not be apparent by people with other viewpoints. A person may heal psychologically via behaviorism or psychoanalysis but eventually he or she must face existential and transpersonal issues. In helping people deal with their existential issues in a humanistic way, Rogers' techniques allowed for the possibility that the goal of enlightenment might emerge. Rogers had no part in the development of specific transpersonal techniques, for example, Assagioli's psychosynthesis or Jung's active imagination. However, in developing his humanistic, client-centered psychology he led the way to a transpersonal "attitude." Rogers' work showed that the attitude and beliefs of the therapist were vital in the patient's healing. Both the humanistic and the transpersonal attitudes regard each patient as unique and worthy of live as a condition of existence. Transpersonalists posit spiritual reasons for this, such as that we are all part of a unity consciousness, while humanists prefer the idea that we are all part of the human community. The patient does not usually see such distinctions. However, he or she does know when the therapist is hopeful and when he or she is not. Rogers clearly inspired patients with his attitude, not just his technique. Though the borderline between humanistic and transpersonal technique is sometimes unclear, the underlying positive attitude, which is far more important, is the same. In aiding the development of the therapeutic attitude, Rogers was a precursor of transpersonal psychology.

A FINAL LOOK AT THE CASE OF "ANGER AND HURT"

In retrospect, we can look at the case of "anger and hurt" as a brief example of Rogers' psychology. The client was seen by Rogers as essentially good, despite his deep distrust of other people and his own emotions. Rogers trusted in the client's innate potential to heal himself under the right conditions and tried hard to provide these conditions.

Rogers also trusted in himself. He interrupted the client's painful and tentative explorations with several intuitive interventions that were counter to his own theory of nondirectiveness. Each time he did this there was some movement, though there was no real catharsis. Rogers accepted all this and trusted that even this "armor-plated man" would heal himself emotionally if the proper therapeutic conditions were provided.

The healing the client needed was emotional, cognitive, and ultimately spiritual. He needed to learn to trust his own feelings, accept himself, and ultimately accept others. Some of Rogers' other therapeutic experiences (see Rogers, 1961) suggest that such emotional healing might well lead to an overt spiritual search. Spirituality starts with emotional healing. As Rogers (1961) and Wilber (1986) have shown, emotional healing at each developmental level provides a different perspective on life, a perspective leading to increased feeling of love for oneself, others, and perhaps the deity or ground of being (which transpersonal psychology, at bottom a unitive philosophy, posits as the source of all life).

In this regard, this case can be seen as an example of the importance of love in psychology and spirituality. The client's allusion to compassion for winos intimates a spiritual kind of love, in the sense that there is a spiritual spark in each person, even a wino. Perhaps, it is this spiritual spark behind the psychically wounded wino that spurred the client's compassion. It is difficult to be sure, but continued sessions of this sort may well have led to further feelings of a spiritually based compassion for others. The transpersonal concept of spirituality varies from the humanistic in one important way: This individual, this wino, is not just an unlucky person. Rather, this wino is a part of myself, others, and, in actuality, the ground of being. For a fourth-force psychologist, God is not seen as separate from humankind. God is seen as the loving energy force pervading everyone and everything. This philosophy could explain the client's feeling of compassion for winos.

From a third-force perspective, the client would be healed if he could find a way to trust and be loved. The client clearly was emotionally blocked in his striving for human love. From a fourth-force perspective, the client could be healed by experiencing transcendental love upon the removal of emotional blockages. His comment about having compassion for winos hints that his pain might even have been leading him to spiritual love. The essence of spirituality, as expressed in both Eastern and Western religious traditions, is love. This is not referring to romantic love, but rather to a more mature conception of love characterized by caring as much for the other person as oneself. This higher, spiritual love of another human being can be a prelude to a more diffuse love for all humankind and a higher power. Third-force psychology emphasizes the role of love in self-actualization. The contribution of fourth-force psychology, as hinted at in Rogers' work, is that psychotherapy can remove the emotional blockages to loving another human being, humanity as a whole, and eventually *God* (in the transpersonal sense expressed above). Thus, it is the further goal of spiritual development that differentiates third- and fourth-force psychology. Once the emotional blockages to love are removed (though not "exorcised" as the client would like) the path to a more peaceful, harmonious, productive (third-force) and indeed spiritual (fourth-force) life is possible. In what appears to be his intuitive connection of the psychological and spiritual dimensions, Rogers, pioneer of third-force psychology, unknowingly became the progenitor of fourth-force psychology.

REFERENCES

Ajaya, S. (1984). *Psychotherapy East and West: A unifying paradigm.* Honesdale, PA: Himalayan Press.

Grof, S.(1985). *Beyond the brain: Birth, death and transcendence in psychotherapy.* Albany: State University of New York Press.

Hoffmann, E. (1988). *The right to be human: A biography of Abraham Maslow.* Los Angeles: J.P. Tarcher.

Hutchins, R. (1987, July). Ten simple ways to explain transpersonal psychology. *PDTP News,* pp. 9–12.

Kreutzer, C. (1984), Transpersonal psychotherapy: Reflections on the genre. *Professional Psychology: Research and Practice, 15,* 868–883.

Lajoie, D., & Shapiro, S. (1992). Definitions of transpersonal psychology: The first twenty-three years. *Journal of Transpersonal Psychology, 24,* 123–139.

Lueger, R., & Sheikh, A. (1989). The four forces of psychotherapy. In A. Sheikh & K. Sheikh (Eds.), *Eastern and western approaches to healing* (pp. 197–233). New York: Wiley.

May, R. (1988). *APA Monitor.*

Miller, A. (1981). *Thou shalt not be aware: Society's betrayal of the child.* New York: Meridian Press.

Miller, A. (1990). *Banished knowledge: Facing childhood injuries.* New York: Doubleday.

Rogers, C. R. (1961). *On becoming a person.* Boston: Houghton Mifflin.

Rogers, C. R. (1977). *Carl Rogers on personal power.* New York: Delacorte Press.

Rogers, C. R. (1980). Growing old—Or older and growing. In *A way of being* (pp. 70–95). Boston: Houghton Mifflin.

Rogers, C. R., Rogers, N., & Fuchs, F. (1986). *Challenging crisis creatively: A three-generation view* [Videotape]. (Available from the Person-Centered Expressive Therapy Institute, Santa Rosa, CA.)

Thorne, B. (1992). *Carl Rogers.* London: Sage.

Wilber, K. (1986). The spectrum of development. In K. Wilber, J. Engler, & D. Brown (Eds.), *Transformations of consciousness.* New York: Random House.

CHAPTER 10

THE CASE OF MARK (1982)

The Dilemmas of a South African White

TRANSCRIPT

On a trip to South Africa [in 1986] Carl Rogers spent one afternoon with a small group of psychotherapists and counselors—psychologists, psychiatrists, and social workers. At their request he agreed to conduct a demonstration therapy interview. The young man who volunteered was told: "You understand that you will bring to it a real concern or problem of yours that is alive for you right now. This is not a conversation or a discussion." He replied, quite simply, "Yes, I have a very real problem. It will be risky, but I'm willing to take the risk."

Carl Rogers (C.R.): Now if you can get your chair settled—this has come rather suddenly. I need to take a minute or two to kind of get with myself somehow, OK? *(Inaudible comment followed by audience laughter)* Then let's just be quiet for a minute or two. *(Pause)* Do you feel ready?

Mark: I'm ready.

C.R.: OK. I don't know what kind of issue or problem you might want to talk about. I'd be very glad to hear whatever you have to say.

Mark: My name is Mark. I'm 37. I am a clinical psychologist and I work in a government institution with other psychologists and social workers. I do evaluations and therapy with a wide variety of cases of people who just don't seem able to cope. So many of these people are just ordinary people who are suffering from reactive conditions—they don't seem to be able to adjust to the demands of society. Because I get my referrals from the district surgeon and often have to do court work, it troubles me that I represent what other people see as an evil system we're perpetuating. I consider myself a good guy, y'know. So I have a dilemma. Some people don't like me. I have a position in the civil service. A cog within the hierarchy. Sometimes in my position of authority I have to make decisions or make recommendations which are not pleasant, not acceptable to others; I'm not clear why.

C.R.: I think—if I'm getting it—you feel within yourself you're a nice guy. It's the attitudes that other people have toward you that disturb you. Is that right? (Mark: Uh-huh.) So that within yourself the nasty jobs you have to do are OK with you. It's simply that others see you as a representative of an evil system.

Mark: Um, yes. I work in an Afrikaans-speaking environment. Culturally I'm English-speaking and the position that I hold has alienated me from my liberal English-speaking friends in the universities. The religious denomination in which I belong also is alienated from my position. You see what I'm trying to say?

C.R.: Yes, I do.

Mark: The students of the University of the North would view me as the oppressor. I don't see myself as that. I have no intention of oppressing anyone. But still I am a civil servant of this system. I have got to remember who is paying my salary. Can you see what the dilemma is?

C.R.: Yes, I think I do. It seems to me that the way you continue to voice it is that it is quite all right with you, but that you feel a greater and greater gulf between yourself and your church, yourself and others, your liberal friends, and so on. But within you—

Mark: Within me? I don't know. I'd like to try and crystallize the whole thing and say, "Who am I? I feel that I'm a South African—I am a South African. I feel responsible for things that happen in the country. It hurts me." Say for example there's a suicide in a police cell. The man might be a political prisoner. He stands for something completely different to what I represent. The police are invariably blamed for not taking adequate precautions in the police cells. Is it really their fault? They are also just civil servants, just carrying out their jobs. I sometimes feel that I'm supporting something I'm not sure of. But I will find my feet somewhere.

C.R.: Two things you said that really hit me—several things. You are hurt by some of these attitudes toward you. You're also raising the question, "Who am *I* really, in this system?"

Mark: Who am *I* in this system.

C.R.: And then you feel that you have your very desperate problems too, and realize how easily you could be attacked and criticized, just as the police are attacked and criticized. But you feel mostly, "Who am I and what am I trying to accomplish?"

Mark: That's right. Who am I, and what I'm trying to accomplish. And I'm so aware that I have a limited amount of energy and that if I use this energy, I want to be effective, correct, appropriate, and so on. I don't want to find that I'm cheated at the end of the road. I don't want to find that I'm watching it from the bunker, that it's the last days of Hitler in his bunker. I thought of myself, "Gee, y'know, here I am involved with civil defense and reading disaster psychology, what happens in times of mass casualties and so on?" Now what would have happened if I woke up one day and I found that the Third Reich had fallen, and I was one of those guards? I wonder, did those troops in Hitler's Germany—what would they think, what would they feel, were their problems like mine? Am I part of a system that's inherently bad? Because I think these people are good. I believe what you believe. I'm client-centered. I believe in the goodness of man. But I see the evil around me, you see. So I can't resolve all these things, and that's why I'm sitting here now, in front of you.

C.R.: I appreciate that. And I also appreciate the fear as I hear it, that "Suppose someday I wake up and I'm on the defeated end of the scale—what am I going to feel? What's it like to be in a bunker in the last days? It would be a disaster. And what will I do, what will I feel? What will I feel about myself?"

Mark: If I believed in what I was doing, OK.

C.R.: Yeah.

Mark: But the point I mean is that, say it's all for nothing. You know, I don't know if you understand it, but a few days in, say, London—the newspapers and the press—we're really an evil country—we stink, you know, we really do. My overseas friend says "Why do you keep asking me, 'What do you think of us?' " I go overseas and I see totally negative responses and I come back feeling it's not that way. What is the right thing, what is the truth?

C.R.: So that outside you see that you belong to a rotten system. Inside it seems quite different to you.

Mark: Right.

C.R.: And which of those views are you going to hold, which are you going to stand by?

Mark: I've noticed the English church, the priests of the churches, they seem to have pulled back. They're not involved so much. I get the impression that, as an English-speaking person, I'm not in. I'm in a minority within a minority within a minority, you see?

C.R.: I do see. You've lost contact with your own subculture, and that makes you wonder again, "What's the right thing to do? What do I believe?" *(Long pause)* It is a real dilemma.

Mark: I want to be honest. And I want to be true to myself. But I have to be a facade, or role. And I've got to accept, I suppose, that not everyone will understand what goes on in me, but will see a facade. People will react to me as if I'm in uniform, people won't really see who I am, so I suppose that it ultimately boils down to what kind of a person I am, you know.

C.R.: There was almost a note of sadness when you said, "I've got to be a facade." (Mark: Um-hmm.) You know the person that lives inside that facade, but you don't know that anyone else will really appreciate that person perhaps.

Mark: Maybe not, no.

C.R.: And you feel you have to play a role.

Mark: Yeah, I have to play a role.

C.R.: That the role you play is something different from the person you are.

Mark: Yeah. *(Pause)* Well maybe I don't have to play a role, you know. Maybe I can play a role or I don't have to play a role. But then of course I might be the eccentric. People might disapprove of me. They might not like me, you see.

C.R.: If you were really yourself, who knows what would happen.

Mark: Who knows what would happen, yeah.

C.R.: People might think you're an oddball, or I don't know what.

Mark: Yeah, they might. But they might do that anyway. *(Audience laughter)* So maybe it's not really an issue at all. Maybe basically it's something I walk around with, but yet my friends have seen through me anyway, and maybe they say, "Oh well, you know, he's just odd. He's crazy," or something like that.

C.R.: So maybe your facade is more transparent.

Mark: Maybe. Maybe more than I realize. That's comforting.

C.R.: That's comforting because you feel, "Maybe I could be the real me, because my friends seem to see the real me anyway."

Mark: Maybe the whole crisis of getting into what's right and what's wrong on a national scale, you know, and the problem of the whites and the blacks, and this and that, that's not my world, you see. *(Long pause)* But maybe it is my world. I'm not sure.

C.R.: I wasn't quite sure whether you were saying, "So the national situation—the black/white situation—that's really not where I live." And then suddenly you raise the question, "Or maybe it is."

Mark: Maybe it is. *(Pause)* Because I would like to live my life in such a way as I wish for my clients to do. I would like them to be able to balance off the demands of the outside world with those of the inner world, the personal world. And it's a very delicate balance.

C.R.: You can see that in the lies of your clients: They have to decide how to be themselves, how to form the delicate relationship with the outside world.

Mark: There is a saying, you know, in Afrikaans, "Vasbyt." It is usually expressed as a word of encouragement or possibly consolation for people in a difficult predicament in which there is no apparent solution apart from passing forward, or rather holding on. Literally, it means "bite fast," like a bulldog, or "stick it out." I find myself saying that to myself. Like giving myself some Reality Therapy. Things won't change. Why should they? They're rough, the world is hard, it is cruel. And either you learn how to make an adjustment or else.

C.R.: So maybe you have to kind of grit your teeth and stick it out, even though it's a bad, rough world.

Mark: Well, I get up in the morning and I say, "Right, Mark. It's 1982. You just happen to be born in this stage of life. Life is rough. There's wars going on all over the place. There's a sort of Godless Marxism sweeping the world. It's a rough world. But I'm alive and I happen to be born in this century." And then I say, "Well we haven't reached the utopia or millennium, or something. This is where we are, and this is what's happening," you know. I'm telling myself we've all got to keep going. Does that sound so extreme?

C.R.: Well, I understand that. You're sounding as though for the moment you're accepting your lot: "Yeah, this is a rough, lousy world, but there I am in it. I didn't choose to be here at this time and place."

Mark: That's right. *(Pause)* I don't feel like being the bad guy, you see.

When the movie's finished I want to be the good guy, you know, the cowboy who does these fine deeds. I don't want to be the evil guy who's caused all the trouble and I don't want history to say, "Ah, but look what you've done." You know what I mean?

C.R.: In a sense you feel that history is looking over your shoulder, and you're going to be either the bad guy or the good guy.

Mark: That's—yeah. I think I know the answer to that. I think I should live up to my own—my own principles, just be true to my own small world.

C.R.: Maybe within the world of your own interpersonal relations—

Mark: Right.

C.R.: You can be the person you are.

Mark: Right. Maybe that's where the answer lies, is in that. Maybe it's no use for me to just look over my shoulder and see what bad things other people are doing, what injustices there are, and worrying so much about that, and then not looking sufficiently after the responsibilities that I have in my little world, you know.

C.R.: I understand that. Maybe what others think or the opinions even of history are less important than "What am I able to do, what kind of a person am I able to be within the circle that I really influence?"

Mark: Hmm. And maybe for me to accept that other people might not agree with me, they might hate me. I don't know if you know what the feeling is like. Here I stand, and it's a party—one of those rather superficial, calculatedly casual English university faculty parties—and some people say, "Where do you work?" And I say, "I work for the government." They say, "Isn't it terribly Afrikaans?" I admit that most of the people I work with are Afrikaans-speaking. And then they sort of float away.

C.R.: So you feel you're sort of a social leper.

Mark: Yeah, yeah. You know what I mean by social distance? (C.R.: Yeah, yeah.) It's not all glamour, you know, it's really tough. It's quite—

C.R.: It's quite something to have people just walk away from you as though they didn't even want to have anything to do with you.

Mark: So it's not so nice. Or the blacks, you know, it's even worse. Say there's a revolution. They're not going to ask me, "How nice are you?" They're enemy. Let's put it that way—they're enemy, who hate the white supremacists, see. They're not going to turn and say, "Hey Mark, you're a nice guy. You can go off, you know, we just want the baddies."

C.R.: So if worse comes to worst, you won't be rewarded for being a nice guy.

Mark: No, I won't. *(Pause)* I've been over to the university and everybody just talks about football scores and student civil rights and things which are all irrelevant, as far as I'm concerned. So I belong here and I'll stick it out. But it's like living out a role which sometimes splits me from what I really want to be, and—

C.R.: That message is really coming through—that you are living out a way of being that may be quite different from the way you usually—you really are inside.

Mark: But I wonder. I think a lot of my friends, or a lot of the people here, feel that way. And I think I'm sort of symptomatic of a large percentage of us here, white or black. I think a lot of us, either civil servants or just ordinary folk, you know, we're not politicians. We just live our lives. We have lived from it—we the "baddies," have lived off the abhorrent system that is suppressing people. You know that propaganda, and we want to say that "Look, we're OK, we're not bad people really." You know what I mean?

C.R.: I do. And it feels—after looking at the other side it makes it worse within yourself. You feel, "I'm not a bad person."

Mark: Hmm. Feelings *(Long pause)*, is our time up?

C.R.: Hmm?

Mark: I think our time is up. Is it the end?

C.R.: No! *(Audience laughter)* It can be up whenever you want it to be up.

Mark: Oh . . . yeah. *(Pause)* You know *(pause)*, you don't ask me any questions. *(Audience laughter)*

C.R.: I think you've partly answered this, but I'll ask it once more, because I'm trying to get a feeling for what it's like to know that you're living a role that is really not you. (Mark: Hmm.) Sounds as though it must be quite tough inside, as I've heard you mention.

Mark: Um *(pause)*, yeah. Do you get that feeling now, you really get into it?

C.R.: Yes, I can really—

Mark: You know that's your problem yourself, that people sort of feel you should be Carl Rogers, big deal, that kind of thing.

C.R.: No, I adopt a somewhat different solution from you, but my problem is different. I feel, to hell with those who want to say, "Ah well, here's Carl Rogers." I'm just Carl. (Mark: Hmm.) I would prefer to be me, to be the person I am.

Mark: Is that the solution?

C.R.: That's for me, in my situation.

Mark: And for me that's my solution too. Do you believe that? For me, so the solution is for me to be me. A lot of books you've written are just about that, just to be me.

C.R.: Yeah.

Mark: People like that. I'd like you to give me permission just to be me. Tell me, Carl—

C.R.: I hear you.

Mark: I'll say, "Carl Rogers said that you can be yourself," you know, you said we can do that. I'll tell them that you're very successful.

C.R.: And the problem which you seem to have raised in the interview: can you tell yourself to be you?

Mark: *(Pause)* Yeah, and maybe I do anyway. Maybe I've just been myself anyway. Because it's going to be harder the more people that don't like what I do and maybe that's how it really is, you know. Getting a bit mixed.

C.R.: Yeah, it mixes one up.

Mark: *(Long pause)* Are you going to summarize for me?

C.R.: *(Immediately)* No. *(Audience laughter)*

Mark: Why?

C.R.: Why? There are very definite reasons. Because the summary that might exist in me is not important in the least. The summary that exists in you is what's important. That doesn't mean that you have to give a summary. I just mean that what the experience means to you is the important thing, not some words that I could say about it.

Mark: When I speak of what I'm feeling now, and it hasn't gone away, it's gotten worse in fact, you know, I'm feeling worse now from having spoken to you than when I first came up here, because I was just relaxing a few minutes ago.

C.R.: In what way are you feeling worse? I'm not quite clear.

Mark: I'm feeling worse in that some of the things that maybe I'd rather not think about have come to the front. Is that OK? I mean, is that—?

C.R.: Things that you really have just put aside and not felt about have come pretty close to the surface *(long pause)*, and it doesn't feel good. *(long pause)*

Mark: No. So honesty would be like for myself, right?

C.R.: Um-hmm. *(long pause)* We probably should come to a stop, but I don't want to rush either of us.

Mark: Well, I'm OK. I'll summarize then: so I'm a guy who has to work out what the really important thing for me is—to be me—and that I must follow my own conscience, to live out the kind of life, make decisions, and to do the type of things I really want, I feel are right, and if I like being the good guy, that's OK. Other people also want to be the good guy, so I'll say, "You can also be good." *(Pause)* I think that the professional role I play within the system is like a challenge for me. It's a challenge, and I think I'm tough enough to handle it. In fact, when I take off my work suit and change into my old relaxing clothes, I really feel I am me. . . . Even before, when I was in private practice, I used to enjoy putting away the work as I put away the clothes.

C.R.: So maybe symbolically you're dropping your role and—

Mark: Yeah.

C.R.: Being you.

Mark: That type of thing. And I think that that's how we give the people permission to be themselves within a context. I think that that's one thing I've learned is to render unto Caesar what is Caesar's and unto God what is God's. And that I must develop what I believe in my life, and likewise my clients who are disturbed, uncertain about this world and psychosomatically ill because of their unhappiness with what they're doing, or even with what they are not doing—

Carl: That's clear to me.

Mark: I must encourage them to live out the purposes they have in themselves. Well, thank you. I appreciate your attention.

AFTER THE INTERVIEW: MARK'S CRITICISMS

C.R.: I really feel very appreciative of talking with you and having you talk with me. And what I would like to do now is for you to take a minute if you want and then tell the group what the experience has seemed like to you, and I'll say what it seemed like to me, and then we'll let them in on the . . . on the show too. OK?

Mark: Do you want me to start telling now what I feel about you?

C.R.: About what's gone on, about me, about anything you've experienced.

Mark: If I'd be really honest now, do you think you can handle it? *(Audience laughter)* You must promise to be honest with me. . . . I definitely feel that *(pause)* as much as I would love this to be a real sort of encounter, I'm trying to ignore, you know, the invisible faces. I still feel that feeling of sort of a structured—I feel I'm being used. I think you follow your rule book, you know, and I'm sure that if you really let go, you'd sort of look at the heart of these things, you'd open up a bit more *(audience laughter)* and wouldn't be so impassive. But if you could say how you really feel, that it's . . . "I know what you mean," "I think I know what you mean." *(Audience laughter)*

C.R.: You seem like a good counselor. *(Audience laughter)*

Mark: I believe you'd like to be, you know, I believe you'd like to be a really good therapist, and I think that everyone else thinks you're a good therapist, but I wonder what you seek for yourself, in yourself, you know, back home, when the show is over. And you must, at this age you must wonder what you've really achieved. I think if I were you, at this stage in my life I'd like to leave these people behind. And I'd like to sit down and just synthesize what my life means to me. And in my last breath that I have at the end of my life, I'd like just to be able to hold that golden thread. I'd let them renovate graduate courses and argue this and that and the other. It's all that "Vanity of vanities. All is vanity." It's all just the wheel of life just going on. I think that's how you'd feel. And I think that what you should do if you feel tired of all this, is that you should just cancel a few appointments, you know. *(Audience laughter)* That's what I would do. *(C.R. is laughing.)* Why do you laugh? And you may think I'm crazy of course.

C.R.: I think you're very eloquent. On a couple of points you're right, and in a number of them you're wrong. What's right is, this seemed to be quite a challenge to me, in that I have not faced the dilemma you're facing. I have had the feelings you have, but I certainly have not faced the dilemma you're facing. So I felt, too, there wasn't as much depth to my response as there would be to some other kinds of problems. And I really learned a great deal from it. I appreciate the fact that you were my client, for this brief period of time, and then also my lecturer for a while. *(Much audience laughter)*

I'm interested in your prescription for my old age. *(Audience laughter)* If what you said had been true, I would have said, "Oh, to hell with this trip to South Africa." I appreciate your advice, but I do keep learning, and when the last moment comes, I hope I die in my boots, not clinging to a golden thread. *(Audience laughter)*

The chapter in my last book that received the most comment is "Growing Old—Or Older and Growing?" and I think I would prefer to be . . . as I said in that chapter, I prefer to die young, or in other words that I do prefer to keep on meeting new experiences and assimilating them.

I appreciate the honesty of your remarks. We come from quite different worlds. We'd have to meet more than once to get really well acquainted. But I did come to appreciate the dilemma that you and, as you say, many others here are undoubtedly facing. I don't think we would agree on everything, but I think it would not be difficult to respect one another deeply.

I want to mention one more specific thing about the interview. One thing you said really moved me and made me feel a little sad. The fact that the interview had brought out things in you that you had sort of put aside, and that they were disturbing for you to think about, because of feelings they brought to the surface. That's the only thing that I don't like about holding an interview like this, because I would like to say to you, "Well, it's all right, never mind that those thoughts are disturbing to you; when we meet next time, we'll really talk out some of those things. I'd like to hear about them." And there's no opportunity for that, so that I feel bad.

C.R.'s REACTION[*]

At the conclusion of the interview and the exchange that followed it, I felt disappointed and baffled. I felt that I had not been so successfully empathic as with other clients. During the interview I thought this was because his position, his political views, his values were so discrepant from mine. When he began to comment after the interview, I recognized another reason. He had been only partially involved in the interview. Part of him was being a clinical observer and critic. As I have had occasion to listen to the tape and

---

[*]In the analysis of the interview material, I am deeply indebted to Dr. Debora Brink. Because of her early years in South Africa, and her continuing interest in that country, she was able to point out to me much of significance that I might have missed. She also initiated the thematic analysis that helped illuminate the dynamics of Mark's struggle.

study the recording, I realize how confused his feelings were, and for this reason too he was difficult to understand.

Mark is full of contradictions, and he was living one of these contradictions in our session. He was expressing some very real attitudes in the relationship and was in fact more revealing of the dilemma of the white South African than any other person we met. At the same time he was standing outside the relationship, looking at it with a critical eye. . . .

At the very point where Mark most clearly defines the dilemma of the white South African, I fail him. I fail to show a real understanding and acceptance, with the result that he wishes to end the interview. Then I compound my error by introducing a different topic, and he runs away from the issue entirely, analyzing and criticizing me.

Let me document these statements. At one point, Mark gives a clear picture of the dilemma of so many whites in his country. "We—the baddies— have lived off the abhorrent system that is suppressing people." He immediately backs off from that statement by saying, "You know that propaganda." He stresses that "we're not bad people really."

Instead of catching that most important feeling of guilt, quickly covered up, I give a weak response, and Mark wants to end the interview—"I think our time is up." He cannot bear to confront these very painful feelings.

Then he complains that I ask no questions, so I compound my error by saying that it must be tough to be "living a role that is really not you."

Mark now runs away completely from the issue by talking about my problem of being Carl Rogers.

Although the interview might have had a more positive ending if I had been quick enough to perceive the picture he was giving me of his inner world, the mistake illuminates the anguish of the honest South African white. Such persons know they are living off of an evil system. They see no clear or simple solution. They feel they are not personally evil. They live with the heavy condemnation of much of the world. They feel trapped in a dilemma too painful, too awful, to face.

The recording of the interview portrays a man who is deeply divided within himself—a man full of uncertainties, doubts, contradictory feelings, searching almost desperately for a resolution, a certainty, an answer to insoluble complexities. When he says after the interview that I should have said to him "I know what you mean," his inflection makes clear that this would be telling him "I understand you perfectly and you're all right!" It would give him the certainty he craves. In the interview when he draws me out, I say "That's the solution for me in my situation." He immediately grasps at it, like the proverbial drowning man and the straw: "And for me, that's my solution too."

Mark demonstrates vividly the nearly impossible situation of the thoughtful white South African. He is upholding a system in which he does not believe. He realizes that many others regard it as evil. He lives surrounded by negative feelings—ranging from disapproval to hatred. He partially recognized that he is guilty of living off of an abhorrent, oppressive system. He is afraid that history will judge him harshly. He sees no clear solution. He knows that he is seen as the bad guy, yet within the small world of family and friends, he experiences himself as an essentially good person. He craves approval, but he cannot fully approve of himself. He knows that the future may end in total disaster, and sees no clear way of avoiding it.

It is not surprising that in the accepting climate of the interview he finds himself feeling worse and worse. He is slowly coming face to face with the pain of his dreadful situation—the pain of realizing the awful things that are happening to people in his country. This may explain why he does not permit himself to become fully involved in the relationship with me. It would mean the experiencing of feelings of pain, guilt, bafflement, which would be unbearable.

When Mark tells me how I should spend my later years, he is undoubtedly speaking for himself. He prefaces his statement with "If I were you," and he seems to be picturing the way he would like his final years to be. But the contradictions still exist. He would like to find the golden thread of meaning in his life, the synthesis that would make sense out of it. Yet perhaps it has no meaning, and is just part of the ceaseless wheel of life, where "all is vanity." Even as he tries to picture an ideal personal future, he is still clearly divided within himself. The split still remains.

I am grateful to Mark for letting us enter, to some small degree, the terrible world in which he lives. It seems, to use the vernacular, a "crazy-making" world.

SIXTEEN MONTHS LATER

Sixteen months after our 30-minute interaction, I wrote to Mark, asking about his recollections of the interview, and whether it had had any lasting impact. Weeks went by, and I began to think I would never know his reactions.

Finally, however, I did receive a lengthy reply giving clear evidence that our brief contact had indeed evoked many deep responses.

After asking "forgiveness for the degree of aggressiveness and impertinence that I projected," he goes on to say, "Coming into personal contact with you brought to the fore deep and painful issues regarding the meaning of my life, which up to that point had only been experienced in a segmented sort of way."

For the first time, he voices the anger he experienced during and after the half-hour. "I also apologize to Ruth—who quickly detected my anger in the interview—in that I refused to speak to either of you after the interview, at the reception."

He also mourns the denigrating of "the Romantic me—which contained my originality and spontaneity—in which I have since lost confidence."

Several excerpts from his letter reveal a sincere, struggling individual:

> It is very difficult for me to write this letter as it always is, when one attempts to face up to realities about oneself which are not easy to digest. It is also not easy to lay oneself bare and to become as vulnerable as I feel now, yet it would serve no purpose to write to you at all if I were not ruthlessly honest with myself. . . .
>
> As I reflect back on my reactions immediately after the interview, I believe that the encounter evoked a number of strong feelings which left me confused and bewildered. Foremost were those angry/hurt feelings of something like "being cheated." You see, you represented in me the lost idealism of my student training and the Child Guidance Clinic where I worked (in a client-centered way). Here I was now, coming into contact with something I was then, with all its magic, mystery and idealism—something so vital to me that it sustained me as does my own breath. I believe I can say this to you Carl, because if anyone knows what this mystery is, it is you. I have experienced it in the therapeutic encounter with my patients as joining forces with that very process of life itself which heals and sustains. Do you see how great was my shock when I came into contact with something I have lost? . . .
>
> I cannot account for why I ever lost that "magic" or idealism. Maybe Romanticism cannot be sustained for any length of time. Maybe I am just a statistic in an inevitable social process. Whatever it was, it was not a specific experience but rather a gradual erosion—and conversely a gradual incursion of something "other" to take its place. Maybe I let it slip out of my hands because I lacked support. At any rate, I began to realize that I had allowed the world around me to swallow me up.

He then tells of several professional experiences that brought him into contact with disasters resulting in great loss of life. His letter continues.

> Going back to your question about my reactions immediately after the interview, I believe I was shocked to discover that I was emotionally wounded, that I, as well as my patients, was contaminated by the fear of death and separation. My emotional description of the Armageddon-like "Bunker" film that I had seen that week on TV, and my desperate search for reassurances (possibly from you) that I was not condemned, has taken on meaningful significance over the past months and has enabled me to work toward some constructive resolution. (Two of his resolutions follow.)
>
> I have recognised my dilemma about the world about me and my

circumstances, as a projection of my inner turmoil. Consequently, because it is "my own" I am not helpless in the face of it, but can work through it.

I have realised that as painful as they may be for me, my experiences have a professional significance and that I must tackle the task of writing as an utmost priority.

Carl, thank you for the opportunity you have given me to both speak with you and write to you. I know you will be glad to hear that it has been of great benefit to me.

I accept Mark's thanks, but I also wish to express my gratitude to him for sharing so profoundly the dilemmas of his life, the dilemmas of the South African white. In the interview these dilemmas were seen as primarily external—the system, the condemnation by others, and the like. Now he has come to accept the fact that the fundamental conflict and confusion lies within himself—the "magic" of his idealism, for example, on the one hand, and permitting others to control him, to swallow him up, on the other. This internal conflict is something he is confident he can work through.

It seems certain that Mark is speaking for a great many white persons in South Africa. The realities of their outward and inner situations are so painful, they can scarcely bear to face them without support. In Mark's case it was a caring understanding that made possible the initiation of a struggling process of inner change in which he is endeavoring to recapture his idealism, his originality, his spontaneity, and his own true self. It is my belief that many of his white countrymen and women are silently calling out for the same sort of caring empathy so that they can make their painful way toward personal, and thus social, transformation.

THREE YEARS LATER

Correspondence continued between Mark and me, and as I was about to submit this manuscript for publication (with Mark's permission), I wrote, asking if he would be willing to indicate the significance, if any, that our interview has for him at the present time. Here is his reply, written three years following our interaction.

Dear Carl,

In bridging the time between the interview and now, there are some reflections that I would like to share with you:

That encounter I had with you had a profound effect on me. It was an extremely painful experience. To the extent that I risked myself in exposure, through verbalizing the dualities, dilemmas, conflicts and confusions of my life, to the extent that I allowed my heart to bleed with emotion as one would let one's tears flow, I began to move into a position of vulnerability and great tenderness.

With the vulnerability and tenderness came a feeling of aliveness. Although words are hard to describe this, at best I can say it is a feeling of remembering who I really am. It is like moving from strange unfamiliar terrain into the well loved precincts of home.

What I am describing is a process that has been taking place with time. It continues today.

It is with deep respect and gratitude to you, Carl, that you did not, as I knew you would not, focus on problem-solving strategies, because I know from the depths of my being that the problems I presented at the level of duality from which they were presented, defy resolution.

> With deep regard, yours,
> Mark

CONCLUDING COMMENT BY CARL

It is nothing short of amazing that the process is still continuing in Mark, three years after our interview. It is even more remarkable in that at the time I found the interview baffling and disappointing. I stand humbled by this additional evidence that it is the *client*, not the therapist, who is the best judge of the significance of an interview, or of a relationship.

ROGERS AND MARK

The Power of the Brief Encounter

Julius Seeman

The client in this interview was a 37-year-old white South African man, a clinical psychologist working for the South African government, who was given the pseudonym "Mark." He volunteered for the interview as part of a workshop offered by Rogers to a group of mental health workers. When the group was told in advance that Rogers wished to interview someone with "a real concern or problem," Mark responded, "Yes, I have a very real problem. It will be risky, but I'm willing to take the risk." In the original preface to this published transcript, Rogers noted that this interview "illuminates the almost unbearable internal conflict of the sensitive white South African. It also indicates the powerful impact that can come from a brief, but intense, half-hour relationship" (Rogers, 1986, p. 15).

Rogers' work with Mark represents what is most characteristic in his approach to psychotherapy. That is, he typically utilized his own total awareness to enter into the client's world in a phenomenological mode—to enter into the client's experiencing process *as lived by the client*. This "living within" is seen to enhance the client's awareness of self and, importantly, to foster enhanced internal communication with self.

Rogers' approach engendered rapid exploration on Mark's part. When we examine the interview we see the rapid emergence of two closely related themes, one having to do with Mark's struggle to define his relationship with other people and with the political system of which he is a part, and the other theme related to Mark's struggle to define himself within this system.

The rapidity with which these themes emerge suggests how close to Mark's central awareness these issues are. Thus, in his very first statements he brings up the troubling facts that whereas he sees himself as a "good guy," he is seen by others as a representative of an evil system, and that he thereby feels alienated from his English-speaking friends. Almost immediately, however, he begins to speak about a troubled feeling having to do with being a white South African ("I feel responsible for things that happen in the country. . . . I sometimes feel that I'm supporting something I'm not sure of").

Once Mark sets out on this path, he continues to explore his inward doubts, doubts that go to the center of his personal system of values. His analogy to Nazi Germany ("what would have happened if I woke up one day and I found that the Third Reich had fallen, and I was one of those guards? I wonder, did those troops in Hitler's Germany—what would they think, what would they feel, were their problems like mine? Am I part of a system that's inherently bad?") symbolizes with special force his fear that he may be part of an evil system. It would be difficult to choose a more powerful metaphor than this to express his inner doubts about his participation in a system that is both evil and doomed.

Throughout the remainder of the interview Mark explores this related pair of themes: "How am I perceived by others? How do I see myself?" And in this exploration there is perceptible movement from the preoccupation with self as outwardly perceived to self as inwardly lived. Thus, in early statements, Mark says, "People won't really see who I am," "People might disapprove of me." As the interview progresses, the self-questioning comes closer to his inward doubts and the possibility of owning his real self. Thus, Mark says, "I think I should live up to my own—my own principles, just be true to my own small world." Later he says, "It's like living out a role which sometimes splits me from what I really want to be."

By the end of the interview Mark has opened up but has not resolved his basic fear of alienation from others and, more pointedly, his fear of alienation from self. He makes his discomfort clear in the final moments, "I'm feeling worse now from having spoken to you than when I first came up here."

It is of interest to note that Rogers, too, feels discomfort and disappointment with himself in the interview. He attributes his feelings to two phenomena: his value differences from Mark and his perception that Mark was only partly involved in the relationship. It is evident, however, that another element of Rogers' dissatisfaction was the very unsettled termination of the interview, a termination in which Mark declared himself more troubled at the end than at the beginning. Such a view might well leave an ethical therapist unsettled. Indeed, Rogers makes it clear that he was saddened by the fact that he had to leave without being able to work further with Mark's unresolved feelings.

THE INTERVIEW SETTING AND ITS EFFECTS

Rogers made frequent use of demonstration interviews as a way of illustrating his clinical style for audiences. In most of these demonstrations there was little visible effect of an audience presence. However, in the interview with Mark there appear to be some significant effects attributable to the interview setting. These effects are worth exploring both as a way of deepening our understanding of this interview and as a way of enhancing sensitivity to an audience's potential impact on a therapy experience.

In the interview with Mark, the mixture of a therapy orientation and an audience-induced social orientation had the effect of blunting Rogers' way of responding to Mark at several crucial points. Mark's own mixture of a therapy-oriented and a socially oriented stance contributed further to the dilution of the therapeutic effect. Finally, the audience itself had a direct role in complicating the therapeutic process.

With respect to the direct audience effects, there was a significant moment when Mark was expressing the thought that he experienced the interview as being stylized ("You follow your rule book"). Along with this view there was a veiled resentment that Rogers did not come through and help Mark when he felt so isolated ("But if you could say how you really feel"). Mark also expressed the view that he was on display ("I feel I'm being used"). It is ironic and unfortunate that precisely at the moment when Mark voiced the view that he was being exploited and wanted a closer relationship the audience laughed. The effect was to veil and deflect Mark's poignant plea for more support from Rogers and his disappointment at feeling left isolated. At this point, Rogers, too, participated in the social climate with the jocular comment to Mark, "You seem like a good counselor," just when Mark was trying to give Rogers some significant information about his distressed feelings.

A FEW METHODOLOGICAL BYWAYS

The dialogue just quoted took place after the end of the formal therapy demonstration, during the postinterview wrap-up, and so it is altogether comprehensible that the psychological climate would shift. Thus, an additional issue here turns on the question of when a therapeutic attitude gives way to a more social–conversational framework. I believe that the episode here with Mark can sensitize us to the value and necessity of maintaining a therapy-oriented listening attitude during a group feedback period, because significant, previously unarticulated feelings can be revealed, as they were here.

That attitude is defined by the concept of *empathy*. What is so special about this concept with respect to client-centered therapy is that empathic listening is the very core of that therapy. The quality of empathy is not owned exclusively by client-centered therapy, and any competent therapist is familiar with the need for empathic understanding of what the client is saying and feeling. But other therapies require the therapist to focus attention and energy on other conceptual structures as well as on empathic listening. For example, psychoanalytic therapy requires that the therapist pay attention to such matters as transference, the potential presence of regressive and narcissistic responses, and so forth; that is, the very structure of the therapy requires that the therapist formulate theoretical constructions as well as empathic responses. Client—centered therapy, on the other hand, focuses precisely on the experiential life of the client as lived by the client at that instant in time.

There is a collateral issue here that surfaces in the session with Mark, an issue that is still the subject of debate among client-centered therapists. It has to do with the depth of empathic listening and the corresponding depth of the therapist's response. There is a point at which intrusion may begin, and therapists differ systematically and importantly as to what that point is.

My own view on this can be illustrated by referring again to the post-interview dialogue that took place between Rogers and Mark. Beneath Mark's manifest demeanor, a stance that had a touch of flippancy, Mark was struggling to voice some deeply felt attitudes. Clients approach serious issues in a variety of ways and may infuse discussion of such issues with sarcasm, flippancy, and humor. At such moments, I feel that it is my responsibility as a therapist to hear the full message, both the manifest embarrassment and the deeper cry. I decline to stop at the level of the client's embarrassment, and instead go on to hear and respond to the deeper message that the client is struggling to voice. It is here that the greatest depth of empathy is most required. Rogers made a different choice with Mark, one that led him in the direction of self-disclosure. That choice was a judgment call, one that was in accordance with the "necessary and sufficient conditions" of therapy as formulated by Rogers. Yet in making that choice Rogers did not deal with Mark's deeper message. We have here an example of a choice therapists are characteristically confronted with. This particular choice of Rogers' is probably best understood in the context of the demonstration interview with all its complexities and dynamics.

THE LONGER-TERM EFFECTS
OF THE BRIEF ENCOUNTER

It would be useful now to take a look at the longer-term effects of the brief encounter between Rogers and Mark, and to speculate more generally about the long-term effects of brief or even one-session therapies.

Mark has given us information that helps in the task set forth here. We note from Mark's comments that there were both strong feelings within the interview and significant developmental processes over a period of 3 years. As to the immediate experience, we note the shock of Mark's coming face to face with a lost aspect of self. He was confronted with his lost idealism, that "sustained me as does my own breath."

The profound recognition and experiencing of this loss created a shock that dislodged the structure of self that had come to immunize him partly from the destructive implications of his life and work. The shock set in motion a fundamental reorganization that in the longer run helped him to reintegrate the most precious aspects of himself. As Mark said in his letter written 3 years after the session, "With the vulnerability and tenderness came a feeling of aliveness, . . . a feeling of remembering who I really am." Integrative experiences of this kind often have a very special kind of effect, paving the way for enduring personal growth.

Yet there is an apparent paradox here. As indicated earlier, the immediate therapy experience left both participants unsettled and dissatisfied. Nevertheless, it is equally evident that there were profound and positive longer-term effects as reported by Mark. How do we begin to account for this discrepancy?

In an effort to address this question, I turn to a qualitative analysis that I made of five brief therapeutic encounters, each of which appeared to be far more powerful in its enduring effects than one would expect from such brief experiences (Seeman, 1992). A distillation of the elements that contributed to the power and durability of these experiences suggests the primacy of several components (the quotations below are from feedback statements made by the clients involved in these brief encounters):

1. The therapist's total concentration on the immediate experience of the client ("Everything about his person seemed focused completely on and available to me to reflect me clearly back to myself").
2. The therapist's unconditional affirmation of the client's perceptions, qua perceptions ("Somehow I felt affirmed by his relationship to me").
3. The client's perception of a distinct sense of crisis that engendered strong motivation ("I'm aware that I went into that relationship in crisis").

4. The client's deep sense of being heard and understood ("In the interview with Dr. X I felt deeply understood"; "The process seems so simple and basic, yet that . . . psychological mirror in front of me seemed entirely necessary").

5. The client's restoration of trust in him- or herself ("There are no words that can express how much you helped me to trust again the things that I really believed all along"; "This issue of trusting myself—my *self*—came through his affirmation").

6. A strong impact of the session on the life of the client ("I want you to know that the session I had with you made a difference in my life").

7. The capacity of the client to maintain the process on his or her own ("After the workshop I wanted to understand more fully and mentally what had happened to me"; "I am aware that the process is continuing for me on my own").

A SYNTHESIS

Several points come together as a way of understanding the impact of these brief encounters. The clients reported that the therapist conveyed a strong and empathic presence, and a deep acceptance and validation of them as persons. The result was a renewed sense of acceptance and trust in self, such that each client was freed to rely upon him- or herself as a source and originator of feelings and plans for action.

As we examine these outcomes, we note that they are quite similar to process and outcome descriptions given for client-centered therapy in general. Thus, the power of the brief encounter lies not in some uniqueness of the process, but rather in two other elements: in the crisis-oriented character of the client's search for understanding and change, and in the *intensity* of the experience as lived by the client during and after the interview. If we note the seven elements enumerated above as touchstones of powerful brief encounters and apply them to the record of Mark's interview and postinterview evaluations, we can see that most, though not all, fit Mark's experience. The most striking exception is criterion 4, the client's sense of being heard and understood. We have already noted that both Mark and Rogers were dissatisfied with this aspect of the process during the interview itself. The later contemplation by Mark of his therapy experience modified this judgment to some extent. But the power of the encounter in Mark's case came from other aspects of the experience and its aftermath.

Mark's reflections on the experience indicate that his work with Rogers had a deep impact on him with respect to both the crisis that he voiced in the session and to the longer-term effects of the session. A crisis orientation (criterion 3) was evident both in his statement at the time of his volunteering for the session and in his use of the metaphor of watching events from Hitler's bunker. Criterion 5, a growing belief and trust in his own experiences, characterized Mark's later development. The intensity of the session's impact (criterion 6) is evident in Mark's statement to Rogers: "Coming into personal contact with you brought to the fore deep and painful issues regarding the meaning of my life." And, the postsession continuity of the process (criterion 7) is clear in Mark's poignant words: "What I am describing is a process that has been taking place with time. It continues today."

It is evident, then, that this brief and complex encounter between Mark and Rogers may fairly be seen as having been an enduring, life-enhancing experience for Mark, an experience that had power far beyond the brevity of the real time that marked its existence.

REFERENCES

Rogers, C. R. (1986). The dilemmas of a South African white. *Person-Centered Review, 1,* 15–35.
Seeman, J. (1992). *The power of the brief encounter.* Unpublished manuscript.

CARL ROGERS' WORK WITH MARK

An Empirical Analysis and Cognitive–Behavioral Perspective

Adele M. Hayes
Marvin R. Goldfried

Carl Rogers was not only an outstanding clinician but was also among the first to subject the process of psychotherapy to scientific scrutiny. He pioneered the use of verbatim transcripts to study the "raw data" of psychotherapy, developed methods to describe and classify therapists' attitudes and behaviors, and began to study the process of change in the client. In this tradition, we will analyze the transcript of Rogers' demonstration session with Mark, a deeply conflicted white South African man.

We will describe what Rogers did in the session by examining the content of his feedback to the client. We conceptualize therapeutic feedback as an important ingredient of change in virtually all approaches to therapy. By providing feedback, therapists help to direct their clients' attention to therapeutically relevant aspects of their intrapersonal and interpersonal functioning. Traditionally, client-centered therapists have used feedback as the primary way to help clients attend to and process facets of their experience that are partly distorted or denied (Anderson, 1974; Rice, 1974; Wexler, 1974). Therapists carefully look for ways to break through perceptual rigidities and distortions that block clients' growth. From within an information-processing model of client-centered therapy

(Wexler, 1974; Wexler & Rice, 1974), therapists play a more directive role than Rogers originally described, continuously directing and redirecting the processing of their clients and helping them organize their responses to experiences. Wexler (1974) even goes as far as to describe client-centered therapists as surrogate information processors for their clients.

Given the theoretical importance of therapist feedback in client-centered therapy, we thought it would be interesting to apply our coding system, specifically designed to study feedback, to this sample session of Rogers' work. In examining how Rogers used feedback, we can look at what he chose to have Mark attend to and what he deemed less important. With this sort of analysis, we can move beyond theory-based discussions of the case to a more generic, transtheoretical description of Rogers' intervention. After describing the specific therapeutic foci, we move to a more general discussion of the case, integrating the findings from our coding of the transcript and considering how a cognitive–behavioral therapist might have intervened.

THE CODING SYSTEM

The Coding System of Therapeutic Focus (CSTF; Goldfried, Newman, & Hayes, 1989) is designed to analyze clinical transcripts from a variety of orientations. The coding system covers a broad range of aspects of client functioning that may be the focus of therapist feedback and is, as much as possible, free of theoretical jargon. It includes six sections: Persons Involved, Time Frames, Specific Components of Client Functioning, Intrapersonal Links, Interpersonal Links, and General Interventions. Table 10.1 lists the six sections of the code and the categories within each.

Briefly, the Persons Involved section identifies the characters focused on in the session and the Time Frames section identifies the temporal aspects of the feedback (e.g., past, current, future). Categories in these two sections provide the overall context of the therapist's feedback. The Specific Components of Client Functioning section classifies the basic elements of functioning, such as the client's Situation, Self-evaluation, General thoughts, Emotions and Actions. An example of a therapist focus on the client's emotions from the case of Mark is, "There was almost a note of sadness [Emotion] when you said, 'I've got to be a facade.'" The two Links sections classify the types of connections that the therapist makes between different components of the client's functioning (Intrapersonal Links) or links that the therapist makes between aspects of the client's functioning and another's functioning (Interpersonal Links). An example of an Intrapersonal Link (in this case, a Difference/incongruity link) is "So maybe you have to kind of grit your teeth and stick it out, even though it's a bad, rough world." An example of an Interpersonal Link (in this case, a

Table 10.1. Description of Categories in the Coding System of Therapeutic Focus

Category	Description
Persons Involved	
Patient/client	Focus is on the patient or client
Therapist	Focus is on the current therapist
Parent	Focus is on the client's parent or guardian
Mate	Focus is on the client's current intimate relationship
Family	Focus is on the client's children or members of the family other than the mate or parent
Acquaintances/strangers/ others in general	People involved in the client's life that are not captured by any of the other persons categories
Time Frames	
Preadult past	Infancy through high school
Adult past	Between completion of high school and beginning of therapy
Current	Immediate past, between the beginning of therapy and the current session
In-session	Within the present session
Future	Following the present session
Unspecified	Time not specified or relevant
Specific Components of Client Functioning	
Situation	Circumstances external to the client that are relevant to understanding his or her functioning
Self-observation	Thought reflecting the client's objective perception of self
Self-evaluation	Client's appraisal, judgment, estimation of own worth and abilities
Expectations	Thought reflecting client's anticipation about the future
General thoughts	Client's thinking that is unspecified
Intentions	Client's future-oriented volition, such as wish, desire, motivation, or need
Emotions	Client's affect
Physiological signs of emotion	Physical status of the client as it relates to his or her affect
Actions	Client's performance of specific behaviors
Unspecified	Client's functioning that cannot be described by any specific component

(cont.)

Table 10.1 *(cont.)*

Category	Description
Intrapersonal Links	
Similarity/pattern	Similarities or recurrences within the client's functioning
Consequences	Therapist implies that a particular component of client's functioning is having an impact on another component
Difference/incongruity	Divergences noted within the client's functioning
Vicious cycle	Focus on the self-perpetuating quality of a problematic aspect of the client's functioning
Interpersonal Links	
Pattern	Therapist highlights client's interpersonal functioning repeated over time, settings, or people
Consequences (self to other)	Client's functioning is impacting on another person
Consequences (other to self)	Another person's functioning is impacting on the client
Compare/contrast	Therapist compares or contrasts the client's functioning with that of another person
General interaction	An interchange between the client and another that cannot otherwise be specified
Vicious cycle	Self-perpetuating interpersonal pattern that has a self-defeating quality
General Interventions	
Choices/decisions	Pointing to the client's options or alternatives
Reality/unreality	Helping clients to step out of their subjective perception and to view experiences more objectively
Expected/imagined reaction of others	Client's subjective view of reaction of another person as it pertains to their interpersonal relationship
Instance/theme	Highlighting a particular example of the client's functioning that is part of an overall trend or pattern
Support	Therapist gives reassurance regarding either specific or general aspects of the client's functioning

Table 10.1 *(cont.)*

Category	Description
Information giving	Providing general facts and knowledge that have therapeutic implications for the client
Changes noted	Therapist refers to client's change associated with treatment
Avoidance	Focus on something the client is doing that interferes with the process or progress of therapy
Encouragement of between-session activity	Therapist encourages some future-oriented experience between sessions or during the course of therapy
Self-disclosure	Therapist shares personal experience that has relevance to the client's situation

Compare/contrast link) comparing the opinions of others with the client's own view of him- or herself is "Maybe what others think or the opinions even of history are less important than 'What am I able to do, what kind of person am I able to be within the circle that I really influence?' " The General Interventions category classifies the form that the feedback takes. For instance, the therapist may point out that the client has choices or can make decisions about a situation (Choices/decisions), can compare the client's subjective view with a more objective perspective (Reality/unreality), or can focus on the reaction that the client expects or imagines of another (Expected/imagined reaction of others).

For our analysis of Rogers' session with Mark, we independently coded the transcript and then met to reach a consensus on the few disagreements we had. The scoring unit for this coding system was the "turn," defined as everything the therapist says between client verbalizations. Each category was scored only once per turn, and each turn was scored for every category it contained.

DESCRIPTION OF THE SESSION

We calculated frequencies for each of the scoring categories and converted them into proportions, based on the number of turns in which a given category occurred, relative to the total number (37) of turns that could be scored. The results are presented using proportions, so as to standardize the frequencies and facilitate comparisons among the categories. The proportions for each of the five sections of the classification system were rank ordered. The most and least characteristic aspects of the feedback

Rogers used are reported in Table 10.2. The most characteristic items are those that were focused on in at least 15% of the turns, and the least characteristic were those that were focused on in fewer than 15% of the turns. Although 15% is an arbitrary cut-off point, we reasoned that any category that occurred less frequently could not be considered characteristic of Rogers' session.

To understand the results of our classification of Rogers' feedback to Mark, it is important to have some context for interpreting the proportions reported. In other research projects using our coding system, we found that categories in the People Involved and Time Frames sections are likely to have the highest proportions, because they set the context for the session. Unlike categories in the other sections of the coding system, they are scored for every turn. The Specific Components of Client Functioning are the next most frequently scored categories, as these deal with the basic aspects of client functioning (e.g., the client's situation, actions, thoughts) that the therapist highlights throughout the course of the session. The therapist is likely to shift from component to component, and it would be rare to focus on any one component throughout most of the session, as may be the case with a given Time Frames or Persons Involved category. The Intrapersonal Links and Interpersonal Links occur less frequently than the Specific Components of Client Functioning, as they are coded when associations are made between the specific components. The General Interventions, which must be more carefully timed than the other categories, are used the most sparingly (e.g., pointing out important themes in therapy). With this context in mind, the results of our coding of Rogers' session are described below.

People Involved

Most characteristic. Most (97%) of the feedback focused on Mark, but as many as 73% of the turns focused on other people (Acquaintances/strangers/others in general). Rogers had Mark explore what others thought of him and of the sociopolitical situation in South Africa, so that these views could be differentiated from his own.

Least characteristic. Rogers was the focus of 14% of the turns because Mark spent most of the end of the session evaluating Rogers' performance and then discussing what it was like to be Carl Rogers. The categories Parent, Mate, and Family were never focused on in the session.

Time Frames

Most characteristic. Most of the session was spent in a Current or Future orientation. Mark's current life situation was the focus of 76% of the session, and the future time frame 27% of the session.

Table 10.2. Proportions of Categories of Rogers' Feedback with Mark Using the Coding System of Therapeutic Focus

Most characteristic		Least characteristic	
Persons Involved			
Patient/client	97%	Therapist	14%
Acquaintances/strangers/ others in general	73%	Parent	0%
		Mate	0%
		Family	0%
Time Frames			
Current	76%	In-session	11%
Future	27%	Preadult past	0%
		Adult past	0%
		Unspecified	0%
Specific Components of Client Functioning			
Unspecified	51%	Situation	11%
General thoughts	38%	Self-observation	3%
Self-evaluation	27%	Expectations	2%
Emotions	27%	Physiological signs of emotion	0%
Intentions	16%		
Actions	16%		
Intrapersonal Links			
Consequences	19%	Similarity/pattern	3%
Difference/incongruity	16%	Vicious cycle	0%
Interpersonal Links			
Compare/contrast	19%	Consequences (self → other)	8%
		Consequences (other → self)	8%
		General interaction	3%
		Vicious cycle	0%
		Pattern	0%
General Interventions			
None		Reality/unreality	11%
		Expected/imagined reaction of others	5%
		Changes noted	3%
		Self-disclosure	3%
		Choices/decisions	0%
		Instance/theme	0%
		Support	0%
		Information giving	0%
		Encouragement of between-session activity	0%
		Avoidance	0%

Least characteristic. The immediate In-session material was the focus of 11% of the turns. Issues were never spoken of in the context of the Preadult past, Adult past, or the Unspecified time frames.

Specific Components of Client Functioning

Most characteristic. The Unspecified category occurred most frequently, being the focus of Rogers' feedback in 51% of the turns. The Unspecified category refers to those aspects of functioning that do not fit cleanly into any one coding category. Examples of this focus on unspecified components are given in Rogers' comment "you are living out a way of being [Unspecified] that may be quite different from the way you . . . really are inside [Unspecified]."

Rogers also spent a significant proportion of the turns (65%) focusing on Mark's perception of his experience and the personal meaning associated with it. Among these turns, 38% were spent on General thoughts, which are the equivalent of Unspecified thoughts, and 27% dealt with Mark's Self-evaluation. The General thoughts, which do not fit into the more specific categories of thoughts (i.e., Self-observation, Self-evaluation, and Expectations), occurred primarily when Rogers had Mark attend to his conflicting views on the situation in South Africa and on his role as a representative of the government. An example of this focus on General thoughts is: "Outside you see [thought] that you belong to a rotten system. Inside it seems [thought] quite different to you. And which of those views [thought] are you going to hold, which are you going to stand by?"

Rogers also spent 27% of the session addressing Mark's Self-evaluation, with questions such as "Who am I?" and exploring his vacillation between feeling like a good person and a bad person. He also compared Mark's view of himself with the view that he thought others had of him, to help him differentiate external views from his own.

Mark's Emotions were addressed in 27% of the turns. The Emotions were highlighted or evoked most often when focusing on his General thoughts about his Situation or his Self-evaluation. An example of an evocative use of feedback on Emotions is when Rogers noted: "There was almost a note of sadness when you said, 'I've got to be a facade.' " Although Mark was not talking about his emotional response, Rogers focused Mark's attention on his affect by giving feedback on this aspect of his experience.

Mark's Actions and Intentions were each addressed in 16% of the turns when Rogers explored what Mark was doing and which beliefs and principles he wanted to uphold.

Least characteristic. Compared to the focus on Mark's General thoughts, Self-evaluation, Emotions, Intentions, and Actions, the external Situation was only focused on by Rogers in 11% of the turns. The other two more specific thoughts—Self-observation and Expectations—received very little attention (3% and 2%, respectively) relative to the other categories. There was no focus on Physiological signs of emotion.

Intrapersonal Links

Most characteristic. The only two types of Intrapersonal Links that were the focus in 15% or more of the turns were Consequences (19%) and Difference/incongruity (16%). An example of a Consequence link, already noted above, is: "There was almost a note of sadness when you said, 'I've got to be a facade.' " Rogers associated the thought of having to be a facade with Mark's feeling of sadness. This particular type of link was most often made when Rogers noted the connection between Mark's construction of his experience and the impact it had on his Self-evaluation or his Emotions. The Difference/incongruity link was used to highlight Mark's internal conflict, as illustrated in: "You feel you have to play a role . . . [and] that the role you play is something different from the person you are."

Least characteristic. The other types of Intrapersonal Links were rarely used. Similarity/pattern links only occurred in 3% of the turns, and the Vicious cycle links were never used.

Interpersonal Links

Most characteristic. The Compare/contrast link was the most frequently used (19%) of the Interpersonal Links. This category describes feedback that focuses on how components of the client may be similar to or different from those of another person. Rogers made such a link when he stated: "You feel within yourself you're a nice guy. It's the attitudes that other people have toward you that disturb you. . . . So that within yourself the nasty jobs you have to do are okay with you. It's simply that others see you as a representative of an evil system." He used this strategy throughout the transcript to differentiate the thoughts of others from Mark's own thoughts and his Self-evaluations.

Least characteristic. The Compare/contrast link was the only Interpersonal Link that characterized Rogers' session with Mark. Interpersonal Consequences, both Mark's impact on others and the effect others had on him, were the focus of only 8% of the turns in the session. Mark's General interaction with others was only addressed in 3% of the turns, and any possible Vicious cycle or Pattern in his life was never addressed.

General Interventions

Overall, General Interventions were not characteristic of this session. Only one type of General Intervention was used in more than 5% of the turns: Reality/unreality, which was highlighted in 11% of the turns. This category involves feedback that serves to compare the client's subjective views of something with more objective ones. Across a number of turns, Rogers focused on Mark's belief that he had to play a facade, but Rogers also highlighted Mark's realization that his friends already saw through his facade and still liked him. What Mark expected or imagined the reaction of others to be was the focus of 5% of the turns, and Changes noted, as well as therapist Self-disclosure, were each the focus of only 3% of the turns. Interventions focusing on Choices/decisions, Instance/theme, Support, Information giving, Encouragement of between-session activity, and Avoidance never occurred.

DISCUSSION OF THE SESSION

Early in the session Mark was looking to Rogers to help him explore and resolve his conflicting values. Consistent with client-centered theory, Rogers did not focus directly on his values nor on the morality of supporting an oppressive government, and he did not attempt to resolve Mark's conflicts. Instead of exploring and clarifying Mark's values, he focused on others' perspectives on the situation in South Africa and on what Mark was experiencing, especially with regard to his view of himself.

The turmoil of this client exemplifies what Rogers viewed as a pervasive problem of modern life—living with absolutely contradictory values, and, thus, divorcing ourselves from ourselves. He believed that the majority of our values are introjected from other individuals or groups, yet are held as fixed constructs that are rarely tested or examined and are then adopted as our own (Rogers, 1983; Rogers & Stevens, 1967). As is vividly illustrated with Mark, we lose touch with our own valuing process and relinquish our locus of Self-evaluation to others, resulting in internal conflict and profound insecurity. The task of the therapist, demonstrated by Rogers, is to explore the fundamental discrepancy between the values that are introjected and what is going on in the client's experience (Rogers, 1983). The goals of therapy are to move the client from an external locus of evaluation to a more internal one, to integrate a fragmented self, to experience more fully and openly, and to have a greater willingness to live by this process (Raskin, 1985). This provides the base from which people become more able to make more satisfying choices, leading to personal growth, the ultimate goal of client-centered therapy.

In line with this approach, Rogers spent a significant portion of the session on the beliefs, values, and emotions of others to get a good picture of Mark's external perspective that he would then use to help Mark elucidate his internal perspective. The other people discussed were those who also worked for the South African government, those who opposed it, those who lived outside the country, and even future generations. Throughout the session, the conflict between the external and internal orientations was highlighted, and the two views were differentiated, using Interpersonal Links, Compare/contrast.

As Rogers moved Mark away from the views of others and the larger issue of the morality of the situation in South Africa, Mark's attention was deployed inward. He began to explore his conflicts, fears, and difficulty accepting himself, as one of the "baddies" who has "lived off the abhorrent system." Rogers had Mark look at what kind of person he thought he was and focus on the isolated "unspeakable" parts of himself. In the supportive, nondirective, and empathic atmosphere created by Rogers, even in a context as difficult as this one, Mark was able to question his actions and intentions, his identity, his role and responsibility as part of an oppressive system, whether he is a good or bad person, and his values in general. In doing so, Mark was able to get in touch with the affect associated with all of this turmoil. He began to look at his guilt, his feelings of being a social leper, his fears of retaliation by the oppressed, and the possibility that the system that he was upholding was evil. He was even able to draw an analogy between himself and a Nazi in Hitler's Germany.

Rogers used the Intrapersonal Links, Consequences category to highlight the connections among these General thoughts, Self-evaluation, Emotions, Actions, Intentions, and the more Unspecified components of Mark's functioning. The Intrapersonal Links, Difference/incongruity category was used to explore and clarify Mark's internal conflict, in much the same way that the Interpersonal Links, Compare/contrast category was used to better understand Mark's perspective as compared to that of others. Rogers had Mark attend to the inconsistency between the way he was feeling inside and the role he was living outwardly, the difference between his views on his situation when inside South Africa and when outside, and to the conflict between viewing himself as a bad person because he worked for a bad system and as a good person in his own little world away from work.

Consistent with Roger's nondirective approach to therapy, none of the General Interventions, which are typically quite directive therapeutic strategies (e.g., Encouraging between-session experiences, Information giving, pointing out that the client can make Choices/decisions), characterized the session. However, it is interesting that as many as 11% of the turns involved the General Interventions, Reality/unreality category, a strategy that typically exemplifies cognitive–behavioral therapy, in that it involves having the client compare his or her subjective experience with a more objective one. In cognitive–behavioral therapy, the therapist actively challenges the client's distorted thoughts, teaches the client cognitive restructuring skills, and even assigns homework to practice these skills (Beck & Weishaar, 1989). However, Rogers' use of Reality/unreality was different, in that he did not initiate the strategy, but rather followed Mark's lead when he began to challenge his own assertion that he had to keep up a facade.

Rogers spent most of the session in the Current and Future Time Frames. Most of the session focused on Mark's current experience, and the session shifted to a Future orientation only when Mark expressed his fears about what could happen to him if the oppressed were to come into power and how future generations would view him. Although not characteristic of the session, there was an In-session focus when Mark shifted from exploring his conflicts and fears to an evaluation of Rogers' performance and what it was like to be Carl Rogers.

AN ALTERNATIVE APPROACH

Rogers was faced with a difficult session in that he was a visitor from the United States, dealing with Mark's dilemma about being a representative of the South African government. Rogers undoubtedly had his own opinions about Mark's participation in such an oppressive system, especially a system not based on the acceptance and valuing of fellow human beings. He had to consider the effect of exploring Mark's dilemma not only on Mark but also on the audience, on himself, and on the interaction of each. He had to consider how much to encourage Mark's exploration of his experience, given the intensity of the affect, the threat to the self, and the brevity of the session. That Rogers could create a warm, supportive, and empathic atmosphere within the threatening environment of an audience of South Africans, some of whom were working in the same capacity as Mark, speaks to the power of his personal and therapeutic style.

The problem that Mark presented was one of overwhelming confusion and conflicting values. The inner turmoil and anguish that he experienced when faced with these conflicts led him to deny these feelings. Rogers' shifted Mark's focus from morality and conflict to his self-evaluation, thus allowing Mark to look at some of the previously denied and unacceptable parts of himself, to decrease his sense of isolation, and to begin the process of integrating and strengthening his fragmented sense of self. Rogers' assumption was that if Mark could accept himself and operate from an internal frame of reference, he would get in better touch with his values, thereby allowing him to make decisions based on his newly integrated belief system. The goal of this session was not to lead Mark to make the "best" or "right" decision, but rather to help him to find his true self. Rogers described this process as beginning in the session and continuing years later. Mark's experiencing became more open, and, theoretically, the growth principle that was previously blocked, could then function effectively.

There is no question that this 30-minute demonstration session had a profound impact on Mark and that he continued his search for himself, even 3 years later. However, this case brings up the questions of the centrality of the *sense of self* in the change process and the limits of a nondirective approach. Rogers' decision to explore Mark's sense of self, rather than to clarify his values and beliefs, reflects Rogers' assumption that the sense of self is the central change mechanism. Rogers viewed growth and therapeutic change as processes that occur when the person's sense of self and values are derived from a firmly established internal orientation (Raskin, 1948), and this focus on self-evaluation is apparent in his session with Mark.

An alternative perspective is that the therapist can focus more directly on the client's perceptual rigidities, distortions, values, and troublesome behaviors toward the goals of improving his or her sense of self and modifying problematic reactions to experiences. This perspective is most consistent with a cognitive–behavioral orientation. In this approach, the road to change is through learning ways to process the world more accurately, to reevaluate thinking, and to behave in more adaptive ways. A more positive evaluation of the self is a product of the cognitive and behavioral changes, rather than the cause of these changes (Goldfried & Robins, 1983). It is interesting to note that when we used our coding system to analyze a demonstration session of Aaron Beck (Goldsamt, Goldfried, Hayes, & Kerr, 1992), in which a depressed client felt worthless and unlovable, we found that Beck spent only 10% of the session on the client's Self-evaluation. In contrast, Rogers 27% of his turns in this session on Mark's view of himself. While the two sessions used different clients with somewhat different problems, theoretically the general strategies applied by each of the therapists should be fairly consistent across the various clients they see.

The cognitive–behavioral therapist takes a much more directive role than Rogers did here. For the cognitive–behavioral therapist, maladjustment is viewed as the result of learning faulty ways of thinking and behaving that can be corrected by teaching the client cognitive and behavioral skills to improve the deficits. Rogers assumed that there is a self-correcting course toward personal growth once the individual develops an internal locus of evaluation and valuing. The cognitive–behavioral therapist assumes that teaching the client new skills is the most expeditious route to change, and that change either will not occur without this new learning or will take much longer than is necessary. The therapist and client collaborate to break old patterns and replace them with new ones that will facilitate growth. The client works to master these skills by practicing them both in and out of session (Arkowitz & Hannah, 1989; Beck & Weishaar, 1989).

Compared to Rogers' session with Mark, Beck maintained an In-session focus twice as often because he was teaching his client ways to examine and challenge his negative thinking during the session (Goldsamt et al., 1992). Cognitive therapy skills involved using the General Interventions, Reality/unreality category of our coding system to compare the client's subjective view with a more objective one. This strategy was used almost twice as much in Beck's session as it was in Rogers'. Because this skill requires practice and is used to help the distressed individual cope, Beck encouraged the client to use it between sessions, which is another of the General Interventions that we code (Encouragement of between-session activity). Beck also used this intervention more frequently than Rogers did. While Rogers highlighted the connections among Mark's Self-evaluation, Emotions, and Actions, in his session, Beck made these connections twice as often. This emphasis is consistent with the theoretical importance placed on the reciprocal relationship between these components in cognitive–behavioral therapy. It is interesting that, unlike Rogers, Beck hardly used the links that are intended to explore, clarify, and differentiate issues such as the Intrapersonal Links, Difference/incongruity, and the Interpersonal Links, Compare/contrast categories. Because Beck did not emphasize the movement of the client from an external to an internal perspective as much as Rogers did, he also focused on other people (Persons Involved, Acquaintances/strangers/others in general) significantly less than Rogers did.

A cognitive–behavioral therapist would probably have picked up on Mark's need for acceptance and approval, and on his sense that he might be a bad person because of the oppressive system he upheld. As Rogers did, the therapist might have helped Mark to see that he is not necessarily a bad person because of his job, and that there is actually substantial evidence to support that he is a good person. This would have been done briefly, to make Mark feel supported and less like a horrible person, to be condemned. This support might allow him to begin to explore his values and thoughts on the sociopolitical situation in his country. Once some of these issues were clarified, the therapist could begin to examine the values that Mark had learned to see whether they were valid and consistent with his beliefs, or whether they had been accepted as truth without careful examination. This strategy is similar to Rogers' differentiation of internally based and externally based views of the self, but would probably involve active hypothesis-testing strategies rather than exploration and clarification of the issues. The therapist would probably summarize what was done in the session, encourage Mark to continue to apply those strategies, and eventually have him move toward a problem-solving stance as his values became more clear. Cognitive–behavioral therapists hold that such an approach would help a client like Mark resolve his conflicts and move beyond the quagmire he was in more quickly than would the more exploratory and nondirective approach of Rogers.

Although Mark continued his self-exploration for at least 3 years after the session, he made no mention in the follow-up letters of any insights into his what *his* values were. He wrote, instead, of the loss of his ideals, of letting others control him, and of being swallowed up by the system. Although Mark felt more in touch with himself and more alive, a resolution of his conflict did not seem to have occurred. He remained in his position, working for a government whose values he did not support. There seemed to be an increase in Mark's self-acceptance but no clear understanding of what his values were and no plan for how he would live a life more consistent with those values.

Still another approach to Mark's dilemma would have been to use the Gestalt two-chair technique to explore different sides of Mark's perspective: the side that had incorporated the values of the government and the side that saw himself as part of an inherently bad system. By having the two sides confront one another, the perspectives could have become more explicit and the exploration more affectively charged, which might have facilitated a deeper level of change. Theoretically, once such conflicts are made explicit, the client can work toward an integration of the two sides of the self (Greenberg, 1984). This approach could accomplish Rogers' goals of contrasting the introjected value system with the individual's experience, and then integrating a fragmented sense of self. The two-chair technique has been demonstrated to be an effective strategy for conflict resolution (Clarke & Greenberg, 1986) and has been recommended as an approach that can be incorporated nicely into a cognitive–behavioral approach to facilitate change (Goldfried, 1988; Goldfried & Hayes, 1989; Robins & Hayes, 1993). Similarly, it may be a useful adjunct to client-centered therapy when exploring and comparing the external and internal perspectives.

CONCLUDING COMMENT

Decades after Rogers began the psychotherapy research movement, we engaged in the interesting task of studying a sample of his clinical work following his model of research. We come from a different perspective, in that we do not study the reactions of the client in therapy, or the attitudes of the client-centered therapist, but rather what the therapist actually does in his or her session with the client. In terms of Rogers' session with Mark, we described what he chose to highlight and what he did not, and presented this within a more general discussion of his therapeutic strategy. The coding of Rogers' session allowed for a comparison with the strategies used by an expert cognitive–behavioral therapist in another demonstration session that we coded with the same coding system. In the spirit of psychotherapy integration, this transtheoretical coding system provides a common language system and facilitates much needed discussions of the similarities and differences across theoretical orientations.

ACKNOWLEDGMENT

Preparation of this commentary was supported, in part, by NIMH Grant No. 40196, awarded to Marvin R. Goldfried.

REFERENCES

Anderson, W. (1974). Personal growth and client-centered therapy: An information processing view. In D. A. Wexler & L. N. Rice (Eds.), *Innovations in client-centered therapy*. New York: Wiley.

Arkowitz, H., & Hannah, M. T. (1989). Cognitive, behavioral, and psychodynamic therapies: Converging or diverging pathways to change? In A. Freeman, K. Simon, L. Beutler, & H. Arkowitz (Eds.), *Comprehensive handbook of cognitive therapy*. New York: Plenum.

Beck, A. T., & Weishaar, M. (1989). Cognitive therapy. In A. Freeman, K. Simon, L. Beutler, & H. Arkowitz (Eds.), *Comprehensive handbook of cognitive therapy*. New York: Plenum.

Clarke K. M., & Greenberg, L. S. (1986). Differential effects of the gestalt two-chair intervention and problem-solving in resolving decisional conflict. *Journal of Counseling Psychology, 33,* 11–15.

Goldfried, M. R. (1988). Application of rational restructuring to anxiety disorders. *The Counseling Psychologist, 16,* 50–68.

Goldfried, M. R., & Hayes, A. M. (1989). Can contributions from other orientations complement behavior therapy? *The Behavior Therapist, 12,* 57–60.

Goldfried, M. R., Newman, C. F., & Hayes, A. M. (1989). *The Coding System of Therapeutic Focus.* Unpublished manuscript, State University of New York at Stony Brook, Stony Brook, NY.

Goldfried, M. R., & Robins, C. J. (1983). Self-schema, cognitive bias, and the processing of therapeutic experiences. In P. C. Kendall (Ed.), *Advances in cognitive-behavioral research and therapy* (Vol. II). New York: Academic Press.

Goldsamt, L. A., Goldfried, M. R., Hayes, A. M., & Kerr, S. (1992). Beck, Meichenbaum, and Strupp: A comparison of three therapies on the dimension of therapist feedback. *Psychotherapy, 29,* 167–176.

Greenberg, L. S. (1984). A task analysis of intrapersonal conflict resolution. In L.

N. Rice & L. S. Greenberg (Eds.), *Patterns of change: Intensive analysis of psychotherapy process.* New York: Guilford Press.

Raskin, N. J. (1948). The development of nondirective therapy. *Journal of Consulting Psychology, 12,* 92–110.

Raskin, N. J. (1985). Client-centered therapy. In S. J. Lynn & J. P. Garske (Eds.), *Contemporary psychotherapies: Models and methods.* Columbus, OH: Charles E. Merrill.

Rice, L. N. (1974). The evocative function of the therapist. In D. A. Wexler & L. N. Rice (Eds.), *Innovations in client-centered therapy.* New York: Wiley.

Robins, C. J., & Hayes, A. M. (1993). An appraisal of cognitive therapy. *Journal of Consulting and Clinical Psychology, 61,* 205–214.

Rogers, C. R. (1983). *Freedom to learn* (Rev. ed.). Columbus, OH: Charles E. Merrill.

Rogers, C. R., & Stevens, B. (1967). *Person to person: The problem of being human.* New York: Simon & Schuster.

Wexler, D. A. (1974). A cognitive theory of experiencing, self-actualization, and therapeutic process. In D. A. Wexler & L. N. Rice (Eds.), *Innovations in client-centered therapy.* New York: Wiley.

Wexler, D. A., & Rice, L. N. (Eds.). (1974). *Innovations in client-centered therapy.* New York: Wiley.

INDEX